THE POLAR PASSION

The Quest for the North Pole

With selections from Arctic Journals

FARLEY MOWAT

An Atlantic Monthly Press Book
Little, Brown and Company: Boston: Toronto

FIRST AMERICAN EDITION
Library of Congress
catalogue card no. 68-11519

Atlantic-Little, Brown Books
Are published by Little, Brown
and Company in Association with
the Atlantic Monthly Press

PRINTED IN CANADA

THE POLAR PASSION

CONTENTS

This volume is dedicated to Alexandrine Ellis whose death, in July of 1966, was as tragic and unnecessary as the deaths of those many men who died for the polar passion. They died in their hundreds because the overweening ambitions and stupidities of others set them to an insane task. Rene Ellis died alone – because the stupidity and callousness of others drove her to her own destruction.

FARLEY MOWAT

To the Indian, who invented pemmican and snowshoes;
To the Eskimo, who gave us the art of sled travel;
To this twin family of wild folk who have no flag
Goes the first credit . . . to these, the pathfinders,
I inscribe my first page. In the ultimate success
There is glory enough to go to the graves of the dead –
And to the heads of the living.

From Dr. Frederick Cook's dedication of
My Attainment of the Pole.

FOREWORD

North Americans have become so preoccupied with the exploitation of the vast riches and resources of the temperate regions that they tend to ignore the almost limitless expanse of sea and land which comprises the northern reaches of their continent.

It was not always so. Until fifty or sixty years ago the North American Arctic was very much a reality to people of every walk of life. It had become real, and it stayed real for them because men of their own kind were venturing into its remote fastnesses unprotected by the elaborate mechanical shields that we now demand whenever we step out of our air-conditioned sanctuaries. Press and magazines followed the fortunes of these men with a good deal more honest enthusiasm than that with which they now follow the exploits of space travellers. Personal accounts of arctic voyages and journeys lined the shelves in book shops. Those who stayed at home identified themselves with arctic travellers, as they can no longer identify themselves with the mechanical heroes of modern times.

It is a measure of the manner in which we have mentally transformed the Arctic into an alien world that most of the great tales of human venturing into it (and they are legion) are no longer current or available. Most of the original books are out of print. A good many of them are so rare that they are not even to be found on public library shelves but are kept in special rooms where they are available only to the eyes of scholars. Where other nations with northern frontiers keep alive the tales of past exploits into the white lands, we have consigned ours to limbo. And in the absence of an enduring and living knowledge we have fostered the growth of a gigantic myth concerning the essentially inimical character of the northlands and their uselessness to modern man.

It is an idiotic myth. In this world of exploding human populations and a fantastically accelerated consumption of natural resources, the Arctic can no longer be written off as a useless wasteland. The Soviets have moved into *their* white world with tremendous vigour and with the same spirit of acceptance which animated the early explorers of our own Arctic. They have already made *their* arctic regions a part of the modern world. Great cities now exist north of the Arctic Circle, rooted in permanently frozen ground. What is more important, great numbers of people live beyond the shelter of the cities, doing all manner of things from fishing and herding to manning power and mining installations. The Soviets have learned, if indeed they ever forgot, that man himself, without technological armour, is the most adaptable of animals and that there is no environment on earth so hostile that it can keep him from seeking his destiny there. By contrast, our exceedingly limited commitment to the North American Arctic consists of tiny clots of human beings living in timid isolation from the world around them, well shielded from the reality of that world, and attempting to create microcosms of *la dolce vita* they left behind them in the yearned-for south.

That man, unarmoured, is competent to be and do, under the most appalling physical conditions, is a fact that we not only forget – we actively reject. Yet we were once well aware of it, as the chronicles of the men who went to the North until only a few decades ago make clear.

It has long been my conviction that these chronicles of high endeavour have a powerful and essential validity for modern man and so, ten years ago, I set myself the task of shaking the dust from some of them and of finding a way to restore them to the mainstream of human experience. In the late 1950's I began the work of gathering, editing and publishing a collection of the most meaningful accounts of exploration and travel in the North American arctic regions. This collection – which, hopefully, will run to other volumes – was intended to provide us with some insight into the true nature of the northern world which we reject, while at the same time demonstrating the magnitude and grandeur of human endeavour in that hard environment. It was not, and is not, intended to be a *history* of exploration in the North American Arctic as such. Rather it is the varied tale of how many individual men endured, and even came to terms with the great polar adversary. It brings the quality of these men into sharp focus so that we recognize them as superb animals, imbued with all the innate strength, derived from struggle with physical adversity, to which we owe ascendancy over all other forms of life.

This is an ascendancy which we may be throwing away. Almost insensibly we appear to be drifting toward a biological condition which can make of us a species of unshelled blobs of protoplasm relying wholly for our survival on the mechanical maintenance of a grossly artificial, and fearfully vulnerable, environment. Witness one of our new supermen – an astronaut, the hero of our times – wombed in his gleaming layers of machinery and about as essential to the success of the electronically controlled robot that carries him as was the chimpanzee that so recently preceded him. If he is not yet completely superfluous to the machine, he is nearly so, and in the near future will be totally so. This is a matter of the flesh, but it is also becoming very much a matter of the spirit. When, and if, man comes to regard himself as being in effect an alien entity in the ancient world that formed him, then he will have become the ultimate egomaniac, imprisoned in an infinitely fragile bubble-world of his own contriving – and unquestionably doomed.

However, *The Polar Passion* is not a tract intended to persuade modern man to turn back the clock, to throw away his technical proficiency and dress himself in skins as he crawls back into a neolithic cave. It is designed to remind him, through the lips, eyes and ears of his fellows of a few short decades ago (fellows who are already beginning to have a strangely foreign look about them) that he dare not put all his future into the keeping of the machine; that he must somehow retain the primal virtues of a tough, unflinching, physically competent, durable and daring animal *in his own right* and *of the world that spawned him.*

We need this reminder and assurance if we are ever to inhabit the rejected third of our continent – the Arctic. We need a recognition of this truth if we are not to go over the evolutionary peak and down the sharp decline leading to the immense graveyard of other species that armoured thmselves too heavily against the physical dangers and challenges, and the reality, of the world around them.

In an earlier book, *Ordeal By Ice* (1960), I dealt with man's efforts to force a sea passage through the ice barriers blocking the water routes to the north of the continent, and to find a way to link Europe with Cathay and the East. This ancient dream was one of surprising strength and viability. It gripped the imaginations of Europeans throughout at least four centuries and it impelled innumerable men and ships into the northwestern reaches to meet and grapple with the trials and agonies posed by a frozen ocean.

The Polar Passion begins roughly where *Ordeal By Ice* leaves off. By about 1850, the dream of finding a usable Northwest Passage was almost dead. Interest in the Arctic had shifted to the pursuit of a new chimera – the North Pole. This also was a development from a much older dream – that of being able to sail direct to China across the very top of the world. It was not until the last half of the 20th century that men gave up the tenacious hope that the central polar ocean would prove to be ice-free – if one could only break through the outer rim of pack ice and reach its spreading waters. By the time it was certain that the polar sea was eternally frozen, men had ventured well out into its wastes, and so they continued probing northward, partly in search of new lands, but mainly in attempts to reach that mathematical point known as latitude 90° N. The search for the Northwest Passage had been rooted in commercial motives; the struggle to reach the Pole was fuelled by national pride – chauvinism, really – coupled with a burning sense of mission on the part of a handful of almost unbelievably intrepid seekers after fame.

A later volume, I hope, will deal with the exploration of the gigantic continental land mass stretching north from the timberline and occupying the top of North America from the Atlantic to the Pacific. This is such a vast area of rock and tundra that it posed almost as great a challenge to the passage of European man as did the polar seas, or the ice-clogged channels between the high Arctic Islands.

These studies are linked by many common themes, but one of them deserves special mention. The European explorers were not the first arrivals on the scene. Ages before their coming, the Arctic had been an abiding home to men. These men were the Eskimos and their forebears who, as early as four thousand years ago, had mastered the arctic environment, despite (or, it may be, because of) the limitations imposed by a stone-age technology. Their story remains unwritten, for they had no written language; but elements of it appear in the accounts of all European venturers into our northern regions. The Eskimo story is integral to the other accounts since, without the physical assistance of the Eskimos, and without the object lessons in adaptation provided by them, European accomplishments in the Arctic would probably have been miniscule. This is by no means a minor theme. The Eskimo was, and is, a living symbol of the tremendous flexibility and the enduring qualities which are man's birthright, and which any species, whether man or mouse, must nurture if it is to maintain its place on the implacable and unforgiving evolutionary treadmill.

The problems involved in assembling the materials for this project have been formidable. The most serious one was the fact that we have been so careless with the stuff of history that we have allowed many of the original accounts of arctic venturing prior to the 16th century to vanish utterly. I have therefore had the choice of ignoring this vast section of the story or of overtly intruding myself into it by writing my own account of the events of that obscure period. I chose the second solution. By gathering the facts that do exist, and by filling in the gaps, I have provided at least a shadow picture of the achievements of many long-forgotten men.

Another problem was that some of the older chroniclers wrote in a style that is hard for a modern reader to comprehend. I have therefore presented such accounts using modern spelling, phraseology and punctuation, wherever there was the possibility that the style or idiom would make easy comradeship between the original author and the modern reader difficult, if not impossible.

Still another difficulty lay in the fact that there was a good deal of repetition in the chronicles. If I had reprinted each account in full, the sheer bulk of the material would have required scores of volumes, and many of the stories would have differed, one from the other, only in detail. So I have selected those parts of each chosen voyage that are particularly revealing, and have condensed or eliminated repetitive material, sometimes substituting brief bridging paragraphs to maintain the narrative flow.

Then there was the primary problem of deciding which of the many accounts I was to include. My decision in every case is arbitrary. I have sometimes ignored famous voyages in favour of little-known ones particularly deserving of our recognition.

The foregoing is in no sense an apology for the liberties I have taken with other men's works. It is a warning that these selections are to be read for what they are – the moving, sometimes humorous, often tragic accounts of enduring men in conflict. Scholars, and those who are interested in the minutiae of history, should go to the original sources, all of which are listed on page 295.

EDITOR'S NOTE: Within the excerpts from the Arctic journals, the author's comments and explanations are preceded and terminated by his initials. E.g. FM

CHAPTER 1 THE FIRST STEPS NORTH

As the needle of the compass is irresistibly attracted to the North Magnetic Pole, so a strange scattering of human beings have been just as irresistibly attracted to that other, chimerical Pole, the geographic one; the imaginary pinpoint which is described in the Oxford Dictionary in the most sublime obscurantism as "one of the two points in the celestial sphere about which the stars seem to revolve; being one of the points at which the earth's axis produced meets the celestial sphere."

Scientific, or at least philosophic, curiosity about the North Pole and its surrounding regions goes so far back into antiquity that we cannot hope to trace its origin. But the Greek mathematician and astronomer Pytheas, who sailed out of Massilia (modern Marseilles) about 330 B.C. seems to have been the first "educated" man to have visited the arctic regions and to have left a record of his voyage. Pytheas reached Iceland and then sailed about a hundred miles farther north before being stopped by slob ice on the edge of the arctic pack.

Here I digress for a brief discussion of arctic climate. Climate is naturally important to explorers, and it is particularly so to those who venture into the Arctic. Yet until very recently historians have assumed that the arctic climate remained more or less unchanged throughout the whole of the historic period. Modern climatological research, however, has upset that applecart. It is now known that about 3000 B.C. the Arctic was experiencing a warming trend under the influence of a warm epoch (rather starchily) known as the period of the Climatic Optimum. This was a time of relatively warm, moist weather which saw the treeline advance far over the tundra plains, and witnessed the total disappearance of ice from the approaches to the high Arctic, and from the Arctic Ocean itself – at least during the summer seasons.

From this peak until well into the Christian era the climate deteriorated and around 500 B.C. it took a sharp turn for the worse, with almost catastrophic results in many northern countries. By the time Pytheas sailed north the polar ice pack extended much farther south than it does today. The treeline (that arbitrary but effective way of defining the boundary between arctic and non-arctic regions) had retreated far to the south of where it now stands. These icy conditions prevailed until about 500 A.D. – a thousand years – before the long-term adverse weather cycle ended and conditions began to improve. By the end of the 9th century the improvement was so marked that once more there was little drift ice in northern seas outside of the basin of the Arctic Ocean itself. The climate had become drier too, and there was a marked shrinkage of glaciers and a reduction in the frequency of the cyclonic storms that have always been one of the prime dangers to northern navigation. All in all, the prospects for successful voyaging into far northern waters had vastly improved, and were to continue improving (with occasional short and temporary setbacks) until about 1000 A.D. By that time the climate had become so benevolent that it has since earned the name of the Little Climatic Optimum. The English meteorologist H. H. Lamb described the Little Climatic Optimum to a UNESCO Symposium on Climate Change, held in Rome in 1961: "The arctic pack ice had melted so far back that the appearance of drift ice in waters near Iceland and Greenland south of 70° N. latitude was rare in the 800s and 900s and apparently unknown between 1020 and 1200, when a rapid increase in frequency [of pack ice] began . . ."

Other climatologists have suggested that the Arctic Ocean itself was partially, if not largely, ice-free in summertime during the peak of this warm period – a possibility we shall return to later.

It is clear that Pytheas chose a rather inopportune time to go exploring in the polar reaches; and conditions were not much better throughout the next thousand years. The whole of the arctic region remained locked in ice, secure from the probing curiosity of men.

We know of only one northern exploring voyage of any importance during the early part of the Christian era, and it is shadowed with myth and obscured by the Irish penchant for exaggeration. Nevertheless it seems probable that about 500 A.D. a peregrinating Irish monk by the name of Brendan sailed north and west from Ireland and, like Pytheas, was stopped by ice. It is impossible to be sure where he went, but Stefansson and other authorities believe he reached south Greenland, Iceland and Jan Mayen Island, which lies about 300 miles north of Iceland. If Brendan *did* reach Jan Mayen, he bettered Pytheas' polar record by about 200 miles. The polar climate had improved a little.

By 860 it had improved considerably, and we do not have to rely entirely on what climatologists have to say about it either. There is excellent independent historical evidence. In 860 a Norseman named Octher (or Ottar) made a remarkable northern voyage, or at least *he* thought it was remarkable, and so did King Alfred of England who recorded it. Yet we would hardly consider it worth a passing mention today. If we did not know about the great fluctuations that have taken place in the arctic climate, we would be inclined to think that Ottar and Alfred had made a great to-do about nothing.

What Ottar did was to sail around the northern tip of Norway. His account of the voyage has survived into our day in considerable detail (which is in itself an indication of its surpassing interest to men of his own time) and even in the following, much-condensed version, there is abundant proof that the climatologists are right.

Ottar said that the country where he lived was called Helgeland (a district in north-central Norway) and that *he dwelt farther north than any other Norseman.*† He said that the land (continued) to stretch far toward the north (from Helgeland) but it was all desert, and not inhabited except in a very few places where Finns (Lapps) dwell on the coasts, who live by hunting in the winter and fishing in the summer.

He said that he once had a fancy to find out how far the land stretched northward and whether any men lived north of the desert stretches. He therefore sailed directly north (along the coast) for the space of three days,‡ which took him as far north as the (Norse) whale hunters used to venture. He then sailed another three days north and found the coast beginning to turn eastward. He sailed eastward four days. At the end of that time the coast bore south and continued southerly for five days. Here was the entrance of a river (evidently the Severnaya Dvina in Russia), which was as far as he went. This was the first peopled land he had come to . . .

†My italics.

‡A sailing day, coastwise navigation, for Norse ships was 60 to 100 miles.

The inference to be drawn from Ottar's voyage is clear enough. Prior to about 860 not even Norsemen were able to sail north *along their own coast* for much more than two hundred miles beyond the Arctic Circle, or to a latitude about midway between that reached by Pytheas and that reached by Brendan. Ottar would have reached about 72° latitude in rounding the top of Norway, and this probably stood as the record (if anyone in those times had been foolish enough to keep records of such a singularly useless nature) until about a century later, by which time climatic conditions in the Arctic had improved dramatically. Ottar's record was eclipsed in 997, in a different part of the Arctic, by accident; but, at least, by a fellow Norseman.

SCARLEG'S FOSTER-SON

Many great voyages of discovery have been more accidental than intentional. The voyage of Thorgisl, Scarleg's Foster-Son (Orrabeinsfostri), was more accidental than most.

Thorgisl was a prosperous Franklin (a minor member of the rude Icelandic aristocracy) toward the end of the first millennium A.D. He had broad holdings of land and a cash surplus measured in the fashion of the day, in "hundreds of three-ells worth of silver." Moreover he had a son, Thorleif, who was either a successful Viking pirate or a well-to-do merchant-adventurer trading between Iceland and Norway.

In his early years Thorgisl was a friend of Erik the Red, before that feuding fellow was forced to leave Iceland in 981 on his famous voyage of discovery and land-taking to southwestern Greenland. Some time about 990, when the Norse settlement in Greenland was getting well established, Erik sent a message inviting his old comrade Thorgisl to give up the (relatively) soft life in Iceland and come out to the new country as a settler. Erik was evidently not aware that, since his departure, Thorgisl had become a rather different sort of man. After being a powerful adherent (and even a priest) of Thor all his life, Thorgisl had fallen into the hands of Christian missionaries who had converted him. Conversion to a belief in White Christ seems to have dampened Thorgisl's Viking spirit somewhat. In any event he made no move to take up Erik's invitation until some years later when his son, Thorleif, returned from abroad and persuaded his father to stir his stumps. In 997 father and son, with wives, dependants and friends, set out for Greenland.

The oral account of this voyage was eventually set down on parchment late in the 13th century by Icelandic Christian priests who were unable to resist the opportunity to make propaganda out of it. Into the original account they intruded a great deal of superstitious nonsense (most of which I have deleted), calculated to redound to the credit of Christ and to the derogation of Thor. Nevertheless the clerics (clerks) were honest in their way. They made every effort to record what had survived of the oral saga, even if they could not resist the temptation to add to it. Consequently the Saga of Thorsgisl Orrabeinsfostri contains the outline and often the intimate details of a truly remarkable voyage into the polar regions nearly a thousand years ago.

Until recently it was automatically assumed that the locale of the voyage was the Greenland Sea and the east coast of Greenland. In my book *Westviking* I have shown that the voyage was into Baffin Bay. Owing to losses in the original text it is not possible to pinpoint the place where the ship was eventually wrecked but the likelihood is that Thorgisl's ship drove ashore somewhere on the northwest coast of the Bay.

The return voyage, in a small boat, started from a place where there was considerable pack ice and where the fiords sometimes stayed frozen all summer long. Since the Little Climatic Optimum was near its peak in 997, and there was little or no pack ice in southern or central Baffin Bay, the wreck must have taken place in a high latitude – probably north of 79°. This is confirmed by the fact that it took the survivors most of two summer seasons to make their way south as far as the Norse colonies in southwestern Greenland.

Reconstructing the beginnings of the voyage, from what the saga tells us, and by analogy with other similar Norse voyages (such as that of Bjarni Herjolfsson) we suppose that during her three months at sea after leaving Iceland the ship was blown south and west of the south tip of Greenland; then was headed north in an attempt to regain lost latitude (the Norse could determine latitude, but not longitude); drove into Baffin Bay, and spent weeks beating about, hopelessly lost, until the combined effects of wind and current set her ashore somewhere on the northwestern coast of the Bay. Such a sequence of events could only have taken place if the weather had been abnormally stormy, and visibility consistently bad. There is much evidence to show that just such conditions prevailed during the summer of 997. The Greenland Norse fishery was a failure that year and there was a famine the following winter as a result of the bad weather, which not only disrupted the fishery but drowned many fishermen. At least one other ship bound from Iceland to Greenland (Thorbjorn Vifilsson's) was nearly lost through fearfully bad weather, and took many weeks to make a landfall in Greenland. A vessel carrying Leif Eriksson, and bound from Greenland to Norway, encountered such bad weather that she was blown south to the Hebrides, where she was forced to spend the winter.

Although we cannot be certain of how far north Thorgisl voyaged, we must credit him with the first really deep penetration into Baffin Bay along the route that later men were to follow in their attempts to reach the North Pole. His is also the earliest existing account of European man's battle for survival in truly arctic regions and, as such, deserves pride of place as the opening story in this volume.

Some time after Thorgisl gave up the worship of Thor and took to himself the belief in Christianity, he dreamed that Thor came to him with a threatening face, declaring that Thorgisl had failed him and that he had been ill-advised. "You have thrown the silver which I gave you into a foul pool, but I will pay you back for that!"

"God will protect me," said Thorgisl, "and I am glad that our partnership is at an end."

When Thorgisl woke in the morning and went out of doors he saw that his yard-boar was dead, and he had it buried so that it would not be used for food.

Once again Thor appeared to Thorgisl in a dream, and told him it would be just as easy to choke him to death as it had been to choke his yard-boar. Thorgisl replied, "God will settle this matter." Thor then threatened to harm his cattle, but Thorgisl said he was not afraid. The next night an old ox of Thorgisl's died. After that he began watching over his cattle himself. One morning when he came back from watching his cattle he was blue all over, and the men of the place took it as a sign that he and Thor must have met. But after that the plague amongst the cattle was stayed.

Thorgisl was the tallest man in Iceland; a dauntless man and very self-willed.

Time passed and, one year, when the ships again began to sail from land to land, Erik the Red in Greenland sent a message to Thorgisl inviting him to come to Greenland and to make his home there. Erik offered to do everything in his power to assist Thorgisl to settle. At first Thorgisl was not very interested. But a few years later a ship came in from seaward bearing Thorleif, Thorgisl's son, who had been on a Viking voyage abroad and brought back great wealth.

Thorgisl was delighted to see his son and he now decided that he would make a trip to Greenland. He asked his wife whether she would go with him, and Thorey replied that it was a great risk to change one's home. Thorgisl said that Erik had sent him an invitation, and he intended to go, "but you may stay behind if you want, and look after our homestead." Thorey still thought it was a mistake to leave home but agreed to go if he was going. Thorgisl then placed his cattle in the hands of his brother and also his lands at Tread-holt; these things to be kept for his heirs if he should fail to come back.

Thorgisl's planned departure was widely reported over the countryside. His son Thorleif was to go with him, and also Col, and Starkad, Col's brother, and Gudrun their sister. Thorarin, the farm foreman, was to go with ten thralls, including Snae-Col and Ozur. Thorgisl had selected his men chiefly on the basis of their usefulness in setting up a homestead in Greenland, and they were all powerful men. Thorgisl took with him all kinds of livestock in case he should set up housekeeping there. His friend Iostan, the owner of Calfholt, decided to join Thorgisl in his voyage and give up his home in Iceland. Iostan had twelve people with him, including Thorgerd his wife, and Thorarin their son, who was a very brisk fellow.

Thorgisl now went and bought a ship in Leiravage. He then gave over the care of his dependants at home to a man named Thorald. Thorgisl intended to take his eight-year-old daughter Thorny with him on the voyage but she fell sick while they were preparing to go aboard the ship. After waiting three nights for her, Thorgisl decided he could not wait any longer and so he gave her forty hundreds of three-ell ounces of silver in case she should need them, saying that perhaps her fate lay there in Iceland. Thorgisl said that he put great faith in the promises made by Erik the Red. However, one of his friends replied, "It is not easy to judge men at a distance, and not least of all when a man is put to great expense over it." Thereupon Thorgisl declared he was rather against going at all, but had not the heart to turn back now.

Thorgisl boarded his ship and waited for a fair wind. While lying at anchor he dreamed that a huge man with a red beard† came to him, saying: "You have got a considerable journey ahead of you and it will be a hard one." The dream figure seemed particularly grim to Thorgisl when he continued: "You have been against me all along, even while you were still a pagan; all the same your change of faith is a great loss to me. Before you changed, the people all sought our help and aid, but now you are against the old gods and you will fare ill unless you change back to a belief in me. Then I will take care of you as I have done in the past."

Thorgisl declared that he wanted no help from Thor and told the god to go away and leave him alone. In his dream Thorgisl thought he replied to Thor saying, "My journey will go as God wills it." Then he thought that Thor brought him to a great cliff where the sea was smashing upon the rocks and said, "You shall find yourself in just such breakers as these, and for a long time, too, you will suffer being tossed about upon the sea and be tormented and in misery and peril, unless you become my man." At this Thorgisl cried out in his dream: "Be gone, you foul fiend!"

After that he woke and told his dream to Thorey, saying: "I would have given up the voyage at once if I had dreamed such a dream before I came on board, but now I am committed. I do not wish you to tell Iostan or any of the others what I have dreamed." Thorey said it was a bad omen but she agreed he was wise to have nothing to do with Thor. "I too would have stayed behind if I had dreamed such a dream," she said.

Then a fair wind came and they sailed out of Faxafiord. Iostan and his people had the forward part of the ship ahead of the mast; and Thorgisl's people had the part of the ship abaft the mast. When they got out of sight of land the fair wind failed and they were tossed about at sea for a long time, until both meat and drink ran short.

One night Thorgisl dreamed again of Thor, who came to him saying: "Has it not gone as I told you it would? This is because you have refused my help. But perhaps even yet your conditions may improve if you will agree to serve me." Thorgisl declared he would not serve Thor even if his life was at stake and ordered his enemy to go and never come back again.

The condition of the people aboard ship grew even more miserable, and it was getting on to harvest time and they were still at sea. Some of the people were now in favour of placating Thor at any cost, saying that other folk had made good voyages in the days when they used to sacrifice to Thor, and the best plan would be to do as had been done in the past. Thorgisl replied by saying: "If I get wind of anyone sacrificing to Thor, and becoming an apostate, it will go very hard with them."

Again Thorgisl dreamed that Thor came to him, speaking thus: "You have betrayed me once again by refusing to let your men serve me! But even though I have delayed you so that many of your shipmates are at the point of death, all the same you will still make safe harbour in seven days time if you will agree to do homage to me." Thorgisl replied: "Though I never make harbour, I will have nothing to do with you." Thor answered, saying: "Even if you refuse to be my man, the least you can do is to pay me back what you owe me."

Thorgisl woke and thought about this dream for a long time before he

†*This was Thor. Thorgisl had been a Godi, or priest of Thor, before becoming a Christian.*

remembered that he had once dedicated a calf to Thor. He told his wife about this and said that nothing belonging to Thor should be allowed to remain aboard the ship. The calf was by now grown to be an old ox, but Thorgisl and Thorey decided to throw it overboard.

When Thorgerd, Iostan's wife, heard about this she begged for the meat of the ox because they were running short of food. Thorgisl flatly denied her request. She grew very angry at him, saying: "It isn't to be wondered at that things have gone so badly, because we have insulted Thor, and that is the reason we have suffered so." Thorgisl went right ahead and threw the ox overboard; but the ship remained at sea for a long time afterward. By this time they had been three months at sea, with long periods of drifting and very little fair wind. Thorarin, the son of Iostan, was the most useful man on board next to Thorgisl; he was only twenty years old at this time.

From the 11th cent. Bayeux tapestry.

Viking ship, from a rock carving.

It is told that one evening they wrecked their ship on the ice mountains of Greenland,† on a sand bank in a certain fiord. The ship broke up and the stern drifted ashore to the south of where they were. All the people and live-stock were saved and the after-boat came safe to shore as well. It was then early in October, a week before winter began. Glaciers ran around the sides of the bay and the most habitable spot lay in the western part of it. Here they all laboured to build a hall which they divided into two parts with a cross-partition. Thorgisl's party had one end of the hall and Iostan's party the other. They had saved a little meal from the wreck and some other flotsam and jetsam, and the two parties shared these things. Most of their surviving cattle died for want of fodder during the winter.

Thorgisl's men were always better at hunting and fishing than Iostan's. Thorgisl made his men be temperate and kept them quiet in the evenings. Good-wife Thorey was far gone with child at this time, and not very strong.

Iostan and his people tended to stay up late at night and make a wild time of it, engaging in mummery and gaming and one thing and another.

On one occasion Iostan spoke to Thorgisl saying that there seemed to be a great difference in their catches. Thorgisl told him this was because they did not work in the same way: "You keep longer at it in the evening," he said, "But we get started earlier in the morning." Iostan then demanded that everything they caught should be shared, and so it was done. Thorgisl was always the luckier, yet neither side ran short. It is said that a coolness sprang up between the two men because Thorgisl and his people were well behaved and quiet, but the others kept up their gaming, with lewd uproar and ribald times.

About midwinter Thorey had her baby. It was a boy, and they called him Thorfinn; but Thorey did not do well on the kind of food they had. Now it drew on toward Christmas time and Thorgisl spoke to his people about it saying that he wished them to be quiet and well behaved.

On the second night of Christmas, Thorgisl and his men went to bed early. They had barely got asleep when Iostan's men came in, very noisy, and ready for meat. Thorgerd was in the midst of all their ribaldry for she was as strong as a man. While they were all eating there came a loud, sharp blow on the door. One of them jumped up, saying: "This must be an announcement of good news." He ran out through the door, and was a long time in coming back. Finally Iostan and his men went out looking for him and discovered that he was stark raving mad. In the morning he died.

Now a general sickness came over Iostan's company and six people died; and then Iostan himself caught the sickness. Thorgerd watched over him but the sickness wore him out and he died, and he and the rest were buried in the

†Greenland, to the early Norse, embraced the lands on both sides of Baffin Bay.

new-fallen snow. Then Thorgerd caught the sickness and died and so, one after another, all the people who had been in Iostan's party died. At the last day of Christmas [the ghosts of] Iostan's company walked again, especially Thorgerd. Thorarin, Iostan's son, died last of all and was buried under the wreck of the ship; and they were all dead by the end of February. There were then great hauntings. The spirits mainly haunted the part of the hall which had been the Iostaners' in life, but they also came into the other part too, and Thorgerd's ghost was particularly troublesome. Finally Thorgisl had all the corpses piled up and burned in a bale-fire, and after that there was no more trouble.

Early in the winter both parties had been working at rebuilding their ship. Now Thorgisl and his men completed a new one out of the wreckage. But they could not get away that summer because the fiord ice did not clear out of the bay. They spent the summer hunting, and building up their stocks of provisions. The next winter began and Gudrun, Col's sister, died. Col buried her under her berth in the house. When the second spring arrived they still could not get away.

One night Thorey had a dream and told it to Thorgisl. She had seen a fair countryside filled with beautiful people and she said: "I have high hopes that we shall finally be released out of this misery." Thorgisl replied: "That is a good dream, but it is just as likely that the things you saw belong to the other world." Thorey then begged them all to try to find a way out of these desert regions if they could. Thorgisl replied that he did not see how it could be done. As for Thorey, she was forced to stay in her bed.

One fine day Thorgisl announced he would walk up to the top of the glacier to see if he could find any sign of the fiord ice loosening. Thorey said she did not like him going any distance away from her, and when he replied that he would only go a short way she answered that she supposed he would have his will this time as always.

The daily routine for the slaves was to go fishing and spend the day at it. Thorarin, the overseer, would see them off each day and then return into the house to stay by Thorey.

Thorleif and Col and Starkad wanted to go with Thorgisl. He told them that, if they did so, there would be none to keep an eye on things at home and: "We should then be trusting the slaves too much if we did that."

Nevertheless they all went off to climb the glacier. Thorgisl had a pole-axe in his hand and had his famous sword, "Earth-house-loom," girded on him.

They walked and climbed most of that day until bad weather caught them. It was late before they got back. When they reached the hut they found the ship had disappeared. They went into the house at once and found all their chests were gone and their stock of supplies had been rummaged, and the slaves had vanished. "This is a black lookout," Thorgisl said. They went on into the dark back part of the hall where they heard a gurgling sound from Thorey's bed.

Thorgisl discovered at once that she was dead, and the noise was the sound of the boy suckling at her even though she was a corpse. They examined her and found that under her arm the flesh was clotted with blood and there was a little wound as if a fine knife-blade had pierced her. All the bed clothes were soaked in blood.

This was the most terrible trial Thorgisl had ever known. They buried Thorey beside Gudrun, and Thorleif did his best to cheer his father up. The slaves had stolen all the provisions; had taken the very doors off their hinges; and all the bed coverings and blankets were gone.

All that night Thorgisl watched over his infant son and he could see that the

In such a ship – this is an artist's conception – Leif Ericsson is thought to have discovered North America.

The hull of a 9th century longship preserved near Oslo. These craft sailed to Greenland with a crew of 90.

Norse fishermen, according to the
Sagas, sailed these sturdy boats
to Markland (probably Labrador).

▼ The longship of war struck fear
into maritime settlements. The
sails were striped, the hull painted.

boy would not survive unless something heroic was done to save him. He did not intend to let his son die if he could help it. He showed his mettle then, for he took a knife and cut his own nipple.† It began to bleed and he let the baby tug at it until blood mixed with fluid came out. He did not stop until milk came out; and the boy was nursed upon that.

When Snae-Col and the other slaves had run off with the ship they had taken the big cooking kettle and left only one small kettle belonging to Thorey. There were also a few augers, although the tool chest and the rest of the tools were gone. Thorarin, the overseer, had disappeared with them.

Thorgisl and his men were very busy for a while, fishing and hunting as hard as they could, to restore the food supplies stolen by the slaves. After that they began trying to build themselves a boat although they had very few tools. They finally built themselves a hide-covered boat, ribbed inside with timber.

So this summer passed, but they could never get enough food to provision their boat for a voyage. They hauled her up as autumn came, and covered her with a shed. They lived then on such small game as ground-squirrels and on whatever drifted ashore.

One morning when Thorgisl came outside he saw a great piece of flotsam drifting in an opening in the ice. It was the body of some kind of sea mammal. Standing beside it were two huge women wearing skin clothing. They were making up bundles of meat from the animal. Thorgisl ran toward them and slashed at one of them with his sword. He cut the woman's arm clean off at the shoulder. Her bundle dropped down and she ran away.‡ They now had the meat for themselves and so were no longer short of provisions, but by the time spring came their food was almost gone.

Thorgisl declared that he was weary to death of this place and now that the ice had loosened at last he gave the order to set out in their boat. They did not wait for the fiord ice to clear away but dragged their boat along the ice-foot near the shore and, when necessary, over the floes between leads of open water.

They got to the Seal Islands but had a hard time surviving on fishing alone. Once they found some black-backed gulls' eggs. They boiled them and the child Thorfinn ate one egg, but would not eat any more. They asked him why he refused and he replied, "You eat little enough of our food, and so I will eat but little too." They spent their nights ashore and the days aboard their boat. They lived on only small amounts of food.

One day they found the stump of an oar on the shore with these runes carved on it:

A lazy fellow had his head washed while wearily I rowed.

Often out of the cold sea, I swung the oar.

The sea gave me sore palms to my hands.

*While the lazy fellow had his head in the lather.**

They dragged their boat ashore over the ice-foot and came to a clifty place where they set up their tent. They were almost out of food. In the morning Col walked out of the tent and found that their boat had vanished. He went back inside and lay down. He would not tell Thorgisl what had happened, thinking that he was depressed enough as things were. But some time later Thorgisl himself got up and went out and saw that the boat had gone. He came back in and said, "Now I can no longer see how we can survive. So take the boy and kill him." He meant that since they would all soon be dead, it would be better for the boy to die quickly.

Thorleif argued that there was no reason to give up and kill the boy, but Thorgisl insisted they obey orders. They took the child away and Thorleif

†*Improbable as this may seem, it is not inherently so. There are a number of reports scattered through medical literature of babies being nursed by their fathers. A very similar occurrence is recorded by the Franklin Expedition as having taken place amongst the Indians of the Great Slave Lake district in northwestern Canada.*

‡*The "huge women" that Thorgisl encountered were almost certainly Eskimoan. The saga gives a perfectly sound description of two Eskimos dealing with a seal, walrus or narwhal which they had harpooned at a lead in the ice. The error in identifying the sex was a common one. Eskimos wore their hair long, and both sexes dressed much alike, with the result that early European explorers frequently mistook men for women.*

The "lazy fellow" referred to is a ship, and the head-washing refers to the "bone at the teeth," or the bow wave. That this incident should be preserved in the saga, where it apparently has no particular relevance, is an example of how faithful to small historical details the saga records could be.

ordered Col to kill him because, "such a deed would not befit me as his brother, and I refuse to do it." But Col would not do it either, for, he said, the effect of the deed on Thorgisl might be to unhinge him completely.

They left the boy outside and went back into the tent, and when Thorgisl asked if the boy was dead, they answered "no." Then he thanked them and was greatly relieved. "I am badly upset," he told them, "but you have prevented me from committing a terrible crime. I should never afterwards have been considered a man of any worth." After this they all had many dreams and visions, because they were starving. Thorleif dreamed that he saw Thorny, his sister, giving him a cheese with the rind off it. "Maybe she would give you one if she could," said Thorgisl. But Thorleif replied: "The hardest part of our luck must be over, since the rind was all off the cheese."

Some time after this they heard a great deal of noise outside and when they went out they saw that their boat had been returned and there were two women near it holding on to it. These people vanished at once.†

Shortly after that the men discovered a bear struggling in an opening in the ice. It could not get out because its forepaw was injured. They ran toward it and Thorgisl hacked at it with his sword until it was dead, then they drew it up on the ice and loaded it into their boat. The beast had been frostbitten on its forepaw, from which it can be judged how hard conditions were for Thorgisl and his men, from frost and cold, when even the beasts were maimed by the cold.

Thorgisl gave a chunk of meat to every man, but they thought it was too little and grumbled amongst themselves, saying that he was niggardly. Thorleif spoke for the rest: "The men say you are stingy with the meat, father." Thorgisl replied: "It has to be done this way, my son, for we are starving and therefore we cannot eat too much for a while."

They now rowed out of a fiord and it took them a long time too. And then they turned towards the open sea and rowed along past many bays, taking the shortest way across the mouth of the bays when the ice permitted. Then the ice began to open and the whole sound began to broaden out and they went straight on out. Sometimes they dragged their boats over the ice between the leads.

They were terribly weary and even Thorgisl was half dead with thirst. There were only five of them left now: the boy Thorfinn, Thorgisl, Thorleif, and the brothers Col and Starkad. There was no drinking water near them and they were almost famished for lack of a drink. Then Starkad spoke up: "I have heard it said that men have mixed salt water and urine together to make a drink." So they took the bilge scoop and made water in it, and they agreed this was the right thing to do if men's lives depended on it. They asked Thorgisl's permission and he replied that he would neither forbid them to drink it nor give them leave to do so, but that he himself would not drink the mixture. So they mixed it up.

Then Thorgisl asked for the scoop, saying he would give them a toast. He took it and spoke like this: "You cowardly and evil beast, Thor, who are holding us up on our journey, you won't get your evil way and persuade me or any of the others to drink this filth!" And with that he threw the stuff overside out of the scoop.

Then Thorgisl said to the rest of them: "This is a poor way for me to reward you after you saved me from committing a fearful crime when I would have killed my son, but the shame and abomination would always have stuck in your minds if I had let you drink. Now maybe our luck will mend."

Later that same day they were able to get drinking water from ice. And at

†Why the natives should have brought the boat back is not established. They may have found it after it had drifted off, and brought it back in the hope of establishing friendly contact with the strangers.

last they came to the mouth of a great fiord and found a berth there. Later they reached a certain island and they were there three days before they found a linen tent. They recognized it as Thorey's tent. When they went in they found Thorarin, the slave overseer, lying sick. They asked him how in the world he had got there. He told them that Snae-Col and the other slaves had given him the choice of going with them or of being killed at the hall where Thorey died. He said they had spent the previous winter not far from the Seal Islands.

They asked him many questions. He told them that he had been forced to take part in everything; that the slaves had all the goods aboard the ship and that it was Snae-Col who had stabbed Thorey. Thorgisl told him he did not know whether he was one of the guilty or not, but in any case he would not abandon him. But before they could get Thorarin out of the tent he died, and they buried him there.

They kept on along the coast and when harvest time was drawing on again they reached a fiord where there was a boathouse. They pulled up their boat and walked up to where they saw a small homestead.

A man was standing out of doors and he greeted them. They told him about their journey. He said his name was Herjolf and invited them to come and stay with him, and they gladly accepted.

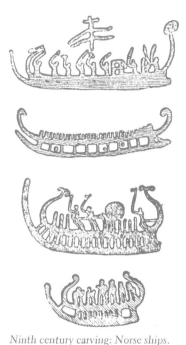

Women of the house tended to Thorfinn and gave him real milk to drink, whereat he said that his father's milk looked quite different.

Herjolf explained that he had been outlawed from the settlement of Greenland because he had committed manslaughter. He was very hospitable to Thorgisl and told him that a ship had come that way in the summer (presumably the stolen ship manned by the runaway slaves) but her people had not come ashore. He also said it was both a long and difficult journey to the settlement which was where Thorgisl wished to go, and so they stayed that winter with him.

Ninth century carving: Norse ships.

In the spring Herjolf told them they could either stay on with him or take any of his boats if they wanted to continue to the settlement. Thorgisl accepted the offer of a boat and said he would do whatever he could to reward Herjolf. Herjolf replied that he hoped Thorgisl would make out well, and requested that he try to get him re-admitted to the settlement.

Thorgisl promised to do what he could and when they parted they blessed each other.

Now they journeyed on southward along the coast, passing Hvarf (probably Cape Desolation, just north of the eastern settlement in the Julianehaab Bight) and they were on their way until harvest time. Early in October, when winter began, they reached Eriksfiord which they entered. They moored their ship and set up their tent ashore.

At this moment they saw a merchant ship sailing into the fiord from seaward. It had the same wind as they had and arrived at the same landing place. Then Thorgisl said: "This is a happy sight! Thorleif and Col, go and meet the men. Perhaps they will have some news to tell us."

Thorleif and Col went to the merchant ship and climbed aboard her. On her afterdeck was a man in a red kirtle who sprang up at once, greeting Thorleif warmly. His name was Thorstan the White, Thorleif's foster-father and step-father. He at once asked after Thorgisl. And they told him where he was.

Thorstan went at once to see Thorgisl and there was a joyful meeting. Thorstan said that he was just arrived from Iceland and that Thorgisl's estate was as he had left it, although he had not been heard of for four winters. He also said that Thorgisl's daughter Thorny had married Bearne-o-Grave.

"When Thorleif did not appear in Norway to visit me I got my ship ready and went out to Iceland and there I spent two winters. But when I heard no news of you there I was determined to find you in Greenland and I am glad now that I have come upon you. Everything that I have, you shall consider as being your own."

Thorgisl replied that no offer could be more timely, but it was only what was to be looked for from Thorstan the White. The next day they sailed to the market harbour in Eriksfiord and fixed their tents on the shore. Men soon came down to them and Erik the Red asked Thorgisl to his house with all those he wished to take along with him.

Thorgisl was given a place of honour beside Erik on the second bench, and Thorstan sat next to him. Thorfinn was given a wet-nurse but would not drink milk before it was night, and shortly afterwards he was weaned from the breast.

Erik was not very gracious to them and the visit did not go off with as much heartiness as Thorgisl had expected. (This was undoubtedly due to the fact that Thorgisl had become a Christian, whereas Erik remained a pagan until his death.) Thorgisl got news that his slaves were living in the land in great estate and telling very little that was true about their voyage.

That winter a polar bear came in amongst the sheep and did a lot of damage. Men from both settlements got together and agreed to pay a price for the bear's death. One day when Thorgisl was in the storehouse the boy Thorfinn called out to his father, saying: "There is a beautiful white dog outside. I never saw one like it, he is so big." His father was busy and told him not to bother about it and not to go out. But the boy ran out anyway.

It was the bear. It had come down off the glacier. It caught the boy and he cried out. Thorgisl ran out with his sword, "Earth-house-loom." The bear was toying with the boy. Thorgisl struck the bear so hard he split its skull in two; then he took up his son, who was not badly hurt.

Thorgisl became famous for this deed and many brought him their share of the bear bounty. But Erik did not like the deed at all. Some say this was because he had an evil and pagan belief in bears.

One day when men were gathered around at Brattalid (Erik's homestead) they got talking about the relative merits of Erik and Thorgisl. One of Erik's servants claimed that Erik was a great chief, but Thorgisl was an unimportant sort of fellow and he wasn't even sure if he was a man or a woman (a reference to Thorgisl's having nursed his son). Whereupon Col snatched up a spear and ran the servant through. Erik ordered his men to seize Col, but a number of traders who were there took Col's side and Thorgisl told Erik it was his personal business to avenge his servant himself. It came close to a battle, but men made peace between them, although it was hard going.

After that Thorgisl went to the western part of the settlement to collect the bear money owing from there. He found Snae-Col and the slaves there. He was going to slaughter them out of hand, but he was persuaded it would make better sense to sell them for hard cash, and this is what he did.

Soon after that, Thorgisl and his men put to sea with Thorstan the White and they had a hard voyage until they neared Iceland. Then they had a southerly gale and made towards the land, but for two days Thorgisl would not let them approach closer for fear of being driven ashore. They lay off for those two days, bailing to keep afloat in the heavy seas. Eight big seas swept the ship and then a ninth came, and it was the biggest of them all. It knocked Thorgisl from the bilge beam where he was bailing, and it picked Thorfinn off his knee and carried the boy overboard.

Then Thorgisl cried out that there was no use bailing any more since the sea which had gone over them had swamped the ship. But at that moment another great wave washed the boy back on deck and he was still alive. Then they all took heart and bailed for all they were worth and managed to save the ship. But Thorfinn vomited blood, and after a while he died.

Thorgisl nearly went out of his mind with grief. He did not sleep nor eat for forty-eight hours and even after they had made land safely he would not part from the body of his son. He had to be tricked into leaving it, and Col took the body to the graveyard and buried it. Thorgisl threatened to kill him for this, but later came to his senses and they were reconciled.

Thorgisl said it was no wonder that women loved the children they had nursed at their own breast better than they could love anyone else.

Thorgisl remarried when he was fifty-five and took over his old estate and prospered. When he was seventy years old he challenged Helge Easterling to personal combat and killed him. When he was eighty-five he took ill and after a week he died, but there are many great men come from his seed and scattered far and wide over the land.

fm Thorgisl seems to have been the first Norseman to voyage so far north into Baffin Bay; but he was not the last. Because few documents survived the ultimate dissolution of the Greenland settlements, it is not to be expected that there should be many written records of Norse explorations high into Baffin Bay; but at least one does exist. This is an account of a voyage made by a party from the Eastern Settlement of Greenland in the year 1266 to discover the "home lands" of the Skraelings (Thule Culture Eskimos) who were then drifting southward down the west Greenland coast and impinging on the Norse. The account is brief but clear and the voyagers seem to have gone as far north as Bylot Island off the northeast coast of Baffin Island.

In addition a rune-stone was found near Upernavik in west Greenland (at about 73° N. latitude) which is believed to date from c. 1330. It tells us that three Norsemen were at this spot on April 24, from which it is clear that they must have wintered in the far north. This is not surprising since there is ample evidence to show that during the 13th and 14th centuries Greenland Norsemen were making annual hunting expeditions far to the north along the coasts of Baffin Bay. In 1876 the British polar expedition, under Sir George Nares, found ancient cairns at 79° 35′ N. latitude on Ellesmere Island, which are probably of Norse origin. Both the Nares party and several later explorers found numbers of eider-duck nesting shelters, of purely Norse pattern, made of slabs of stone, in Jones Sound and near the mouth of Smith Sound. These would appear to have been built by Greenland Norse hunters who may even have wintered this far north. □ FM

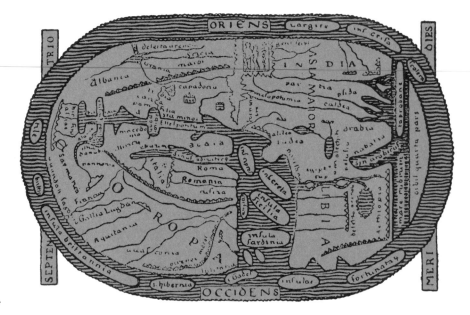

In this 8th century map, after
the Pole came the abyss. This
version was drawn about 1050 A.D.

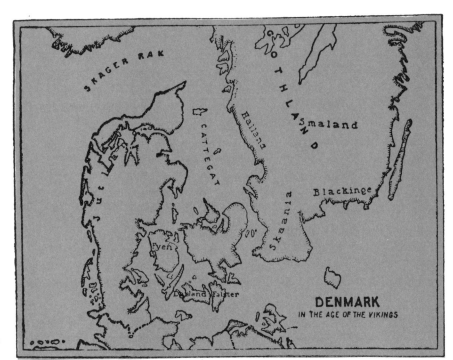

Considerable cartographic skill is
shown in this early map of Denmark.
This was the Viking homeland.

Sigurdur Stafansson, 16th century
Bishop of Iceland, drew this chart
depicting North American coast.

The first explorers in far northern
waters (this is a 16th century
map) navigated "by guess and by God."

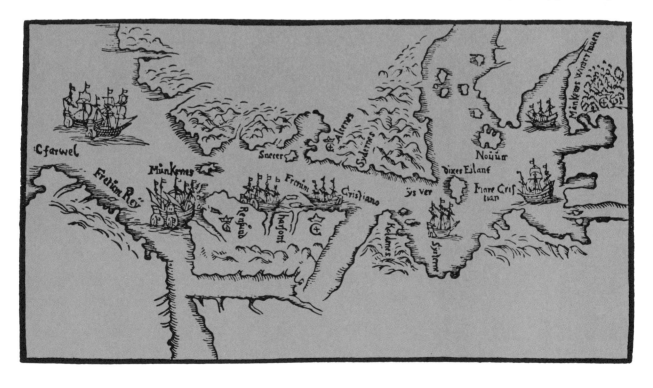

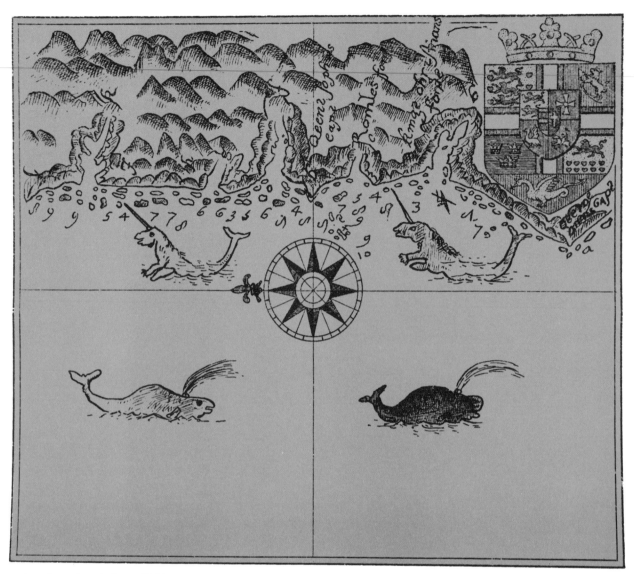

The title on Captain James Hall's map,
circa 1612, reads: "The Coast of
Groineland." Hall sailed with Davis.

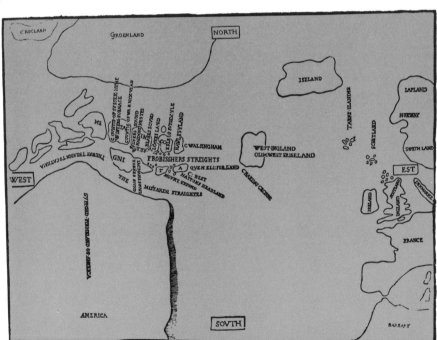

Frobisher's discoveries as charted
by George Best. "Mistaken Straightes"
were, of course, Hudson Strait.

CHAPTER 2 THE BAY OF DISBELIEF

The Icelandic Norse had not been sitting idly at home. An ancient Icelandic geography tells us that before 1300 they had explored the east coast of Greenland at least to 80° N. latitude, and probably right to the northern tip of that great island. They also seem to have reached Spitsbergen, or to have seen the island archipelago, for they knew there was land at the top of the Greenland Sea. Some of them deduced that there must be a land bridge stretching from Greenland right across to Russia; but others evidently believed there was a polar sea to the north of the Greenland Sea and, moreover, they believed it to be an open and ice-free ocean.

About 1360 a monk or scholastic named Nicholas of Lynne, reputedly a mathematician at Oxford, made several voyages into the "northern regions" and wrote two books about his findings. Unhappily both have perished, leaving us only their titles. But the books themselves were still available in the 1500s when the great cartographer Gerardus Mercator was doing his best work. Mercator used Nicholas's findings when, in 1569, he drew a chart of the north polar region. This chart shows a complete circlet of land lying north of Asia, America and Europe, pierced by four great "gulfs" through which pour the waters of an ice-free polar ocean that surrounds the Pole itself.

The concept of an ice-free polar ocean seems to have had its genesis in actual observations made by the Norse during the Little Climatic Optimum. When Henry Hudson set out to sail across the Arctic Ocean to Cathay in 1607, he carried with him sailing directions for arctic waters written by Ivar Bardarsson, a Greenland Norseman of c. 1350. Considering that Nicholas of Lynne appears to have brought back news of an open polar sea after his visits to the Norse-dominated regions in the mid-1300s we can believe that Bardarsson's directions also indicated the existence of an open ocean in the north, and that was why Hudson attempted to reach the Far East by sailing north up the east coast of Greenland.

One thing is certain: the concept of an open polar sea was ancient, deep-rooted, widespread, and tenaciously preserved.

Columbus knew about it, and seems to have thought that the polar route offered great possibilities, although he personally preferred a passage in a more comfortable climate.

In 1527, *before* Mercator drew his polar map, an Englishman named Robert Thorne was doing his best to persuade King Henry VIII that the way to short-circuit Spanish and Portuguese control of the temperate sea routes was to sail straight to the Indies across the Polar Sea. Thorne was responsible for an expedition setting out about 1527 "to set forth a discovery even to the North Pole." All that we know about the voyage is that one of the vessels was said to have been wrecked "on entering a dangerous gulf between the north of Newfoundland and Greenland." The north of Newfoundland, in those days, was the north of Labrador, so the ship was either lost in Davis Strait or, perhaps, somewhere farther north in Baffin Bay. In any event Thorne seems to have moved the lethargic business minds of England to definite action, and in 1553 Sir Hugh Willoughby was sent out to try for a polar passage or a northeast passage to the Indies. He and his own ship's crew, to a man, died of scurvy on the Russian arctic coast, although two ships of his squadron managed to make it back to England.

This was a bit discouraging, so English eyes shifted back to the west. Between 1576 and 1578 the bucaneering Martin Frobisher led three expeditions into the northwest waters, but they were blunted against Baffin Island. Then, in the 1590s, John Davis made three tries to broach the ice barriers that lay across the northern passage on both sides of Greenland. He made his best northing on the west Greenland coast at 72° 41′ and gained recognition for the discovery of Davis Strait in the process. But neither Davis nor Frobisher had broken through to the open polar sea, and so interest shifted to the east again. In 1596 Willem Barents piloted two ships straight north from Norway to discover the Spitsbergen archipelago. Barents coasted these islands to about 80° north latitude and there met the implacable ice. It cost him his ships and his own life.

By this time it should have been apparent that climatic conditions had changed radically since the days when the Norse had found it possible to sail so far north that they believed in the existence of an open polar ocean. From c. 1250 on there had been a steady deterioration in the arctic climate. The Arctic Ocean had become its old, frozen self – the *Mare Glaciale*. Great streams of pack ice were once again surging south in the East Greenland Current and down through Baffin Bay and Davis Strait. Conditions continued to grow steadily worse, culminating, between 1650 and 1850, in what has been called The Little Ice Age; but apparently nobody living in those times noted any great change in climatic conditions.

During the first decade of the 1600s the Danes joined the polar "puscht" by sending three expeditions up the west coast of Greenland under the direction of the English ice pilot, James Hall, who had been out with Davis. The best these voyages accomplished was 67° N. latitude. This seemed to prove that the Davis Strait–Baffin Bay route was hopelessly blocked by ice, and so the next polar expedition tried a different tack entirely.

In 1607 Henry Hudson set out to sail across the Pole on behalf of the Muscovy Company. The voyage is not one of his better-known ones, for Henry Hudson sticks in our minds mainly because he ascended the Hudson River and is credited with discovering Hudson Bay. Yet the voyage of 1607 was his greatest exploit. In an old and leaky ship, and with a rag-tail crew, Hudson fought his way north up the east Greenland coast to 76° 38′. Then, baffled by the ice, he bore away to the northeastward until he raised Barents's Newland (Spitsbergen) at 79°. For weeks he beat around in this uncharted maze of islands, reefs and rocks, bedevilled by fog and ice, but persistently trying to work his wreck of a vessel northward. In the end he managed to reach 81° or perhaps a little better. Although he never caught a glimpse of the open polar sea that he was seeking, two centuries were to slip away before his record northing was surpassed.

Instead of laying the beckoning ghost of the open polar sea, Hudson's voyage only seems to have fleshed it out. It was now assumed that there was a ring of pack ice around the outer edge of the open arctic sea, and that if a ship could only squeeze through this icy girdle, the rest of the way would be clear sailing.

Jens Munk's Danish expedition wintered in the mouth of Churchill River, Hudson Bay, in the year 1619.

When scurvy struck, Munk's voyage turned to tragedy; of 64 men, only three survived – but they sailed home.

But the problem of getting through the girdle seemed insoluble. For a time men turned to an alternative – the idea of a Northwest Passage around North America. In 1610 the Muscovy Company sent Hudson on his final, fatal voyage to Hudson Bay; but when subsequent voyages indicated that Hudson Bay was a cul-de-sac, the Muscovy Company shifted its interest back toward the north. This time it chose Davis Strait as the avenue through which to launch a new attack.

The two men picked to lead the attack, and the ship that was to bear them, represented a formidable trio.

Robert Bylot was an illiterate from a working-class background, who had worked his way from the forecastle to the rank of master. He was first mate to Henry Hudson on the fatal voyage to Hudson Bay and it was entirely due to him that the mutiny-racked *Discovery* ever got back to England. Bylot was tried as a mutineer, but even the myopic Lords of Admiralty, who would hang a man on the merest suspicion of disobedience to an officer, seem to have recognized his worth, and he was freed. Thereupon the Muscovy Company hired him to go as master on the *Discovery* in a second and then a third voyage into Hudson Bay, in a fruitless attempt to find a passage out of it to the northwest. On the last of these voyages he had with him as pilot (a rank roughly equivalent to chief officer, or navigating officer in modern parlance) a man named William Baffin.

Baffin was of a different cut. Well educated, he was a first-rate mathematician and could write fluent prose. But he too was an old arctic hand. He had served as pilot with Captain James Hall on a voyage to Greenland in 1612, during which Hall was murdered by Eskimos in reprisal for a kidnapping perpetrated by the Danes a few years earlier. Returning to England in command of Hall's ship, Baffin was hired by the Muscovy Company and made two voyages, in 1613 and 1614, to Spitsbergen where he extensively explored and charted that polar maze of rocks and islands.

The *Discovery* was a bluff-bowed, fantastically strongly-built ship (she was almost a solid mass of wood below decks) that had made at least five arctic voyages and had suffered almost every imaginable danger but had always managed somehow to bring her people back to England, even when they were incompetent or when they were so reduced by hunger and disease that the old ship practically had to sail herself.

The men and the ship were well tried and well matched when, in the spring of the year 1616, they put out from England to seek the elusive passage to the north.

In the name of God, Amen. The ship *Discovery* being in full readiness upon the 26th of March, 1616, we set sail from Gravesend, being in number seventeen persons and having very fair weather. The 20th of April, in the morning, we passed between Land's End and the Scilly Isles with a fair wind.

Nothing worthy of note happening [during the sea voyage]. We had a good passage, and the first land we saw was in Davis Strait, on the coast of Greenland, in latitude 65° 20′ [Sukkertoppen].

On the 14th of May, in the morning, six of the local people (Eskimos), being fishing, came to us. We gave them small pieces of iron, they keeping us company and being very joyful, supposing that we intended to come to anchor; but when they saw us stand off from shore they followed us awhile, and then went away discontented.

We continued our voyage being loth to come to anchor as yet, although the wind was contrary. We still plied to the northward until we came into 70° 20′ when we came to an anchor in a fair sound near the place Master [John] Davis called London Coast [Disco Island]. On the 20th of May at evening time, the people, espying us, fled away in their boats, climbing up on the rocks and wondering and gazing at us; but after this night we saw no more of them, they leaving behind many dogs to run to and fro on an island.

At this place we stayed two days during which time we took in fresh water and other necessaries. On the 22nd of May we set sail and plied still to the northward, the wind being right against us as we stood off and on. On the sixth and twentieth day we found a dead whale about twenty-six leagues from shore, having all her whalebone attached. Making our ship fast to the whale we used the best means we could to get the whalebone and with much toil got a hundred and sixty pieces that evening. The next morning the sea rose very high and, the wind arising, the whale broke from us and we were forced to leave her and set sail. We had not stood three or four leagues to the northwestward when we came to the ice. We then tacked and stood to shoreward and a sore storm ensued.

By the 30th we came to Hope Sanderson, the farthest land Master Davis was at, lying between 72° and 73°. That evening we came to much ice, which we put into, plying all the next day to get through it.

The first of June we were clear of the ice and not far from shore, the wind blowing very hard from north-northeast and we put in amongst diverse islands. The people, seeing us, fled away in all haste leaving their tents behind. Upon a small rock [reef] they hid two young maids, or women. Our ship lying not far off, we espied them, and our master, Robert Bylot, went to them with some others of our company in our boat. The maids made signs to be carried to the island where their tents were, close adjoining. When they came to the island they found two old women, the one very old, in our estimation little less than four score years, and the other not so old. The next time we went on shore there was another woman with a child at her back who had hid herself amongst the rocks till the others told her how we had used them, by giving them pieces of iron and suchlike, which they highly esteemed. In exchange they gave us seal skins; other riches they had none save dead seals and the fat of seals, some of which fat or blubber we afterwards carried aboard. The poor women were very diligent to carry the blubber to the waterside to put it in our casks, making show that their men were over at the mainland and at another small island somewhat more to the eastward.

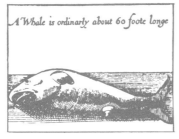

A Whale is ordinarly about 60 foote longe

When the whale comes aboue water y ballop rowes towards him and being within reach of him the harpoiner darts his harpingiron at him out of both his hands and being fast they lance him to death

When the whale is killed hee is in this mann towed to the shipps by twoe or three shal: lops made fast one to another.

Making signs to them that we would show them our ship and carry them to where the men were, the four youngest [were persuaded] to come into our boats. When they were aboard they wondered very much to see our ship and furniture. We gave them some of our meat, which they, tasting, would not eat. Then two of them were set on that island where they supposed the men to be; the other two were carried back to their tents again. Those that went to seek the men could not find them but came as near the ship as they could and at evening we set them over with the others.

This place we called Women's Islands. It lies in the latitude of 72° 45' [Upernavik]. The inhabitants were poor, living chiefly on the flesh of dried seals, which they ate raw. They clothed themselves with the skins and also made covers for their tents and boats. They dress the skins very well. The women are marked in the face with diverse black strokes or lines, the skin being raised by some sharp instrument when they are young, and black colour put therein that will by no means be gotten forth again.

Concerning their religion I can say little, only that they have a kind of worship or adoration of the sun, which they will continually point to while striking their hands on their breast crying "Ilyout." They bury their dead on the side of the hills, commonly on small islands, making a pile of stones over them; yet the stones are not put so close but that we could see the dead body within. The air being so piercing, it keepeth them from stinking. So, likewise, I have seen their dogs buried in the same manner.

Upon the 4th day of June we set sail from there, having very fair weather, although the winds were contrary, and plied to and fro between the ice and the land being, as it were, in a channel seven or eight leagues broad. On the ninth day, being in latitude 74° 4' and much pestered with ice we came to anchor near one of three small islands [the Baffin Islands, north of Cape Shackleton] lying eight miles from the shore. These islands are sometimes frequented by the people in the latter part of the year, as it seemed to us by the houses, and places where the tents had stood; but this year, as yet, they had not come.

The tenth day we set sail from thence and stood through much ice to the westward to see if, at a further distance from the shore, we might proceed more easily. This attempt was soon abandoned, for the more ice we went through, the thicker it was, till we could see no place to thrust in the ship's head.

Seeing that as yet we could not proceed we determined to stand in for the shore, there to abide some few days until such time as the ice was more wasted and gone, for we plainly saw that it was [being] consumed very fast. With this resolution we stood in and came to anchor amongst many islands in latitude 73° 45' [near Cape Shackleton] on the 12th of June.

Here we stayed two days without seeing any sign of people until on the fifteenth day, in the morning, there came forty-two of the inhabitants in their boats or canoes and gave us seal skins and many pieces of the bone or horn of the sea-unicorn [narwhal] and showed us diverse pieces of sea-morse [walrus] teeth. They made signs that to the northward were many of them. In exchange thereof we gave them small pieces of iron, glass beads and suchlike. Several times the people came to us and at each time brought us the aforesaid commodities, by reason of which we called this place Horne Sound.

Here we stayed six days and on the 18th of June we set sail having very little wind. Being at sea we made the best way we could to the northward. Although the winds had been contrary for the most part of this month it was strange to see the ice so much consumed in so little space of time, for now we might come to the three islands before mentioned, and stand off to the westward almost twenty leagues, without being stopped by ice, until we were north to 74° 30′ when we put in amongst much scattered ice. Yet every day we got something farther on our way. Nothing worthy of note but that at diverse times we saw the fishes with long horns, many and often, which we call the sea-unicorn.

fm By following the west coast to Greenland they had taken the only feasible way up through Baffin Bay. They were now entering the open water which, at this season of the year, lay north of the main Baffin Bay ice pack and which later voyagers, particularly the whalers, came to know as the "North Water." ☐ FM

It would be superfluous to write of the weather because it was so variable; there were few days without snow and it was often freezing, insomuch that on Midsummer Day our shrouds, ropes and sails were so frozen that we could scarce handle them; yet the cold is not so extreme but that it cannot be endured.

In the first of July we were come into an open sea on the latitude of 75° 40′, which revived our hopes of finding a passage [to the north]. Because the wind was contrary we stood off twenty leagues from the shore before we met the ice, then standing in again, when we were near the land, we let fall an anchor to see what tide there was, but we found small comfort in that.

fm By anchoring the ship and seeing whether there was a strong tidal current, they hoped to discover if there was a major inlet, or gulf, connecting with the arctic sea, in the vicinity. This procedure clearly shows that Baffin and Bylot must have held to some variant of the theory illustrated by Mercator, of a central arctic sea communicating (through a ring of lands) with the more southerly oceans, by means of gulfs or straits through which flowed strong currents. ☐ FM

Shortly afterwards the wind came to southeast and blew very hard, with foul thick weather and fog. We set sail and ran along by the land. The next morning we passed by a fair cape, or headland, which we called Sir Dudley Digges Cape. It is in latitude 76° 35′. The wind still increasing, we passed by a fair sound twelve leagues distant from the cape, having an island in the middle [Saunders Island, off the entrance of Wolstenholme Sound]. Under this island we came to anchor, but had not ridden [to anchor] more than two hours when our ship dragged, although we had two anchors out. We were forced to set sail and stand forth. This sound has many inlets in it and is a fit place for the killing of whales.

The 4th day of July the storm began again from west and south, so vehement that it blew away our forecourse [sails] and being unable to bear any sails we lay drifting till about 8 o'clock when it cleared up a little and we found ourselves embayed in a great sound. We set sail and stood over to the southeast side where, in a little cove, we let fall an anchor which we lost, cable and all, the wind blowing so extremely hard from the top of the hills that we could get no place to anchor in. We were forced to stand to and fro in the sound, at the bottom of which it was all frozen over.

In this sound we saw great numbers of whales, therefore we called it Whale Sound, and doubtless if we had been prepared for killing of them, we might have struck very many.

All the 5th of July it was fair weather and we kept along by the land until 8 o'clock in the evening, by which time we were come to a great bank of ice, it being backed with land, which, when we saw it, we determined to stand back some eight leagues to an island we called Hakluyt's Isle. It lies between the two great sounds, Whale Sound and the other called Sir Thomas Smith's Sound. This last runs north of 78° and is remarkable because in it is the greatest

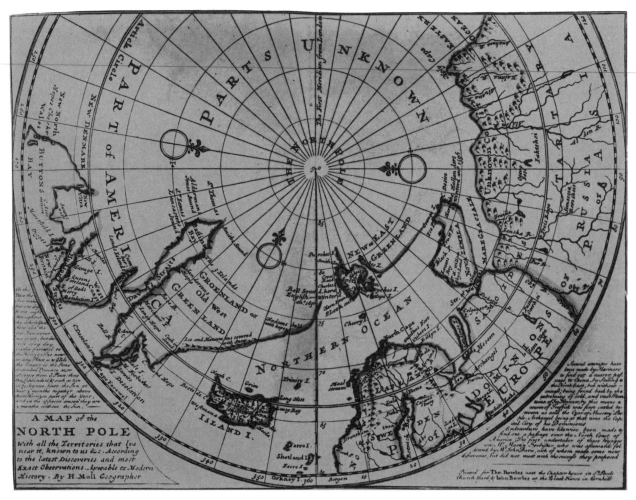

"Parts Unknown" covered half of this map
included in the book Moll's Maps, published in London,
1712. The development of geographic names can be
traced in "Artick Circle" and "Island I." (Iceland).
Note that Ungava was then "New Britain."

Whalers weren't bent on exploration
but their intrepid voyages after
oil added to navigators' knowledge.

In the earliest days, man didn't
always win. This illustration
was first published in France in 1741.

variation of the compass of any part in the known world. I found it to be about 56° varied to the westward. This sound seems to be good for the killing of whales also, it being the greatest and largest in all this bay.

The reason we were of a mind to stand back to Hakluyt's Isle was to see if we could find any whalebone on the shore, and so we came to anchor, but the weather was so foul our boat could not land. The next day we were forced to set sail; the sea was grown so high and the wind came more outward. We spent two days beating back and forth and could get no good place to anchor in. On the 8th of July it cleared up and we, seeing a company of islands lying off from the shore twelve or thirteen leagues, were minded to go to them to see if we could anchor. When we were near, the wind took us short, and being loth to waste more time we took advantage of the wind and abandoned the search of these islands, which we called Carey's Islands.

So we stood to the westward in an open sea with a stiff gale of wind all the next day and until the 10th day at two o'clock in the morning, at which time it fell calm and very foggy, and we were near the land in the entrance of a fair sound which we called Alderman Jones Sound. We sent our boat to the shore, the ship remaining under sail, and as soon as the men were on shore the wind began to blow. They returned again declaring that they saw many sea-morse amongst the ice but, as far as they went, they saw no sign of people nor any good place to anchor.

Having an easy gale of wind at east-northeast we ran along by the shore which now trended much to the south and began to look like a bay.

On the 12th we opened another great sound in the latitude of 74° 20′ and called it Sir James Lancaster's Sound. Here our hope of finding a passage began to lessen every day, for from this sound to the southward we had a ledge of ice between the shore and us, although it remained clear to seaward.

fm The irony is that Baffin and Bylot were so sure the passage north or northwest must be marked by a great current that they never guessed Lancaster Sound could be the passage they were seeking. It was through Lancaster Sound that the Northwest Passage was finally accomplished, but not until almost three centuries after Baffin and Bylot's time. □ FM

We kept close by this ledge of ice till the 14th day, in the afternoon, by which time we were in latitude 71° 16′ [about halfway down the coast of Baffin Island] and perceived the land to the southward of us. Now having so much ice around us, we were forced to stand more to the eastward, expecting to be soon clear of the ice and to keep outside it until we reached 70°, then to have stood in again to the west. But this proved contrary to our expectations, for we were forced to run nearly three score leagues through very much ice which was often so thick that we could go no ways, although we kept our course due east.

When we had gotten into the open sea we kept so near the ice that many times we had much ado to get clear, yet we could not come close to the land until we were about 68°, where we saw the shore, but could not reach it for the great abundance of ice. This was on the fourth and twentieth day of July.

We spent three more days to see if we could come to anchor to make a trial of the tides; but the ice drove us into the latitude of 65° 40′. We then left off seeking to reach the western shore because we were in the indraft of Cumberland [Sound] and knew that there could be no further hope of a passage.

Seeing that we had made an end of our discovery, and the year being too far spent to make a trip to the bottom of the bay [Hudson Bay?] to search for dressed whalebone, we therefore determined to go for the coast of Greenland to see if we could get some refreshment for our men. Master Herbert and two more had kept to their cabins above eight days, besides our cook, Richard Waynam who died the day before. And diverse more of our company were so weak that they could do but little labour. [they were suffering from scurvy]

The wind favouring us we came to anchor [on the Greenland coast] in the evening of the 28th of July.

The next day, going ashore on a little island, we found great abundance of the herb called scurvy grass which we boiled in beer, and drank thereof, using it also in salads with sorrel and orpin, which here grow in abundance. By means of these, and the blessings of God, all our men were in perfect health within the space of eight or nine days.

We stayed in this place three days before any of the people came to us. On the 1st of August, six of the inhabitants in their canoes brought us salmon peeles (grilse) and suchlike, which were a great refreshment to our men. The next day the same men came again, but after that we saw them no more until the sixth day when we had weighed anchor and were almost clear of the harbour. We gave them glass beads, counters, and small pieces of iron, which they do as much esteem as we Christians do gold and silver.

The 6th of August we were clear of this place and the Lord sent us a speedy and good passage homeward. In nineteen days after, we saw land on the coast of Ireland.

fm This was *Discovery*'s sixth, and Bylot's fourth, voyage into the ice – it was the final recorded one for both; but what a period it makes to the career of ship and man: the complete circumnavigation of that ice-bound sea we call Baffin Bay; and the discovery of the two channels, by one of which (Smith) men would eventually reach the Pole itself, while through the other (Lancaster) they would find the long-sought Northwest Passage. The quality of the achievement is underlined by the fact that two centuries passed before another exploring ship could gain a comparable victory over the ice of Baffin Bay.

So startling was the voyage of the *Discovery* that future generations concluded that it was an impossible feat and, consequently, that the whole thing had been a hoax. As late as 1812 charts of this portion of the Arctic did not show Baffin Bay at all, but only a dotted bulge north of Davis Strait in which the legend was printed: *Baffin's Bay according to the relation of W. Baffin in 1616, but not now believed.*

When the Bay was at last officially rediscovered by Sir John Ross in 1818, and the old charts of the voyage were found to be amazingly accurate, something rather odd took place. Under the ægis of the Royal Navy's arctic voyagers and of the historians at home, the entire credit for the discovery was given to Baffin, while Bylot was condemned to almost total obscurity. There were probably two reasons for this. First, although Bylot was master of the ship and unquestionably in command of the expedition, he was an uneducated fellow from the lower strata of English society, while his pilot, Baffin, was a well-educated and accomplished individual, and the account of the voyage that survived into our time was written by him. Consequently it was easy for an uncritical, or biased historian of the 19th century to dispose of Bylot. And the historians were certainly biased. The "definitive" account of the voyage was written by Sir Clements Markham, R.N., in 1881; and Markham just mentions Bylot, and that is all. The reason for this bias was that the Navy and Victorian England could never forgive Bylot for the part he played during the last voyage of Henry Hudson. They felt, and many arctic historians still seem to feel, that it would be almost immoral to allow Bylot his due place in the sun in view of the fact that he chose to remain with, and eventually save, the *Discovery* and those aboard her, rather than volunteering to share a futile death with Hudson in an open boat. So the Victorians of yesterday – and of today – cocked a snoot at Robert Bylot, and did their level best to ignore him out of existence. □ FM

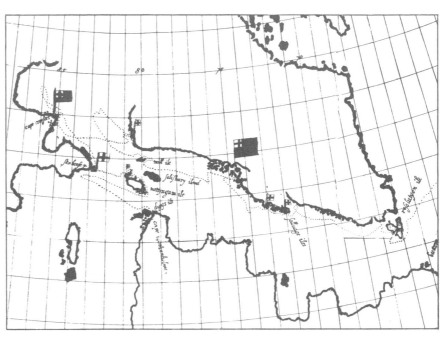

William Baffin's own map of his fourth voyage, 1615. The original is in the British Museum.

CHAPTER 3 A MOTH TO THE FLAME

Attempts to find a way into, and through, the arctic ocean after Bylot and Baffin were spasmodic and scattered. The dream was not dead, but from about 1615 to 1740 interest again shifted to Hudson Bay, from which salient it was still hoped that a passage might be found leading to the west. Only the Russians were really busy in the Arctic during this period. In 1728 a thrust was made by Vitus Bering, out of the Pacific and through the strait that now bears his name. It hardly qualified as a polar voyage, but in 1765 Czarina Catherine sent Admiral Tschitschagoff to penetrate the polar sea via Spitsbergen. The Admiral did his best, but the ice stopped him at 80° 28'. Less than ten years later it also stopped Constantine Phipps sailing out of London for Spitsbergen and the Pole with two ships, *Carcass* and *Racehorse* (ex-whalers both), and accompanied by Horatio Nelson as a boat's coxswain. Phipps reached 80° 23'. Clearly conditions had not improved in the Spitsbergen area since Hudson's time – if anything they had grown worse.

So for a time the fires of the polar passion burned low. Great efforts were being made to find a northeast passage, while exploration in the northwest had almost ceased, having been replaced by a determined effort to exploit the resources of the native peoples and new lands that had been discovered around the shores of Hudson Bay. Ships were still sailing northward (there were as many as 200 of them in some years) but these were commercial vessels and, as such, were of no interest to historians and had no place in the pages of history. They were the whalers, Dutch, American, English and Scots, who had been working the pack at Davis Strait for a hundred years and were now moving north into Baffin Bay itself, as well as plying along the very edge of the pack in the northern reaches of the Greenland Sea. One minor result of the presence of all these whaling ships was that, in 1776, HMS *Lion* was sent out to convoy the British whalers to Davis Strait and give them protection from American privateers. *Lion* was then to proceed "through the Northwest Passage" and meet Captain Cook in the Pacific! *Lion* sailed north to 68° before being turned back by the ice. The following year she went out again with the same tasks and the same instructions and got almost to 73°, which was well into Baffin Bay in the vicinity of Upernavik.

The whalers themselves had done better than that. In 1806 the most famous of all whaling skippers, Captain William Scoresby Sr., made what was in part a working trip and in part a voyage to satisfy his own curiosity, and took his whaler north along the east Greenland coast to 81° 12', thereby surpassing Henry Hudson's record of two centuries earlier, and setting one of his own which was to endure for many years. Scoresby was a realist. He did not expect to find an open polar ocean, and he was not at all disappointed when the ice finally became too much even for him.

The next recorded (in the sense of historical) attempt to reach the open polar sea came in 1812 and took its genesis from the voyages of the *Lion* and of Scoresby. But by then something new had been added to the impetus for polar conquest. With the end of the Napoleonic War the British Navy was left with great numbers of unemployed ships and officers (the men, mostly impressed, were delighted to return to civilian life), and some form of peacetime employment for them was desperately needed. Polar exploration seemed a possible solution. So, in 1812, a four-ship squadron of the Royal Navy was dispatched to make a two-pronged assault on the polar reaches. Aboard the ships went a formidable array of names soon to be famous in arctic annals: John Franklin, Edward Parry, George Back, Edward Sabine, John Ross and James Clarke Ross amongst them.

Captain Buchan in the *Dorothea*, and Lieut. John Franklin commanding the *Trent*, were ordered to reach the North Pole (and this is the first time in history that we hear of anyone actually setting out specifically to *find* that nebulous objective) by way of Spitsbergen, and then to continue on into the Pacific. Full of "wind and vinegar" – to use an old sailors' phrase – the navy took up the challenge. Bravely the two ships bore to the north. They reached Spitsbergen and drove forward with colours flying, but . . . not very far forward. The best they could manage was 80° 40′, less than either Hudson or Scoresby had achieved, and they spent the balance of the summer weather-bound among the islands. There is something faintly pathetic in their bewilderment at finding that the way to the open polar sea was still closed to them.

The second pair of ships, *Isabella* and *Alexander*, under Captain John Ross, did better. Ross took them north up the west Greenland coast, either with a whaler as ice-pilot or making use of sailing information derived from the whalers, into the North Water. He then veered west to the mouths of Jones and Lancaster Sounds and so southward and home again. He had not found an exit from the great bay but he *had* restored Bylot and Baffin's discoveries to the realm of fact.

Lieut. Edward Parry was Ross's second-in-command on this voyage. He was a most ambitious, if not unscrupulous, man (these qualities appear to have been common among true explorers). On his return to England he went behind Ross's back to accuse him of having failed to properly examine Lancaster Sound. At Ross's expense he then managed to obtain command of an expedition of his own to do the job. He sailed in 1819 and made a deep westward penetration into the Sound, with the result that the whole emphasis on arctic venturing underwent a drastic change. A gateway had now been discovered which was presumed to lead to the Pacific. It remained but to prove that ships could navigate this apparent passage. For the next twenty-five years, until a good many men and ships had been lost and the ardour for the passage had been cooled by the frigid arctic wilderness, the search for the passage (and consequent searches for those who had become victims of the search) dominated arctic exploration. The true polar passion almost flickered out . . . but there was one notable exception.

The exception was Edward Parry, now become inordinately famous and having been promoted to the rank of captain. On his first voyage west he had been favoured by a brilliant success, due largely to the fact that he happened to strike an exceptionally good year as far as ice conditions were concerned. But his two follow-up voyages were both dismal failures. Meanwhile, for some inscrutable purpose of its own, the British Parliament had offered a handsome reward for the first person to reach the North Pole. On his return from his third expedition into the northwest, during which he lost one of his two ships and

DISCOVERY OF THE NORTH POLE AND THE POLAR GULF SURROUNDING IT.

A large Ark riding at anchor; her crew starving, and nothing but a drowned horse left for them to eat.
The Pole is a topaz or diamond. The water around the Pole never freezes.

JOHN B. SHELDEN,
DISCOVERER,
MILLVILLE, N. J.

I made this discovery on the night of the 25th of October, 1869.
The Pole is ten degrees high, and ten degrees wide, and round.
The outer wall is ice. The centre of the Gulf is ninety degrees north.

A polar curiosity. But the fallacy of an ice-free sea on the top of the world lasted for centuries, and led to tragedy.

very nearly lost the other without accomplishing anything of note, Parry was delighted to give up the increasingly unrewarding western venturing and try for the Pole instead.

In the spring of 1827 he set sail toward Spitsbergen in command of HMS *Hecla*, the survivor of his last Lancaster Sound voyage of 1824. Parry had learned something from the many futile thrusts made by his predecessors, which had been blunted against the ice around Spitsbergen. He did not expect *Hecla* to breach the girdle of ice. Instead he planned to have his British tars manhandle boats across the intervening pack until they could be launched on the inner, ice-free ocean.

About all one can say of his attempt is that it demonstrated, beyond any shadow of a doubt, the indomitable and enduring qualities of British naval ratings of those times. The men hauled two very heavy boats and a mountain of supplies over the ice from June 21, when they left *Hecla* and Spitsbergen, until August 11. They worked, quite literally, like dogs. And they succeeded in hauling their fantastic load north to 82° 45′, which put them just 172 miles north of where the *Hecla* lay. No open water ever met their yearning gaze until they turned back and were in sight of the black peaks of Spitsbergen.

Again the polar passion flickered low. It did not revive until the middle of the 1800s when it began to be fed with a new and volatile fuel. The central arctic basin no longer interested anyone as a potential trade route to the Indies. It had become, instead, the site of a purely symbolic objective whose attainment offered fame and fortune to some intrepid arctic venturer. The North Pole itself had become *the* lure. It was a cold, white, dazzling lure; and there were to be many men of many nations who would rise to it. The first of them was an American by the name of Elisha Kane.

Between his birth in 1820, and his death thirty-seven years later, Dr. Elisha Kent Kane did so many things in so many different fields of action that it is hard to believe one man could have crowded so much into so short a life. Even before graduating from medical school he fell wildly in love with a 13-year-old spiritualist from Rochester, Margaret Fox, and his passion for her reached such a pitch of notoriety that it became the subject of a wickedly scandalous book called *The Love-Life of Dr. Kane* – a book that became so popular in the United States that Elisha saw fit to leave home for a bit of foreign travel. It turned out to be quite a bit. Before he was thirty he had explored an unknown volcanic crater in the Philippines; had visited Madeira, Ceylon, Brazil, Borneo, Sumatra, China, Nubia, Sennar, Persia, Greece, Mexico, the West Indies, and points between. Along the way he had contracted lockjaw, plague, coast fever, and had been wounded by an irate Mexican armed with a lance.

In his thirtieth year he elected to try a cold climate for a change, and signed on as doctor with an American arctic expedition under Lieut. Edwin DeHaven, USN, which was sent north in 1850 by Henry Grinnell (of whom more later) to join in the search for Sir John Franklin's missing ships and men. DeHaven's ships, *Advance* and *Rescue*, got as far as Griffiths Island in Lancaster Sound, the operations base for a major part of the British searching fleet, before turning about and scudding for home. But both ships were caught in the ice and forced to spend the winter drifting aimlessly about Lancaster Sound and Baffin Bay. The expedition contributed little to the Franklin search, but it did give young Dr. Kane a strong inclination for arctic venturing. Back in New York he began raising funds to support a Franklin search expedition of his own; but while engaged in this he heard about the feat of Captain Edward Augustus Inglefield, RN. In 1852 Inglefield took the steam-auxiliary vessel *Isabel* into Smith

Sound to 78° 35′ and he reported that ice had posed no problem, and that he could have sailed further north if he had had the time. However, this was only a side trip for the *Isabel*, which was under orders to proceed to Lancaster Sound to join the Franklin search.

Kane was a very acute fellow, and he instantly saw the significance of Inglefield's report. He knew, of course, of the ancient belief in an ice-free polar ocean lying north of the girdling pack. Now he surmised that the girdle could perhaps be penetrated by way of Smith Sound. His interest in the Franklin search faded rapidly before the rising flame of a new ambition. Elisha Kane would be the first to reach the Pole!

Kane was far too astute to announce his change of plan. Publicly he remained committed to the Franklin search, but now he let it be known that he had reason to believe the Franklin expedition (which, it will be remembered, was under orders to sail through the Northwest Passage by going *west* around the top of Canada) had got its signals crossed and had gone sailing off due north toward the Pole. Riding the wave of emotion roused by the Franklin search, Kane got the support he wanted.

Henry Grinnell was a New York shipping magnate of recent vintage (part of his fortune had come from buying up the establishment of a man named Preserved Fish) who, like the *nouveau riche* of any age, was desperately anxious for prestige. He had a great deal of money and he was, as we would say, a sucker for a good pitch, particularly when it happened to be a polar one. Having already backed DeHaven, he now agreed to place the *Advance* at Kane's disposal. The newly formed American Geographical Society (of which Grinnell was the first president) also supported Kane. The U.S. Navy agreed to supply a contingent of ten men; and a Mr. Peabody of London, England, was inveigled into putting up quite a lot of cash.

It may not be too early in our story to briefly consider why so many "philanthropists" were willing to spend such vast amounts of money on the polar expeditions of the late 1800s. The reason was simple, although most historians avoid mention of it for fear, perhaps, that the heroic tales of polar adventure may be somewhat besmirched by mundane human motives. The fact is that the rich men expected to buy a degree of immortality by having newly discovered geographical features named after them. And the bigger their investment, the bigger the monument they expected in return. It was, quite literally, by pre-selling the names of as-yet-undiscovered islands, bays, capes, etc., to wealthy men avid for a more lasting fame than mere riches gave, that many seekers after the North Pole financed their expeditions. This was true from the time of Kane to the time of Peary, and it explains why the map of the top of the world is defaced by hundreds of utterly ridiculous personal names applied to some of the most magnificent, if forbidding, natural features to be found anywhere.

With a crew of seventeen aboard, the stoutly-built *Advance* – a 140-ton brig originally built for carrying heavy iron castings, and later strengthened even more for ice navigation – set off from New York on May 30, 1853, carrying Kane northward on his "mission of mercy."

The *Advance* took a lethargic eighteen days to reach St. John's, Newfoundland; but this may not have been her fault. There is reason to suspect that her captain was not quite the seasoned mariner he aspired to be. Captain Kane was captain, apparently, solely by virtue of his own appointment to the post, and, as he notes: "We did not sail under the rules that govern our National ships; but we had our own regulations . . . These included absolute subordination to the officer in command . . . abstinence from all intoxicating liquors except when dispensed under special orders (and) the habitual disuse of profane language. We had no other laws."

Advance spent two days at St. John's where Kane took aboard a team of Newfoundland dogs. Poor beasts! They were as unfit for the future that faced them as were their human shipmates, and they had less luck.

The brig did a little better on the next lap of her voyage, reaching Fiskenaesset in southwest Greenland on July 1. Here Kane bought some Eskimo dogs, and procured the services of the most important member of his expedition – a 19-year-old Eskimo youth named Hans. He also took aboard, either here or farther up the coast (he does not say which) his second most important member, a Danish-Eskimo named Petersen.

Following the usual practice of whalers working north into Baffin Bay, *Advance* kept close to the Greenland coast so she could take advantage of the north-flowing current while at the same time remaining clear of the main pack ice. In the last days of July she reached Melville Bay, the greatest spawning ground of icebergs in the north, and the most dreaded spot on the entire coast. Here the land swings westerly and ships must leave the safe shore passage to risk both the icebergs and the remnants of the spring ice pack. We take up the story from here in Kane's own words.

On the morning of the 27th of July, as we neared the entrance of Melville Bay, a heavy ice fog settled round us. We could hardly see across the decks. By the time the sun had scattered the mist, the bergs, which infest this region and which have earned for it among the whalers the title of "Bergy Hole," showed themselves all around us: we had come in among them in the fog. It was a whole day's work, towing the brig with both boats; but toward evening we had succeeded in crawling off shore.

Two days later we entered the ice intending to work to the northward and eastward. The breeze freshened off shore, breaking up the floes; the leads rapidly closing. Fearing a besetment I determined to fasten to an iceberg and, after eight hours of very hard labour, warping, heaving and planting ice-anchors, succeeded in effecting it.

We had hardly a breathing spell, before we were startled by a set of loud, crackling sounds above us; and small fragments of ice began to dot the water like the first drops of a summer shower. We had barely time to cast off before the face of the berg fell in ruins, crashing like near artillery.

Our position had become critical, a gale blowing off the shore, and the floes closing rapidly. We lost some three hundred and sixty fathoms of whale-line, which were caught in the floes and had to be cut away to release us from the berg. It was a hard night for boat-work, particularly for those of the party who were taking their first lessons in floe navigation.

On Saturday we again moored alongside of an iceberg. We had a rough time working to what the whalers term an open hole. We drove into a couple of bergs and carried away our jib-boom and shrouds, and destroyed one of our quarter-boats.

August 1, Monday: Beset thoroughly with drifting ice. But for our berg, we would now be carried to the south; as it is, we drift with it to the north and east.

2 a.m. – The continued pressure against our berg has begun to affect it; and it has taken up its line of march toward the south. At the risk of being entangled, I ordered a light line to be carried out to a much larger berg, and after four hours labour, made fast to it securely. This berg is a moving breakwater of gigantic proportions; it keeps its course steadily toward the north while the loose ice drifts by on each side, leaving a wake of black water for a mile behind us.

Our brig went crunching through all this crystal jewellery; and, after a tortuous progress of five miles, arrested here and there by tongues of ice which required the saw and ice-chisels, fitted herself neatly between two floes. Here she rested till toward morning when the leads opened up again and I was able, from the crow's-nest, to pick our way to a larger pool some distance ahead. In this we beat backward and forward, like a fish seeking an outlet from a glass jar, till the fog caught us again. But at midnight we were at last clear of Melville Bay and its myriads of discouragements. The "North Water," our highway to Smith's Sound, lay fairly ahead.

We passed the "Crimson Cliffs" of Sir John Ross in the forenoon of August 5th. The patches of red snow,† from which they derive their name, could be seen clearly at the distance of ten miles from the coast. I determined to leave a cairn on Littleton Island and to deposit a boat with a supply of stores in some convenient place near it. Selecting from our stock of provisions and field equipage such portions as we might by good luck be able to dispense with, and adding with reluctant liberality some blankets and a few yards of India-rubber cloth, we set out in search of a spot for our first depot.

We found that we were not the first human beings who had sought a shelter in this desolate spot. A few ruined walls here and there showed that it had once been the seat of a rude (Eskimo) settlement; and in a little knoll which we cleared away we found the mortal remains of the former inhabitants.

Nothing can be imagined more sad and homeless than these memorials of extinct life. Hardly a vestige of growth was traceable on the ice-rubbed rocks; and the stone huts so much resembled the broken fragments that surrounded them, that at first sight it was hard to distinguish one from the other. From one of the graves I took several rudely fashioned pieces of walrus ivory, evidently part of sledge and lance gear. Wood must have been more scarce with them even than with the natives of Baffin's Bay north of the Melville glacier. We found a child's toy spear which, though elaborately tipped with ivory, had its wooden handle pieced out of four separate bits, all carefully patched and bound with skin.

It may be noted among our little miseries that we have more than fifty dogs on board, the majority of whom might rather be characterized as "ravening wolves." To feed this family, upon whose strength our progress and success depend, is really a difficult matter. Accordingly I started out this morning to hunt walrus, with which the Sound is teeming. We saw at least fifty of these dusky monsters and approached many groups within twenty paces; but our rifle balls reverberated from their hides like cork pellets from a pop-gun target. Later in the day Ohlsen found the dead carcase of a narwhal or sea-unicorn — a happy discovery which has secured for the dogs at least six hundred pounds of good foetid wholesome flesh.

August 12, Friday: After careful consideration I determined to try for a further northing by following the coastline. At certain stages of the tides — generally from three-quarters flood to the commencement of the ebb — the ice relaxes enough to give a partial opening along the land. The strength of our vessel we have tested pretty thoroughly; if she will bear the frequent groundings that we must look for, I am persuaded we may seek these openings and warp along them from one lump of grounded ice to another. I am preparing the little brig for this novel navigation, clearing her decks, securing things below with extra lashings, and getting out spars, to serve in case of necessity as shores to keep her on an even keel [when the tide falls].

The day closed with a northerly progress, by hard warping, of about three-quarters of a mile. The men were well tired; but the weather looked so threatening that I had them up again at three o'clock this morning. My immediate aim is to attain a low rocky island which we see close in to the shore, about a mile ahead of us. If we can only reach the little islet, make a lee of its rocky crests, and hold on there until the winds give us fairer propects!

Midnight: We did reach it; and just in time. At 11:30 p.m. we had a whale-line made fast to the rocks. Ten minutes later the breeze freshened directly in our teeth. It is blowing a gale now, and the ice driving to the northward before it; but we rely on our hawsers. All behind us is now solid pack.

August 16, Tuesday: Fast still; the wind dying out and the ice outside closing steadily. Here, for all I can see, we must hang on for the winter unless providence shall send a smart ice-shattering breeze to open a road for us to the northward.

More bother with these wretched dogs! Worse than a street of Constantinople emptied upon our decks; the unruly, thieving, wild-beast pack! Not a bear's paw, nor an Esquimaux skull, or basket of mosses, or any specimen whatever, can leave your hands for a moment without their making a rush at it and,

†Caused by wind-blown red sandstone dust.

after a yelping scramble, swallowing it at a gulp. I have seen them attempt a whole feather bed; and this very morning one of my brutes has eaten up two entire birds' nests which I had just before gathered from the rocks.

August 20, Saturday 3½ p.m. – By Saturday morning it blew a perfect hurricane. We had seen it coming and were ready with three good hawsers out ahead, and all things snug on board.

Still it came on heavier and heavier, and the ice began to drive more wildly than I had ever seen it. I had just turned in to warm and dry myself during a momentary lull, when I heard the sharp twanging snap of a cord. Our six-inch hawser had parted and we were swinging by the two others; the gale roaring like a lion to the southward.

Half a minute more, and "twang, twang!" came a second report. I knew it was the whale-line by the shrillness of the ring. Our noble ten-inch manilla still held on. I was hurrying my last sock into its seal-skin boot when McGary came waddling down the companion-ladders: – "Captain Kane, she won't hold much longer: it's blowing the devil himself."

The manilla cable was proving its excellence when I reached the deck. We could hear its deep Eolianne chant, swelling through all the rattle of the running gear and moaning shrouds. It was the death song! The strands gave way with the noise of a gun; and we were dragged out by the wild sea, and at its mercy.

There was but one thing left for us – to keep in some sort of command of the helm by going freely where we must otherwise be driven. We allowed her to scud under a reefed fore-topsail.

At seven in the morning we were close upon the piling masses of ice. We dropped our heaviest anchor, but there was no withstanding the ice-torrent that followed us. We had only time to fasten a spar as a buoy to the chain, and let the anchor slip. So went our best bower!

Down we went with the gale again, helplessly scraping along a lee of ice seldom less than thirty feet thick. One floe, measured by a line as we tried to fasten to it, was more than forty. One upturned mass rose above our gunwale, smashed our bulwarks and deposited half a ton of ice in a lump upon our decks. Our staunch little brig bore herself through all this wild adventure as if she had a charmed life.

But a new enemy came in sight. Directly in our way, just beyond the line of floe-ice against which we were alternately sliding and thumping, was a group of bergs. We had no power to avoid them; and the only question was whether we were to be dashed to pieces against them or whether they might offer us some providential nook of refuge from the storm.

The memory flashed upon me of one of our escapes in Melville Bay; and as a berg moved rapidly alongside us, McGary managed to plant an anchor on its slope and hold on to it by a whale-line. It was an anxious moment. Our noble tow-horse hauled us bravely on; the spray dashing over his windward flanks, and his forehead ploughing up the lesser ice as if in scorn. The other bergs encroached upon us as we advanced; our channel narrowed to a width of perhaps forty feet; we braced the yards to clear the impending ice-walls.

. . . We passed clear; but it was a close shave (so close that our port quarter-boat would have been crushed if we had not taken it in from the davits) and found ourselves under the lee of a berg in a comparatively open lead. Never did heart-tried men acknowledge with more gratitude their merciful deliverance from a wretched death . . .

But the gale was unbroken and the floes kept pressing heavily upon our berg;

at one time so heavily as to sway it on its vertical axis and make its pinnacle overhang our vessel. My poor fellows had but a precarious sleep before our little harbour was broken up. We were driven astern, our rudder splintered, and the pintles torn from their boltings.

Now began the nippings. The first shock took us on our port quarter; the brig bearing it well and, after a moment of the old-fashioned suspense, rising by jerks handsomely. The next was from a veteran floe, tongued and honeycombed, over twenty feet in thickness. Of course no wood or iron could stand this; but the shoreward face of our iceberg happened to present an inclined plane descending deep into the water; and up this the brig was driven as if some great power was forcing her into a dry dock.

As our brig, borne up by the ice, commenced her ascent of the berg, the suspense was oppressive. The immense blocks piled against her, range upon range, pressing themselves under her keel and throwing her over on her side as she rose slowly, with convulsive efforts, along the sloping wall. Shock after shock jarring her to her very centre, she continued to mount steadily. But for the groaning of her timbers and the heavy sough of the floes, we might have heard a pin drop. Finally, as she settled back into her old position, quietly taking her place among the broken rubbish, there was a deep-breathing silence as though all were waiting for some signal before the clamour of congratulation and comment could burst forth.

It was not until the 22nd that the storm abated and we could return to the coast. We took advantage of the flood-tide to rig our tow-lines and, harnessing ourselves like mules on a canal, made a good three miles by tracking along the coast.

August 26, Friday: My officers and crew are staunch and firm men; but the depressing influences of want of rest, the rapid advance of winter and, above all, our slow progress, make them sympathize but little with this continued effort to force a way to the north. One of them volunteered an expression of opinion this morning in favour of returning to the south and giving up the attempt to winter. Not being able to take the same view, I explained to them the importance of securing a position which might expedite our sledge journeys in the future. The warping began again, each man, myself included, taking his turn at the capstan. The ice seemed less heavy as we penetrated into the recess of a bay; track-lines and shoulder-belts replaced the warps. Our success, however, was not complete. At high water the brig took the ground while close under the walls of the ice-foot.

August 27, Saturday: We failed to get the brig afloat with last night's tide; and as our night tides are generally the highest, I have apprehensions as to her liberation. We have landed everything we could get up on the rocks. Heavy hawsers are out to a grounded lump of berg-ice, ready for instant heaving. Last night she heeled over so abruptly that we were all tumbled out of our berths. At the same time the cabin stove with a full charge of glowing anthracite was thrown down. The deck blazed smartly for a while; but, by sacrificing Mr. Sontag's heavy pilot-cloth coat to the public good, I choked it down till water could be passed from above to extinguish it. It was fortunate we had water near at hand, for the powder was not far off.

5 p.m. – She floats again, and our track-lines are manned! The men work with a will, and the brig moves along bravely. We now had a breathing spell, and I could find time to look out again upon the future. I had seen no place combining so many of the requisites of a good winter harbour as this bay we were now in and which we named Rensselaer Bay. Lofty headlands walled it in

Dr. Elisha Kent Kane explored Borneo
before he succumbed to the polar
passion. He reached a record 80° 10' N.

Kane's book, Arctic Explorations, had
a huge sale in 1856. An illustrator
depicted the expedition's "observatory."

"By the 30th (May, 1616) we came to Hope Sanderson,
the farthest land Master Davis was at. . . . That
evening we came to much ice, which we put
into, plying all the next day to get through it."
– Robert Bylot's fourth voyage.

Kane's own sketch of the Advance amid bergs. The
140-ton brig, especially strengthened to withstand
floes, was donated by shipping magnate Henry Grinnell.
It sailed from New York on May 30, 1853. Grinnell's
reward was to have a portion of Ellesmere Island named for him.

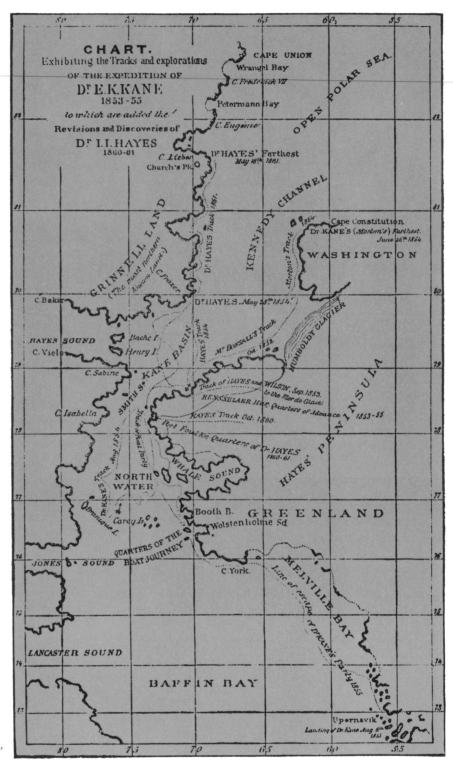

Isaac Hayes travelled as ship's surgeon on the second Kane expedition, then made his own polar venture in 1860-61. Map shows that Hayes believed in an "open polar sea."

beautifully to seaward, enclosing an anchorage with a moderate depth of water; yet it was open to the sunlight and guarded from winds, eddies and drift. The space enclosed was only occupied by a few rocky islets. We found seven-fathom soundings and we laid our little brig in harbour.

FROZEN IN

fm Preparations to spend the winter at Rensselaer Bay were now begun in earnest. Most of the stores of salt meat were moved to a hut built on nearby Butler's Island, where a shelter was also erected for the Eskimo dogs. The Newfoundland dogs were kept aboard ship, sheltered by a large wooden "house" erected over most of the deck space. The ship herself was strongly moored until she should freeze in. An "observatory" was built on shore and a meteorological station upon the ice of the Bay. But Kane's chief interest lay in preparing advance parties charged with establishing depots of supplies as far to the northward as they could get so that, when conditions were ripe, he could make his dash for the heart of the polar regions. □ FM

The thermometer has fallen by the 10th of September to 14°F., and the young ice has cemented the floes so that we can walk and sledge round the brig. The long "night in which no man can work" is close at hand: in another month we shall lose the sun.

We have seen little or no game as yet in Smith Sound. The salmon-trout and salt codfish which we bought at Fiskernaes [Greenland] are placed in barrels, perforated to permit a constant circulation of fresh water through them. Our pickled cabbage is similarly treated, after a little potash has been used to neutralize the acid.

September 13, Tuesday: Besides preparing our winter quarters, I am engaged in the preliminary arrangements for setting out my provision depots along the Greenland coast. My plans for the future are directly dependent upon the success of these operations of the fall. With a chain of provision depots along the coast of Greenland, I could readily extend my travel by dogs, both Esquimaux and Newfoundlanders. Of these last I had ten: they were to be carefully broken to travel by voice without the whip and were expected to be very useful for heavy draught. The Esquimaux dogs were reserved for the great tug of the actual journeys of search.

September 30, Friday: We have been terribly annoyed by rats. Some time ago we made a brave attempt to smoke them out with the vilest imaginable compound of vapours: brimstone, burnt leather, and arsenic, and spent a cold night in a deck-bivouac to give the experiment fair play. But they survived the fumigation. We now determined to dose them with carbonic acid gas. Dr. Hayes burnt a quantity of charcoal and we shut down the hatches after pasting up every fissure that communicated aft, and starting three stoves in the forepeak.

Our French cook, good Pierre Schubert, who with a considerable share of bull-headed intrepidity unites a commendable portion of professional zeal, stole below, without my knowledge or consent, to season a soup. Morton fortunately saw him staggering in the dark and reached him with great difficulty as he fell; both were hauled up in the end, Morton, his strength almost gone, and the cook perfectly insensible.

The next disaster was of a graver sort. I record it with emotions of mingled awe and thankfulness. We have narrowly escaped being burnt out of house and home. I had given orders that the fires should be regularly inspected; but Pierre's misadventure had made the watch careless for a time. A suspicious odour reached me as of burning wood. I descended at once. Reaching the deck of the forecastle, a glance towards the fires showed me that all was safe there. But, while passing near the door of the bulkhead which leads to the carpenter's room, the gas began to affect me. My lantern went out as if quenched by water; and as I ran by the bulkhead door I saw the deck near it a mass of glowing fire. I could not tell how far it extended, for I became quite insensible at the foot of the ladder and would have sunk had not Mr. Brooks seen my condition and hauled me out.

When I came to myself, which happily was very soon, I confided my fearful secret to the four men around me, Brooks, Ohlsen, Blake and Stevenson. It was all-important to avoid confusion: we shut the doors of the galley so as to confine the rest of the crew and officers aft, and then passed up water from the fire-hole in the ice alongside. It was done very noiselessly. Ohlsen and myself went down to the burning deck; Brooks handed us the buckets; and in less than ten minutes we were in safety.

October 1, Saturday: Upon inspecting the scene of yesterday's operations we found twenty-eight dead rats of all varieties of age. A circumstance that happened today is of serious concern to us. Our sluts have been adding to our stock. We have now on hand four puppies of peculiar promise; six have been ignominiously drowned, two devoted to a pair of mittens for Dr. Kane, and seven eaten by their mammas. Yesterday the mother of one batch, a pair of fine white pups, showed peculiar symptoms. We recalled the fact that for days past she had avoided water, or had drunk with spasm or evident aversion; but hydrophobia never occurred to us. The animal walked up and down the deck with a staggering gait, her head depressed, and her mouth frothing. Finally she snapped at Petersen and fell foaming and biting at his feet. It was quite an anxious moment, for my Newfoundland dogs were around the housing, and the hatches open. We shot her, of course.†

October 10, Monday: Our first depot party has been out twenty days, and it is time they were back: their provisions must have run very low, for I enjoined them to leave every pound at the depot they could spare. I am going out with supplies to look for them. I take four of our best Newfoundland dogs, now well broken, in our lightest sledge; and Blake will accompany me with his skates.

I found little or no trouble in crossing the ice until we passed beyond the northeast headland. But, on emerging into the channel, we found that the spring tides had broken up the great area around us, and that the passage of the sledge was interrupted by fissures which were beginning to break in every direction through the young ice.

The dogs began to flag; but we had to press them. In the event of the animals failing to leap any of the rapidly-multiplying fissures we could hardly expect to extricate our laden sledge. Three times in less than three hours my hinder dogs went in; and Blake and myself, who had been trotting alongside the sledge for sixteen miles, were nearly as tired as they were. This state of things could not last, and I therefore made for the old ice to seaward.

We were nearing it rapidly when the dogs failed in leaping a chasm that was somewhat wider than the others, and the whole concern came down in the water. I cut the lines instantly and, with the aid of my companion, hauled the poor animals out.

We rested on the floe. We could not raise our tent, for it had frozen as hard as a shingle. But our buffalo-robe sleeping bags gave us protection; and, though we were too wet inside to be absolutely comfortable, we managed to get something like sleep.

†*Rabies occurs throughout the Arctic in wolves and foxes, who pass it to the dogs.*

The nights which followed were not so bad as one would expect from the saturated condition of our equipment. By alternately exposing the tents and furs to the air, and beating the ice out of them, we dried them enough to permit sleep. The dogs slept in the tent with us, giving it warmth as well as fragrance. What perfumes of nature are lost at home upon our ungrateful senses!

On the morning of the 15th, about two hours before the late sunrise, I perceived far off upon the white snow a dark object which not only moved but altered its shape strangely – now expanding into a long black line, now gathering itself up into a compact mass. It was the returning sledge party.

They had made a creditable journey and were, on the whole, in good condition. They had no injuries worth talking about, although not a man had escaped some touches of the frost. Bonsall was minus a big toe-nail, plus a scar upon the nose. McGary had attempted, as Tom Hickey told us, to pluck a fox, it being so frozen as to defy skinning by his knife. They reached their highest latitude on the 6th October in latitude 79° 50′, and longitude 76° 20′. They buried here six hundred and seventy pounds of pemmican, forty of Borden's meat biscuit, and some articles of general diet; making a total of about eight hundred pounds.

November 7, Monday: The darkness is coming on with insidious steadiness. Our darkness has ninety days to run before we shall get back again even to the contested twilight of today. Altogether, our winter will have been sunless for one hundred and forty days.

November 16, Wednesday: The great difficulty is to keep up a cheery tone among the men. Poor Eskimaux Hans has been sorely homesick. Three days ago he bundled up his clothes and took his rifle, intending to bid us all good-bye. It turns out that besides his mother there is another one of the softer sex at Fiskenaesset that the boy's heart is dreaming of. He looked as wretched as any lover of a milder clime. I hope I have treated his nostalgia successfully, by giving him first a dose of salts, and secondly, promotion. He has now all the dignity of a henchman. He harnesses my dogs and walks with me on my ice-tramps; and, except hunting, is excused from other duty. He is really attached to me, and as happy as a fat man ought to be.

November 27, Sunday: I sent out a volunteer party some days ago with Mr. Bonsall, to see whether any local Esquimaux have returned to the huts we saw empty at the cape. The thermometer was in the neighbourhood of 40° below zero, and the day was too dark to read at noon. I was hardly surprised when they returned after camping one night on the snow. Their sledge broke down and they were obliged to leave everything else behind them. It must have been very cold, for a bottle of Monongahela whisky of good stiff proof froze under Mr. Bonsall's head.

My journal for the first two months of 1854 is so devoid of interest, that I spare the reader the task of following me through it. In the darkness and consequent inaction, it was almost in vain that we sought to create topics of thought, and by a forced excitement to ward off the encroachments of disease. Our observatory and the dogs gave us our only regular occupations.

The first traces of returning light were observed at noon on the 21st of January, when the southern horizon had for a short time a distinct orange tint.

This morning at five o'clock – for I am so afflicted with the insomnium of this eternal night that I rise at any time between midnight and noon – I went upon deck. It was absolutely dark. Not a glimmer came to me through the ice-crusted window-panes of the cabin. While I was feeling my way, two of my Newfoundland dogs put their cold noses against my hand, and instantly commenced the most exuberant antics. It then occurred to me how very dreary and forlorn must these poor animals be, living in darkness, howling at an accidental light, as if it reminded them of the moon, and with nothing either of instinct or sensation to tell them of the passing hours or to explain the long-lost daylight. They shall see the lanterns more frequently.

January 25, Wednesday: The leaders of my Newfoundland team have for the past fortnight been nursed like babies. No one can tell how anxiously I watched them. They are kept below, tended, fed, cleansed, caressed, and doctored, to the infinite discomfort of all hands. Today I give up the last hope of saving them. Their disease is as clearly mental as in the case of any human being. They eat voraciously, retain their strength and sleep well. But they bark frenziedly at nothing, and walk in straight and curved lines with anxious and unwearying perseverance. Their most intelligent actions seem automatic: sometimes they claw you, as if trying to burrow into your sealskins; sometimes they remain for hours in moody silence, and then start off howling as if pursued, and run up and down for hours.

The month of March brought back to us the perpetual day. We needed it to cheer us. The scurvy-spots that mottled our faces gave sore proof of the trials we had undergone. It was plain that we were all of us unfit for arduous travel on foot at the intense temperatures of the nominal spring; and the return of the sun, by increasing evaporation from the floes, threatened us with a recurrence of still severer weather.

But the great object of the expedition challenged us to a more northward exploration. My dogs, that I had counted on so largely, the nine splendid Newfoundlanders and thirty-five Esquimaux of six months before, had perished; there were only six survivors of the whole pack, and one of these was unfit for draught. Still, they formed my principal reliance, and I busied myself from the very beginning of the month in training them to run together.

March 9, Thursday: How do we spend the day? At six in the morning McGary is called. The decks are cleaned, the ice-hole opened and things aboard put to rights. At half-past seven all hands rise, wash on deck, open the doors for ventilation, and come below for breakfast. We are short of fuel and therefore cook in the cabin. Our breakfast is hard tack, pork, stewed apples frozen like molasses-candy, tea and coffee, with a delicate portion of raw potato. After breakfast the smokers take their pipes till nine; then all hands turn to, idlers to idle and workers to work; Ohlsen to his carpenter's bench, Brooks to work with canvas, McGary to play tailor, Whipple to make shoes, Bonsall to tinker, Baker to skin birds, and the rest to the "Office!" Take a look into the Arctic Bureau! One table, one salt-pork lamp with rusty flame, three stools, and as many waxen-faced men with their legs drawn up under them, the deck at zero being too cold for their feet. Each has his department: Kane is writing, sketching and projecting maps; Hayes copying logs and meteorologicals; Sontag reducing his surveying work. At twelve a round of inspection, and orders enough to fill up the day with work. Next, the drill of the dogs – my own peculiar recreation – a dog-trot specially refreshing the legs that creak with every kick, and rheumatic shoulders that chronicle every descent of the whip. And so we get on to dinner-time, which misses the tea and coffee of breakfast, but rejoices in pickled cabbage and dried peaches instead.

At dinner as at breakfast the raw potato comes in, our hygienic luxury. Like doctor-stuff generally, it is not as appetizing as desirable. Grating it down, leaving out the ugly red spots and adding oil as a lubricant, it is as much as I can do to persuade the men to shut their eyes and bolt it, like Mrs. Squeer's molasses and brimstone at Dotheboys Hall. Two absolutely refuse to taste it.†

†*It was intended as an anti-scorbutic.*

Sleep, exercise, amusement, and work at will, carry on the day till our six o'clock supper, a meal something like breakfast and something like dinner, only a little more scant; and the officers come in with the reports of the day. Dr. Hayes shows me the log, I sign it; Sontag the weather, I sign the weather; Mr. Bonsall the tides and thermometers. Thereupon comes in mine ancient, Brooks; and I enter in his journal all the work done under his charge, and discuss his labours for the morrow.

McGary comes next, with the cleaning-up arrangements, inside, outside, and on decks; and Mr. Wilson follows with ice-measurements. And last of all comes my own record of the day gone by; every line, as I look back upon its pages, giving evidence of a weakened body and a harassed mind.

March 11, Saturday: Our fuel is limited to three bucketfuls of coal a day, and our mean temperature outside is 40° below zero; 46° below as I write. London Brown Stout, and somebody's Old Brown Sherry freeze in the cabin lockers. Our lamps cannot be persuaded to burn salt lard; our oil is exhausted and so we work by muddy tapers of cork and cotton floated in saucers. We have not a pound of fresh meat, and only a barrel of potatoes left. Not a man now, except Pierre and Morton, is exempt from scurvy.

THE SLED JOURNEY

March 20, Monday: I saw a depot party off yesterday. They gave the usual three cheers, with three for myself. I gave them the whole of my brother's great wedding-cake which he had sent along for me and my last two bottles of Port, and they pulled the sledge they were harnessed to famously. But I was not satisfied. I could see it was hard work. I followed them and found that they encamped at 8 p.m. only five miles from the brig.

When I overtook them I said nothing to discourage them, and gave no new orders for the morning; but after laughing at good Ohlsen's rueful face, and listening to all Petersen's assurances that the cold and nothing but the cold retarded his Greenland sledge, I quietly bade them good-night, leaving all hands under their buffalo-robes.

March 21, Tuesday: All hands at work house cleaning. Thermometer −48°. Visited our fox-traps with Hans in the afternoon and found one poor animal frozen dead. He was coiled up with his nose buried in his bushy tail, like a fancy foot-muff. A hard thing about his fate was that he had succeeded in effecting his escape from the trap but, while working his way underneath, had been frozen fast to a smooth stone by the moisture of his own breath. These saddened thoughts did not impair my appetite at supper, when the little creature looked handsomer than ever. McGary brings from the traps two foxes, a blue and a white. Afternoon passes, and we skin them. Evening passes, and we eat them. Never were foxes more welcome visitors.

March 31, Friday: We were at work cheerfully, sewing away at the skins of some moccasins by the blaze of our lamps when, toward midnight, we heard the noise of steps above, and the next minute Sontag, Ohlsen, and Petersen came down into the cabin. Their manner startled me even more than their unexpected appearance on board. They were swollen and haggard, and hardly able to speak.

Their story was a fearful one. They had left their companions on the ice, risking their own lives to bring us the news: Brooks, Baker, Wilson, and Pierre were all lying frozen and disabled. Where? They could not tell; somewhere in among the hummocks to the north and east; it was drifting heavily around them when they parted. Irish Tom had stayed by to feed and care for the others; but the chances were sorely against them. It was in vain to question them further. They had evidently travelled a great distance, for they were sinking with fatigue and hunger and could hardly be rallied enough to tell us the direction in which they had come.

Ohlsen seemed to have his faculties rather more at command than his associates, and I thought that he might assist us as a guide; but he was sinking with exhaustion. There was not a moment to be lost. Ohlsen was strapped on a sled, his legs wrapped in dog-skins and eider down, and we went off upon the ice. Our party consisted of nine men and myself. We carried only the clothes on our backs. The thermometer stood at −46°, seventy-eight below the freezing point.

We knew that our lost companions must be somewhere within a radius of forty miles. Mr. Ohlsen, who had been without rest for fifty hours, fell asleep as soon as we began to move, and woke now with unequivocal signs of mental disturbance. It became evident that he had lost the bearing of the icebergs, which in form and colour endlessly repeated themselves; and the uniformity of the vast field of snow utterly forbade the hope of local landmarks.

The thermometer had fallen by this time to −49.3°, and the wind was setting in sharply from the northwest. It was out of the question to halt; it required brisk exercise to keep us from freezing. The strange manner in which some of us were affected I now attribute as much to shattered nerves as to the direct influence of the cold. Men like McGary and Bonsall were seized with trembling fits and short breath; and in spite of all my efforts to keep an example of sound bearing, I fainted twice on the snow.

We had been nearly eighteen hours out without water or food when a new hope cheered us. I think it was Hans, our Esquimaux hunter, who thought he saw a broad sledge-track. The drift had nearly effaced it and we were some of us doubtful at first whether it was not one of those accidental rifts which the gales make in the surface-snow. But as we traced it on to the deep snow among the hummocks, we were led to footsteps; and following these with religious care we at last came in sight of a small American flag fluttering from a hummock, and lower down a little Masonic banner hanging from a tent-pole hardly above the drift. It was the camp of our disabled comrades; we reached it after an unbroken march of twenty-one hours.

We were now fifteen souls; the thermometer 75° below the freezing point; and our sole accommodation a tent barely able to contain eight persons. More than half our party were obliged to keep from freezing by walking outside while the others slept. We could not halt long. Each of us took a turn of two hours' sleep; and we prepared for our homeward march. It took us no less than four hours to strip and refresh the sufferers and then to embale them in robes. Few of us escaped without frost-bitten fingers: the thermometer was 55.6 below zero, and a slight wind added to the severity of the cold. We made, by vigorous pulls and lifts, nearly a mile an hour and reached the new floes before we were absolutely weary. Ohlsen, restored by hope, walked steadily at the leading belt of the sledge-lines; and I began to feel certain of reaching our half-way station of the day before, where we had left our own tent. But we were still nine miles from it when, almost without premonition, we all became aware of an alarming failure of our energies.

Bonsall and Morton, two of our stoutest men, came to me begging permission to sleep: "they were not cold: the wind did not enter them now: a little sleep was all they wanted." Presently Hans was found nearly stiff under a drift;

and Thomas, bolt upright, had his eyes closed and could hardly articulate. At last John Blake threw himself on the snow and refused to rise. They did not complain of feeling cold; but it was in vain that I wrestled, boxed, ran, argued, jeered, or reprimanded: an immediate halt could not be avoided.

We pitched the one tent with much difficulty. Our hands were too powerless to strike a fire: we were obliged to do without water or food. Even the spirits (whisky) had frozen at the sick men's feet, under all the coverings. We put Bonsall, Ohlsen, Thomas, and Hans, with the other sick men, well inside the tent and crowded in as many others as we could. Then, leaving the party in charge of Mr. McGary with orders to come on after four hours' rest, I pushed ahead with William Godfrey, who volunteered to be my companion. My aim was to reach the half-way tent and thaw some ice and pemmican before the others arrived.

I cannot tell how long it took us to make the nine miles for we were in a strange sort of stupor and had little apprehension of time. It was probably about four hours. We kept ourselves awake by imposing on each other a continued articulation of words; they must have been incoherent enough. I recall these hours as among the most wretched I have ever gone through: we were neither of us in our right senses and retained a very confused recollection of what had preceded our arrival at the tent. We both of us, however, remember a bear who walked leisurely before us and tore up as he went a jumper that Mr. McGary had improvidently thrown off the day before. He tore it into shreds and rolled it into a ball, but never offered to interfere with our progress. I remember this, and with it a confused sentiment that our tent was undergoing the same unceremonious treatment.

Probably our approach saved the contents of the tent; for when we reached it the tent was uninjured though the bear had overturned it, tossing the buffalo-robes and pemmican into the snow. We missed only a couple of blanket bags. What we recollect, however, and perhaps all we recollect, is that we had great difficulty in raising it. We crawled into our reindeer sleeping-bags and for the next three hours slept a dreamy but intense slumber. When I awoke my long beard was a mass of ice, frozen fast to the buffalo-skin: Godfrey had to cut me out with his jack-knife.

We were able to melt water and get some soup cooked before the rest of the party arrived: it took them five hours to walk the nine miles. They were doing well and, considering the circumstances, in wonderful spirits. The day was almost providently windless, with a clear sun.

The hummocks we had now to meet came properly under the designation of squeezed ice. A great chain of bergs stretching from north-west to south-east, moving with the tides, had compressed the surface floes and, rearing them upon their edges, produced an area more like the volcanic basin of Mexico than anything else I can compare it to.

It required desperate efforts to work our way over it – literally desperate, for our strength failed us anew and we began to lose our self-control. We could not abstain any longer from eating snow; our mouths swelled and some of us became speechless. Our halts multiplied and we fell half-sleeping on the snow. I could not prevent it. I ventured upon the experiment myself, making Riley wake me at the end of three minutes; and I felt so much benefited by it that I timed the men in the same way. They sat on the runners of the sledge, fell asleep instantly, and were forced to wakefulness when their three minutes were out.

By eight in the evening we emerged from the floes. The sight of the familiar

Kane was a romantic figure, an
authentic hero in his own time. He
fought in Mexico where he was
wounded by a lance. A scandalous
book, The Love Life of Dr. Kane, was
published before his death at 37.

Pinnacly Berg revived us. Brandy, an invaluable resource in emergency, had already been served out in tablespoon doses. We moved on like men in a dream. Bonsall was sent staggering ahead and reached the brig, God knows how, for he had fallen repeatedly at the track-lines, but he delivered with punctilious accuracy the messages I had sent by him to Dr. Hayes. I thought myself the soundest of all, for I went through all the formula of sanity, and can recall the muttering delirium of my comrades when we got back into the cabin of our brig. Yet I have been told since of some speeches and some orders too of mine which I should have remembered for their absurdity if my mind had retained its balance.

Petersen and Whipple came out to meet us about two miles from the brig. They brought my dog-team, with the restoratives I had sent for by Bonsall. I do not remember their coming. Dr. Hayes entered with judicious energy upon the treatment our condition called for, administering morphine freely, after the usual frictions. Mr. Ohlsen suffered some time from strabismus and blindness; two others underwent amputation of parts of the foot. This rescue party had been out for seventy-two hours.

April 4, Tuesday: Four days have passed and I am again at my record of failures, sound but aching still in every joint. The rescued men are not out of danger, but their gratitude is very touching. Pray God that they may live!

The week that followed has left me nothing but anxieties and sorrow. Nearly all our party, as well the rescuers as the rescued, were tossing in their sick-bunks, some frozen, others undergoing amputations, several with dreadful premonitions of tetanus. I was myself among the first to be about; the necessities of the others claimed it of me.

Early in the morning of the 7th I was awakened by a sound from Baker's throat, one of the most frightful and ominous that ever startled a physician's ear. The lockjaw had seized him; that dark visitant whose foreshadowings were on so many of us. His symptoms marched rapidly to their result; he died on the 8th of April.

THE UNKNOWN PEOPLE

We were watching in the morning at Baker's death-bed when one of our deck-watch came hurrying down into the cabin with the report, "People hulloaing ashore!" I went up, followed by as many as could mount the gangway; and there they were on all side of our rocky harbour, dotting the snow-shores and emerging from the blackness of the cliffs'—wild and uncouth, but evidently human beings.

As we gathered on the deck they rose upon the more elevated fragments of the land-ice, standing singly and conspicuously like the figures in a tableau. They were vociferating as if to attract our attention, or perhaps only to give vent to their surprise; but I could make nothing out of their cries.

There was enough light for me to see that they brandished no weapons and were only tossing their heads and arms about in violent gesticulations. A more unexcited inspection showed us that their numbers were not as great nor their size as Patagonian as some of us had been disposed to fancy at first. In a word, I was satisfied that they were natives of the country; and calling Petersen from his bunk to be my interpreter I proceeded unarmed and waving my open hands, toward a stout figure who made himself conspicuous and seemed to have a greater number near him than the rest. He evidently understood the movement for he at once, like a brave fellow, leaped down upon the floe and advanced to meet me fully half-way.

He was nearly a head taller than myself, extremely powerful and well-built, with a swarthy complexion and piercing black eyes. Although this was the first time he had ever seen a white man he went with me fearlessly; his companions staying behind on the ice. Hickey took them out what he esteemed our greatest delicacies – slices of good wheat bread, corned pork, and lumps of white sugar; but they refused to touch them. They had evidently no apprehension of open violence from us. I found afterward that several among them were singly a match for the white bear and the walrus, and they thought us a very pale-faced crew.

Being satisfied with my interview in the cabin I sent out word that the rest might be admitted to the ship; and some nine or ten of them followed with boisterous readiness upon the bidding. Others in the meantime, as if disposed to give us their company for the full time of a visit, brought up from behind the land-ice as many as fifty-six fine dogs, with their sledges, and secured them within two hundred feet of the brig, driving their lances into the ice and picketing the dogs to them by the seal-skin traces. The sledges were made up of small fragments of porous bone admirably knit together by thongs of hide; the runners, which glistened like burnished steel, were of highly polished ivory obtained from the tusks of the walrus.

The only arms they carried were knives concealed in their boots; but their lances were quite a formidable weapon. The staff was of the horn of the narwhal, or else of the thigh-bones of the bear, two lashed together, or sometimes the penis bone of the walrus, three or four of them united. This last was a favourite material also for the cross-bars of their sledges. They had no wood. A single rusty hoop from a current-drifted cask might have furnished all the knives of the party; but the tips of their lances were of unmistakable steel and were riveted to the tapering bony point with no mean skill. I learned afterward that the metal was obtained in traffic from the more southern tribes.†

When they were first allowed to come aboard they were very rude and difficult to manage. They spoke three or four at a time, to each other and to us, laughing heartily at our ignorance in not understanding them, and then talking away as before. They were incessantly in motion, going everywhere, anxious to touch and handle everything they saw, and asking for everything they touched. It was the more difficult to restrain them, as I did not wish them to suppose that we were at all intimidated. But there were some signs of our disabled condition which it was important they should not see; it was especially necessary to keep them out of the forecastle where the dead body of poor Baker was lying; and, as it was in vain to reason or persuade, we had at last to employ the "gentle laying-on of hands" which, I believe, the laws of all countries tolerate, to keep them in order.

Our whole force was mustered and kept constantly on the alert; but though there may have been something of discourtesy in the occasional shoulderings and hustlings that enforced the policing of the ship, things went on good-humouredly. Our guests continued running in and out and about the vessel until the afternoon; when like tired children they threw themselves down to sleep. I ordered them to be made comfortable in the hold; and Morton spread a large buffalo-robe for them, not far from a coal-fire in the galley-stove.

They were lost in barbarous amaze at the coal – too hard for blubber, too soft for firestone – but they were content to believe it might cook as well as seals' fat. They borrowed from us an iron pot and some melted water and parboiled a couple of pieces of walrus-meat; but the real *pièce de resistance*, some

†*This was only the second meeting between the Smith Sound Eskimos and Europeans since the disappearance of the Greenland Norse three centuries earlier. Capt. Inglefield had met the Etah people in 1852 when he entered Smith Sound.*

five pounds a head, they preferred to eat raw.

In the morning they were anxious to go; but I had given orders to detain them for a parting interview with myself. It resulted in a treaty, brief in its terms that it might be certainly remembered, and mutually beneficial that it might possibly be kept. I tried to make them understand what a powerful Prospero they had for a host, and how beneficial he would prove himself so long as they did his bidding. And as an earnest of my favour I bought all the walrus-meat they had to spare, and four of their dogs, enriching them in return with needles and beads and a treasure of old cask staves.

In the fullness of their gratitude they pledged themselves emphatically to return in a few days with more meat, and to allow me to use their dogs and sledges for my excursions to the north. They did not return. I had read enough of treaty makings not to expect them too confidently. But the next day came a new party of five, on foot – two old men, one middle aged, and a couple of gawky boys. We had missed a number of articles soon after the first party left us, an axe, a saw, and some knives. We found afterward that a storehouse we had erected at Butler Island had been entered; we were too short-handed to guard it by a special watch. Besides all this, reconnoitering stealthily, we discovered a train of sledges drawn up behind the hummocks.

There was cause for apprehension in all this; but I felt that I could not afford to break with the rogues. They had it in their power to molest us seriously in our sledge-travel; they could make our hunts around the harbour dangerous; and my best chance of obtaining an abundant supply of fresh meat, our greatest need, was by their agency. I treated the new party with marked kindness and gave them many presents; but took care to make them aware that, until all missing articles were restored, no member of the tribe would be admitted again as a guest on board the brig. They went off with many pantomimic protestations of innocence; but McGary, nevertheless, caught the incorrigible scamps stealing a coal-barrel as they passed Butler Island, and expedited their journey homeward by firing among them a charge of small shot.

Still, one peculiar worthy – we thought it must have been the venerable of the party, whom I knew afterwards as a staunch friend, old Shang-huh – managed to work round in a westerly direction and to cut to pieces my India-rubber boat which had been left on the floe and to carry off every particle of the wood.

A few days after this an agile, elfin youth drove up to our floe in open day. We asked him about the boat; but he denied all knowledge of it and refused either to confess or repent. He was surprised when I ordered him to be confined to the hold. At first he refused to eat and sat down in the deepest grief; but after a while he began to sing, and then to talk and cry, and then to sing again; crying and talking by turns till a late hour of the night. When I turned in he was still noisily disconsolate.

There was a simplicity and *bonhomie* about this boy that interested me much; and I confess that when I made my appearance the next morning I was glad to find my bird had flown. Some time during the morning watch he had succeeded in throwing off the hatch and escaping. We suspected that he had confederates ashore, for his dogs had escaped with as much address as himself.

ATTEMPT TO TRAVEL NORTH

April 19, Wednesday: I have been out on the ice again, breaking in my dogs. My reinforcement from the Esquimaux makes a noble team for me. For the last five days I have been striving with them, just as often and as long as my

Lieut. Edwin DeHaven's ship Rescue was nipped in
the ice of Melville Bay in 1850. His expedition
was one of the many sent north in the hope of
finding the vanished Sir John Franklin. Elisha
Kent Kane shipped as doctor with DeHaven.

strength allowed me; and to-day I have my victory. The Society for Preventing Cruelty to Animals would have put me in custody if they had been near enough; but thanks to a merciless whip freely administered I have been dashing along twelve miles in the last hour, and am back again; harness, sledge, and bones all unbroken. I am ready for another journey.

The worst thought I have in setting out is that of the entire crew, I can leave but two behind in able condition, and the doctor and Bonsall are the only two officers who can help Ohlsen. This is our force, four able-bodied, and six disabled, to keep the brig; the commander and seven men, scarcely better upon the average, out upon the ice.

fm So Kane set out on his attempt toward the Pole. His narrative account of what transpired was written after his return. □ FM

It is now the 20th of May and for the first time I am able, propped up by pillows, and surrounded by sick messmates, to note the fact that we have failed again to force a passage to the north.

Godfrey and myself overtook the advance party under McGary two days after leaving the brig. Our dogs were in fair travelling condition and, except snow-blindness, there seemed to be no drawback to our efficiency. In crossing Marshall Bay we found the snow so accumulated in drifts that we could not force our sledges through. We were forced to unload and carry forward the cargo on our backs, beating a path for the dogs to follow in.

This progress was dearly earned. As early as the 3rd of May the winter's scurvy reappeared painfully among our party. As we struggled through the snow along the Greenland coast we sank up to our middle; and the dogs, floundering about, were so buried as to preclude any attempt at hauling. It obliged us to unload our sledges again and carry their cargo – a labour which resulted in dropsical swellings with painful prostration. Here three of the party were taken with snow-blindness, and George Stevenson had to be condemned as unfit for travel altogether on account of chest-symptoms accompanying his scorbutic troubles. On the 4th Thomas Hickey also gave in. Perhaps we would still have got on; but to crown all we found that the bears had effected an entrance into our depot pemmican casks and thus destroyed our chances of reinforcing our provisions. The pemmican was covered with blocks of stone which had required the labour of three men to adjust; but the extraordinary strength of the bear had enabled him to force aside the heaviest rocks, and his pawing had broken the iron casks, which held our pemmican, literally into chips. Our fuel alcohol cask, which had cost me a separate and special journey in the late fall to deposit, was so completely destroyed that we could not find a stave of it.

Off Cape James Kent, while taking an observation for latitude, I was myself seized with a sudden pain and fainted. My limbs became rigid and certain obscure tetanoid symptoms of our late winter's enemy disclosed themselves. In this condition I was unable to make more than nine miles a day. I was strapped upon the sledge and the march continued as usual; but my powers diminished so rapidly that I could not resist even the otherwise comfortable temperature of 5° below zero.

On the 5th, becoming delirious, and fainting every time that I was taken from the tent to the sledge, I succumbed entirely. My comrades would kindly persuade me that, even had I continued sound, we could not have proceeded on our journey. The snows were very heavy and increasing as we went; some of the drifts perfectly impassable, and the level floes often four feet deep in yielding snow. The scurvy had already broken out among the men, with symptoms like my own; and Morton, our strongest man, was beginning to give way. All that I should remember with pleasurable feeling is that, to five brave men, Morton, Riley, Hickey, Stevenson, and Hans, themselves scarcely able to travel, I owe my preservation. They carried me back by forced marches.

I was taken into the brig on May 14th. Since then, fluctuating between life and death, I have by the blessing of God reached the present date, and see feebly in prospect my recovery. Dr. Hayes regards my attack as one of scurvy, complicated by typhoid fever. George Stevenson is similarly affected. Our worst symptoms are dropsical effusion and night sweats.

Poor Pierre Schubert is gone. Our gallant, merry-hearted companion left us some ten days ago for, I trust, a more genial world. It is sad, in this dreary little homestead of ours to miss his contented face and the joyous troll of his ballads.

The health of the rest of us has, if anything, improved. Their complexions show the influence of sunlight, and I think several have a firmer and more elastic step. Stevenson and Thomas are the only two besides myself who are likely to suffer permanently from the effects of our breakdown. Bad scurvy both; symptoms still serious.

The first thing I did after my return was to send McGary southward to the Life-boat Cove, to see that our boat and its buried provisions were secure. He made the journey by dog-sledge in four days and has returned reporting that all is safe: an important help for us should this heavy ice of our more northern prison refuse to release the brig.

THE RETURN OF SPRING

As soon as I had recovered enough to be aware of my failure on the northern journey, I began to devise means for remedying it. But I found the resources of the party shattered. There were only three men able to do duty. Of the officers, Wilson, Brooks, Sontag, and Petersen were knocked up. There was no one except Sontag, Hayes, or myself who was qualified to conduct a survey; and of us three Dr. Hayes was the only one on his feet.

May 23, Tuesday: We have had superb weather, thank Heaven! – a profusion of the most genial sunshine, bringing out the seals in crowds to bask around their breathing-holes. A ptarmigan was killed today. The winter is gone! The Andromeda has been found on shore under the snow, with tops vegetating and green! I have a shoot of it in my hand.

May 28, Sunday: Our day of rest and devotion. It was a fortnight ago last Friday since our poor friend Pierre died. The last offices were rendered to him with the same careful ceremonial that we observed at Baker's funeral. There were fewer to walk in the procession; but the body was encased in a decent pine coffin and carried to Observatory Island where it was placed side by side with that of his messmate. Neither could yet be buried; but it is hardly necessary to say that the frost has embalmed their remains.

By means of the Esquimaux stratagem of a white screen pushed forward on a sledge until the concealed hunter comes within range, Hans has shot four seals. We have more fresh meat than we can eat. For the past three weeks we have been living on ptarmigan, rabbits, two reindeer, and seal. They are fast curing our scurvy.

June 8, Thursday: Hans brings us in today a couple of seals. When raw the meat has a flabby look, more like coagulated blood than muscular fibre; cooking gives it a dark soot-colour. It is close-grained but soft and tender, with a flavour of lamp-oil. The blubber, when fresh, is at this season sweet and delicious.

Mr. Ohlsen and Dr. Hayes are off on an overland tramp. I sent them to inspect the open water to the southward. The immovable state of the ice-foot

Shooting seal through a blind.

gives me anxiety. This morning, to my great surprise, Petersen brought me quite a handful of scurvy-grass. I felt grateful to him for his kindness and, without the affectation of offering it to any one else, ate it at once.

fm Although the hard winter had sadly reduced the effectiveness of Kane's party, the summer was not entirely wasted. On May 22 Dr. Hayes and Godfrey began a sled journey north into Kane Basin, crossing to the shore of Ellesmere Island at Cape M'Clintock and then circling south and east to return to Rensselaer Bay on June 1. Three days later Morton and the Eskimo, Hans, began sledding north to pass the mighty face of the Humboldt Glacier and enter Kennedy Channel. They followed its eastern shore north to Cape Constitution (incorrectly shown on modern maps as Cape Ressner) and then turned back, reaching the ship on June 28. Someone, either Morton or Kane himself, later claimed that this party had got as far north as latitude 82° 30′, and had reached the shore of an "ice-free" polar ocean! Actually Morton turned back at 80° 40′ and, although Kennedy Channel had indeed been clear of ice, it was hardly to be confused with the Arctic Ocean, which lay nearly two hundred miles farther north. □ FM

IN SEARCH OF HELP

The summer was wearing on, but still the ice did not break up as it should. As far as we could see it remained inflexibly solid between us and the North Water of Baffin's Bay. The questions and speculations of those around me began to show that they too had anxious thoughts for the coming year. There was reason for all our apprehensions.

I have to remember that I am much further to the north than any of my predecessors, and that by the 28th of last August I had already, after twenty days of unremitting labour, forced the brig nearly forty miles through the pack, and that the pack began to close on us only six days later, and that on the 7th of September we were fairly frozen in. Yet last summer was a most favourable one for ice-melting. Putting all this together it looks as if the winter must catch us before we can get halfway through the pack, even though we should begin warping to the south at the earliest moment that we can hope for water.

It is not a pleasant prospect; for there never was, and I trust never will be, a party worse armed for the encounter of a second arctic winter. We have neither health, fuel, nor provisions. Dr. Hayes, and indeed all I have consulted about it indirectly, despond at the thought; and when I look round upon our diseased and disabled men and think of the fearful work of the last long night, I am tempted to feel as they do.

The alternative of abandoning the vessel at this early stage, even though it were possible, would, I feel, be dishonouring; but revolving the question as one of practicability alone, I would not undertake it. In the first place, how are we to get along with our sick and newly amputated men? It is a dreary distance at the best to Upernavik or Beechy Island, our only seats of refuge, and a precarious traverse if we were all of us fit for moving; but we are hardly one-half in efficiency of what we count in number. Besides, how can I desert the brig while there is still a chance of saving her? There is no use of noting pros and cons: my mind is made up; I will not do it.

I have determined to attempt in person to communicate with Beechy Island, or at least make the effort. If I can reach Sir Edward Belcher's squadron,† I am sure of all I want. I will take a light whaleboat and pick my companions for a journey to the south and west. I may find stores at the Wolstenholme Islands, or by great good luck come across some passing vessel of the squadron and make known our whereabouts and wants; or, failing these, we will try and coast along to Wellington Channel.

Our equipment has been getting ready for some time. The boat we chose was our old *Forlorn Hope*, mended up and revised for her new destinies. She was 23 feet long, had 6½ feet beam, and was 2 feet 6 inches deep. Her build was the characteristic one of American whaleboats, too flat-bottomed for ordinary use, but much improved by a false keel which Ohlsen had given her throughout her entire length. But after all, she was a mere cockle-shell.

We lifted our boat over the side in the afternoon of July 11th, and floating her to the crack at the Observatory Island, mounted her there on our large sledge, stowed in everything but the provisions and carried her on to the bluff of Sylvia Headland – and the next morning a party consisting of all but the sick was detailed to transport her to open water. In the next four days we carried the boat across twenty miles of heavy ice-floe, and launched her in open water. The straits were much clogged with drift ice, but I followed the coast southward without difficulty. We travelled at night, resting when the sun was hottest. I had every reason to be pleased with the performance of the whaleboat, and the men kept up their spirits well. We landed at the point where we left our life-boat a year ago and to our great joy found it untouched: the cove and the inlet were still fast in ice.

We now neared Littleton Island where a piece of good fortune awaited us. We saw a number of ducks, and it occurred to me that by tracking their flight we should reach their breeding-grounds. There was no trouble in doing so, for they flew in a bee-line to a group of rocky islets, above which the whole horizon was studded with birds. A rugged little ledge was so thickly colonized that we could hardly walk without treading on a nest. We killed with guns and stones over two hundred birds in a few hours.

On Wednesday, the 19th, we left Flagstaff Point where we fixed a beacon last year; and stood west 10° south under full canvas. My aim was to take the channel obliquely at Littleton Island; and push on for Kent Island and leave a cairn there.

Toward night the wind freshened from the northward and we passed beyond the protection of the straits into the open sea-way. My journal gives no picture of the life we now entered on. The oldest sailor, who treads the deck of his ship with the familiar confidence of a man at home, has a distrust of open-boat navigation. The feeling grew upon us as we lost the land. McGary was an old Bering's Straits whaler, and there is no better boatman in the world than he; but I know that he shared my doubts as the boat buried herself again and again in the trough of a short chopping sea.

Baffin passed round this gulf in 1616 with two small vessels; but they were giants beside ours. I thought of them as we crossed his track steering for Cape Combermere, then about sixty miles distant, with every prospect of a heavy gale.

We were in the centre of this large area of open water when the gale broke upon us from the north. We were soon near foundering. Our false bow of India-rubber cloth was beaten in and our frail weather-boarding soon followed it. With the utmost exertion we could hardly keep our boat from broaching to: a broken oar or an accidental twitch would have been fatal to us at any time. But McGary handled the whalers' marvel, the long steering-oar, with admirable skill. None of us could pretend to take his place. For twenty-two unbroken hours he stuck to his post without relaxing his attention or his efforts.

I was not prepared for such a storm. I do not think I have seen a worse sea raised by the northers of the Gulf of Mexico. At last the wind hauled to the eastward and we were glad to drive before it for the inshore floes. We had passed several bergs; but the sea dashed against their sides so furiously as to negate all hopes of protection at their base; the pack or floe, so much feared before, was now looked to for a refuge.

I remember well our anxiety as we entered the loose stream of drift after four hours' scudding and our relief when we felt their influence upon the sea. We fastened to an old floe, not 50 yards in diameter and, with the weather-surf breaking over our heads, rode out the storm under a warp and grapnel.

The obstacle we had now to encounter was the pack that stretched between us and the south. When the storm abated we commenced boring into it – slow work at the best of times; but my companions encountered it with a persevering activity quite as admirable as their fortitude in danger. It had its own hazards too; and more than once it looked as if we were permanently beset.

We were still labouring on, hardly past the middle of the bay, when the floes began to relax. On Sunday, the 23rd of July, the whole aspect around us changed. The sun came out cheeringly, the leads opened more and more and, as we pulled through them to the south, each ice-tongue that we doubled brought us nearer to the Greenland shore. A slackening of the ice to the east enabled us after a while to lay our course for Hakluyt Island.

For the next three days we worked painfully through the half-open leads, making in all some fifteen miles to the south. We had very seldom room enough to row; but, as we tracked along, it was not difficult to escape nippings by hauling up the boat on the ice. Still she received some hard knocks, for she began to leak; and this, with the rain which fell heavily, forced us to bail her out every other hour. Of course we could not sleep, and one of our little party fell sick with the unmitigated fatigue.

On the 29th it came on to blow, the wind still keeping from the southwest, but cold and almost rising to a gale. We had had another wet and sleepless night, for the floes still baffled us by their capricious movements. But at three in the afternoon we had the sun again and the ice opened just enough to tempt us. It was uncomfortable toil. We pushed forward our little weather-worn craft, her gunwales touching on both sides, till the toppling ice began to break down on us and, sometimes, critically suspended, met above our heads.

One of these passages I am sure all of us remember. We were in an alley of pounded ice-masses such as the receding floes leave when they have crushed the tables that were between them, and had pushed our way far enough to make retreat impossible, when the fields began to close in. There was no escaping a nip, for everything was loose and rolling around us and the floes broke into hummock ridges as they came together. They met just ahead of us and gradually swayed in toward our boat. The fragments were already splitting off and spinning over us when we found ourselves borne up by the accumulating rubbish, like the Advance in her winter drift; and after resting for twenty minutes high out of the water, we were quietly lowered again as the fields relaxed their pressure.

It was a time of almost unbroken excitement; yet I am not surprised, as I turn over the notes of my meagre diary, to find how little of stirring incident it records. The story of one day's strife with the ice-floes might serve for those which followed it; I remember that we were four times nipped before we succeeded in releasing ourselves, and that we were glad to haul upon the floes as often as a dozen times a day. We attempted to drag forward on the occasional fields; but we had to give it up, for it strained the boat so much that she was barely seaworthy; it kept one man busy the last six days bailing her out.

On the 31st, at the distance of ten miles from Cape Parry, we came to a dead halt. A solid mass lay directly across our path, extending onward to our furthest horizon. There were bergs in sight to the westward and by walking for some four miles over the moving floe in that direction, McGary and myself succeeded in reaching one. We climbed it to the height of a hundred and twenty feet and, looking out from it with my excellent spy-glass to the south and west, we saw that all within a radius of thirty miles was a motionless, unbroken, and impenetrable sea of ice.

If was obvious that a further attempt to penetrate to the south must be hopeless till the ice-barrier before us should undergo a change. I had observed, when passing Northumberland Island, that some of its glacier-slopes were margined with verdure, and as my men were much wasted with diarrhea, and our supplies of food had become scanty, I resolved to work my way to the island and recruit there for another effort.

Tracking and sometimes rowing through a heavy rain, we traversed the leads for two days, working eastward; and on the morning of the third gained the open water near the shore. Here a breeze came to our aid, and in a couple of hours more we passed with now unwonted facility to the southern face of the island. We met several flocks of little auks as we approached it, and found on landing that it was one enormous homestead of the auks, dovekies, and gulls.

We encamped on the 31st on a low beach that had evidently been selected by the Esquimaux for a winter settlement: five well-built huts of stone attested this. The droppings of the birds had fertilized the soil, and it abounded with grasses to the water's edge. The foxes were about in great numbers, attracted by the abundance of birds.

fm From Northumberland Island open water stretched to the northward, and Kane and his party had little difficulty making their way back to Rensselaer Bay, arriving there August 8. □ FM

It was with mingled feelings that we neared the brig. Our little party had grown fat and strong upon the auks and eiders and scurvygrass; and surmises were rife among us as to the condition of our comrades and the prospects of our ice-bound little ship.

In the midst of the greeting which always met our returning parties, and which gave to our little vessel the endearing associations of a homestead, our thoughts reverted to the feeble chances of our liberation, and the failure of our recent effort to secure the means of a retreat.

The brig had now been imprisoned by closely-cementing ice for eleven months, during which period she had not budged an inch from her icy cradle.

TRAPPED

August 18, Friday: Reduced our allowance of wood for fuel to six pounds a meal. This allows us coffee twice a day, and soup once. Our fare besides this is cold pork boiled in quantity and eaten as required. This sort of thing works badly; but I must save coal for other emergencies. I see darkness ahead.

I inspected the ice again today. Bad! Bad! – I must look another winter in the face. I do not shrink from the thought; but while we have a chance it is my first duty to have all things in readiness to meet it. It is *horrible* – yes, that is the word – to look forward to another year of disease and darkness to be met without fresh food and without fuel. I should meet it with a more tempered sadness if I had no comrades to think for and protect.

I determined to place upon Observatory Island a large signal-beacon or cairn, and to bury under it documents which, in case of disaster to our party, would convey to any who might seek us intelligence of our proceedings and our fate. A conspicuous spot was selected upon a cliff looking out upon the icy desert, and on a broad face of rock the words: ADVANCE, A.D. 1853-54 were painted in letters which could be read at a distance.

So now came the question of the second winter: how to look the enemy in the face and how to meet him. Anything was better than inaction; and in spite of the uncertainty which yet attended our plans, a host of expedients were to be resorted to, and much Robinson Crusoe labour ahead. Moss was to be gathered for eking out our winter fuel, and willow-stems and sorrel-grass, as anti-scorbutics, collected and buried in the snow. But while all these were in progress came other and graver questions.

Some of the party had entertained the idea that an escape to the south was still practicable; and this opinion was supported by Mr. Petersen, our Danish interpreter. They even thought that the safety of all would be promoted by a withdrawal from the brig.

August 24, Thursday: At noon today I had all hands called, and explained to them frankly the considerations which have determined me to remain where we are. I endeavoured to show them that an escape to open water could not succeed and that the effort must be exceedingly hazardous; I advised them strenuously to forgo the project. I then told them that I should freely give my permission to such as were desirous of making the attempt, but that I should require them to renounce in writing all claims upon myself and the rest who were resolved to stay by the vessel. Having done this, I directed the roll to be called, and each man to answer for himself.

In the result, eight out of the seventeen survivors of my party resolved to stand by the brig. It is just that I should record their names. They were Henry Brooks, James McGary, J. W. Wilson, Henry Goodfellow, William Morton, Christian Ohlsen, Thomas Hickey and Hans Christian. I divided to the others their portion of our resources justly and even liberally; and they left us on Monday, the 28th, with every appliance our narrow circumstances could furnish to speed and guard them.

The party moved off with the elastic step of men confident in their purpose, and were out of sight in a few hours. As we lost them among the hummocks the stern realities of our condition pressed themselves upon us anew. The reduced numbers of our party, the helplessness of many, the waning efficiency of all, the impending winter with its cold, dark night, our penury of resources, the dreary sense of increased isolation – these made the staple of our thoughts.

September 6, Wednesday: We are at it, all hands, sick and well, each man according to his measure, working at our winter's home. We are none of us in condition to brave the frost and our fuel is nearly out. I have determined to borrow a lesson from our Esquimaux neighbours, and am turning the brig into an igloo.

The sledge is to bring us moss and turf from wherever the men can scrape it. This is an excellent non-conductor and when we get the quarter-deck well padded with it we shall have a nearly cold-proof covering. Down below we will enclose a space some eighteen feet square, and pack it from floor to ceiling with inner walls of the same material. The floor itself we are caulking with plaster of Paris and common paste, and will cover it, when we have done, with Manilla oakum a couple of inches deep, and a canvas carpet. The entrance is to be from the hold, by a low moss-lined tunnel with as many doors and curtains to close it up as our ingenuity can devise. This is to be our apartment of all uses – not a very large one; but we are only ten to stow away, and the closer the warmer.

When three Esquimaux visited us near the end of August I established them in a tent below deck, with a copper lamp, a cooking-basin, and a liberal supply of slush for fuel. I left them under guard when I went to bed at two in the morning, contentedly eating and cooking and eating again without the promise of an intermission. An American or a European would have slept after such a debauch till the recognized hour for hock and seltzer water. But our guests managed to elude the officer of the deck and escape unsearched. They repaid my liberality by stealing not only the lamp, boiler, and cooking-pot† they had used for the feast, but Nanook also, my best dog. If the rest of my team had not been worn down by over-travel, no doubt they would have taken them all. Besides this, we discovered the next morning that they had found the buffalo-robes and India-rubber cloth which McGary had left a few days before on the ice-foot near Six-mile Ravine, and had added the whole to the spoils of their visit.

I was puzzled how to inflict punishment, but saw that I must act vigorously, even at a venture. I despatched my two best walkers, Morton and Riley, as soon as I heard of the theft of the stores, with orders to make all speed to a place they called Anoatok, and overtake the thieves who, I thought, would probably halt there to rest. They found young Myouk making himself quite comfortable in a stone hut there, in company with two women; and my buffalo-robes already tailored into parkas on their backs.

A continued search of the premises recovered the cooking utensils, and a number of other things of greater or less value that we had not missed from the brig. With the prompt ceremonial which outraged law delights in among the officials of the police everywhere, the women were stripped and tied; and then, laden with their stolen goods and as much walrus-meat besides from their own stores as would pay for their board, they were marched on the instant back to the brig.

The thirty miles was a hard walk for them; but they did not complain, nor did their constabulary guardians, who had marched thirty miles already to apprehend them. It was hardly twenty-four hours since they left the brig with their booty before they were prisoners in the hold, with a dreadful white man for keeper, who never addressed to them a word that had not all the terrors of an unintelligible reproof, and whose scowl, I flatter myself, exhibited a well-arranged variety of menacing and demoniacal expressions.

The women had not even the companionship of Myouk. Him, I had despatched to Metek, head-man of Etah (their settlement), and others, with the message of a melodramatic tyrant, to negotiate for the ransom. For five long days the women had to sigh and sing and cry in solitary converse. At last the great Metek arrived. He brought with him Ootuniah, another man of elevated social position, and quite a sledge-load of knives, tin cups, and other stolen goods, refuse of wood and scraps of iron, the sinful prizes of many covetings.

I may pass over our peace conferences and the indirect advantages which I, of course, derived from having the opposing powers represented in my own capital.

This treaty — which, though I have spoken of it jocosely, was really an affair of much interest to us — was ratified, with Hans and Morton as my accredited representatives, by a full assembly of the people of Etah. All our future intercourse was conducted under it. It was not solemnized by an oath; but it was never broken. We went to and fro between the villages and the brig, paid our visits of courtesy and necessity on both sides, met each other in hunting parties

† *Which they doubtless thought were gifts to them.*

A walrus kill often meant life
itself to explorers caught in the
polar ice. A bull can weigh as much
as 3,000 lbs. but, although walrus look
fierce, they are easy victims.

Near-nudity in Eskimo homes
surprised the early travellers, but in
semi-sealed igloos or earthen huts
body heat and a small oil lamp can
raise temperature to 60°.
Children are invariably pampered.

on the floe and the ice-foot, organized a general community of interests, and really, I believe, established some personal attachments deserving of the name. As long as we remained prisoners of the ice, we were indebted to them for invaluable council in relation to our hunting expeditions; and in the joint hunt we shared alike, according to their own laws. Our dogs were in one sense common property; and often have they robbed themselves to offer supplies of food to our starving teams. They gave us supplies of meat at critical periods; we were able to do as much for them.†

THE SECOND WINTER

October 5, Thursday: We are nearly out of fresh meat again, one rabbit and three ducks being our sum total. We have been on short allowance for several days. What vegetables we have – dried apple and peaches and pickled cabbage – have lost much of their anti-scorbutic virtue by constant use. Our spices are all gone. Except four small bottles of horse-radish, our menu is comprised in three lines – bread, [salt] beef, and [salt] pork.

I must be after the Esquimaux. They certainly have meat and wherever they have gone we can follow. Once upon their trail, our hungry instincts will not risk being baffled. I will stay [aboard]only long enough to complete my latest root-beer brewage. Its basis is the big crawling willow, the miniature giant of our Arctic forests, of which we laid in a stock some weeks ago. It is quite pleasantly bitter, and I hope to get it fermenting in the deck-house without extra fuel, by heat from below.

October 7, Saturday: Lively sensation, as they say in the land of olives and champagne. "Nanook, nanook! – A bear, a bear!" – Hans and Morton in a breath. To the scandal of our domestic regulations, the guns were all unworkable. While the men were loading and capping anew, I seized my six-shooter and ran on deck. A medium-sized bear with a four months' cub was in active warfare with our dogs. They were hanging on to her skirts, and she with wonderful alertness was picking out one victim after another, snatching him by the nape of the neck, and flinging him many feet, or rather yards, by a barely perceptible movement of her head.

Tuda, our master dog, was already *hors de combat*; he had been tossed twice. Jenny, just as I emerged from the hatch, was making an extraordinary somerset of some eight fathoms, and alighted senseless. Old Whitey, staunch, but not bear-wise, had been the first in the battle; he was yelping in helplessness in the snow.

It seemed as if the controversy was adjourned; and Nanook evidently thought so; for she turned off to our beef-barrels and began in the most unconcerned manner to turn them over and nose out their fatness. She was apparently devoid of fear.

I lodged a pistol-ball in the side of the cub. At once the mother placed her little one between her hind-legs and, shoving it along, made her way behind the beef-house. Mr. Ohlsen wounded her as she went, with my Webster rifle; but she scarcely noticed it. She tore down by single efforts of her forearms the barrels of frozen beef which made the triple walls of the storehouses, mounted the rubbish, and snatching up a half barrel of herrings carried it down by her teeth and was making off. It was time to close, I thought. Going up within half pistol range, I gave her six buckshot. She dropped, but instantly rose and getting her cub into its former position, moved off once more.

This time she would really have escaped but for the admirable tactics of our new recruits from the Esquimaux. The dogs of Smith's Sound are educated

†The truth is that, without the help of the Eskimos, particularly in supplying meat, the Kane expedition would have perished to a man.

more thoroughly than any of their more southern brethren. Unlike the dogs we had brought with us from Baffin's Bay, these dogs acted not to attack but to embarrass. They ran in circles round the bear, effecting a diversion at the critical moment by a nip at her hind-quarters.

The poor animal was still backing out, yet still fighting, carrying along her wounded cub, embarrassed by the dogs, yet gaining distance from the brig, when Hans and myself threw in the odds in the shape of a couple of rifle-balls. She staggered in front of her young one, faced us in death-like defiance, and only sank when pierced by six more bullets.

Another article of diet, less inviting at first, but which I found more innocuous, was the rat. We had failed to exterminate this animal by our varied and perilous efforts of the year before, and a well-justified fear forbade our renewing the crusade. It was marvellous in a region apparently so unfavourable to reproduction, what a perfect warren we soon had on board. Their impudence increased with their numbers. It became impossible to stow anything below decks. Furs, woollens, shoes, specimens of natural history, everything we disliked to lose, however little valuable to them, was gnawed into and destroyed. They harboured among the men's bedding in the forecastle, and showed such boldness in fight and such dexterity in dodging missiles that they were tolerated at last as inevitable nuisances. I find in my journal for the 10th of October an anecdote that illustrates their boldness:

"We have moved everything movable out upon the ice, and besides our dividing moss wall between our sanctum and the forecastle we have built up a rude barrier of iron sheathing to prevent these abominable rats from gnawing through. It is all in vain. They are everywhere already, under the stove, in the steward's lockers, in our cushions, about our beds. If I was asked what, after darkness and cold and scurvy, are the three besetting curses of our Arctic sojourn, I should say, *rats, rats, rats*. A mother-rat bit my finger to the bone last Friday, as I was intruding my hand into a bear-skin mitten which she had chosen for a homestead for her little family. I withdrew it of course with instinctive courtesy; but among them they carried off the mitten before I could suck the finger.

"Last week I sent down Rhina, the most intelligent dog of our whole pack, to bivouac in their citadel forward: I thought she might at least be able to defend herself against them, for she had distinguished herself in the bear-hunt. She slept very well for a couple of hours in a bed she had chosen for herself on the top of some iron spikes. But the rats would not forgo the horny skin about her paws and they gnawed her feet and nails so ferociously that we drew her up yelping and vanquished."

Before I pass from these intrepid and pertinacious visitors, let me add that on the whole I am personally much their debtor. Through the long winter night Hans used to beguile the lonely hours of his watch by shooting them with the bow and arrow. The repugnance of my associates to share with me the table luxury of "such small deer" gave me the frequent advantage of a fresh-meat soup which contributed no doubt to my comparative immunity from scurvy.

October 26, Thursday: The thermometer was at 34° below zero, but fortunately no wind blowing. We go on with outdoor work. We have passed wooden steam-tubes through the deck-house, to carry off the vapours of our cooking-stove and the lighter impurities of the crowded cabin. We burn but seven pounds of fuel a day, most of it in the galley – the fire being allowed to go out between meals. We go without fire altogether four hours of the night; yet such is the excellence of our moss walls that the thermometer indoors never indicates less than 45° above zero, with the outside air at 30° below. When the main hatch is secured with a proper weather-tight screen of canvas, we shall be able, I hope, to meet the extreme cold of February and March without fear.

Darkness is the worst enemy we have to face; but we will strive against the scurvy in spite of him, till the light days of sun and vegetation.

October 27, Friday: We are ripping off the extra planking of our deck for fuel during the winter. The cold increases fast, verging now upon 40° below zero, and in spite of all my efforts we will have to burn largely into the brig.

November 15, Wednesday: The last forty-eight hours should have given us the annual meteoric shower. We were fully prepared to observe it; but it would not come off. It would have been a godsend variety. Our fox traps have been empty for ten days past; but for the pittance of excitement which the visit to them gives, we might as well be without them. The men are getting nervous and depressed. McGary paced the deck all last Sunday in a fit of home-sickness, without eating a meal. I do my best to cheer them; but it is hard work to hide one's own trials for the sake of others who have not as many.

December 2, Saturday: Had to put Mr. McGary and Riley under active treatment for scurvy. Gums retracted, ankles swollen, and bad lumbago. Mr. Wilson's case, a still worse one, has been brought under [control]. Morton's is a saddening one. His tendon Achilles has been completely perforated and the surface of the heel-bone exposed. An operation in cold, darkness, and privation, would probably bring on lockjaw. Brooks grows discouraged: the poor fellow has scurvy in his stump, and his leg is drawn up by the contraction of the flexors at the knee-joint.

December 3, Sunday: I have now on hand twenty-four hundred pounds of chopped wood, a store collected with great difficulty; and yet, how inadequate a provision for the sickness and accident we must look for through the rest of the dark days! It requires the most vigorous efforts of what we call a healthy man to tear from the oak-ribs of our stout little vessel a single day's firewood. We have but three left who can manage even this. Two thousand pounds will barely carry us to the end of January, and the two severest months of the Arctic year, February and March, will still be ahead of us.

To carry us over these, our days of greatest anticipated trial, we have the outside oak sheathing – a sort of extra skin to protect the brig against the shocks of the ice. Although nearly three inches thick it is only spiked to her sides, and carpenter Ohlsen is sure that its removal will not interfere with her seaworthiness. Cut only to the water-line, it will give me at least two and a half tons; and with this – God willing – I may get through this awful winter, and save the brig besides.

I was asleep in the forenoon of the 7th when I was called to the deck by the report of "Esquimaux sledges." They came on rapidly, five sledges with teams of six dogs each, most of the drivers strangers to us; and in a few minutes were at the brig. Their errand was of charity: they were bringing back to us Bonsall and Petersen, two of the party that left us on the 28th of August.

The party had many adventures and much suffering to tell of. They had verified by painful and perilous experience all I had anticipated for them. But the most stirring of their announcements was the condition they had left their associates in, two hundred miles off, divided in their counsels, their energies broken, and their provisions nearly gone. My first thought was of the means of rescuing and relieving them.

I resolved to despatch the Esquimaux escort at once with such supplies as our miserably imperfect stores allowed, they giving their pledge to carry them

with all speed and, what I felt to be much less certain, with all honesty. But neither of the gentlemen who had come with them felt himself in condition to repeat the journey. Mr. Bonsall had evidently broken down, and Petersen, never too reliable in emergency, was for postponing the time of setting out. Of our own party – those who had remained with the brig – McGary, Hans, and myself were the only ones able to move, and of these McGary was now fairly on the sick-list. We could not be absent for a single day without jeopardizing the lives of the rest.

December 8, Friday: I am much afraid these provisions will never reach the wanderers. We were busy every hour since Bonsall arrived getting them ready. We cleaned and boiled and packed a hundred pounds of pork, and sewed up smaller packages of meat-biscuits, bread-dust, and tea; and despatched the whole, some three hundred and fifty pounds by the returning convoy. But I have no faith in an Esquimaux under temptation, and I almost regret that I did not accompany them myself. It might have been wiser. These Esquimaux left us some walrus-beef; and poor little Myouk made me a special present of half a liver. These go of course to the hospital. God knows they are needed there!

December 12, Tuesday: Brooks awoke me at three this morning with the cry of "Esquimaux again!" They stopped at the gangway and, as I was about to challenge, one of them sprang forward and grasped my hand. It was Dr. Hayes. A few words, dictated by suffering, certainly not by any anxiety as to his reception, and at his bidding the whole party came up on deck. Poor fellows! I could only grasp their hands and gave them a brother's welcome.

The thermometer was at minus 50°; they were covered with rime and snow, and were fainting with hunger. It was necessary to use caution in taking them below; for after an exposure of such fearful intensity and duration as they had gone through, the warmth of the cabin would have prostrated them completely. They had journeyed three hundred and fifty miles; and their last run from the bay near Etah, some seventy miles, was through the hummocks at this appalling temperature.†

One by one they all came in. Poor fellows! As they threw their Esquimaux garments by the stove, how they relished the scanty luxuries which we had to offer them! The coffee and the meat-biscuit soup, and the molasses and the wheat bread, even the salt pork which our scurvy forbade the rest of us to touch – how they relished it all! For more than two months they had lived on frozen seal and walrus-meat. I resigned my own bunk to Dr. Hayes who is much prostrated: he will probably lose two of his toes, perhaps a third. The rest have no special injury.

December 23, Saturday: This uncalculated accession of numbers makes our little room too crowded to be wholesome. We are using the Esquimaux lamp as an accessory to our stove: it helps out the cooking and water-making, without encroaching upon our rigorously-meted allowance of wood. But the odour of pork-fat, our only oil, we have found to be injurious; and our lamps are therefore placed outside in a small room bulkheaded off for their use.

This new arrangement gave rise yesterday to a near fatal disaster. A watch had been stationed in charge of the lamp, with the usual orders of "No uncovered lights." He deserted his post. Soon afterward Hans found the cooking-room on fire. It was a horrible crisis; for no less than eight of our party were absolutely nailed to their beds and there was nothing but a bulkhead between them and the fire. I gave short but instant orders, stationing a line between the tide-hole and the main hatch, detailing two men to work with me. Before we reached the fire the entire bulkhead was in a blaze as well as the dry timbers and skin of the brig. Our moss walls, with their own tinderlike material and their light casing of inflammable wood, were entirely hidden by the flames. Fortunately the furs of the recently returned party were at hand and with them I succeeded in smothering the fire.

December 28, Thursday: I have fed the dogs the last two days on their dead brethren. Spite of all proverbs, *dog will eat dog* if properly cooked. I have been saving up some who died of fits, intending to use their skins, and these have come in very opportunely. I boil them into a sort of bloody soup and deal them out twice a day in chunks and solid jelly; for of course they are frozen like quartz rocks. Salt meats are absolutely poisonous to the Northern Esquimaux dog. We have now lost fifty-odd, and one died yesterday in the very act of eating his reformed diet.

January 6, Saturday: If this journal ever gets to be inspected by other eyes, the colour of its pages will tell of the atmosphere it is written in. We have been emulating the Esquimaux for some time in everything else; and now, last of all, this intolerable temperature and our want of fuel have driven us to rely on our lamps for heat. Counting those which I have added since the wanderers came back, we have twelve constantly going, with grease and soot everywhere in proportion. I can hardly keep my charts and registers in anything like decent trim. Our beds and bedding are absolutely black, and our faces begrimed with fatty carbon. The heat given out by these burners is astonishing. One four-wicked lamp not very well attended gives us six gallons of water in twelve hours from snow and ice of a temperature minus 40°, raising the heat of the cabin to a corresponding extent, the lamp being entirely open. With a line-wick—another Esquimaux plan—we could bake bread or do other cookery.

January 14, Sunday: Our sick are about the same; Wilson, Brooks, Morton, McGary, and Riley unserviceable. Dr. Hayes getting better rapidly. How grateful I ought to be that I, the weakling of a year ago, am a well and helping man. I found an overlooked godsend this morning—a bear's head, put away for a specimen, but completely frozen. There is no inconsiderable quantity of meat adhering to it and I serve it out raw to Brooks, Wilson and Riley.

I do not know that my journal anywhere mentions our habituation to raw meats, nor does it dwell upon their strange adaptation to scorbutic disease. Our journeys have taught us the wisdom of the Esquimaux appetite and there are few among us who do not relish a slice of raw blubber or a chunk of frozen walrus-beef. The liver of a walrus eaten with little slices of his fat—it is a delicious morsel. Fire would ruin the curt, pithy expression of vitality which belongs to its uncooked juices. I wonder that raw beef is not eaten at home.

January 17, Wednesday: There is no evading it any longer; it has been evident for the past ten days that the present state of things cannot last. We require meat, and cannot get along without it. Our sick have finished the bear's head and are now eating the condemned abscessed liver of the animal, including some intestines that were not given to the dogs. We have about three days' allowance; thin chips of raw frozen meat, not exceeding four ounces in weight for each man per diem. Our poor fellows eat it with zest; but it is lamentably little.

Although I was unsuccessful in my last attempt to reach the Esquimaux huts with the dogs, I am far from sure that with proper equipment it could not be managed by walking. The thought weighs upon me. Foot-travel does not seem to have occurred to my comrades; at first sight the idea of making for a point [the Eskimo settlement of Etah] seventy-five miles by the shortest line from our brig, in this awfully cold darkness, is gloomy enough.

January 22, Monday: Busy preparing for a trip to the Esquimaux settlement. Petersen caught a providential fox. We divided him into nine portions, three for each of our scurvied patients. I am off.

The dogs carried Hans and me to the lower curve of the reach before breaking down. It was just beginning for an easy voyage, when Toodla and Big Yellow gave way nearly together—the latter frightfully contorted by convulsions. There was no remedy for it; the moon went down and the wretched night was upon us. We groped along the ice-foot, and after fourteen hours painful walking reached an old igloo.

Here, completely excluded from the knowledge of the things without, we spent many miserable hours. We could keep no note of time and except by the whirring of the drift against the roof of our kennel, had no information of the state of the weather. We slept and cooked coffee, and drank coffee, and slept and cooked coffee, and drank again; and when by our tired instincts we thought that twelve hours must have passed, we treated ourselves to a meal — that is to say we divided impartial bites out of the raw hind-leg of a fox, to give zest to our biscuits spread with frozen tallow.

We then turned in to sleep again, no longer heedful of the storm, for it had now buried us deep in the snow.

In the morning — that is to say when the combined light of the noonday dawn and the circumpolar moon permitted our escape — we had been pent up nearly two days. Under these circumstances we made directly for the hummocks, en route for the bay. But here was a disastrous change. The snow had accumulated under the windward sides of the inclined ice tables to a height so excessive that we buried sledge, dogs, and drivers in the effort to work through. It was all in vain that Hans and I harnessed ourselves to, or lifted, levered, twisted, and pulled. Utterly exhausted and sick, I was obliged to give it up. The darkness closed in again, and with difficulty we regained the igloo.

I now determined to try the land-ice by Fog Inlet; and we worked four hours upon this without a breathing spell — utterly in vain. My poor Esquimaux, Hans, adventurous and buoyant as he was, began to cry like a child. Sick, worn out, strength gone, dogs floundering, I am not ashamed to admit that, as I thought of the sick men on board, my own equanimity also was at fault.

We took the back-track next morning and reached the brig by 4:00 p.m. on Friday.

January 30, Tuesday: My companions on board felt all my disappointment at bringing back no meat; but infinite gladness took the place of regret when they heard the great news that we had at least found a passage through the hummocks. Petersen began at once to busy himself with his wardrobe; and an eight-day party was organized almost before we turned in, to start as soon as the tempestuous weather subsides and the drifts settle down. It is four days since, but as yet we dare not venture out.

That there is no time for delay, this health-table will show:—

Henry Brooks: Unable any longer to go on deck: we carry him with difficulty from his berth to a cushioned locker.

McGary: Less helpless; but off duty and saturated with articular scurvy.

Mr. Wilson: In bed. Severe purpuric blotches and nodes in the limbs. Cannot move.

George Riley: Abed; limbs less stiff, gums better, unable to do duty.

Thomas Hickey (our cook): Cannot keep his legs many more days; already swelled and blistered.

William Morton: Down with a frozen heel; the bone exfoliating.

Henry Goodfellow: Scurvied gums, but generally well.

Dr. Hayes is prostrate with his amputated toes; Sontag just able to hobble. In a word, our effective force is reduced to five.

January 31, Wednesday: Our sick are worse; for our traps yield nothing and we are still without fresh food. The absence of raw meat for a single day shows itself in our scurvy. Haemorrhages are becoming common. My crew – I have no crew any longer – the tenants of my bunks, cannot bear me to leave them for a single watch. Yet I cannot make Petersen try the new path which I discovered and found practicable. Well, the wretched month is over. It is something to be living, able to write. No one has yet made the dark voyage, and January 31st is upon us.

February 2, Friday: The weather clears, the full moon shows herself, the sledge is packed, and Petersen will start tomorrow with Hans.

February 4, Sunday: Mr. Ohlsen breaks down: the scurvy is in his knee, and he cannot walk. This day too, Thomas Hickey, our acting cook, gives way completely. I can hardly realize that among these strong men I alone should be the borne-up man – the only one except Mr. Bonsall on his legs.

I made a dish of freshened codfish-skin for Brooks and Wilson; they were hungry enough to relish it. Besides, I had kept back six bottles of our Scotch ale, to meet emergencies, and I am dealing these out to them by the wine-glass. It is too cold for brewing in our apartment: water freezes two feet above the floor.

February 6, Tuesday: At ten last evening I heard voices outside. Petersen and Hans had returned. I met them silently on deck, and heard from poor Petersen how he had broken down. The snows had been increasing since my own last trial – his strength had left him; the scurvy had entered his chest; in a word, he had failed, and Hans could not do the errand alone.

February 10, Saturday: Three days' respite! Petersen and myself have made a fruitless hunt; but Hans comes in with three rabbits. Distribution: the blood to Ohlsen and Thomas; and to the other eight of the sick men full rations; consuming a rabbit and a half. I cannot risk the depression that a death would bring upon the whole party, and have to deal unfairly with those who can still keep about to save the rest from sinking. Brooks and Ohlsen are in a precarious condition: they have lost the entire mucous membrane of the alveoli; and Mr. Wilson requires special attendance every hour to carry him through.

February 23, Friday: Esquimaux Hans was out early this morning on the trail of a wounded deer. Rhina, the least barbarous of our sledge-dogs, assisted him. He was back by noon with the joyful news, "The *tuktuk* [a caribou] dead only two miles up big fiord!" The cry found its way through the hatch and came back in a broken huzza from the sick men.

We are so badly off for strong arms that our deer threatened to be as great an embarrassment to us as the auction-drawn elephant was to his lucky master. We had hard work with our dogs carrying him to the brig, and still harder, worn down as we were, in getting him over the ship's side. But we succeeded and were tumbling him down the hold when we found ourselves in a dilemma. It was impossible to drag the prize into our little moss-lined dormitory and it was equally impossible to skin him anywhere else without freezing our fingers in the operation. It was a happy escape from the embarrassments of our hungry little council to determine that the animal might be carved before skinning as well as he could be afterward; and in a very few minutes we proved our wisdom by a feast on his quartered remains.

The second Grinnell Expedition in winter quarters
in Smith Sound, 1853. Left to right: Amos Bonsall,
Henry Brooks, Dr. Kane, Dr. Hayes, William Morton.
The moss-chinked quarters were built over the
frozen-in Advance which was eventually abandoned.

It was a glorious meal, such as the compensations of providence reserve for starving men alone. We ate, forgetful of the past, and almost heedless of the morrow; cleared away the offal wearily: and now at 10 p.m. all hands have turned in to sleep, leaving to their commanding officer the solitary honour of an eight hours' vigil.

February 24, Saturday: A bitter disappointment met us at our evening meal. The flesh of our deer was nearly uneatable from putrefaction; the liver and intestines, from which I had expected so much, utterly so. The rapidity of such a change in a temperature so low as minus 35° seems curious; but the Greenlanders say that extreme cold is rather a promoter than otherwise of the putrefactive process.

February 28, Wednesday: Two attempts have been made by my orders, since the month began, to communicate with the Esquimaux at their huts. Both were failures. Petersen, Hans, and Godfrey came back to denounce the journey as impracticable. I know better: the experience of my two attempts in the midst of darkness satisfies me that at this period of the year the thing can be done; and if I might venture to leave our sick-bay for a week I would prove it. But there are dispositions and influences here around me, scarcely latent, yet repressed by my presence, which make it my duty at all hazards to stay where I am.†

On the 6th of March I made the desperate venture of sending off my only trusted and effective huntsman on a sledge-journey to find the Esquimaux of Etah. Should Hans come back with a good supply of walrus, and himself unsmitten by the enemy, our sick would rise under the genial specific of meat, and our strength probably increase enough to convey our boats to the North Water.

March 10, Saturday: Hans has not yet returned, so that he must have reached the settlement. His orders were, if no meat be obtained of the Esquimaux, to borrow their dogs and try for bears along the open water. In this resource I have confidence. The days are magnificent.

. . . I had hardly written the above, when "Bim, bim, bim!" sounded from the deck, mixed with the chorus of our returning dogs. The next minute Hans and myself were shaking hands. He had much to tell us; to men in our condition Hans was as a man from cities. We of the wilderness flocked around him to hear the news. Sugar-teats of raw meat are passed around. "Speak loud, Hans, that they may hear in the bunks."

He had reached Anoatok on the first night after leaving the brig: no Esquimaux there of course; and he slept not warmly at a temperature of 53° below zero. On the evening of the next day he reached Etah Bay and was hailed with joyous welcome. But a new phase of Esquimaux life had come upon its indolent, happy, blubber-fed denizens. Instead of plump, greasy children, and round-cheeked matrons, Hans saw around him lean figures of misery: the men looked hard and bony, and the children shrivelled in the hoods which cradled them at their mother's backs. Famine had been among them; and the skin of a young narwhal, lately caught, was all that remained to them of food. Even their dogs, their main reliance for the hunt and for an escape to some more favoured camping-ground, had fallen a sacrifice to hunger. Only four remained out of thirty: the rest had been eaten.

Hans behaved well and carried out my orders in my full spirit. He proposed to aid them in the walrus-hunt. They smiled at first with true Indian contempt; but when they saw my Marston rifle, which he had with him, they changed their tone.

†*Mutiny and desertion were both brewing at the time.*

I have not time to detail Hans's adventurous hunt. Metek speared a medium sized walrus, and Hans gave him no less than five Marston balls before he gave up his struggles. The beast was carried back in triumph, and all hands fed as if they could never know famine again. The less severe cases on our sick-list are beginning to feel the influence of their new diet; but Wilson and Brooks do not react. Their inclination for food, or rather their toleration of it, is so much impaired that they reject meat in its raw state, and when cooked it is much less prompt and efficient in its action.

PREPARING TO ABANDON THE SHIP

April 19, Thursday: The open water has not advanced from the south more than four miles within the past three weeks. It augurs ill not only for the possible release of the brig, but for the facility of a boat-voyage if we shall be obliged to forsake her, as everything seems to say we must do soon. Last year, on the 10th of May, the water was free around Littleton Island and coming up to within two miles of Refuge Inlet. It is now forty miles further off!

Petersen and Ohlsen are working by short spells at the boats and sledges. I will not leave the brig until it is absolutely certain that she cannot thaw out this season; but everything shall be matured for our instant departure as soon as her fate is decided.

April 20, Friday: Nearly all our beams have been used up for fuel; but I have saved enough to construct two long sledges of 17 feet 6 inches each. I want sledges sufficiently long to bring the weight of the whaleboats within the line of the runner; this will prevent their rocking and pitching when crossing hummocked ice, and enable us to cradle them firmly to the sledge. The men are at this moment breaking out our cabin bulkhead to extract a beam. Our cabin dormitory is full of cold vapour. Everything is comfortless: blankets make a sorry substitute for the moss-padded wall which protected us from –60°.

DEPARTURE FOR THE SOUTH

Our last farewell to the brig was made with solemnity. The entire ship's company was collected in our dismantled winter chamber to take part in the ceremonial. It was Sunday. Our moss walls had been torn down and the wood that supported them burned. Our bedding was off at the boats, already on their way across the ice. The galley was unfurnished and cold. Everything about the little den of refuge was desolate.

I had prepared a brief memorial of the considerations which justified our abandonment of the vessel. I now fixed it to a stanchion near the gangway, where it must attract the notice of any who might seek us hereafter, in case we should be overtaken by disaster. It closed with these words:–

"I regard the abandonment of the brig as inevitable. We have by actual inspection but thirty-six days' provisions, and a careful survey shows that we cannot cut more firewood without rendering our craft unseaworthy. A third winter would force us, as the only means of escaping starvation, to resort to Esquimaux habits and give up all hope of remaining by the vessel and her resources.

"I hope, speaking on the part of my companions and myself, that we have done all that we ought to do to prove our tenacity of purpose and devotion to the cause which we have undertaken. This attempt to escape by crossing the southern ice on sledges is regarded by me as an imperative duty – the only means of saving ourselves and preserving the laboriously-earned results of the expedition.

E. K. KANE,
Com. Grinnell Expedition.
"ADVANCE, RENSSELAER BAY, May 20, 1855."

Our figurehead – the fair Augusta, the little blue girl with pink cheeks, who had lost her breast by an iceberg and her nose by a nip off Bedevilled Reach – was taken from our bows and placed aboard a sled. "She is at any rate wood," said the men, when I hesitated about giving them the additional burden; "and if we cannot carry her far we can burn her."

Excluding four sick men, who were unable to move, and myself who had to drive the dog-team [carrying the smaller of the boats] and serve as common carrier and courier, we numbered but twelve men – which would have given but six to haul each sledge or too few to move it. It was therefore necessary to concentrate our entire force upon one sledge at a time.

Up to the evening of the 23rd of May, the progress had been a little more than a mile a day for one sledge: on the 24th, both sledges had reached the first ravine, a distance of seven miles from the brig, and the dog-sledge had brought on to this station the buffalo bags and the other sleeping appliances which we had prepared during the winter.

In the meantime I had carried Mr. Goodfellow to an advance sick station with my dog-sledge, and had managed to convey the rest one by one to the same spot. Mr. Wilson, whose stump was still unhealed, and who suffered besides from scurvy; George Whipple, whose tendons were so contracted that he could not extend his legs, and poor Stephenson, just able to keep the lamps burning and warm up food for the rest, were the other invalids, all incapable of moving without assistance. Dr. Hayes, though still disabled from his frozen foot, adhered manfully to the sledges.

On Saturday, June 6, we still had all hands at the drag-ropes. The ice ahead of us bore the same character as the day before – no better; we were all perceptibly weaker, and much disheartened. We had been tugging in harness for about two hours when a breeze set in from the northward, the first that we had felt since crossing Bedevilled Reach. We got out our long steering-oar as a boom and made sail upon the boats. The wind freshened almost to a gale and, heading toward the depot on Littleton Island, we ran gallantly before it.

It was a new sensation to our foot-sore men, this sailing over solid ice. Levels which, under the slow labour of the drag-ropes, would have delayed us for hours, were glided over without a halt. We thought it dangerous work at first, but the speed of the sledges made rotten ice nearly as safe as sound ice. The men could see plainly that they were approaching new landmarks and leaving old ones behind. Their spirits rose; the sick whom we were now carrying with us mounted the thwarts, the well clung to the gunwale and, for the first time for nearly a year, broke out the sailors chorus, "Storm along my hearty boys!"

We must have made a greater distance in this single day than in the five that preceded it. We encamped at 5:00 p.m. near a small berg which gave us plenty of fresh water, after a progress of at least eight miles.

From this time we went on for some days aided by our sails, meeting with accidents occasionally – the giving way of a spar or the falling of some of the party through the spongy ice – and occasionally, when the floe was altogether too infirm, labouring our way with great difficulty upon the ice-belt. To mount this solid highway, or to descend from it, the axes were always in requisition.

An inclined plane had to be cut — ten, fifteen, or even thirty feet long, and along this the sledges were to be pushed and guided by bars and levers with painful labour. These are light things, as I refer to them here; but in our circumstances, at the time I write of, when the breaking of a stick of timber was an irreparable harm, and the delay of a day involved the peril of life, they were grave enough. Sometimes too we encountered heavy snowdrifts which were to be shovelled away before we could get along; and within an hour afterward, or perhaps even at the bottom of the drift, one of the sledge runners would cut through to the water.

It was saddening to our poor fellows when we were forced to leave the shore-ice and put out into the open pack field, to look ahead at the salt ice-marshes, as they called them, studded with black pools, with only a white lump rising here and there through the lead-coloured surface. The labour would have been too much for us, weary and broken as we were, but for the assistance we derived from the Esquimaux. I remember once a sledge went so far under, carrying with it several of the party, that the boat floated loose. Just then seven of the natives came up to us – five sturdy men and two almost as sturdy women – and without waiting to be called on, worked with us most efficiently for more than half a day, asking no reward.

Still, passing slowly on day after day, we came at last to the unmistakable neighbourhood of the open water.

Though the conditions of the ice assured us that we were drawing near the end of our sledge-journey, it by no means diminished their difficulty or hazards. The part of the field near the open water was so transparent that we could even see the gurgling eddies below it; while in others it was worn into open holes that were already the resort of wild fowl. This continued to be its character as long as we continued to pursue the Littleton Island channel and we were compelled, the whole way through, to sound ahead with the boat-hook or narwhal-horn. We learned this precaution from the Esquimaux, who always move in advance of their sledges when the ice is treacherous and test its strength before bringing on their teams. Our first warning impressed us with the policy of observing it. We were making wide circuits with the whaleboats to avoid the tide-holes, when signals of distress from the men scrambling on the ice announced to us that the boat called *Red Eric* had disappeared.

It was by great good fortune that no lives were lost. Stephenson was caught, as he sank, by one of the sledge-runners, and Morton, while in the very act of drifting under the ice, was seized by the hair of the head by Mr. Bonsall and saved.

We were now close upon Life-boat Cove, where nearly two years before we had made provisions for just such a contingency as that which was now before us. Buried under the frozen soil our stores had escaped even the keen scrutiny of our savage allies, and we now turned to them as essential to our relief. Mr. McGary was sent to the cache with orders to bring everything except the salt-beef. This had been so long a poison to us that, tainted as we were by scurvy, I was afraid to bring it among those who might be tempted to indulge in it.

On the 12th of June the boats and sledges came to a halt in the narrow passage between the islands opposite Cape Misery. I ascended some eight hundred feet to the summit of Pekiutlik and, looking out, beheld the open water, so long the goal of our struggles, spread out before me. It extended seemingly to Cape Alexander and was nearer to the westward than the south of my position by some five or six miles. But the ice in the latter direction led into

A female bear tossed several of the
Kane expedition dogs in her
determination to get at the stores.

On their sled journey south, the
explorers negotiate an ice chasm.
Poor diet weakened them; three died.

the curve of the bay, and was thus protected from the wind and the swell. My jaded comrades pleaded anxiously in favour of the direct line to the water; but I knew that this ice would give us both safer and better travel. I determined to adopt the inshore route.

I was with the advance boat, trying to force a way through the channel, when the report came to me from Dr. Hayes that Ohlsen was no more. Petersen had gone out to kill a few birds, in the hope of possibly sustaining him by a concentrated soup. But it was in vain: the poor fellow flushed up only to die a few minutes after.

We had no time to mourn the loss of our comrade, a tried and courageous man who met his death in the gallant discharge of his duty. It cast a gloom over the whole party; but the exigencies of the moment were upon us, and we knew not whose turn would come next, or how soon we might all of us follow him together. Without the knowledge of my comrades I encroached on our little store of sheet-lead, which we were husbanding to mend our leaky boats with and, cutting on a small tablet his name and age: *CHRISTIAN OHLSEN, aged 36 years*, laid it on his manly breast. The cape that looks down on him bears his name.

We gave two quiet hours to the memory of our dead brother, and then resumed our toilsome march. As we neared [Etah] the Esquimaux came in flocks to our assistance. They volunteered to aid us at the drag-ropes. They carried our sick upon hand-sledges. They relieved us of all care for our supplies of daily food. The quantity of little auks that they brought us was enormous. They fed us and our dogs at the rate of eight thousand birds a week, all of them caught in their little hand-nets. All anxiety left us for the time. My little note-book closes for the week with this gratefully expounded record:—

"*June 16, Saturday:* Our boats are at the open water. We see its deep indigo horizon, and hear its roar against the icy beach. Its scent is in our nostrils and our hearts."

THE BOAT JOURNEY

We had our boats to prepare now for a long and adventurous navigation. They were so small and heavily laden as hardly to justify much confidence in their buoyancy and they were split with frost and warped by sunshine, and fairly open at the seams. They were to be caulked and swelled, and launched, and stowed, before we could venture to embark in them.

July 18, Monday: The Esquimaux are camped by our side – the whole settlement of Etah congregated to bid us good-bye. There are Metek, and Nualik his wife, "Mrs. Eider-duck," and their five children, commencing with Myouk, my body-guard, and ending with little Accomodah. There is Nessark and Anak his wife; and Tellerk the "Right Arm" and Amaunalik his wife; and Sip-su, and Marsumah and Aningnah – and who not? I can name them every one, and they know us as well. We have found brothers in a strange land.

My heart warms to these poor dirty, miserable, yet happy beings, so long our neighbours, and of late so staunchly our friends. Theirs is no affectation of regret. There are twenty-two of them around me, all busy in good offices to the Docto Kayens. Ever since we reached Pekiulik, these friends of ours have considered us as their guests. They have given us hand-sledges for our baggage, and taken turn about in watches to carry us and it to the water's edge. But for them our dreary journey would have been prolonged at least a fortnight, and we are so late even now that hours may measure our lives.

And now it only remains for us to make our farewell to those desolate and confiding people. I gathered them round me on the ice-beach, and talked to them as brothers for whose kindness I still had a return to make.

But we were not yet to embark, for the gale which had been long brooding now began to dash a heavy sea against the floe, and obliged us to retreat before it, hauling our boats back with each fresh breakage of the ice. It rose more fiercely, and we were obliged to give way before it still more. Our goods, which had been stacked upon the ice, had to be carried further inward. We worked our way back step by step, before the breaking ice, for about two hundred yards. At last it became apparent that the men must sleep and rest, or sink; and, giving up for the present all thoughts of embarking, I hauled the boats at once nearly a mile from the water's edge, where a large iceberg was frozen tight in the floes.

But here we were still pursued. All the next night it blew fearfully, and at last our berg crashed away through the broken ice and our asylum was destroyed. Again we fell to hauling back the boats until, fearing that the continuance of the gale might induce a ground-swell, which would have been fatal to us, I came to a halt near the slope of a low iceberg on which I felt confident that we could haul up in case of the entire disruption of the floes. The area was already intersected with long cracks, and the surface began to show a perceptible undulation beneath our feet.

I climbed to the summit of the berg; but it was impossible to penetrate the obscurity of the mist and spray further than a thousand yards. The sea tore the ice up almost to the very base of the berg and all around it looked like one vast tumultuous cauldron, the ice-tables crashing together in every possible position with deafening clamour.

The gale died away to a calm, and the water became as tranquil as if the gale had never been. All hands were called to prepare for embarking. The boats were stowed and the cargo divided between them equally; the sledges unlashed and slung outside the gunwales; and on Tuesday the 19th, at 4:00 p.m., with the bay as smooth as a garden-lake, I put off in the *Faith*. She was followed by the *Red Eric* on our quarter, and the *Hope* astern.

So we stood away for Hakluyt. It was an ugly crossing: we had a short chopping sea from the southeast and, after a while, the *Red Eric* swamped. Riley and Godfrey managed to struggle to the *Faith*, and Bonsall to the *Hope*; but it was impossible to remove the cargo of our little boat; it was as much as we could do to keep her afloat and let her tow behind us. Just at this time, too, the *Hope* made a signal of distress and Brooks hailed us to say that she was making water faster than he could free her.

The wind was hauling round to the westward, and we could not take the sea abeam; but as I made a rapid survey of the area around me studded already with floating shreds of floe ice, I saw ahead the low grey blink of the pack. I remembered well the experience of our Beechy Island trip, and knew that the margin of these large fields is almost always broken by inlets of open water which gave much the same sort of protection as the creeks and rivers of an adverse coast. We were fortunate in finding one of these, and fastening ourselves to an old floe alongside of which our weary men turned in to sleep without hauling up the boats.

When Petersen and myself returned from an unsuccessful hunt upon the ice, we found them still asleep in spite of a cold and drizzling rain that might have stimulated wakefulness. I did not disturb them until eight o'clock. We then retreated from our breakwater of refuge, generally pulling along by the boat-hooks, but sometimes dragging our boats over the ice; and at last, bending to our oars as the water opened, reached the shore of Hakluyt Island. It snowed hard in the night, and the work of caulking went on badly though we expended on it a prodigal share of our remaining white lead. We rigged up a tent for the sick and reinforced our bread-dust and tallow supper by a few birds. We had shot a seal in the course of the day, but we lost him by his sinking.

In the morning of the 22nd we pushed forward through the snow-storm for Northumberland Island, and succeeded in reaching it a little to the eastward of my former landing-place. Myriads of auks greeted us, and we returned their greeting by the appropriate invitation to our table.

We crossed Murchison Channel on the 23rd and encamped for the night on the land-floe at the base of Cape Parry; a hard day's travel, partly by tracking over ice, partly through tortuous and zigzag leads. The next day brought us to the neighbourhood of Fitz-Clarence Rock, rising from a field of ice like an Egyptian pyramid surmounted by an obelisk.

The next day gave us admirable progress. The ice opened in leads before us, and for sixteen hours I never left the helm. We were all of us exhausted when the day's work came to a close. Our ration allowance had been small from the first; but the delays we seemed fated to encounter had made me reduce them to what I then thought the minimum quantity, six ounces of bread-dust and a lump of tallow the size of a walnut. A paste or broth made of these before setting out in the morning, and distributed occasionally through the day in scanty rations, was our only fare. We were all of us glad when, running the boats under the lee of a berg, we were able to fill our kettles with snow and boil up for our great restorative, tea.

The imperfect diet of the party was showing itself more and more in the decline of their muscular power. They seemed scarcely aware of it themselves but as we endeavoured to renew our labours through the morning fog, belted in on all sides by ice-fields so distorted and rugged as to defy our efforts to cross them, the truth seemed to burst upon every one. We had lost the feeling of hunger and were almost satisfied with broth and the large draughts of tea which accompanied it.

We were sorely disheartened [when] I climbed on the iceberg; and there was nothing in view except Dalrymple Rock, with its red brassy face towering in the unknown distance. But I hardly got back to my boat before a gale struck us from the northwest, and a floe began to close slowly in upon our narrow resting-place.

At first the floe we were upon also was driven before the wind; but in a while it encountered the stationary ice at the foot of the very rock itself. On the instant the wildest imaginable ruin arose around us. The men sprang mechanically each one to his station, bearing back the boats and stores; but I gave up for the moment all hope of our escape. It was not a nip, such as is familiar to arctic navigators; but the whole platform where we stood, and for hundreds of yards on either side of us, crumbled and crushed and piled, and tossed itself madly under the pressure. I do not believe that our little body of men, all of them disciplined in trials, able to measure danger while combating it —I do not believe there is one who this day can explain how or why we found ourselves afloat. We only know that in the midst of a clamour utterly indescribable, through which the braying of a thousand trumpets could no more have been heard than the voice of a man, we were shaken and raised, and whirled and let down again in a swelling waste of broken hummocks, and as the men grasped their boat-hooks, the boats eddied away in a tumultuous screed of ice and snow and water.

We were borne along in this manner as long as the unbroken remnant of the in-shore floe continued revolving – utterly powerless, and catching a glimpse now and then of the brazen headland that looked down on us through the snowy sky. At last the floe brought up against the rocks. The looser fragments that hung around it began to separate and we were able by oars and boat-hooks to force our battled little flotilla clear of them. To our joyful surprise we soon found ourselves in a stretch of the land-water wide enough to give us rowing room, and with the assured promise of land close ahead.

As we neared it we saw a forbidding wall of shore-ice. We pulled along its margin, seeking in vain either an opening of access or a nook of shelter. The gale rose and the ice began to drive in again; but there was nothing to be done but get a grapnel out to the ice-wall and hold on for the rising tide. The *Hope* stove her bottom and lost part of her weather-boarding, and all the boats were badly chafed. It was an awful storm, and it was not without constant exertion that we kept afloat, bailing out the scud that broke over us, and warding off the ice with boat-hooks.

At three o'clock the tide was high enough for us to scale the ice-cliff of the shore-ice. One by one we pulled up the boats upon a narrow shelf, the whole sixteen of us uniting at each pull. We were too much worn down to unload; but a deep and narrow gorge opened in the cliffs almost at the spot where we clambered up; and, as we pushed the boats into it on an even keel, the rocks seemed to close above our heads until an abrupt turn in the course of the ravine placed a protecting cliff between us and the gale. We were completely encaved.

Just as we had brought in the last boat, the *Red Eric*, and were shoring her up with blocks of ice, a familiar sound startled and gladdened every ear, and a flock of eiders, flecking the sky for a moment, passed swiftly in front of us. We knew that we must be at their breeding-grounds; and as we turned in wet and hungry to our long-coveted sleep, it was only to dream of eggs and abundance.

We remained almost three days in our crystal retreat, gathering eggs at the rate of twelve hundred a day. Outside the storm raged without intermission, and our egg-hunters found it difficult to keep their feet; but a merrier set of gourmands than were gathered within never surfeited on a more genial diet.

On the 3rd of July the wind began to moderate, though the snow still fell heavily; and the next morning after a patriotic egg-nog – the liquor borrowed grudgingly from our alcohol-flask and diluted till it was worthy of temperance praise – we lowered our boats, and bade a grateful farewell to "Weary Man's Rest."

For some days after this we kept moving slowly to the south along the lanes that opened between the shore-ice and the floe. The weather continued dull and unfavourable, and we were off a large glacier before we were aware that further progress near the shore was impracticable. Great chains of bergs presented themselves as barriers in our way, the spaces between choked by barricades of hummocks. It was hopeless to bore. We tried for sixteen hours together without finding a possibility of egress.

I climbed one of the bergs to the height of about 200 feet and, looking well to the west, was satisfied that a lead which I saw there could be followed. But on conferring with Brooks and McGary I was startled to find how much the boats had suffered in the encounters of the last few days. The *Hope* was altogether unseaworthy and it required nearly all our wood to repair her.

In the meantime the birds which had been so abundant when we left Dalrymple Island and which we had counted on for a continuous store seem to have been driven off by the storm. We set out keeping in-shore, in the hope of renewing to some extent our supplies of game. We were fifty-two hours in forcing this rugged passage.

Once through the barrier the leads began to open again, and on the 11th we found ourselves approaching Cape Dudley Digges. It looked for some hours as if our troubles were over, when a glacier came in sight not laid down on the charts, whose tongues of floe-ice extended still farther out to sea. Our first resolve was to double it at all hazards, for our crew were too much weakened to justify hauling through the hummocks and the soft snow which covered the land-floe. We forced our way into a lead of sludge, but the only result was a lesson of gratitude for our escape from it. Our frail and weather-worn boats were quite unequal to the duties.

I climbed the nearest berg and surveyed the ice. My eyes never looked on a spectacle more painful. We were in advance of the season and the floes had not broken up. There was no "western water." Here in a cul-de-sac between two barriers, both impassable to men in our condition, we were to wait [at Cape Dudley Digges] until the tardy summer should open to us a way.

I could not allow fuel for a fire, our slush and tallow was reduced to very little more than a hundred pounds. We made experiments upon the organic matter within reach, the dried nests of the kittiwake, the sods, the mosses, and the fatty skins of the birds around us. But none of them would burn. Nevertheless it was one glorious holiday, a week at Providence Halt, so full of refreshment and happy thoughts that I never allowed myself to detract from it by acknowledging that it was other than premeditated. There were only two of the party who had looked out with me at the bleak icefield ahead, and them I had pledged to silence.

My journal tells of disaster at our eventual setting out. In launching the *Hope* she was precipitated into the sludge below carrying away rail and bulwark, losing overboard our best shotgun, and our kettle.

Our descent of the coast followed the margin of the fast ice. The birds along it were rejoicing in the young summer and when we halted it was upon some green clad cape.

We reached Cape York on the 21st after a torturous but romantic travel through a misty atmosphere. Here the land lead ceased, and everything bore proof of the late development of the season. A fast floe extended with numerous tongues far out to the south and east. The only question was between a new prolonged rest, while we waited for the shore-ice to open, or a desertion of the coast and a trial of the open water to the west.

I called my officers together, explained to them the motives which governed me, and prepared to re-embark into the open water. The boats were hauled up, examined carefully, and as far as our means permitted, repaired. The *Red Eric* was stripped of her outfit and cargo, to be broken up for fuel when the occasion should arise.

By degrees the ice through which we were moving became more and more impacted, and sometimes required all our knowledge to determine whether a particular lead was practicable. I was awakened one evening from a weary sleep to discover that we had lost our way. The officer at the helm of the boat, misled by the irregular shape of a large iceberg, had lost the main lead and was steering shoreward out of our true course.

Without apprising the men of our misadventure I ordered the boats hauled up, on the pretence of drying the clothing. A few hours later the weather cleared enough to allow me to climb a berg some 300 feet high. We were deep in the recesses of a bay, surrounded on all sides by icebergs and tangled floe-ice.

There was but one thing to be done, cost what it might. We must harness our sledge again and retrace our way to the westward. One sledge had already been used for firewood so that it was not until the third toilsome day was well spent that we reached the berg which had bewildered our helmsman. We hauled over its tongue and again joyously embarked.

Our little squadron was now reduced to two boats. The land to the northward was no longer visible and whenever I left the margin of the shore-ice I was obliged to trust entirely to the compass. We had at least eight days' allowance of fuel on board, but our provisions were running very low and we met few birds and failed to secure any larger game.

Our next land was to be Cape Shackleton, one of the most prolific bird colonies of the coast, but, reckoning our stores to the number of days that must elapse before we could expect to reach its hospitable welcome, I found that 5 ounces of bread-dust, 4 of tallow, and 3 of bird meat must from this time form our daily ration.

I now determined to try the more open sea. For the first two days the experiment was a failure. We were surrounded by heavy fog. We were thus carried to the northward and lost about 20 miles. Nevertheless I held to my purpose, steering south-south-west as nearly as the leads would admit, and looking constantly for the thinning out of the pack that bounds the "western water."

Things grew worse and worse with us, the old difficulty of breathing came back again and our feet swelled to such an extent that we were obliged to cut open our canvas boots. A form of low fever hung over us. It must be remembered that we were now in the open bay, and in full line of the great ice drift to the great Atlantic, and in boats so frail and unseaworthy as to require constant bailing to keep them afloat.

It was at this crisis of our fortune that we saw a large seal floating on a small patch of ice. It was so large that I at first mistook it for a walrus. Trembling with anxiety, we prepared to crawl down upon him.

He was not asleep, for he reared his head when we were almost within rifle-shot, and to this day I can remember the hard, care-worn, almost despairing expressions of the men's thin faces when they saw him move. Their lives depended on his capture. I depressed my hand nervously for Petersen to fire. McGary hung upon his oar, and the boat slowly but noiselessly sagged ahead. Looking at Petersen I saw that the poor fellow was paralyzed by his anxiety, trying vainly to obtain a rest for his gun against the cutwater of the boat. The seal rose on his fore flippers, gazed at us for a moment with frightened curiosity and prepared himself for a plunge. At that instant, with the crack of our rifle, he relaxed his full length on the ice at the very brink of the water, his head falling helpless to one side.

I would have ordered another shot but no discipline could have controlled the men. With a wild yell they urged both boats upon the ice. A crowd of hands seized the seal and bore him up to safer ice. The men seemed half crazy; I had not realized how much we were reduced by absolute famine. They ran over the floe crying and laughing, and brandishing their knives. It was not five minutes before every man was sucking his bloody fingers or eating long strips of raw blubber.

This was our last experience of the disagreeable effects of hunger. I need not detail our journey any farther. Within a day or two we shot another seal and from that time forward had a full supply of food.

On the 1st of August we sighted the Devil's Thumb and were again amongst the familiar localities of the whaler's battling grounds. Now, with the apparent certainty of reaching home came that nervous apprehension which follows upon hope long deferred. I could not trust myself to take the outside passage but timidly sought the quiet water channels running deep into the archipelago which forms a sort of island labyrinth along this coast.

Thus it was at one of our sleeping halts amongst the rocks that Petersen awoke me with a story. He had just seen and recognized a native who, in his frail kayak, was seeking eider ducks amongst the islands. The man had once been an intimate of his family. "Paul Zacharias, don't you know me? I am Carl Petersen!" "No," said the man; "his wife says he's dead"; and with a stolid expression of wonder he stared for a moment at the long beard that loomed at him through the fog, and paddled away with all the energy of terror.

Two days afterwards we were rowing around the shadow of Karkamoot. Just then a familiar sound came to us over the water. It died away in the cadence of a "halloo." "Listen, Petersen! Oars, men!" "What is it?" He listened quietly at first, and then trembling said in a half whisper, "Dannennarkers!"

By and by (we must have been pulling a good half hour) the single mast of a small shallop showed itself and Petersen, who had been very quiet and grave, burst out into an incoherent fit of crying only relieved by broken exclamations of mingled Danish and English. "'Tis the Upernavik oil boat! Carlie Mossyn must be on his road to Kingatok for blubber. The *Mariane* (the one annual ship) has come!"

fm Kane did not have much to show for the expedition's long ordeal. He wintered his ship only nine miles farther north than had been reached by Commander Inglefield, RN, in 1852. He lost his ship and three of his men; and many of the survivors were crippled for life. His pretence that he had gone north to search for the Franklin expedition had been exposed. Despite all this, Kane became a great hero at home. He was publicly praised as "the outstanding American polar idol of the mid-century." His wishful reporting of the existence of an "open polar sea" was greeted with respect and taken seriously.

The charm of his personality gave Kane a hero's aura; but if there is a real hero in the tragedy of errors that marks the second Grinnell expedition, it is the Eskimo Hans Hendrik, or Hans Christian as he was sometimes called. Hans saved the lives of the members of the Kane expedition, not once, but many times. It was due to his ability and efforts that the only worthwhile sledge journey was made – to Cape Constitution. And he did all that he did in exchange for two barrels of flour and fifty-two pounds of salt pork, his salary, paid in advance before he left Fiskenaesset.

Hans was not the single-handed saviour of the Kane expedition. He was ably assisted by Petersen; but the efforts of both men would probably not have been enough to avert a catastrophe had it not been for the assistance given by the Thule Eskimos. One wonders what the Thule people thought of it all. Kane and his men certainly gave the Eskimos sufficient reason to suspect that they were a band of dangerous lunatics; yet instead of withdrawing and leaving the madmen in a vacuum to live or die as luck went, the Eskimos rallied to them time after time. They got precious little credit for it and, through the next sixty years during which they served as the indispensable mainstays to a never-ending succession of white men, all hell-bent on reaching the Pole at any cost, the Thule Eskimos were always short-changed on credit for their efforts, and were usually short-changed in terms of more material rewards as well. This did not bother them. They were kind people.

Back at Fiskenaesset Hans married a girl named Markut and settled down –

but not for long. During the next twenty years he was called upon to guide and help the polar expeditions of Dr. Hayes; C. F. Hall; and the massive British effort under Sir George Nares. *Somebody* had to get the white men out of trouble once they got into it, and a fair number of times that somebody was Hans Hendrik. We shall hear of him again.

Elisha Kane, the first modern man to covet the glory of reaching the North Pole, had his faults as a polar explorer, but he was an engaging fellow. Gay, inconsequential, and cursed (or blessed) with a short interest span, he was a true adventurer. Two years after the fiasco of the second Grinnell expedition he turned his back on the Arctic and was in Havana when he was struck down by a heart attack. He did not live to hear of the sorry failure of his old companion, Dr. Hayes, to find the "open polar sea" and sail across it to the Pole. □ FM

CHAPTER 4 LIFE ON AN ICE-FLOE

The most important result of Kane's expedition was to plant the germ of an *idée fixe* in the hearts of his countrymen. The dash and daring with which he had carried off his polar journey had a tremendous impact on the public, and from this time forward the pursuit of the Pole became a major American theme.

Kane's immediate successor was his second-in-command, Dr. Isaac Hayes. The loss of several toes from frostbite during the Kane expedition had not taken the edge off Hayes's enthusiasm, and in 1860 he launched his own attempt to reach the Pole. "Accepting the deductions of many learned physicists that the sea about the North Pole cannot be frozen; that an open area must be found within the Ice-belt, which is known to invest it . . . I entertained the expectation of being able to push a vessel into the Ice-belt to about the 80th parallel (via Smith Sound) and then transport a boat over the ice to the open sea . . ."

Hayes was not the promoter Kane had been, or else Mr. Grinnell was growing stingy. In any event Hayes's plans for a two-ship flotilla had to be pared to the purchase of one small schooner originally called the *Spring Hill*, which he grandiloquently renamed *United States*. Accompanying him as second-in-command went August Sontag, who had been the astronomer with Kane.

The little schooner could be pushed no further north than Etah, where she went into winter quarters. Hayes started work by making a hundred-mile trek to the east across the Greenland Ice-cap. It was a brave start; but the omens were bad. During the early winter Sontag froze to death as a result of breaking through thin ice. This disaster was followed by an epidemic disease which killed all of Hayes's sled-dogs. Nevertheless, in April of 1861 he set out for the north with his men hauling the sleds by hand, and after enduring the miseries and hardships inevitable with this kind of travel, they reached (so Hayes claimed) Lady Franklin Bay at the mouth of Kennedy Channel, in 81° 35' N. latitude.

When the *United States* broke free of the ice at Etah in July, Hayes turned her head for home, his dreams unfulfilled but his faith unshaken. In his book, which he forthrightly called *The Open Polar Sea*, he firmly stated his conviction that an open polar sea existed and that, by following in his tracks, the next expedition would have no difficulty in reaching it and passing onward to the Pole.

Unfortunately for Hayes and his ambitions, his countrymen had started a civil war during his absence; a war of such ferocity it put a halt to American polar expeditions for the next several years.

However, these two American attempts had brought a new element into the story – international competition. The British were indignant that anyone should have dared to enter *their* polar preserves. The Germans were determined to demonstrate that they were the *only* race competent to capture the Pole. Hungarians, Austrians and Italians began to feel that they were being upstaged.

The North Pole suddenly became *the* place to go, and the pursuit of it became *the* way to demonstrate feelings of national superiority.

The Germans opened this new phase of polar explorations in 1869 by sending two ships, the schooner *Hansa* and the steamer *Germania*, to follow the trail of Englishman William Scoresby and to try to burst the ice-girdle by a thrust delivered from the northeastern coast of Greenland.

Alas, they were hardly up to their self-imposed task. The two ships early separated and the *Hansa* got trapped in the East Greenland Pack which wrecked and sank her. Her crew drifted south on the pack from September 27 until May 7 of the following year before managing to launch their boats and gain the shore in southeast Greenland. The *Germania* had meanwhile managed to harbour on the coast at about 75°. For some reason her people seemed to rouse a violent antipathy on the part of the polar bears – normally rather inoffensive animals. One bear very nearly finished off the expedition's astronomer, a man named Borgen:

One winter's night on my return from the observatory, about 50 steps from the vessel, I heard a noise and became aware of the proximity of a bear. There was no time to think or to use my gun. The attack of the bear was so sudden and rapid that I am unable to say how it was done; whether he rose and struck me down with his forepaw, or whether he ran me down. The next thing I felt was the tearing of my scalp, which was only protected by a cloth cap. This is their method of attacking seals, but owing to the slipperiness of my skull the teeth glided off. The cry for help I uttered frightened the animal for a moment; but he turned again and bit me several times in the head. The alarm had meanwhile been heard by the Captain. He hurried on deck, roused the crew and hastened to the ice.

The noise frightened the bear and he trotted off with me, dragging me by the head. A shot fired to frighten the creature effected its purpose, and he dropped me and sprang a few steps aside; but he immediately seized me again by the arm and, the hold proving insufficient, he then seized me by the right hand. This gave the pursuers time to come up with the brute. He was now making for shore and would certainly have escaped with me had he climbed the bank. However he turned along the coast on the rough and broken ice, which greatly retarded his speed and allowed his pursuers to gain rapidly. After being dragged this way for three hundred paces, almost strangled by my shawl which the bear had also seized in his teeth, he dropped me. Immediately afterwards Koldewey was bending over me with the words, "Thank God! He is still alive!"

The main injuries were in my head where, amongst other wounds from the bites, two especially from 4 to 6 inches long ran along the scalp, the edges of which hung loose, leaving the skull bare. The other wounds, about twenty in number, were in part caused by striking against the rough broken ice. It is worth mentioning that I did not experience the smallest pain.

fm In the spring of 1870 the Germans mounted a sled expedition to the north, and it laboured along to 77° before turning back. The most notable result was the meticulously detailed account of what life was like during such an expedition. □ FM

Amongst other disagreeables is monotony. The ideas contained within the limited horizon of life in the arctic world pass as quickly away as the eye is wearied by the monotony of the landscape. Conversation cannot be very animated. The frost prevents smoking, for the pipes freeze. There is a continued conflict against the loss of warmth, and the cold penetrates in a hundred different ways. Now the chin is numb, or a painful straining of the forehead sets in, or a violent pricking of the nostrils. One stands in constant danger of the heels, the toes or the hands being frostbitten. The hair of the face and eyelashes gets hoar with frost. When frozen hands or feet are not rubbed with snow before too late, the fingers and toes swell up into lumps and become quite numbed.

Under ordinary circumstances the tent was pitched in a hole dug in the snow around 7:00 p.m. When the sleeping sack had been laid down, our personal baggage settled, the kettle filled with blocks of snow by the cook, the lamp lit and the rations given out, our comrades who owing to the intense cold had been running and jumping to keep themselves warm, were allowed to enter. Each man had been busy thawing his beard with his hands for it had changed into a lump of ice and if allowed to melt while the cooking was going on it would wet their clothes and coverings.

Our stiff sail-cloth boots, fast-frozen to the stockings, were to form our pillows; but first had to be thawed between the hands and, with difficulty, taken off our feet. The stockings, thick with snow, were scraped, then wrung, then laid upon our naked breasts to dry by the only available means – our body heat. At last we all wriggled into the sleeping bag, each one lying partly on his neighbour, and in this modest space waited for the evening meal.

The first hour was spent in melting snow, the second in cooking the meal. The steam during the cooking put us into such a vapour bath that we could not even see our neighbour. The tent walls became completely wet through as the temperature rose. The condensation resulted in everything being coated with ice or a crust of snow before the cooking was over.

Only occasionally did our supply of fuel allow us to prepare sufficient drinking water. During the march each man carried an India-rubber or tin bottle full of snow on his bare body, turned as much as possible toward the sun. After many hours only a few spoonfuls, and sometimes no water at all, could be obtained from it.

The cook, after cleaning the kettle, fights his way into the sleeping bag which thus attains its full complement. The side position is the only one possible. Tonight all lie to the left; tomorrow all lie to the right. When at length silence falls upon us the eight men form one single lump. The nose becomes a cold-pole but leaving it outside the rimy and icy covering is preferable to burying it in the questionable atmosphere of the sack. The mouth must remain open but the teeth get so cold that they feel like icicles and the mask, which one must wear in the night, freezes to the long beard. In spite of all efforts to the contrary the cutting cold soon penetrates the sleeping sack, within a tent where the temperature sinks to 60° or 65° below zero.

During the day the sack gets thoroughly frozen on the sled, being frozen into thick folds as hard as iron. Whoever lies upon these seems to be lying on laths which, toward morning only, begin to lose their sharpness. For hours together we are in a state of suffocation, pressure on either side causing a feeling as though the collar bone was being forced into the chest and the shoulders crushed. Each lies on his arm (which of course goes to sleep) and is often prevented from breathing by the smell of putrid oil proceeding from his neighbours' sealskins.

The misery of tent life reaches its maximum during an uninterrupted snowstorm of sometimes three days' duration. The wind would greatly lessen the already small space by pressing in the walls. A small flood of the finest snow would come in through the walls until a covering of snow at least an inch thick lies on top of the sack, under which we must patiently wait till the storm ceases.

We waited through these periods with an indifference bordering on stupidity. Woe to the unfortunate man who is driven to go outside during a lull. He is almost torn to pieces by the gale. Numbed with cold, white as a miller, he returns to the tent where he is a subject of horror to his neighbours in the sack, who he intends robbing of their warmth to thaw himself. The disturbance consequent on someone going into the open air does not subside for many hours. Those of us who were snow-blind suffered the most in such a state of things, and out of consideration for them smoking had to be dropped.

fm The German expedition had been less than a success, but its mere gesture in the direction of the North Pole was enough to fire the United States to mount another expedition. By this time the Americans had begun to feel the same sort of proprietary interest in the Pole that they now feel for the moon. Nobody else was going to be allowed to get there first, if they could help it. In 1871 Charles Francis Hall became the chosen man whose task it was to carry the Stars and Stripes to the North Pole.

Hall was one of the most remarkable of all the strange figures who have stalked across the white wilderness –and he was also one of the least understood. He was the antithesis of the explorers who sallied north at the head of complex and formidable expeditions, determined to beat down the defences of the north by brute strength, or through sheer stubbornness. The essence of Hall's method was to divest himself of as much as possible of the usual exploring paraphernalia and adapt himself to circumstances. He was a simple man, and he began his arctic work in a simple manner.

Of obscure antecedents, Hall had been, among other things, a blacksmith's apprentice and the editor of a penny paper. He was something of a mystic, and in the late 1850s God told him to take up the now abandoned search for survivors of the Franklin expedition.

The support he obtained for this purpose was so meagre it barely sufficed to provide a small open boat and a completely inadequate stock of food – one of the major items of which was a gift of hog-cracklings from a friend in Cincinnati. To get north at all he had to beg free passage aboard a New England whaler bound for two summers and a winter on the east coast of Baffin Island. In the spring of 1860, at the same time Hayes was proudly sailing north in the *United States* to capture the Pole, every inch the explorer, Charles Hall was hitch-hiking *his* way north. East Baffin Island was a long, hard way from the area of the Franklin tragedy, but Hall was undismayed. He boarded the whaler *George Henry*, determined to leave her when he reached the Baffin coast and make his way in his open boat to King William Island. It was a fantastic scheme – but then Hall was a fantastic person.

In any event, the little boat was destroyed in a hurricane a short time after the *George Henry* reached Baffin Island. This abrupt end to his hopes did not destroy Hall's faith. He at once began making plans for a second expedition, but these were for the future. Meanwhile he was condemned to spend two years on Baffin Island. He did not intend to waste those years. He seems to have grasped intuitively the cardinal fact which had eluded his predecessors, and many of his successors too, that victory could only be achieved in the North if the explorer learned how to become an integral part of the country. He needed an intimate knowledge of the land, its beasts, its people, and their ways of life. Hall went directly to the obvious source of such information, which almost every white man before his time had totally neglected. He went to the Eskimos, and he became the first white man of whom we have any certain knowledge who deliberately chose to live for an extended period as an Eskimo himself. □ FM

Towards the end of October 1860, I was visited by two Eskimos, man and wife, together with a child, all three of whom later accompanied me to the States. The man's name was Ebierbing – otherwise called Joe by us; his wife's name was Tookoolito, or Hannah.

I was told that this couple had been taken to England in 1853, and presented to Her Majesty Queen Victoria, and that the female was a remarkably intelligent, and what might be called an accomplished woman. They had remained nearly two years in Great Britain, and were everywhere well received. Hannah was the sister of an Eskimo who was well known in England from a visit there in 1839: Joe was a good pilot for this coast and had brought many whaling ships through the channels into the harbour where we now were. My first interview with this couple is recorded in my journal as follows:

Horns of a musk ox killed by C. F. Hall.

While occupied in my cabin writing I heard a soft, sweet voice say "Good morning, sir." The tone in which it was spoken – musical, lively and varied – instantly told me that a lady of refinement was there greeting me. I was astonished. Could I be dreaming? No! I was wide awake and writing. Had a thunderclap sounded on my ear, though it was snowing at the time, I could not have been more surprised than I was at the sound of that voice. I raised my head: a lady was indeed before me, and extending an ungloved hand.

Of course, my welcome to such an unexpected visitor in these regions was as befitting as my astonished faculties for the moment could make it. The doorway in which she stood leads from the main cabin into my private room. Directly over this entrance was the skylight admitting a flood of light, and thus revealed to me crinoline, heavy flounces, an attenuated toga, and an immensely expanded "kiss-me-quick" bonnet, but the features I could not at first make out.

I immediately tried to do honour to my unknown visitor. But, on turning her face, who should she be but a lady Eskimo! Whence, thought I, came this civilized refinement? But, in a moment more I was made acquainted with my visitor. She was the Tookoolito I had so much desired to see, and directly I conversed with her she showed herself to be quite an accomplished person. She spoke my own language fluently, and there, seated at my right in the main cabin, I had a long and interesting conversation with her. Ebierbing, her husband – a fine and also intelligent looking man – was introduced to me and, though not speaking English so well as his wife, yet I could talk with him tolerably well. From them I gleaned many interesting particulars of their visit to England, and was gratified to hear that they had actually dined with Prince Albert, who treated them kindly and with much consideration.

Ebierbing, in speaking of the Queen, said he liked her very much and she was quite pretty. He also said that Prince Albert was "very kind, good man, and he should never forget him."

I asked Hannah how she would like to live in England. She replied that she would like it very much.

"Would you like to go to America with me?" said I. "I would indeed, sir," was the ready reply.

In reference to the Queen of England she said: "I visited her, and liked the appearance of Her Majesty and everything about the palace. Fine place, I assure you, sir."

As Tookoolito continued speaking I could not help admiring the exceeding gracefulness and modesty of her demeanour. Simple and gentle in her way, there was a degree of calm intellectual power about her that more and more astonished me. I felt delighted beyond measure, because of the opportunity for becoming better acquainted with these people through her means.

Some days later I visited Ebierbing's igloo. He himself had gone out but Tookoolito welcomed me as usual, soon entering into lively and instructive conversation. Two native boys were present at the time, and Tookoolito herself was busy knitting *socks for her husband!* Yes, to my surprise, she was thus engaged as if she had been in a civilized land and herself civilized, instead of being an Eskimo in her own native wilds of ice and snow!

It was a strange contrast. Knitting stockings for her husband! How much of dear home was in that domestic occupation. I have before said that she was peculiarly pleasing and refined in her style and manner; and now, while sheltering me beneath her hospitable roof, with the bright oil lamp before me, the lively prattle of the two boys came in strong contrast to the soft tones of her civilized tongue. What she said and what my impressions were are found in the following extract from my journal:

November 14th, 1860. Tookoolito after returning from England five years ago, where she and her *Wing-a* (husband) spent twenty months, commenced diffusing her accomplishments in various ways, to wit, teaching the female portion of the Eskimo nation to knit, and the various useful things practised by civilization. By dressing her hair, keeping her face and hands clean, and wearing civilized dresses – others of her sex, in considerable numbers, follow these fashions imported by her. This shows me what one person like Tookoolito could accomplish in the way of the introduction of schools and churches amongst this people.

"While in the tent, Tookoolito brought out a book I had given her and desired to be instructed in reading. She has got so she can spell words of two letters, and pronounce most of them properly. Her progress is praiseworthy. She is far more anxious to learn to read and write than Ebierbing. I feel greater confidence (allowing it were possible to feel so) in the success of my mission now that I have engaged these two natives to help me. They can talk with me in my own vernacular, are both smart, and will be useful each in the department they will be called upon to fill. Tookoolito, I have no doubt, will readily accomplish the differences in language between the Eskimos of Boothia and King William's land, and that of her own people around Northumberland Inlet and Davis Strait.

"Tookoolito now had the tea kettle over the friendly fire-lamp, and the water boiling. She asked me if I drank tea. Imagine my surprise at this, the question coming from an Eskimo in an Eskimo tent! I replied, "I do, but you have no tea here, have you?" Drawing her hand from a little tin box she displayed it full of fine flavoured black tea saying, 'Do you like your tea strong?' Thinking to spare her the use of much of this precious article away up here, far from the land of civilization, I replied, 'I'll take it weak, if you please.' Seeing she had but one cup, I induced her to share with me its contents. There, amid the snows of the north, under an Eskimo's hospitable roof, for the first time I shared with them in that cheering, invigorating emblem of civilization – tea!"

fm For nearly two years Hall lived and travelled with the Eskimos on Baffin Island. Although he made no startling geographical discoveries he did solve one long-standing mystery of the Arctic by rediscovering and correctly identifying Frobisher's Strait (incidentally proving that it was actually a bay) and thereby transferring it back to its correct location from a mythical position on the map of South Greenland. Hall also unearthed a number of relics of the Frobisher expedition – a matter which delighted his romantic soul.

H.H. NICHOLS.

Boat camp of the Polaris expedition, which tried (and failed) to reach the Pole in 1871. They attained 82° 11′.

Charles Francis Hall: he proved the best chance of survival lay in adapting to the Arctic, not fighting it.

Eskimo ladle from musk ox horn.

But the major result of his stay on Baffin Island was that Hall conclusively demonstrated how best to surmount the basic problems of existing in the Arctic. The knowledge and experience which he gained by actually living as an Eskimo made it clear that the secret of survival lay in adapting oneself to the conditions of that hard land; in abandoning, in effect, the entire superstructure of "civilized" attitudes and methods. It was a conclusion which would have meant salvation to scores of expeditions from the time of Jens Munk to that of Franklin, had those earlier explorers been able to arrive at it. Yet the principle behind it, that of acquiescing to existing conditions, rather than of attempting a conquest by brute force, was one that few of Hall's predecessors could have accepted or even tolerated. It was to be a different matter with his successors. Most of the major victories gained over the Arctic during the next half century were to be accomplished by an adherence to the principle which Hall had demonstrated. It was a principle that was to be applied even to the major problem of surmounting that last and most formidable barrier of all – the polar ice itself.

As for Hall, his discovery of the key to Arctic travel served him well during his second expedition – a five-year journey through the area where the Franklin party perished. That it did not serve him on his third and last expedition was no fault of his.

This final venture of Hall's to the Arctic was made in 1871, when he took a converted U.S. Navy tugboat named the *Polaris* up through Baffin Bay in an attempt to reach the Pole. It was an ill-starred voyage. Hall was accompanied by a crowd of cowards, incompetents and worse, and though he was able to force a recalcitrant crew to sail his little ship farther north than any other vessel had ever reached before, he did so only at the price of signing his own death warrant. Shortly after *Polaris* reached a winter berth in Hall Basin, almost on the lip of this central polar sea, Hall died – suddenly and mysteriously. There is not much doubt that he was poisoned, probably with arsenic, by a dissident portion of his crew who neither shared his ambitions nor his belief in the adequacy of his new methods of coping with the defences of the Arctic.

Although Hall did not survive to write an account of the *Polaris* venture, there was one who did, Captain George Tyson. Tyson gives us the nearest approximation to the report of a detached observer of the *Polaris* fiasco. He provides a great deal of specific information about what actually happened; but he intimates a great deal more, which the ethics of his time forbade him to put in print. Through his eyes we shall see Hall being victimized by the savage internecine jealousy which, unhappily, has cast its pall over many voyages of exploration. We also watch the progress and fate of a polar venture, described without the adornments of contrived bravado, forced humour, or suitably becoming modesty. Here, in the words of a master mariner, is the essence of what it was like to be part of a polar expedition during those times.

Tyson is new to us, but the Eskimos who dominate the story of the ice drift are old friends. Hans is the same Hans Christian who was with Hayes and Kane. Joe and Hannah are, of course, the two Canadian Eskimos who were with Hall almost continuously from the time he met them in 1860 until the hour he died.

□ FM

I sailed in the spring of 1867 in the whaling schooner *Era*, to Hudson Bay, on which voyage the schooner broke out of winter quarters in December in the ice, and drifted out to sea. Two other vessels in company with us were caught in the same drift; one was abandoned, the other ran ashore. The *Era* finally drifted in amongst some bergs and froze in for the winter. During this voyage I met Captain Hall again. He was living with the Eskimos in "training" as a sportsman would say, for the great work which he even then had in mind. This was the attempt upon the Pole. I supplied him with provisions of various kinds and he, when he had opportunity, sent the natives with fresh meat to the ships.

I sailed again in the *Era* in the spring of 1869, returning home in the fall of 1870. In referring to my old logbooks as well as in recalling the events themselves, I find that the experiences of whaling are not essentially different from those of polar exploring parties – I mean as the exposures and dangers are concerned. We were always in continual risk of getting beset, and often were closed in by ice and unable to move for days and weeks, and sometimes compelled to remain and winter, being unable to break out or bore our way free. On one occasion my ship remained frozen in all winter while I and my crew lived ashore in a hut built of stones covered with the sails taken from the vessel, watching anxiously all the time for a break-up, which would either relieve the ship or crush her to pieces. I could not tell what would happen, but fortunately in February the ice began to break, and I got to the ship, found she was still seaworthy, repaired the damages, got our provisions aboard again, and finding a lead out finished my intended voyage.

When I arrived home in New London in October 1870 Captain Hall called to see me.† He informed me that he had succeeded in getting an expedition started for the North Pole and wished me to go with him as sailing master, but at that time I had a project of my own on hand, having opened negotiations with a party expecting to get a vessel for the white whale fishery. Hall called on me several times to persuade me to go with him but I felt obliged to decline. I then heard that he had engaged S. O. Budington.

In the end I did not arrange an agreement about the whale fishing and shortly thereafter I called on Captain Hall. He again requested me to join his expedition. At that time all positions were filled, but he was not to be denied and declared he would make a position for me.‡ At last I consented to go, and in forty-eight hours from the time I agreed to accompany him I had made all my arrangements, procured my outfit, bade farewell to friends and was on my way to the North Pole.

THE POLARIS EXPEDITION

The *Polaris* was a screw-propelled steamer of only three hundred and eighty-seven tons; but in addition to steam power she was fitted as a fore topsail schooner, so that she could be propelled both by steam or wind. To guard against accident to the propeller by contact with heavy ice the screw was arranged so that it could be unshipped and raised to the deck through a shaft in the stern. The hull was specially prepared for Arctic work by being planked all over with solid six-inch white oak timber, the bows being made almost solid and then sheathed with iron which terminated in a sharp prow with which to bore her way through the ice. She had four boats similar to whaleboats, one flat-bottomed scow and a patent portable folding canvas boat. In the cabin was a cabinet organ

† *"Captain" was purely a courtesy title. Hall had no seafaring experience.*

‡ *Which Hall did; as "Assistant Navigator."*

The U.S. Government's Polaris
pressing northward. Insubordination
developed among the mixed crew.

Hall with his Eskimo companions
Tookoolito (left) and Ebierbing. The
natives had already met the Queen.

Members of Hall's first party
shoot narwhals, the tusked whale of
the Arctic. The meat is nutritious.

A comical encounter sketched for
Capt. Hall's journal, Life Among
the Esquimaux, published in 1864.

The funeral of Charles Hall, on the rim of the
Arctic Ocean, 1871. The author says: "There is
not much doubt he was poisoned, probably with
arsenic, by a dissident portion of his crew."

An artist's concept of Capt. Hall's grave. The floral tributes were most unlikely at that high latitude!

After Hall's death, the Polaris was hitched to a huge berg which nearly wrecked it. Water spoiled the stores.

generously presented to Captain Hall by the Smith Organ Company with the hope that its sweet strains would assist in regular Sunday service aboard *Polaris*, and on other occasions would help while away the tedious hours.

The Secretary of the Navy put the *Polaris* formally in commission, placing the command of the expedition, the vessel, officers, and crew under the orders of Captain Charles Francis Hall. This point it is well for the reader to remember, as on its subsequent interpretation the welfare and success of the whole expedition turned. Except for the chief engineer, Emil Schuman, the officers were mostly Americans or English. However, the seamen were mostly Germans and the head of the scientific party, Mr. Emil Bessel, as well as the meteorologist, Mr. Frederick Meyers, were also Germans. In addition to this crew we took on board several Eskimos, including Joe and Hannah and their child Puny. Joe and Hannah had accompanied Captain Hall on most of his Arctic expeditions. We also had Hans Christian and his wife and their three children who were Greenland Eskimos that we picked up at Upernavik.

As for Captain Hall much – far too much – has been said in his disparagement on account of his lack of what is technically called a "liberal education." He had all the education which was needed to carry him to the end of his enterprise, had he not been thwarted by the cowardice of one man, and the jealousy of others. He was energetic, persevering and courageous and, above all, unselfish. The extent to which he was able to overlook the insolence and impertinence of those who owed him duty and allegiance was something marvellous to consider. Indeed he carried this too far. Had he dealt more sternly with the beginnings of insubordination, we might have had a far different story to tell; but every other feeling and sentiment seemed swallowed up in his absorbing desire to get north.

CAPTAIN TYSON'S JOURNAL

July 3, 1871: Left New London harbour – so recently my home. Some of my old friends here think I have started on a wild goose chase. But as to that all depends on good management.

July 9th: We sighted the coast of Newfoundland today, encountering loose floating ice as we approached Saint John's. In the harbour were two good sized icebergs. There is no perfect harmony between Captain Hall and the Scientific Corps, nor with some others either. I am afraid things will not work out well. It is not my business, but I am sorry for Hall: he is fearfully embarrassed. The sailing master, Captain Budington, talked of resigning and going home, but matters have been smoothed over.

July 31st: Reached Holsteinborg. Like most of the Greenland settlements it is a small place. You can stand on the deck of *Polaris* and count not only all the houses, but almost all the people, for everyone that can walk gets out to look at a vessel in the harbour. Someone has been at the ship's stores. Captain Hall told me he would not have any liquor on board; but Dr. Bessel procured an order for some for medical purposes and the "thirsty" have found where it is stowed.

August 10th: Disco. United States store ship *Congress* arrived from New York with provisions and coal. After storing the *Polaris*, the rest was landed at Disco as a depot in case the expedition should need it hereafter. Captain Davenport, who came up in the *Congress*, is having his hands full trying to straighten things out between Captain Hall and the disaffected members of our crew. Some of the parties seem bound to go contrary, and if Hall wants a thing done that is just what they won't do. There are two parties already, if not three, aboard. All the foreigners hang together and expressions are freely made that

Hall shall not get any credit out of this expedition. Already some have made up their minds how far they will go and when they will get home again – queer sort of explorers these! Hall tells me that Captain Davenport was prepared to take one party home in irons for insolence and insubordination, but then another said he would leave too and then all the Germans of the crew would leave and that would break up the expedition. Was ever a commander so beset with embarrassments, from which there seemed no way to free himself except by giving up all for which he has worked so long and hopefully?

August 24th: Tessuisak. Sailed today. This is the last settlement we expect to stop at. Now we may say we are at the entrance of our work. Only a few days more and, if the ice does not beset us, we shall be into Smith Sound.

August 27th: Evening. We have reached a latitude 78° 51′ N., just past Kane's winter quarters. The sailing master wanted the *Polaris* to go into Port Foulke [Etah] and lie up there; then he can stay there and take care of the ship while the others can go up north in sledges if they want to. But I am glad to see that Hall perseveres and will have his way about that; and indeed there is nothing to hinder us going on into the north.

One revelation after another. Seeing Captain Hall constantly writing, I asked him if he was writing up his Franklin Search book, about which he had often told me. He said, "No. I left all those papers at Disco." I did not like to ask him, but I looked "why?" A sort of gloom seemed to spread over his face, as if the recollection of something with which they were associated made him uncomfortable, and presently, without raising his head he added, "I left them there for safety's sake." I saw that the subject was not pleasant, and I made no further remark but I could not help thinking about it.

August 28th: Last night First Mate Chester came down and reported that an "impassable barrier of ice" lay ahead of us. I went up and found the vessel had been slowed down; I met our sailing master, who was in a fearful state of excitement at the thought of going forward. I went aloft and looked carefully around. There was a great deal of ice in sight coming down with a light northerly wind. It looked bad, but off to the westward I saw a dark streak which looked like water and I believed it was. I went down and reported to Captain Hall that the ship could skirt round the ice by sailing a little southerly and then steering west-northwest.

Later: We have reached the west side of the sound and I hope we shall get much farther north. But there is one, at least, on board who thinks we have come too far already. Out on such cowards, I say! I keep aloft much of the time. Crossed Kennedy Channel to Cape Lieber, where we brought up in a fog. Here a copper cylinder was thrown overboard containing a record of our progress. We have now reached a latitude 81° 35′. I can't make anything out of the charts.† As old Captain Scoresby used to say, "They are more of a snare than a guide." But we are now at the head of Kennedy Channel and ought soon to see Captain Kane's "open sea."

Still sailing north working through the ice. This should be open sea, but there is land on both sides of us; we have got into a channel similar to Kennedy Channel, only wider. This channel is seventeen or eighteen miles wide and obstructed by heavy ice. I hope we shall be able to get through but I don't like the look of it. I see some rueful countenances around me. I believe some of them think we are going to sail off the edge of the world. So far we have seen no worse than I have seen scores of times in Melville Bay. Captain Hall has called this new channel Robeson Channel. If the *Polaris* should get no farther, her keel has at least plowed through waters never parted by any ship before.

†*The charts drawn by Hayes on his sled journey north.*

August 30th: Drifting out of Robeson Channel to the southwest with the wind from the northeast. Steamed in under the land and came to anchor behind some bergs. It is blowing a gale.

September 2nd: Captain Hall requested Captain Budington, Mr. Chester and myself to come to the cabin to consult about attempting to proceed farther north. Mr. Chester wanted to go as far as it was possible but the senior officer was opposed. I could have told that before. He was very set, and walked off as if to end the discussion. Captain Hall followed him and stood some time talking to him. After a while Captain Hall came toward me and ordered us to see to the landing of provisions. These puerile fears distress me.

Evening: Captain Hall spoke to me again. He seemed to feel worried. I told him that I gain nothing by it, but it would be a great credit to him to go two or three degrees farther. He appears to be afraid of offending someone. I don't speak my mind. It might be misunderstood. God knows I care more for the success of the expedition than I do for myself. But I see it's all up, and here we must stop. We reached 82° 29′ N., but have now drifted nearly a degree southward again.

September 7th: We weighed anchor and stood in nearer to the shore. There was some discussion as to going over to the west side to look for a harbour but the sailing master declared she should not move from here. So Captain Hall gave up. We have now brought the ship round behind an iceberg which is aground. After service this morning Captain Hall announced that we would name our winter quarters Thank God Harbour in recognition of His kind providence over us so far.

September 11th: Commenced housing the ship over with canvas and, after the ice becomes strong enough, we shall bank her up with snow and ice.

Eskimos have evidently lived here; circles of stone indicate where their tents have been placed, but we have seen none of them. Perhaps they used to come here in summer and now emigrated to the south.

October 2nd: In consequence of [danger to the ship from] the pressure of the ice a considerable quantity of provisions and stores have been taken ashore. Today they were covered up with snow and some of the men are ordered to haul them off the flat ground and place them under the lee of the hill. There ought to be a house built to shelter them. Captain Hall is talking of preparing a sledge party to go north.

October 3rd: Captain Hall feeding the dogs and looking over his things to decide what he will take. Had a conversation with him. He told me he would like to have me go with him, and then he stopped and, pointing to the sailing master said, "But I cannot trust that man. I want you to go with me, but don't know how to leave him alone with the ship. I want to go on this journey, and to reach a higher latitude than Parry before I get back." I told him I would like to go, but of course I was willing to remain and take what care of the ship I could. I did not tell him how *much* I wanted to go.

October 6th: Preparations going forward for the sledge expedition. Captain Hall told me that he would take Chester with him instead of me, giving as his (official) reason that, "If the vessel should break out of the ice, it would be better for you to be aboard to assist the sailing master."

October 10th: Everything ready at last. There are two sledges, each sled has seven dogs. Captain Hall and Joe with one and Mr. Chester and Hans with the other. I understand the journey is preliminary to a more extended journey in the spring. Hall wants to get a general idea of what will be the best route north.

Evening: Saw Captain Hall on his journey. I watched them as long as I could

Abandoned by the Polaris when the ice broke in
a gale, Captain George Tyson heroically gathered
stragglers from drifting floes in the stormy sea.
Twenty-seven were rescued. The party reached safety after
seven perilous months on a small ice floe.

see them and hope he will have a successful and safe trip, but I have no doubt he has forgotten something; he is rather peculiar that way.

October 11th: As soon as the snowstorm is over I shall try to get material to build a house ashore to put our stores in, otherwise we shall have to dig them out of the snow whenever they are wanted. Hans has returned with a letter from Captain Hall; it seems he has forgotten several things and is now waiting five miles off for them.

October 24th: Engaged in banking the ship with snow, it is heavy work as we are making the bank about ten feet thick.

Afternoon: Captain Hall and the rest returned today about one o'clock, all well. Have been gone just two weeks. Captain Hall looks very well. They expected to go one hundred miles, but only went fifty. I saw them coming and went to meet them. Captain Hall seems to have enjoyed his journey amazingly. He said he was going again soon and that he wanted me to go with him. He went aboard and I resumed my "banking."

Evening: I kept at work until it was too dark to see and then came aboard. Captain Hall is sick; it seems strange, he looked so well. I have been in the cabin to see him. He is lying in his berth and says he feels sick at his stomach. This sickness came on immediately after drinking a cup of hot coffee. I think it may be a bilious attack, but it is very sudden. I asked him if he thought he was bilious and told him I thought an emetic would do him good. He said if it was biliousness it would. Hope he will be better tomorrow.

October 25th: Captain Hall is no better. Mr. Morton and Mr. Chester watched with him last night; they thought part of the time he was delirious.

Evening: Captain Hall is certainly delirious; I don't know what to make of what he says. He sent for me as if he had something particular to say but – I will not repeat what he said. No talk of anything in the ship but Captain Hall's illness; if it had only been the "heat of the cabin," which some of them say overcame him, he could have got out in the air and felt better. I cannot find out that he ate anything to make him sick; all he had was that cup of coffee.

November 1st: Captain Hall is a little better and has been up attempting to write, but he doesn't act like himself – he begins a thing and doesn't finish it. He begins to talk about one thing and then goes off on something else. His disease has been pronounced (by Mr. Bessel) paralysis and also apoplexy. I can't remember of anyone dying of apoplexy in the north except Captain McClintock's engineer, and he died very suddenly. I always thought that it might have been heart disease. Hope the Captain will rally.

November 3rd: Captain Hall very bad again. He talks wildly – seems to think someone means to poison him; calls for first one and then another, as if he did not know who to trust. When I was in, he accused —— and —— of wanting to poison him. When he is more rational he will say, "If I die you must still go on to the Pole," and such remarks. It is a sad affair; what will become of this expedition if Captain Hall dies, I dread to think.

November 5th: No change for the better – worse, I think. He appears to be partially paralyzed. This is dreadful. Even should he recover his senses, what can he do with a paralyzed body?

November 8th: Poor Captain Hall is dead. He died early this morning. Last evening Chester said the Captain thought, himself, that he was better and would soon be around again. But it seems he took worse in the night. Captain Budington came and told me he "thought Captain Hall was dying." I got up immediately and went to the cabin and looked at him. He was quite unconscious – knew nothing. He lay on his face and was breathing very heavily, his face hid in the pillow. Assisted in preparing the grave which is nearly half a mile from the ship, inland, but the ground was so frozen that it was necessarily very shallow. Even with picks it was scarcely possible to break it up.

November 11th: As we went to the grave this morning, the coffin hauled on a sledge over which was spread the American flag, we walked in processional. I walked on with my lantern a little in advance, then came the captain and officers, the engineer, Dr. Bessel and Meyers, and then the entire crew hauling the body by a rope attached to the sledge. One of the men on the right holding another lantern. Nearly all are dressed in skins and, were there other eyes to see us, we should look like anything but a funeral cortege. There is a weird sort of light in the air, partly boreal or electric, through which the stars shone brightly while on our way to the grave.

Thus ends poor Hall's ambitious project; thus is stilled the effervescing enthusiasm of as ardent a nature as I have ever known.

Captain Budington has passed to the command without question, it being understood by all that such was to be the case if Captain Hall died or was disabled.

November 19th: Sunday. After prayers this morning it was announced that the service would be discontinued in the future. It was suggested that "each one could pray for himself just as well." I think the Sunday service has a good influence; it seems a pity to discontinue it. Perhaps the cabin is needed for something else.

November 22nd: Yesterday the ice broke all around us, the snow drifting so that we could not see our condition or how to remedy anything. However we put out another anchor; but the ship drifted closer toward the berg. Toward noon some of the men succeeded in getting over the floe to the iceberg and with the aid of hatchets they fastened three ice anchors to which the ship was secured by hawsers. These held her more steady, and in the afternoon the gale abated. When the weather cleared, we found that the water was open all around us.

November 28th: In the latter part of the day the barometer fell and in the evening a snowstorm with a gale set in from the south. The floe ice was pressed against our berg so violently that it broke in two. We swung to our anchors but the ship was forced upon the foot of the berg, which lay to the southwest of us, shaking and straining the vessel badly. At ebb tide she keeled over and lay nearly on her beam-ends; careening so much that it is difficult to keep one's footing on deck. The foot of the iceberg is now pushed beneath her, raising her stem. I sent Hannah and Hans's wife with the children to the observatory on shore for safety. Also sent some stores ashore in case we have to abandon the vessel. Think the vessel could be hauled off but no orders are given. If she is left in this way she will get farther and farther on to the spur of the berg and get such a straining as will set her leaking.

December 16th: The other evening I had wandered away from the ship, disgusted with the confusion and noise and longing for a moment's quiet. Once beyond range of the men's voices there was no sound whatever. It was calm with no wind; no movement of any living creature; nothing but a leaden sky above, ice beneath my feet, and silence everywhere. It hung like a pall over everything. So painfully oppressive did it become at last that I was tempted to shout aloud to break the spell.

The men have had revolvers and other firearms issued to them by the commanding officer; what use they are expected to make of them I have not enquired. The time drags heavily. I shall be glad when we can get out and do something if it is only to bob for shrimps.

December 18th – 24th: Nothing occurred that is pleasant or profitable to record. I wish I could blot out of my memory some things which I see and hear. Captain Hall did not always act with the clearest judgment but it was heaven compared to this. I have not had a sound night's sleep since the eleventh of November. Would he had lived till spring! If I can get through this winter I think I shall be able to live through anything. Mr. Bryan (astronomer and chaplain) does not say much, but I think he feels it as much as I do. He is naturally a gentleman with the true instincts of right and wrong.

December 28th: A futile attempt was made to break up the foot of the berg and free the ship by blasting, but the berg was too strong. The amount of powder necessary to blast it successfully would endanger the ship.

January 1, 1872: The first day of the new year and eighty days since we have seen the sun. Considering the heterogeneous elements of which this expedition is composed it is something to be thankful for that we all commenced the new year in good health and without any open disagreement, which I think remarkable. Well, all I can do is keep silence; my position does not warrant interference. Last month such an astonishing proposition was made to me that I have never ceased thinking of it since. The time may come when it may be proper for me to narrate all the circumstances. It grew out of a discussion as to the feasibility of attempting to get farther north next summer. My own opinion is that we ought to do all we can to carry out Captain Hall's wishes. It would be a lasting disgrace not to use to the utmost a ship fitted out with such care and expense. It is enough to make Captain Hall stir in his ice-cold grave to hear some of the talk that goes on.

February 28th: A glorious day. The sun has shown himself once more. If it had not been for the hills we should have seen him yesterday. Never was expected guest more warmly welcomed; it is 135 days since we have seen his disc. Poor Hall! How he would have rejoiced in the return of the sun. His enthusiasm would have broken loose today had he been with us. And to think there are those who are glad that he cannot come back to control their movements!

April 19th: Dr. Bessel wishes to go in sledges to the north. I believe he got for answers that "he" (Budington) "intended to take the boats and go north himself." No one thinks he will do it. Had a talk with Chester about the astounding proposition made to me in the winter. We agreed that it was monstrous and must be prevented. Chester said he is determined, when he got home, to expose the matter.†

May 9th: I have at last got a couple of sledges to try to get to the northward; Mr. Meyers, Joe and Hans will accompany me. We start now (4:00 a.m.). Shall go to Lunan Bay if possible.

May 15th: Evening. Got back to the ship having been gone six days. I paid my principal attention to getting game as the ship's company was in want of fresh meat. I soon noticed the tracks of musk-oxen, all showing that they had come from the southeast. One day we came upon a large herd of them. They act very curiously when attacked. They form round in a circle, stern to stern, and so wait an attack. The dogs surround them and keep them at bay. Now and then a dog gets tossed. Joe and I fired and reloaded as fast as we could; the animals made no rush at us; we killed eight and the rest ran off. These cattle develop a great weight on what looks like a very slender diet; their food is the moss and lichens that grow on the rocks and to obtain it they first have to scrape away the snow with their hoofs. I forgot to mention that there were some calves with the herd. We did not see them at first for at the approach of danger the young ones get under the parent's body, and the hair of the musk-ox

†There seems to have been a proposal made that a select few of the senior members of the expedition should take a journey to a very high latitude, if not to the Pole itself.

is so long that, almost touching the ground, it hangs like a curtain before the young, completely concealing them from view. At a later date two of the crew, Siemen and Coogar, encountered two musk-oxen. One of the animals made for them and the two men retreated to a considerable distance. They then opened fire, killing the female while the male, with the calf, took to flight. We afterward discovered that in accomplishing this feat they had expended three hundred shots.

June 3rd: The ship has made so much water that the donkey engines have been started; after four hours' work she was pretty well free for the time being, but unless the leak is stopped it will get worse.

July 8th: Mr. Schuman, the engineer, reports that the pumps have become choked and that some water has got into the lower hold injuring a quantity of provisions. As there is no probability that we shall be allowed to do anything more – the Captain only waiting for an opportunity to get us out – I have been over to see if Captain Hall's grave had been put in order; when he was buried it was too dark to work and the ground frozen too hard to do much except to cover it with stones for security. There was an ordinary board at the head with an inscription written in pencil.

July 25th: The bay partially open and much water in the hold of the ship. I wanted the Captain to divide the crew into three watches so as to have all hands take a turn at the pumps to save fuel. Shortly after that there was a sudden increase in the hold and it was suggested to the Captain that someone in the engine room had wilfully opened the stop-cock and flooded her so that those in favour of hand-pumping "should have enough of it." Captain Budington went down to the engine room to see about this but had the door shut in his face for his pains.

I talked with Chester about fixing Captain Hall's grave and he got a board and shaped it out properly and cut an inscription very nicely. We fixed it up so that the grave now looks, though dreary enough, not quite so neglected as it did.

August 1st: Still in Polaris Bay. What opportunities have been lost! Someone some day will reach the Pole, and I envy not those who have prevented the *Polaris* having this chance.

August 12th: The wife of Eskimo Hans has added a male member to the expedition. These natives have not outgrown some of their customs. The women are left alone at childbirth and free themselves by severing the umbilical cord with their teeth. The boy has been named "Charlie Polaris." Thus combining a remembrance of our late commander and the ship.

This afternoon, the ice opening, and a good lead of water appearing, we weighed anchor and steamed out of Polaris Bay.

August 19: Fog hung about us for twelve hours and then cleared with a fresh breeze. There is no lead visible and we are drifting in the floe. Tried to shift the position of the vessel, as we are in danger of being nipped. There is now a quantity of stores, clothing and some bags of coal kept on deck so that they may be at hand to throw overboard in case of necessity.

September 13th: Beset in the ice we have reached latitude 79° 21′. Some walrus have been seen. Hans has shot a seal and Joe fired at a walrus but their hides are so thick, and their heads so impenetrable that it is difficult either to kill or secure them without harpoons.

September 30th: Open water can be seen to the southward but we can not get at it. Water is also visible to the north, but we are trapped in the pack. During the last six weeks we have done little except drift, with now and then a spurt from the engines. In this time we have made about sixty miles – about two miles a week, and mostly drifting.

October 4th: October came in fair and clear. Have past Rensselaer Harbour where Dr. Kane wintered. The ice keeps groaning as if change of some kind were impending. There is little chance of getting home this fall. We shall have to spend another winter here, I expect. If we were heading the other way I should not mind, but to go home without having done all we could is galling.

I have commenced work on a house on the ice in which to store provisions, as there is no telling when the ship may get nipped. I wanted some lumber from the ship to build it but could get only poles and canvas.

ADRIFT

October: Blowing a strong gale from northwest. I think it must have been about 6:00 p.m. on the night of the sixteenth, when we were nipped by the ice. The pressure was very great. The vessel did not lift to it much; she was not broad enough – she was not built flaring, as the whalers say. Had she been built so, she would have risen and the pressure would not have affected her so much; but considering it all she bore it nobly.

At the start of the nip I came out of my room which was on the starboard side of the ship, and looked over the rail and saw that the ice was pressing heavily. I walked over to the port side. Most of the crew were at this time gathered in the waist of the ship looking at the floe to which we were fastened. I saw that the ship rose somewhat to the pressure and then immediately came down. The ice was very heavy and the vessel groaned and creaked in every timber.

At this time the engineer came running from below amongst the startled crew saying that "the vessel had started to leak aft, and that the water was gaining on the pumps." The vessel had been leaking before this and they were already pumping.

I walked over to my room on the starboard side. Behind the galley I saw Captain Budington and told him what the engineer said. He threw up his arms and yelled out to "throw everything out on the ice!" Instantly everything was confusion, the men seizing everything and throwing it overboard. Most of these things had previously been placed on the deck in anticipation of such a catastrophe, but as the vessel was constantly breaking the ice, and as no care was taken as to how or where these things were thrown, I decided I had better get overboard, calling some of the men to help me, and try to carry whatever I could away from the ship so that it would not get crushed and lost. I also called out to the men on board to stop throwing things till we could get what we had clear and out of the way. Much of what was thrown overboard was run under the ship.

It was a dark night and I could scarcely see the stuff – whether it was on the ice or in the water, but we worked away three or four hours, when the ice on the starboard side suddenly let the ship loose. We had been tied to the floe by ice anchors and hawsers, but when the piece on the starboard side drifted off she righted herself from her beam-ends and broke away. I had been aboard just before she broke loose and asked Budington "how much water the vessel was leaking," and he told me no more than usual. The engineer's statement was a false alarm. The vessel was strong, and no leak had been made, but as the ice lifted her up what little water was in the hold was thrown over so that it made a rush and he thought that the vessel was leaking badly. I returned to

Polaris broke away in a snowstorm.
She was in no real danger but
she never returned for the castaways.

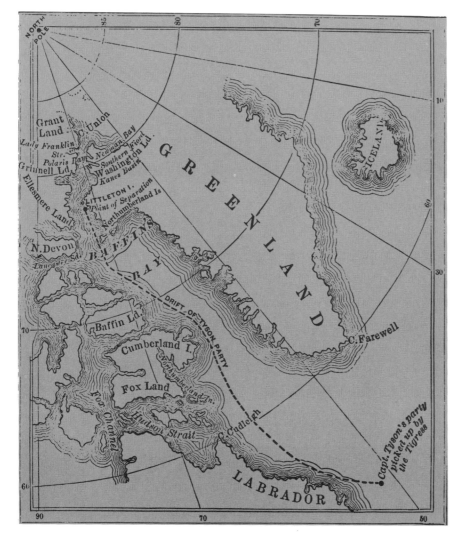

Map charts Tyson's incredible drift
from Oct. 16, 1872, to April 30, 1873.
His party included five children.

Ebierbing (usually called "Joe") stalks
a seal for the Tyson party. The group
of Eskimos kept the Europeans fed.

Sectional view of a seal chimney.
Seals surface for air every seven
minutes but can stay below for 20.

"A native will sometimes remain
watching a seal hole 36 or 48 hours
before getting a chance to strike
and if the first strike is not
accurate the game is gone forever."

Polaris, needlessly beached at Etah.

the ice. Budington called out to me to get everything back as far as possible away from the ship on to the solid ice. Very shortly afterward the ice exploded under our feet and broke in many places, and the ship broke away in the darkness and we lost sight of her in a moment.

It was snowing at this time and it was a terrible night. We did not know who was on the ice or who was on the ship, but I knew some of the children were on the ice because almost the last thing I had pulled away from the crushing heel of the ship was some musk-ox skins. They were lying across a wide crack in the ice and as I pulled them toward me I saw that there were two or three of Hans's children rolled up in one of the skins. A slight motion of the ice, and in a moment more they would either have been in the water and drowned in the darkness or crushed.

Some of the men were on smaller pieces of ice. I took the small scow and went for them, but the scow was almost instantly swamped. Then I shoved off one of the whaleboats and took what men I could see, and some of the men took the other boat and helped their companions, so that eventually we were all on firm ice together.

We did not dare move about much after that, for we could not see the size of the ice-cake we were on, on account of the storm and darkness. All but myself – the men, women and children – sought what shelter they could from the storm by wrapping themselves in skins and so laid down to rest. I walked the floe all night.

Morning came at last. I could then see what had caused the immense pressure on the ship. The floe to which she was fastened was crushed and pressed upon by heavy icebergs which was the cause of it breaking up.

Fortunately we had two boats on our piece of the floe, which was a nearly circular piece four miles in circumference. The ice was of varying thickness. Some of the mounds were probably thirty feet thick, and the flat parts about ten or fifteen. It was very rough, with hillocks covered with snow. Some of the men whom I now found on the ice were those I had picked off the smaller pieces last night in the darkness. These men were thirty or forty yards from the main floe when I pushed off the boat and went for them. Those who had laid down on the ice to sleep were snowed under – but that helped to keep them warm.

October 16th: Why does not the *Polaris* come to our rescue? The gale had abated; it was almost calm. I looked around the company. Besides myself there were eighteen persons. Frederick Meyers, meteorologist, and John Herron, steward, with six of the German members of the crew. There were also all of the Eskimos including Joe, Hannah, Joe's wife, the child Puny, Hans and his wife, and their four children.

To feed all these we had but fourteen cans of pemmican, eleven and a-half bags of bread, one can of dried apples, and fourteen hams. If the ship did not come for us we might have to support ourselves all winter or die of starvation.

As soon as I could see I walked across the floe to the best lead, intending that we should try and get ashore. I ordered the men to get the boats ready. I thought that perhaps the *Polaris* had been lost in the night, as I could see nothing of her. I told the men that we must reach the shore. They thought so too, but seemed very inert and in no hurry; they were "tired" and "hungry and wet"; nothing could induce them to hurry. I might have got off by myself with the Eskimos but I knew that, in that case, if the *Polaris* did not come and pick them up they would all perish in a few days; so I waited and waited. Not satisfied to eat what was at hand they must set about cooking. They had nothing to cook in but some flat tins in which they tried to cook canned meat and make coffee or chocolate. Then some insisted on changing their clothes; for several had found their bags of clothing. But everything has an end, and at last I got started at 9:00 a.m. but, as I feared, it was now too late. The leads were closing and a change in the wind soon made it impossible to reach the shore. When we got half way to the shore, the loose ice which I had seen coming crowded on our bows so that we could not get through and we had to haul up on the ice. Soon after this I saw the *Polaris*! I was rejoiced indeed, for I thought assistance was at hand.

She came around a point eight or ten miles distant. I wondered why she did not come in our direction. Thinking perhaps she did not know in what direction to look – though the set of the ice must have told which way it would drift – I determined to attract her attention by setting up the colours which I had with me, and a piece of India-rubber cloth. With my spy glass I then watched the vessel. She was under both steam and sail; I could not see anybody on deck. She kept along down by the land and instead of steering towards us, dropped in behind Littleton Island. Our signal was dark and would surely be seen that distance on a white ice floe. I do not know what to make of this.

Somewhat later I sent some of my men to another part of the floe to get some sticks that were there and they reported seeing a vessel tied up behind the island. I took my spy glass and ran to a point of ice where I could see her, and sure enough there she was tied up – at least her sails were furled and there was no smoke from her stack.

Our piece of ice, which had been stationary, now commenced drifting. I did not feel well about the vessel not coming for us. I began to think she did not mean to. I could not believe she was disabled, because we had recently seen her steaming, so I told the men we must get to the other side of the floe and try to reach the land, perhaps lower down than the vessel was, so that we might eventually reach her.

There was a great deal of murmuring – the men did not seem to realize the crisis. They seemed to think more about saving their clothes than their lives. But I seemed to see the whole winter before me. Either, I thought, the *Polaris* is disabled and cannot come for us or else, God knows why, Captain Budington does not mean to help us. And then there flashed through my mind the remembrance of a scene and a fearful experience which had happened earlier, in which his indifference had nearly cost me my life, and those of all my crew.

I was trying to force the men to move, but they stood muttering and grumbling, because I did not want the boats overloaded. They insisted on carrying everything they had. They were under no discipline – they had been under none since Captain Hall's death. They loaded one boat full of all sorts of trash which they wished to carry. And we spent hours dragging the boat across the floe to an open lead. I would have shoved off, but when I looked for the oars there were only three, and there was no rudder. I had told the men to prepare the boat while I was gone to look for the lead, and this was the way they had done it.

Night was now coming on, the day was lost and our opportunity with it. We had to leave the boat where she was, being too tired to attempt to drag her back. We also left in her the clothing and other things the men had been so anxious to save in the morning. Near the centre of the floe we put up a little canvas tent and I was glad enough to creep in, pull a musk-ox skin over me, and get what rest I could.

I slept soundly until I was awakened by hearing a loud cry from the natives.

The ice had broken all around us! We were separated from the boat which we had been unable to haul back the night before. Most of our supplies were still on part of the old floe, leaving us on a very small piece of ice. As soon as I saw the position I called the men out of their tent, desiring them to go for the boat and the food. It could have been done with safety, for there was no sea yet running, and the floe had not yet separated very much. I could not move them, however – they were afraid.

So we drifted, having one boat on our piece of ice while another boat, part of our provisions, and the house of poles and canvas that I had built during the winter remained on the main part of the original floe. Our piece of ice is perhaps one hundred and fifty yards across.

October 17th: A heavy sea is running. Piece after piece is breaking away from our floe. God grant we may have enough left to stand upon. The vessel could now come to us in clear water. If we can only get enough seal we can live; but without seal we can have no warm food, for we shall have to cook with blubber oil as the natives do. The natives have caught three seals and could have caught more but for the thoughtlessness of our men who gathered round and frightened them off.

October 21st: This morning Joe, who had been out on the now re-cemented floe, discovered our abandoned boat. He called me and I started off with him to try to recover it. Eventually we got it back with all the things, and also loaded into it what bread I could carry. I had five dogs with me. We harnessed them to the boat and they dragging, we pushing over the bad places, we got it safely to the piece of ice where we are now encamped. We have now both boats, the natives' kayaks, and are all together again.

October 23rd: We have now given up all hope of the *Polaris* coming to look for us. All we can do is wait for the ice to get strong enough so that we can attempt to get to shore. The piece of ice we are on will not do to winter on. The ice appearing strong enough today, I got the boats loaded, harnessed on the dogs, and started to try and regain the large floe. I succeeded with the first boat and went back for the second. It is fortunate that we have the boats. They are our salvation. Got the second one over safe and am rejoiced at that, and they do not appear to have received any injury except what can be easily repaired.

We have now got all our principal things on the large floe. I wanted the crew to try to save the kayaks and other things, but could not get them to do anything. At last Joe started alone and one of the kayaks was saved, but the other was lost. These little boats are invaluable to the Eskimos, who are accustomed to manage them.

The weather has come on very bad, but we have built several snow houses. We now have quite an encampment – one snow house, or rather half a house, for Mr. Meyers and myself; Joe's house for himself, Hannah, and their adopted daughter Puny; a snow house for the men; a storehouse for our provisions, and a cookhouse, all united by arched alley-ways built of snow. One main entrance, and smaller ones branching off to the several apartments or huts, connect them up. Joe did most of the work of building these huts, but we others assisted. They are made in the regular Eskimo style and the natives call them igloos. The walls and arched roof are composed of square blocks of snow, packed hard by the force of the wind. A square of about eighteen inches of thin, compressed snow or ice, or sometimes a piece of animal membrane, is fixed in for a window. The entrance is very low and is reached through the alley-way so that one has to almost crawl in. There is hardly room to turn around in these huts, and an ordinary size white man can only just stand up straight in them. In the men's hut the dais, or raised platform on which they sleep, just accommodates them lying like herrings in a box.

We did not have a proper lamp but soon contrived one out of an old pemmican can, and having no moss for a wick we cut up a piece of canvas. But somehow the men could not seem to understand how to use it, and they either got the blubber all in a blaze or else got it smoking so badly that they were driven out of their hut. They have begun to break up one of the boats for fuel. This is a bad business, but I cannot stop them, situated as I am without any other authority than such as they choose to concede to me. It will not do to thwart them too much even for their own benefit. These boats are not designed to carry more than six or eight men, and yet I foresee that all this company may have yet to get into one boat to save their lives, for the ice is very treacherous.

October 24th: We only allow ourselves two meals a day, and Mr. Meyers has made a pair of scales on which to weigh out each one's portion so that there should be no jealousy. Our allowance is very small – just enough to keep body and soul together; we must economize or our little stock will soon give out altogether.

One bad symptom has appeared: we have only had chocolate prepared for the party four times, and the supply is nearly all gone! Someone has made free with the storehouse. Our present daily food allowance is eleven ounces for each adult and half rations for the children. There appears to be a good deal of discontent in some quarters, but I fear they will get less before any of us get more.

Hans has just taken two of the dogs, killed and skinned them, and we will eat them. I give each of the natives the same amount of bread, and whatever else we have, as I deal out to myself.

October 26th: We lost sight of the sun's disc three days ago. May God have mercy on us and send us seals or I fear we must perish. We are growing very weak from having to live on such small allowance, and the entire loss of the sun makes us all despondent. We are only about eight or ten miles off shore. I should judge our latitude to be about 77° 30′ [about opposite Northumberland Island and Whale Sound]. We have not drifted any distance the last three days. If the ice remains firm it may still be possible for us to endeavour to find the vessel.

October 28: We are out of seal meat and today dine on pemmican and bread. The bread, of course, is simply biscuit. It is "bread" on board ship and "biscuit" to landsmen. We have very little blubber and must try to save what there is for the lamps. It is not easy to find seal in winter. They live under the ice and can only be seen when the ice cracks. Being warm-blooded they cannot remain under the ice without breathing and in consequence make air holes through the ice and snow. At the surface these holes are so small – not more than two and one-half inches across – that they are not easily distinguished. A native will sometimes remain watching a seal hole thirty-six or forty-eight hours before getting a chance to strike, and if the first stroke is not accurate the game is gone forever. The natives use barbed spears and, as the skull of the seal is exceedingly thin, if the blow is well aimed it is sure to penetrate and the seal can then be held securely until the hole is enlarged enough to pull the body through.

November 8th: I started on the morning of the first of November to try to reach the shore. We had loaded the boat with provisions and necessary articles and succeeded in dragging it nearly halfway to the shore on the old ice. Then the ice broke and we were adrift again. Saw the Carey Islands twelve miles to the southeast of us. Since then it has been such thick weather I have seen nothing. Fate, it seems, does not mean that we shall get back to the *Polaris* or even reach the shore. To help the matter, bad weather came on and it has been so bad ever since there has been no possibility of another attempt. Here we are, and here, it seems, we are doomed to remain. On the sixth, Joe caught a seal, for which I was truly thankful, for our blubber was almost gone. The weather is so bad no one pretends to leave the hut. We are all prisoners.

November 19th: I am down with rheumatism, hardly able to hold a pencil. By the movement of the ice I judge we are now drifting to the southward very fast. The natives tell me they have seen two bear tracks and five seal holes but they brought home nothing. I wish they had better fortune, for we need the fresh meat very much.

November 21st: The last few days the weather has been clear and cold but I have been confined to the hut with rheumatism. It has been very difficult for the natives to hunt this month, except for the few times the moon shone, on account of the darkness. Some days it was quite impracticable. But today, thank God, they have brought in two seals. Without them we should have no fire, one boat being already cut up. We must go without fire or warm food if there are no seals caught. It will never do to cut the other boat; the time must come – if we live to see it – when the boat will be our only means of safety.

We are now living on as little as the human frame can endure without succumbing. Some tremble with weakness when they try to walk. Mr. Meyer suffers much from this cause; he was not well when he came on the ice and the regimen here has not improved him. He lives with the men now. They are mostly Germans and so is he, and the affinity of blood draws them together, I suppose. Since he has gone with the men I have lived in the hut with Joe, Hannah, and Puny. Puny, poor child, is often hungry, indeed, all the children often cry with hunger. We give them all that is safe to use. I can do no more, however sorry I may feel for them.

The seals which Joe got today will help us very much. In our situation he is "the best man," for without him we should get little enough game, I fear. I am the worst hunter of all for I have neither gun nor pistol. This is a disadvantage in other respects. The men know it; they are all armed, and I am not. After Captain Hall's death, for some reason unknown to me, arms were distributed amongst the men. They have now moved to a new larger igloo. The bread has disappeared very fast lately: more of this hereafter. We have only eight bags left.

For the first time since separating from the ship I have eaten enough; but it was raw, uncooked seal meat – skin, hair and all.

November 22nd: The situation is very unpleasant. I can only advise the men and have no means of enforcing authority. But if we live to get to Disco there they will have to submit, or I shall leave them to shift for themselves. I will not continue to live as I have lived here. Here I am forced to live for the present: there is no escape. It is not altogether their fault, they were good men but have been spoiled on board the *Polaris*. For the last year there has been no discipline. There also appears to be some influence at work on them now. It is natural, no doubt, that they should put confidence in one of their own blood; but they will probably find out that "all is not gold that glitters" before they get through this adventure.

November 27th: The natives have not attempted hunting, it being too dark. Joe has used the time well, however, in enlarging the igloos. I prefer living with him, as both he and his wife, and even the child, can speak English while in the men's hut I hear nothing but German, which I do not understand.

November 28th: Thanksgiving Day. To satisfy my hunger I was compelled to eat strips of frozen seal's entrails, and sealskin – hair and all – just warmed over the lamp. But I am thankful for what I get. No doubt many of my friends who read this will exclaim "I would rather die than eat such stuff!" You think so, no doubt. But people can't die when they want to and when one is in full life and vigour and only suffering from hunger he doesn't want to die. Neither would you.

November 30th: It is a long time – nearly a month – since we lost sight of land. All hopes of seeing the *Polaris* have long since vanished but the hope of getting to land is not entirely abandoned. I have been over the floe to the remains of the old pole house, after canvas. I wanted it to line the hut of the Eskimo, Hans. He has worked late and early to make the men comfortable, and their snow hut is comfortably lined and the Eskimos' ought to be too, especially as the little children are there.

I do not write every day – it would take too much paper. I had some blank notebooks in one of the ship's bags. In looking for them a few days ago I found they were all gone. Some of these men seize hold of anything they can lay hands on. But no wonder, they were taught that on board the *Polaris*; they saw so much stealing going on there. It would have demoralized worse men than these.

No change in our way of living. We still lie in our snow burrows much of the time, partly because there is nothing else to do – it is now too dark to do anything – but also because stirring around and exercising makes us hungry, and we cannot afford to eat. Moreover, my clothing is very thin and light, quite unfit for exposure in this cold. Being hard at work when the *Polaris* parted from us I did not have time to collect even the usual amount of clothing. The natives have been endeavouring to hunt but it is in vain.

Mr. Meyers has taken an observation and thinks we are going close to the Greenland Coast. In truth, unless the currents have changed their natural course, we must be going towards the southwest. It would not matter what opinion was entertained, only that it makes the men uneasy, thinking they are approaching the coast and nearing the latitude of Disco, where they know there is a large store of provisions left for the expedition. I am afraid they will start off and endeavour to reach the land. If they do it will mean death to some or all of them. The possibility has occurred to me they might take the boat, load it with provisions, and leave us and Hans's family without resource. But I will not harbour such thoughts without proof.

One thing set me on this train of thinking: Joe, who has all along kept his gun and pistol, and did not seem willing even to lend me the latter, has voluntarily brought it to me. He says, "I don't like the look out of the men's eyes." I know what he fears: he thinks they will first kill and eat Hans and family, and then he knows Hannah's, Puny's and his turn would be next. God forbid that any of this company should be tempted to such a crime. However, I have the pistol now and it will go hard with any who harm even the smallest child on this raft. Hannah seems much alarmed.

Setting aside the crime of cannibalism, it would be the worst possible policy to kill the poor natives. They are our best, and I may say only, hunters. No white man can catch seal like an Eskimo, who has practised it all his life.

December 12th: No change in the last five days. Hans has fixed up an ice trap and yesterday caught a fox; it was a small white one. If there is any way to catch an animal, these Eskimos will do it. Now he has made a hole in the ice and set a seal net but, so far, without success.

"Most of our supplies were still on part of the old floe. . . . Our piece of ice is perhaps 150 yards across. . . . Piece after piece is breaking away. God grant that we have enough left to stand on. If we can only get enough seal we can live."

The men are organized now and appear determined to take control. They were masters of the *Polaris* and want to be masters here. They go swaggering about with pistols and rifles. I see the necessity of being very careful, though I shall protect the natives at any cost. I must be wary as well as firm. They think the natives a burden and would gladly be rid of them. They think there would then be fewer to consume the rations and, if they moved toward shore, there would not be the children to lug.

December 16th: The fear of death has long ago been starved and frozen out of me, but if I perish, I hope that some of this company will be saved to tell the truth of the doings on the *Polaris*. Those who have baffled and spoiled this expedition ought not to escape. They cannot escape their God!

Christmas Day: I have just finished breakfast. My breakfast consisted of four ounces of bread and two and a half ounces of pemmican warmed over the lamps. This is a full ounce over the usual allowance. Even that additional morsel of meat was a treat and very welcome. Our Christmas dinner was gorgeous. We had each a small piece of frozen ham, two whole biscuits of hard bread, a few mouthfuls of dried apples and a few swallows of seal's blood.

December 27th: The gale which has been blowing has moderated. The natives are out as usual looking for seals, and found the ice broken up in many places. They saw two seals but could not get them.

From the talk in the men's hut I hear they plan great things; but when they get outside and face the cold, and feel their weakness, they are glad to creep back again to their shelter and such safety and certainty as we have.

We had in our hut saved a few pieces of dried sealskin for repairing clothing, but Hannah has just cooked some pieces and we are trying to make a meal of it. The natives have very strong teeth and can go through almost anything. I ate some of it, but it made my jaws ache to chew it. We ate up the refuse out of the oil lamp – tried-out blubber. In fact we eat anything we can get that teeth can masticate.

January 12: The last three days the temperature has stood at 35° to 37° below zero. Today I looked for a few shirts and drawers which I had in a bag, there was also a pair of pants and several pairs of stockings. But they are not to be found; bag and all have disappeared. This, my little store which I had relied on for travelling, had been stolen. I have thus far wintered without either coat or pants, wearing only short breeches. I was saving the pants to walk in when we set out for the shore.

January 16th: A glorious sound – a life inspiring shout! It was the natives calling for their kayak. That means they have found open water, and water means seals. The natives had shot a seal, which we got, and with which we returned in triumph. This seal appears to have come just in time to turn the men away from their purpose of travelling. If we can get enough to feed them they will stay content.

I ordered the seal to be taken into Joe's hut. As he did the most toward getting food I thought this was right. One of the men, however, took upon himself to take it into their hut. They have divided the seal to suit themselves. It seems hard on the natives who have hunted day after day, in cold and storm, while these men lay idle on their backs, or sat in the shelter of their huts, which were mainly built by these same natives they are wronging. The men kept the largest proportion of the meat from this last seal, which discourages the natives very much. But they dare not say much for they are afraid for their lives. Joe and Hans say that they have very often suffered before for the want of food but have never been obliged to endure anything like the present experience. Considering that they are out of the hut so much more than the rest, hunting around, they ought to have a larger allowance of food. I would gladly give it to them but it would cause open mutiny amongst the men.

How our two remaining dogs live I know not. A few days ago Joe discovered where one of them had been off hunting on his own account and had evidently encountered two bears, indicated by the appearance of the ice, and held them at bay for some time. One of the bears must have hit him for he came bleeding to the hut. The wound, however, will soon heal.

January 19th: Joe and Hans hunting. Yesterday they saw a number of seals but it was blowing heavy and was very cold. Joe says he tried to shoot but he shook so with the cold he could not hold his gun steady and his fingers were so numb he could not feel the trigger; and so the seal escaped. These Eskimos work hard for themselves and for us.

Afternoon: A great event has occurred: the sun has reappeared after an absence of eighty-three days. The sun means more than light to us: it means better hunting, better health, relief from despondency. It means hope in every sense. The sun has come this time earlier than I expected. We must have drifted faster than I had realized.

January 20th: I thought yesterday I could see the Baffin Island coast but I am not sure. Mr. Meyers, the fountain of all knowledge for his German brethren, places us within a few miles of Greenland. His inexperience in these waters has made great trouble in misleading the men and inspiring them with the confidence of what they can do, which has no basis in fact. When Meyers says "We are within a few miles of Greenland" they believe him and some think if they should start now they could get to Greenland in two days. They little know the labour that would be. They would get to their deaths – that's where they'd get.

I expect we shall drift by Disco, but if the weather permits I hope we will be able to make Holsteinborg in the boat some time in March. It is not safe to start this month or next – not with these men. They have been housed all winter and, when inside their huts, are valiant and brave and talk of great things, but let them get out in the cold for a short time and the pluck is gone.

Joe is not very well. I hope he will not get down sick for we depend greatly on him. For such a little fellow he is a mighty hunter. Our provisions are going fast. I know they are stolen but cannot stop it without shedding blood, and I shall avoid that unless to prevent an event that I suspect has been contemplated.

4:00 p.m. – Joe has just returned bringing a small seal. He found no open water but after watching at a blow-hole for a long time this fellow came and put up his snout to breathe and Joe was fortunate enough to spear him. He is now divided up and I have eaten a little of the raw meat.

January 25th: I should like very much to accompany the natives on their hunting excursions but cannot, for want of clothing. Like Miss Flora M'Flimsy, "I have nothing to wear." I may say that I am almost without clothing – at least anything suitable to be exposed all day to temperatures of 30° or 40° below zero. Joe and Hans have deer and dogskin clothing and even they complain of the cold, and they have a change too, which I have not. They can take theirs off and dry them over the lamp but I have not been able to change my clothing for nearly three months. It sickens me to think of it, saturated as it is with all the vile odours of this hut. I have to sleep in my clothing as well, for I should freeze to the wretched skins under which I sleep if I did not. Today is our 103rd day on the ice.

The two Eskimos have hunted nobly all winter through darkness, cold and storm. They saw the necessity of it as well as I. They knew the men could not live without fresh meat or without fire to warm their food and melt ice for drink. However, it has happened that when the Eskimos have been tramping about for hours on the hunt for seals, and at last get one, they are very hungry and since they know that when they bring it in they will get no more than those who have stayed home all day, they sometimes open the seal and eat the entrails, kidneys or heart. Who is to blame them – they must do it to keep life in them. Yet the men complain of this, and say they do not get their full share.

I fear we have lost our best bear-dog. Hans had the dog with him yesterday and let the dog go and he has not yet found his way back. I fear he is lost. The thermometer is 42° below zero, the coldest day yet we have had on the floe.

January 27th: The mercury is frozen. The Eskimos returned early, the severe weather proving too much for them, inured to it from childhood though they are. If they could have enough of the seal meat to keep up their circulation they would have gone on.

I do not yet see my way clear as to what to do. Can see no land either to east or west, so we must be far from both shores and are probably near the middle of the strait. We cannot be near Disco, yet the "German Count" makes his countrymen believe we are near to it. Disco can be seen on a clear day eighty miles distant, and I have seen it when one hundred miles off, raised by refraction.

I know not whether I can keep the men quiet until the temperature rises. It may moderate in March and then they may yet be saved, but should they start for shore in January or February they are lost. They will find no water to drink, have but little to eat, must sleep unprotected except for their wet musk-ox skins, if they have the strength to drag them along.

The natives have returned again without success, and we have lost our only dog. The poor animal was taken sick and died. I fed him last night what I was eating myself, seal skin and well-picked bones. It may be that the bones caused his death, as they swallow such large pieces.

January 29th: The Eskimos are off as usual on the hunt. They do not stop for fog, cold, or wind. Were it not for "Little Joe" many if not all of this party must have perished before now. He has built our snow huts and hunted constantly for us; and the seals he has captured have furnished us not only with fresh meat but with oil from the blubber, without which we could neither have warmed our food nor have any means of melting ice for drink.

We are all well but one – Hans's child, Tobias. I can doctor a sailor but I don't understand what is the matter with this poor little fellow. His stomach is disordered and very much swollen; he has been sick now for some time. He cannot eat pemmican so he has to live on dry bread, as we have nothing else to give him. The wonder is not that one is sick, but that there are any well. The mercury is still frozen. The men seldom go outside their hut. From the nature of the food we live on and the small quantity of it there is no imperative necessity which calls them outside – perhaps not more than once in fourteen days.

Oh but it is depressing in the extreme to sit crouched up all day, with nothing to do but try to keep from freezing. It is 107 days since I have seen a printed word. What a treat a bundle of old papers would be. I have told Joe and Hannah, should anything happen to me, to save these pocket books on which I am making my notes and carry them home. They are very badly written with pencil, in a dark hut, with very cold fingers, but, so help me God, it is all true. However, although my present life is perilous enough, I can truly say that I feel more secure sleeping on this floe, notwithstanding the disaffection of some of the men, than I did the last eleven months on board the *Polaris.*

February 1st: It is blowing very heavy from the northwest; too much wind for any hunting. We keep closely housed in our dens. Should an accident happen to our floe, serious enough to turn us out of our burrows, we should none of us live long. The Eskimos inform me that the cracks in the ice where they have been sealing are not limited to the young ice but cut clear through the old floes, which is an intimation that our floe may now split up at any time if the wind continues. We have thus far floated safely yet we know the ice must break up sometime; and whether we shall survive the catastrophe we cannot tell.

An old can cut in half has served for a cooking vessel this winter in which all our food has been warmed. I dare not look to see with what Hannah has mended the holes in this can. It is dark enough inside this igloo but nevertheless I am compelled to shut my eyes on many occasions. Joe and Hannah are sitting in front of the lamp playing checkers on an old piece of canvas, the squares marked out in pencil. They use buttons for men, as they have nothing better. Little Puny is sitting wrapped in a musk-ox skin. Every few minutes she says to her mother, "I am so hungry!" The children often cry with hunger. It makes my heart ache, but they are obliged to bear it with the rest of us. The breeze still blowing from the northwest makes it impossible for Joe and Hans to hunt. Poor fellows, they know our situation is desperate.

I went into Hans's hut the other day to see the sick boy, Tobias; the miserable group of children there made me sad at heart. The mother was trying to pick a few scraps of tried-out blubber out of the lamp to give them. A little girl, Succi, about four years old, was crying – a kind of chronic hunger whine – and I could just see the baby's head in the mother's hood or capote. The babies have no clothing whatever, and are carried about in this hood which hangs down the mother's back, like young kangaroos in the maternal pouch.

February 3rd: A continuing gale with drifting snow has covered everything. We were all snowed under the other night and had some little difficulty in digging our way out to the air and daylight. The Eskimos are on the hunt once more, and we who stay at home are praying for success. The men now know that they have lost Disco, and appear more reasonable.

In the afternoon the storm cleared off and I looked anxiously for land but saw only ice and icebergs. The ice and the sky is our only view. Dreary, yet beautiful.

Mr. Meyers promulgates the statement that the straits are only eighty miles wide. He would find it a long eighty miles walk over the ice! This man is very troublesome, the more so that I have no chart to show the men to the contrary. His interference destroys all discipline.

Evening: A stroke of luck. Joe has brought home a seal. He shot two others but lost them in the young ice. This seal is a very little fellow but there will not be hide or hair left of him, nor anything inside or out, but bone and the gall.

Joe shot this seal, but Hans was the one who got him in the kayak. It was interesting to see how this was done. The kayak was pushed out over the young ice and Hans, by sticking his paddle in the ice and by movements of his body, propelled the kayak towards the seal. The ice would not have borne him had he attempted to walk over it. After this seal was gone we cooked the skin and drank the greasy water. Joe says "anything is good that don't poison you."

Narwhals are appearing through the thin ice. Hans shot one and Joe shot one but both sank before they could be caught. Narwhals are sometimes called sea-unicorns, on account of the long horn – six to eight feet long – which projects from the upper jaw.

February 8th: I think I have not recorded hitherto the fact that since we have had sufficient daylight we have had our house-cleaning day. The moisture which arises from cooking as well as the exhalations of our own lungs, condenses and clings to the inside lining of our hut. It gets so thick it falls on our bedding, making it very uncomfortable. As we beat it from the walls it falls on the carpet; which is a bit of old canvas spread over our ice floor. This carpet is a sight to behold, encrusted with the accumulated drippings of grease, blood, saliva, ice and dirt of four weary months – all of which cannot be removed by our limited means of cleaning, namely taking it out of the hut and shaking and beating it. We shake our carpet every day now that the weather permits. During the night the wind hauled from south to north and is blowing very heavy. Our huts are nearly buried in the drift and we shall have to do much more digging to get out. Should the gale continue it will send us past Holsteinborg. We are making a very rapid drift. Heaven only knows where we shall get to before the weather will permit us to start for the land.

February 12th: An almost continuous hurricane is still blowing. We are completely buried in the snow drift. Joe attempted to get out this morning but failed. Our communal passageway is in a most filthy condition. Joe came back into the hut very indignant saying, "They talk about Eskimos being dirty and stinking, but sailors are worse than Eskimos."

February 14th: The sun is shining for the first time through our little ice window. Though the sun is welcome it reveals too plainly our filthy condition. I thought I knew the worst before, but the searching sun has made new revelations. This morning Puny seemed to be enlightened by the sun. She sat looking at me for some time and then gave the remark, "You are nothing but bone!" And, indeed, I am not much else.

February 19th: Clear and cold. The Baffin coast is in sight! I think it in the vicinity of Cape Seward, and distance thirty or forty miles. If the ice were in condition I would try to reach the shore. I could find Eskimos and we could live as they do until June, when we could get to Pond Bay and find English whalers. But these are castles in the air. The state of the ice forbids the attempt; we must bide our time.

February 22nd: Our situation is getting desperate – plenty of ammunition but no game. Everything is now ready to push for the shore, but how to get there I know not, there seems to be no feasible way either by boat or foot. The ice is in such a fearfully rough condition that it could not be traversed with even a light back load. The men are frightened. They seem to see death staring them in the face. Joe is frightened too. He feels that if he and his family were alone without this company of men he could catch game enough for his own use; but to catch a living for eighteen discourages him and indeed it seems impossible without some great change occurring. We are now on an allowance of one meal a day. Well, a man can be trained to live on the rations of a canary, but I do not like the training.

Yesterday a bear passed by our igloo, knocking down a spear and gun. Having no dogs to give the alarm he escaped us. However, the hunters gladdened our eyes tonight with thirty-seven dovekies (robin-sized seabirds). We take two apiece, the children have one each.

March 2nd: We were off at crack of dawn this morning hunting for seal or dovekies. I decided to try hard to get a narwhal.

5:00 p.m. – I did not get my narwhal, but Joe has shot a monster oogjook – a large kind of seal – the largest I have ever seen. It took all hands to drag him to the huts. The men fairly danced and sang for joy. No one who has not been in a similar position to ours can tell the feeling of relief. How we rejoiced over the

death of this oogjook it would be impossible to describe. This fellow weighed
six or seven hundred pounds and will furnish, I should think, thirty gallons of
oil. We are rich indeed.

The men after such long fasting cannot restrain their appetites and some of
them have eaten until they are sick. One cannot find fault with them, for they
have been living on nine ounces a day. When first killed the warm blood of the
seal is scooped up in tin cans and relished like milk. The mammary glands of the
female seal, especially when distended with milk, is very delicate. Our glorious
oogjook proved, on measurement, seven feet nine inches in length. Our hut now
looks like a slaughter house. Meat, blood, entrails, dirt all over everything. Our
hands and faces are smeared with blood, and one coming amongst us now would
take us for carnivorous animals just let loose upon their prey.

I think we are now approaching the Cumberland Gulf – my old whaling
ground. Should the weather prove favourable I shall have no hesitancy trying
to get clear of the floe, for there we will find ships. But should we drift past the
Gulf, why then we can try Hudson Strait, and try to get to Resolution Island
where we can wait for Hudson's Bay Company vessels or American whalers.

March 6th: For the last few days we have had the most severe gale of any,
with temperatures of minus thirty-two degrees and very heavy snow drifts. We
dined on part of oogjook's head this evening. It was very tough, but with the
addition of a pot of blood we contented ourselves. Oh what a wretched life to
live. Sometimes I feel almost tempted to end my misery at once. For some days
past, and all last night, the ice has been cracking and snapping around us, sound-
ing like distant thunder. This betokens the breaking up of the floe. It received
a great shaking during the last great storm. I think the noise and commotion is
partly caused by loose pieces of ice underneath our floe rolling along. These
noises startle me from my sleep. I begin to have some idea how people in earthquake countries must feel when the ground is trembling and shaking beneath
their feet, especially on a dark night when one cannot see a foot before him and
knows not which way lies danger and which safety. It is impossible to convey an
idea of the overwhelming power of these pushing and grinding masses.

March 12th: Another twenty-four hours of care, watching, anxiety and great
peril. We have been having a terrible gale. Yesterday evening the large floe piece
on which we have lived all winter was suddenly shattered into hundreds of
pieces, leaving us on a piece of about seventy-five by one hundred yards. We
passed a dreadful night expecting every moment that our little piece would
follow the fate of the larger ones and be broken up. Thank God it still holds
together.

When I selected the place for erecting the igloos I picked out what seemed
the thickest and most solid. If it is thick enough it may be able to endure the
shock of riding amongst these loosened bergs and other fragments. But it is all
uncertain, and I fear it cannot hold together after the heavy thumping it has
already received and which it still must bear with such a heavy sea as is now
running. Most fortunately our boat remains uninjured. For sixty hours, amidst
this fearful turmoil of the elements, with our foundations breaking up beneath
our feet, we could not see ten yards around us. But now the wind is abating,
the snow has ceased to fall, and the terrible drift has stopped. We can now look
around and see the position we are in.

We see a great change in the condition of the ice. The floes have become a
broken pack, and great blocks of ice of all sizes are piled and jammed together.
On my last walk before this storm the floe appeared to extend for many miles;
it is now all broken up, and the pieces heaped over each other in the most tre-

mendous disorder. With the return of moderate weather we can commence shooting. Seals are scarce but, there being open water around us, we can now shoot all we see. Today Joe shot two, Hans one, and I one.

March 14th: Yesterday and last night it was blowing heavy from the north again. This morning it suddenly ceased and the day has been fine. Joe and myself were out looking for seals before anyone else was up. Our domain is wearing away at the edges; we can stand in our own hut door and shoot seals now, for our piece is so reduced that it is only twenty paces to the water.

March 22nd: It is cooler and pleasant with a light west wind. Joe, Hans and myself went off early to the sealing hole and Joe shot two seals – only one day's fare if there was no restriction put upon the men. These Germans are outrageous eaters and tremendous grumblers. They also seem to be possessed of the idea that they can improve on everything. In consequence nearly every rifle we had upon the ice but Joe's which they could not get hold of, had been ruined by their tinkering. They must work away at everything and never stop till it is rendered useless.

Spearpoint of an Eskimo lance.

Spring is here, according to the astronomers, and the thermometer has marked 10° to 15° above zero. Oh how I wish that two more months were past. This is a dreadful life and we have been a long time in it – over five months now; but we still live.

March 25th: New ice has formed and there is no open water within a mile. By observation today our latitude is 61° 59'. We are down now where I expect to find the large hooded seal. A very few of these large seals and there would be no more risk of starving.

March 26th: The hooded seals are here! Shot nine large ones today and saved four – five of them sank. Thank God we now have meat enough for eighteen to twenty days. Also saw a whale today.

We are now in the strong tides off the mouth of Hudson Strait but can see no land. The ice is on the move, but without any present sign of new disruption.

March 28th: We have got a bear at last! Shortly after dark we heard a noise outside our hut. Joe thought it was the ice breaking and decided to go and see. He was not gone ten seconds before coming back pale and frightened, exclaiming, "There is a bear at my kayak." The kayak was within ten feet of the entrance to the hut and Joe's rifle and mine were outside lying close to it. But Joe had the pistol. We crept out and could plainly see his bearship. Joe crept into the sailors' hut to alarm them while I tried to get my rifle. The bear heard me, but the rifle was already on him. He growled, I pulled the trigger, but the gun did not go. Pulled a second and third time – it did not go. But *I* did, for the bear now came for me. Getting back in the hut I tried another cartridge. This time, to my joy and his sorrow, the rifle ball went straight to its mark. The bear ran about two rods and fell dead.

March 30th: Night before last we had another great gale. Huge bergs were plowing their way through the ice. The floe ice had re-frozen mostly together again, after the break-up in the middle of March, but was now once more in fragments. The gale continued heavy through the night of the 29th. It is still blowing heavy with considerable swell. In the night I felt a great thump as if a hammer a mile wide had hit us, and getting out to see what was the cause found we had drifted foul of a large berg. We thumped a while on the berg and I did not know but whether we should go to pieces and founder; but we finally cleared it.

April 1st: We have been the "fools of fortune" now for five months and a-half. Our piece of ice is now entirely detached from the main pack, which lies to the west of us. We have determined we must take to the boat and regain the main pack. To do this we must abandon all our store of meat, although we have sufficient now to last a month. We will also have to leave much of our ammunition behind on account of the weight.

We got launched and made some twenty miles to the west but were very nearly swamped for, notwithstanding all we had abandoned, we were excessively overloaded, what with nineteen persons and their heavy sleeping gear. When it is considered that this boat was intended for six or eight people it is not surprising that we did not make much headway. We were so crowded that I could scarcely move my arms sufficiently to handle the steering ropes without knocking over a child – and these children were frightened and crying all the time. Having got about twenty miles we were compelled to climb on the first piece of good ice we could find.

April 4th: After a desperate struggle we have at last regained the main pack and are now encamped. Our tent is not as good a protection from the wind as the snow huts. Joe, with a little help, can build a hut in an hour if the right kind of snow blocks can be procured but there are none here.

April 5th: Blowing a gale from the northeast and a fearful sea running. Two pieces broke from our floe this morning. We had to haul all our things back toward the centre. Soon after, another piece broke off, carrying Joe's hut away with it. Fortunately the cracking of the ice gave some warning for they had time to escape and were able to throw out and save some few things. No telling where it will split next. It has been a dreadful day – the more so that we can do nothing to defend ourselves. This sort of real estate is getting to be very "uncertain property."

April 6th: Blowing a gale. We are at the mercy of the elements. Joe lost another igloo today. The ice, with a great roar, split across the floe, cutting Joe's hut right in two. We have such a small foothold left that we cannot lie down tonight. We have put our things in the boat and are standing by for a jump.

April 7th: Wind still blowing a gale with a fearful sea running. At six o'clock this morning, while we were getting a morsel of food, the ice split right under our tent. We were just able to scramble out, but our breakfast went into the sea. We very nearly lost our boat – and that would be equivalent to losing ourselves.

While this storm and commotion has been raging we could not shoot seals and so are obliged to starve again, hoping it will not be for long. The worst of our present dearth of seals is that we have no blubber for the lamp and cannot even melt a piece of ice for water. We have therefore nothing to drink. Everything looks very gloomy again. We have set up a tent again and half the men have got in under to get a little rest while the others walk around outside. This is a very exciting period. It is possible to rest the body but not the mind. One after another will spring up from their sleep and make a wild dash outside as if avoiding some sudden danger.

April 8th: Worse and worse! Last night at midnight the ice worked right between the tent and the boat, so close that a man could not walk between them. There the ice split, separating the boat and the tent, and with the boat was the kayak and Mr. Meyers, who was on the ice beyond the boat. We could only stand helpless looking at each other drifting off.

The weather was blowing, snowing, and very cold with a heavy sea running and the ice breaking and crushing. It was a grand sight but most fearful in our position. Meyers could manage neither the boat nor the kayak – the boat being too heavy. He cast the kayak adrift, hoping it would come to us and that Joe or Hans could get in and come for him. Unfortunately the kayak drifted to lee-

Head of lance was detachable.

ward. However, Joe and Hans took their paddles and ice spear and went for the kayak, springing from one piece of loose ice to another. It was a dangerous business. We may never see them again, but we will all be lost without the boat so they are as well off as we. After an hour's struggle, through what little light there is, we could just make out that they have reached the boat. There they appear to be helpless.

Daylight at last! We see them now with the boat, but they can do nothing with her. The kayak has drifted about the same distance away in another direction. They have not strength to manage the big boat. We must therefore venture off and try to get to them. We may as well be crushed in the ice as remain here without a boat. Taking my stick in my hand to support myself I make a start and Kruger follows me. We jump or step, as the case may be, from one slippery piece of ice to another – a few steps level and then a piece higher or lower so that we have to spring up or down. Eventually we arrive where the boat is and find our combined strength could not stir it. I called to the other men and two others got over the way we had, and still our strength was insufficient. At last all came over but two who were afraid to venture, and after a long struggle we got the boat safe back to camp again, bringing Mr. Meyers with us.

April 9th: Things have been quiet the last twelve hours. However, the sea is running very high again and threatening to wash us off our floe at any moment.

Evening: The sea washed us out of our tent, and the natives out of their hut, and so we got everything into the boat ready for a start. But I fear she cannot live in such a sea. The women and children stay in the boat for safety. The ice may split up so suddenly there may not be time to get them if they are scattered about. The sea keeps washing over the floe so that there is not a dry place to stand upon. We are suffering badly from thirst. Not until midnight did things quiet down sufficiently to allow us to risk setting up the tent once more.

April 16th: One more day without a catastrophe. The men are too weak to keep up long together. Someone has been stealing the pemmican. I know the men; there are three of them. One of them was caught at it on the seventh of the month. We have but a few days' provisions left. We came down still lower on our allowance this morning. The idea that cannibalism can be contemplated by any human being troubles me very much.

April 18th: This morning Joe spied a seal. He shot, and called loudly for the kayak for the water was making rapidly. It took an hour to get the kayak to him – an hour of intense anxiety, for we were afraid the seal would float away; but at last it was accomplished and a nice sized seal rewarded our exertions. We shall have to eat it raw, but are thankful to get that. It will save us from starving, perhaps worse.

We had visitors today – a raven, some other land birds and a large flock of ducks. I wished we could shoot some of them for a meal or two; we have eaten up every scrap of that seal, everything but the gall.

April 20th: This morning while resting in our tents we were alarmed by an outcry from the watch and almost at the same moment a heavy sea swept across our floe carrying away everything that was loose. This was but a foretaste of what was to follow. We began shipping sea after sea. Finally a tremendous wave carried away our tent, skins, most of our bed clothing, and left us destitute. Only a few things were saved which we had managed to get into the boat. The women and children were already in the boat, or the little ones would have been swept into a watery grave. All we could do under this flood of disaster was try to save the boat. All hands were called to man it in a new fashion – namely to hold

"We must venture off and try to get
to them ...We may as well be crushed
as remain here without a boat . . ."

"There's a steamer!" The survivors
gave three cheers when they were
seen and rescued by the Tigress.

on to it with might and main to prevent it being washed away. Fortunately we had a boat warp and another strong line made out of strips of oogjook skin and with these we secured the boat as well as we were able to projecting points of ice; but having no ice anchors these fastenings were frequently unloosed and broken, and the boat could not for one moment be trusted to their hold. All our strength was needed and we had to brace ourselves and hold on.

As soon as possible I got the boat to the edge of the ice where the seas first struck, for I knew if she remained toward the farther edge the momentum of the waves would more than master us and the boat would go. As it was we were nearly carried off, boat and all, many times during this dreadful night.

We stood from nine at night till seven in the morning enduring what I should say few, if any, have ever gone through and lived. Every little while one of the tremendous seas would lift the boat up bodily and us with it and carry it and us forward almost to the extreme opposite edge of our piece of ice. Several times the boat got partly over the edge and was only hauled back by super-human strength, which the knowledge of our desperate condition gave us. Had the water been clear it would have been hard enough. But it was full of loose ice rolling about in blocks of all shapes and sizes, and with almost every sea would come an avalanche of these, striking us on our legs and bodies and bowling us off our feet like so many pins in a bowling alley. We were all black and blue with bruises for many a day after.

So we stood, hour after hour, the sea as strong as ever, but we weakening from fatigue so that before morning we had to make Hannah and Hans's wife get out and help hold on too. This was the greatest fight for life we had yet had. Had it not been for the strength imparted to us by that last providential gift of seal meat it does not seem possible that we would have lasted the night. For twelve hours there was scarcely a sound uttered save and except the crying of the children and my orders to "hold on," "bear down," "put on all your weight," and the responsive "Aye, aye, sir," which for once came readily enough.

When daylight came I perceived a piece of ice riding quite easy near to us, and made up my mind we must reach it. The sea was fearfully rough and the men hesitated, thinking the boat would not live in such a sea. But I knew that the piece of ice we were on was still more unsafe and told them they must risk it and launch away. And away she went, the women and children being all snugly stowed in first and the rest all succeeding in getting in safely but the cook, who went overboard, but managed to cling to the gunwale of the boat and was dragged in and saved. We succeeded in reaching the other piece of ice without other accident, and having eaten a morsel of food, lay down on our new bit of floe in our wet clothes to rest. And we are all today well and sound except the bruises we received from the blows and falls.

April 22nd: If something does not come along soon I do not know what will become of us. Fearful thoughts go through my brain as I look at these eighteen souls, without a mouthful to eat. Meyers is actually starving. He cannot last long in this state. Joe has been off on the soft mushy ice a little way, but cannot see anything. We ate some dried skin this morning that had been tanned and saved for clothing, – tough and difficult to sever with the teeth.

Joe ventured off for the fourth time during the afternoon and, after looking for a while from the top of a hummock, saw a bear coming slowly towards us. He returned as fast as possible for his gun, all hope and anxiety lest the creature should turn another way. All the party were ordered to lie down and keep perfectly still while Joe climbed to the hummock and Hans secreted himself near-by, both with rifles ready.

It was a period of intense, anxious excitement. Food seemed within our reach but it might yet escape. The bear came slowly on thinking, undoubtedly, that we were seals and expecting to make a good dinner upon us. A few steps more and he was within range of the rifles. Both fired, killing him instantly. We arose with a shout. The dread uncertainty was over. Poor polar bear! He meant to dine on us, but we shall dine on him. The blood of the bear was exceedingly acceptable, for though we had more water than enough on the outside of us we had nothing to drink and were very thirsty.

April 28th: We have had three days of gale winds. Water again washing over our little bit of floe. Had to stand-to by the boat all night. The ice seeming unsafe, we again launched our boat at daylight but could get nowhere for the small ice, a heavy sea, and a head wind blowing a gale in our teeth. Had to haul up on a piece of ice after an hour's exhausting but useless effort. At least we are now among the seals.

In the afternoon we were threatened by some heavy bergs. These bergs were having quite a battle amongst themselves and beating right down for us. The gale has set everything that can float moving – a grand and awful sight. The sounds accompanying these ice collisions are frightful, combined with the roar of waves. Seeing the bergs were coming too near we launched the boat to try to get out of the way.

4:30 p.m. – A joyful sight – *a steamer right ahead and bearing north of us!* We hoisted our colours and pulled toward her. She is a sealer apparently working through the ice. For a few moments what joy filled our breasts. But we have lost it! She did not see us and we could not get to her! Evening came down and she was lost to sight.

Instead of the hopes for a steamer, we boarded a small piece of ice and made our camp. The sea is quiet and we can rest in peace. We take the blubber of three seals which Joe shot and build fires on the floe so that if a steamer approaches us in the night she will see us. We keep a good watch this evening. To see the prospect of rescue so near, though so quickly withdrawn, has set every nerve thrilling with hope.

April 29th: All on the lookout for steamers. Sighted one about eight miles off. Called the watch and launched the boat and made for her. After an hour's pull we had gained on her a good deal but they did not see us. Another hour and we are beset in the ice and can get no farther.

Landed on a small piece of ice and hoisted our colours, then getting on the highest part of the ice, we mustered our rifles and pistols and all fired together, hoping by this means to attract her attention. We fired three rounds and heard a response of three shots; at the same time the steamer headed towards us. Now we feel sure that the time of our deliverance has come.

Presently the steamer changes her course and heads south then north, then west. We do not know what to make of it. So she keeps on all day as though she were trying to work through the ice but could not force her way.

We repeat our experiment of firing several rounds but she comes no nearer than four or five miles off. All day we watched, making every effort within our means to attract attention. Whether they saw us or not we do not know but late in the afternoon she steamed away and reluctantly we abandoned the hope which had upheld us all day.

While looking at her, another steamer hove in sight so we had two steamers near – one on each side of us. Some of these sealers will surely come by us or we may be able to work down to them.

Sunset: Sighted land this evening in the southwest about 35 miles distant.

The survivors: Led by George Tyson, fed by the
Eskimo members, they had drifted – by direct
line – 1,800 miles on an ice floe. They were
rescued by members of the Newfoundland Bartletts,
a famous sealing family.

April 30th: Evening. At 5:00 a.m. as I was lying in the boat the watch on lookout espied a steamer coming through the fog and the first I heard was a loud cry, "There's a steamer! There's a steamer!" I sprang up ordering all guns to be fired and we sent up a loud shout. I started Hans off with his kayak which he himself had proposed to do, to intercept her if possible, as it was very foggy. To my great joy and relief the steamer's head soon turned towards us. But Hans kept on and paddled up to the vessel singing out in his broken English, the unmeaning words "American steamer," meaning to tell them that an American steamer had been lost, and he tried to tell them where we came from but they did not understand him. In a few minutes she was alongside our piece of ice.

On her approach I took off my old Russian cap which I had worn all winter and gave three cheers, in which all the men most heartily joined. It was instantly returned by one hundred men who covered her top gallant mast, fo'c'sle and foredeck. She proved to be the sealer *Tigress*, Captain Bartlett commanding, out of Conception Bay, Newfoundland.

The crew got out on our bit of ice and peeped curiously into the dirty pans we had used over our blubber fire. We had been making soup out of the blood and entrails of a last little seal. They soon saw enough to convince them that we were in sore need.

Taking the women and children in their boats, we tumbled into our own and were soon alongside her. We left all we had behind and our all was simply a few battered smoky tin pans and the debris of our last seal.

On stepping on board I was at once surrounded by a curious lot of people. I told them who I was and where we were from. But when they asked me "how long have you been on the ice?" and I answered "since the fifteenth of last October" they were so astonished that they looked fairly blank with wonder. One of the party looked at me with open-eyed surprise and exclaimed, "And was you on it night and day?"

The peculiar expression and tone, with the absurdity of the question, was too much for my politeness. I laughed in spite of myself.

At this time the Captain came along and invited me into the cabin. After a couple of pipes of tobacco, breakfast came along – codfish, potatoes, hard bread, and coffee! Never in my life did I enjoy a meal like that. No subsequent meal can ever eclipse this to my taste, so long habituated to raw meat.

fm After breaking clear from the floe, the *Polaris* with fourteen men aboard drove off into the darkness until she was eventually brought up in slob ice, where she lay till morning. She was making water, but there is no indication that her leaks were any worse than they had been when she sailed from Polaris Bay. The dawn broke calm and clear and the ship lay near Littleton Island. She had steam up on one boiler and was using her steam-driven pump to keep the leaks under control. Captain Budington said later that he: "believed the propellor was smashed and the rudder broken." The official account adds: "Since there was only coal enough to keep the fires alive for five days, it was evident that the vessel must be abandoned."

The mate, Mr. Chester, climbed to the crow's-nest and reported that he could see "provisions and stores" on a floe about four miles from the ship; but "others who saw the same thing felt sure it was black ice, or stones, or debris." A breeze sprang up, sail was made; and with the help of the engine the ship was headed for shore, where she was deliberately beached not far from Etah. Nothing was wrong with the propellor and the ship answered her rudder satisfactorily, as the official report admits. Furthermore the *Polaris* was perfectly able to proceed under sail alone, even if she ran out of coal for her boiler fires. The plain fact of the matter is that Budington and Bessel turned their backs on the castaways and made no attempt to search for, or rescue them. Whatever the grounds may have been for Captain Tyson's fear of being deserted by Budington, they were evidently firmly founded.

Having run the vessel so far up on the shore that she was heeled over on her beam-ends, a total wreck, Budington took time to examine the bows. He found them to be damaged but: "the Captain was greatly surprised that the vessel did not leak more, and could only explain it by the many thicknesses of timbers in the bows, which were solid for some distance from the stem."

Since, in their panic, they had deprived themselves of the vessel, the *Polaris* people were now forced to stay where they were. They had thrown overboard onto the ice (where it had been crushed) most of their bedding, spare clothing, and much of their food, and were in poor condition to face another arctic winter. Fortunately for them they were soon discovered by the Etah Eskimos, who kept the party alive through the ensuing winter. In early June of 1873 the fourteen set off in two boats for the south. They had not gone far before they were picked up by the Scots whaler *Ravenscraig* in Melville Bay.

The ice-drift party was picked up off Grady Harbour on the southeast coast of Labrador by one of the skippers of the famous Bartlett family of Brigus. In the years ahead Bartletts of Brigus were to command many polar exploring ships, which were often Newfoundland vessels, manned by Newfoundland crews.

The point at which Tyson's group was rescued was only about fifty miles north of the Strait of Belle Isle, and Newfoundland. They had drifted eighteen hundred miles, calculated on a *direct* course, to accomplish what must be one of the most remarkable voyages, of any sort, in the human record. Yet it is a voyage that is seldom mentioned, except in a most perfunctory manner, by orthodox arctic historians. The same treatment is meted out to Charles Hall's accomplishments. It is almost as if the whole *Polaris* episode is considered too embarrassing to discuss.

The fact remains that Hall took the *Polaris* much farther north than any other ship had ever sailed. He penetrated right through the straits dividing Greenland from Ellesmere Island and brought his ship to the lip of the polar ocean – which, he established, was firmly frozen.

It is worth noting that Hall recorded the highest latitude reached as 82° 29′, a figure confirmed by Captain Tyson who was the official assistant navigator. But in Washington, three years later, Meyers (the man who could not even begin to get an accurate position while with the ice-floe party) stated that Hall had actually only reached 82° 16′. This was the official figure accepted by the Navy and all subsequent authorities. It was a thoroughly typical attempt to diminish Hall's exploits.

Anyone who has bothered to study Hall's record as a sled traveller, in company with Joe and Hannah, has no doubt that he would have been able to go a great deal farther north the following spring – if he had lived.

But Hall died – of apoplexy. At least that is the official verdict, based on the diagnosis of the saturnine Dr. Bessel. The U.S. Navy and the United States Government alike were at great pains to credit what Dr. Bessel, Captain Budington, and others of the disaffected section of the expedition had to say. They were resolutely disinclined to listen to what Tyson, Chester and some others said. One sees their point. If they had given credence to the charges levelled against Bessel and Budington they would have unleashed a most unsavoury scandal – and the Establishment is notoriously averse to scandal. Hall was dead.

The ood-loo, the Eskimo woman's knife, is a combined cutter, chopper, scraper.

He died of apoplexy, and the good Dr. Bessel and the sturdy Captain Budington were commended for their loyalty and dedication to the *Polaris* expedition.

Vilhjalmur Stefansson once suggested that, since Hall had been buried in permafrost, it was possible that his body might have been preserved in a frozen state. He thought it might prove useful to have someone go and see, and if possible bring the remains back for an autopsy. Even if Hall's corpse had completely decomposed, traces of arsenic would still be detectable if they were present. No great difficulty would have been involved, or would be involved today, since the United States then maintained, and still maintains, a major military air base at Thule, only a few hundred miles south of the place Hall died. But the suggestion has been greeted with a silence almost as frigid as that which surrounds the lonely grave upon the shore of Polaris Bay.

Hall was dead; but three of the people whose efforts prevented the *Polaris* fiasco from becoming a terrible catastrophe remained alive. They were Hans Christian, whose career has already been sketched, and Joe and Hannah. Professor Nourse, the official chronicler of the *Polaris* voyage, wrote this brief, sad biography of these two aboriginal Canadians.

It may be conceded as something due in simple justice to the two Eskimos who have been so frequently named in connection with C. F. Hall that a few items of their personal history be recorded. Through all the trials of Hall's three expeditions – a period of more than ten years – they were not only his steadfast friends, but indispensable supporters without whom he could never have carried on his investigations or have kept, in some emergencies, even his life. Joe Ebierbing was, as frequently appeared in Hall's narratives, Hall's great dependence as a hunter. On repeated occasions, by his native skill in the use of lance and line and by his readily learned use of the rifle, he procured food in the darkest days of want, not for Hall alone, but often for the less skilful and suffering Eskimos and white men around him. Hannah, or Tookoolito, was perhaps the more intelligent and, as a woman, naturally of quicker perception in the things of everyday life which would serve the necessities of the white man among strangers. She proved an interpreter without whom every effort to understand the natives of Cumberland Gulf, Repulse Bay, Igloolik, Pelly Bay, or the country en route to King William's Land would have been hopeless. Every one of Hall's journeys and talks with the Eskimos would have been nearly useless without her.

Beyond all this, the heroic conduct of these two on the last of Hall's voyages claims special tribute. It must be very plain to every reader of the narrative of the *Polaris* voyage that these Eskimos saved the lives of Tyson's party on the fearful ice-floe drift. In the early days of that suffering, when the floe was drifting past Cumberland Sound and was very nearly opposite their native place, the temptation presented itself to this native couple to escape to the mainland. "Father Hall" was gone from them and at that time there were just grounds of fear within their breasts that, in the almost famished condition of the white men, some of them might make the Eskimos the first victims, if the direst necessity should come.

Hannah listened to no such words of persuasion, but strengthened Joe's purpose to remain; a hunter for seal and bear was thus still to be at hand for the saving of men whose skill in such hunts was plainly as unequal to their need as was their diminished strength.

Joe and Hannah were originally natives of Cumberland Inlet, where Captain S. O. Budington first met them in the fall of 1851. Hannah, who was born at Cape Serrel on the west side of Davis Strait, was, at the time of Budington's visit, only about twelve years of age. Joe was then married to another woman, and seemed to Budington at that time "as old as he does today." Cape Serrel was a whaling station much frequented by English and American sailors and by the Eskimos of the Cumberland Gulf for trade. A few years later, Mr. Bolby, a merchant of Hull, became much interested in Joe and Hannah and took them with him in his own vessel on his return voyage from the Gulf. In England he treated them as his guests with great liberality. They were married in his house in the presence of a large company, and with Mr. Bolby visited, in their native costume, many places in England and Scotland and were presented to Queen Victoria, and dined with her and the Prince Consort.

Two years later they returned to Cumberland Inlet and there Hall first met them in 1860. Joe had just piloted two English vessels into Cornelius Grinnell Bay through a narrow channel more than one hundred miles long. Both Joe and Hannah next accompanied Hall through all the investigations that led to the discovery of Frobisher's Bay and the Frobisher relics. In 1862 they returned with him to the United States, where they assisted him to raise funds for his next expedition by appearing with him on the lecture circuit, in their native costumes.

Hannah's willingness to leave her country seemed to have been produced by her desire to keep her husband, who was at that time being persuaded to leave her for another wife. His uncle, Ugack, was reported as having had twenty wives, three of them living with him at one time. At the time of Hall's return to the United States, Joe, who had been sick, was ordered by the angekok (shaman) to take another wife as the only way to get well; but to his own best future success, as is well known, he came with Hannah to the United States.

After assisting Hall in his preparations for the second expedition Joe and Hannah closely attended him through the years 1864 to 1869; they again accompanied him on his last voyage in the *Polaris* in 1871 and returned to the United States with the floe party. In a home purchased for them by Hall in Groton, Connecticut, they commenced housekeeping in 1873, readily adapting themselves to the customs of civilized life. Joe became a good carpenter and farmhand, retaining his old love for fishing. Hannah was soon skilful in making up, with the help of her sewing machine, furs and other saleable articles for the people of New London and Groton.

Their first child, Tukeliketa, died in New York in the winter of 1863; the second died and was buried on the first sled journey to King William's Land in 1866; a third, which Joe adopted in 1868, came with him to the United States in 1869. Hannah named this child Sylvia.† The girl was an intelligent scholar at the Groton school until her death in 1875.

The health of this couple had been repeatedly broken during the long period of suffering of the years 1864 to 1869, and they do not seem to have been readily acclimated in the United States. The terrible experience of the ice-floe especially had left severe traces on them. During the year 1876, Hannah suffered much with that fatal disease consumption; a disease which carries off the larger number of her race. She bitterly felt the loss of her last child and the absence of her husband, who, after having been again out in the arctic regions with Captain Sir Allan Young of the *Pandora*, was then doing service aboard a vessel belonging to the United States Fish Commission. After a season of protracted suffering she breathed her last as the old year went out, December 31, 1876, at the age of thirty-eight.

In June, 1878, Joe again sailed for the Arctic with a party commanded by Lieutenant Schwatka to prosecute a renewed search for the record of Sir John

†*This was "Puny" of the ice-drift*

Franklin's expedition. He served Schwatka as effectively as he had served so many white men, but when the time came for the Lieutenant to return to the United States, Joe was no longer with the expedition. Joe had found himself another wife and with the memory of the deaths of two of his children and of Hannah still strong in his mind, he had no desire to risk losing a second family in the unfamiliar wastelands of civilization. With his new wife he returned to Baffin Island, to Cumberland Sound, and in that place of frozen mountains, of the seal, the walrus and the caribou, he lived out the final years, died, and was buried under a cairn of rocks in the land where he belonged. □ FM

Captain Tyson, portrayed by a contemporary artist after the rescue.

CHAPTER 5 LIEUT. GREELY SEES IT THROUGH

While Captain Tyson was still adrift on his ice floe a new polar expedition, and one with a distinct touch of the comic opera about it, was under way far to the eastward.

This was the Austro-Hungarian Expedition of 1872-74, consisting of a polyglot agglomeration of nationalities. The nominal command lay with two lieutenants of the Austrian Navy, of whom one, Lieut. Payer, had served with the German expedition on the east coast of Greenland. The remaining officers and crew numbered twenty-three, of whom some spoke only German, some Italian, some Slavonic, some Hungarian, and one – Norwegian.

The ship was the *Tegetthoff*, a ridiculously inadequate little steamer of barely two hundred tons. This new expedition determined to reach the Pole via Novaya Zemlya, a great sickle-shaped sweep of barren rock stretching north from European Russia. As ice-pilot they shipped a whaler, Capt. Olaf Carlsen, who had earned considerable fame by circumnavigating both Spitsbergen and Novaya Zemlya.

Carlsen's skills turned out to be of very little use. Within a few hours of leaving the coast of Novaya Zemlya the under-powered *Tegetthoff* was trapped in the ice. All that winter the ship drifted slowly northward while her Tower-of-Babel crew lived in a state of terror, expecting her to sink under them at any moment. To propitiate the Ice Gods some of the crew sacrificed a set of reindeer antlers to the deep and, when this had no effect, they offered up (or down) the skull of a polar bear.

The ship continued to drift throughout the following summer, making slight northerly progress. On August 20, having reached latitude 79° 43′, the glum prisoners were cheered by the totally unexpected discovery of new land. Gazing at the blue blur on the northern horizon, they patriotically named it Kaiser Franz Josef Land.

The second winter was slightly more pleasant than the first, since the ship no longer drifted on the wide ice-sea, but stayed quietly in one place not far off the new lands. In the spring of 1874 Payer undertook a sled journey along the shores of Franz Josef Land, with a team of dogs of whom two came from Lapland while the other six were natives of Vienna. He reached 82° 5′ before returning to the ice-girt ship.

By this time all on board had had enough of each other's company and of the quest for the North Pole. In May they decided to abandon ship and began making their way south across the ice towing their boats on sleds. Their progress was not notably rapid. After two months they had advanced forty-seven miles. Fortunately for them they struck open water in mid-August, launched their boats, and were able to row to Novaya Zemlya. There they were rescued by two Russian fishing ships from Archangel. The Russians cheerfully carried these odd bods, who had appeared from God knew where, to Vardo in Norway.

*Playing the keeloun,
a native tambourine.*

Meanwhile Victorian England had determined that the British must re-establish their ascendency in polar exploration. Her Majesty's Government ordered the Navy to do the job, with two ships, *Alert* and *Discovery*, supported by the supply ship *Valorous*. The Lords of Admiralty intended to do the thing properly with a full-scale naval assault before which the defences of the Pole must crumble. It was to be a fine, old-fashioned effort in the spirit of Franklin. The only concessions to new ideas were the inclusion of a few (far *too* few) Eskimo dogs, and the employment of the indefatigable Greenland Eskimo, Hans Christian (Hendrik). In all other respects, including food, the Royal Navy intended to rely on tried-and-true methods which, while they had admittedly failed to work in the past, were at least properly hallowed by tradition. The powers behind the expedition still believed in the myth of the open polar ocean, although they must have been among the few remaining people in the world who did.

The plan called for Capt. George Nares to ram his ships as far north as possible, whereupon officers and men were to take to the ice, manhandling heavy boats and sleds across the floes to the inner arctic sea, and so onward to the Pole. It was a straightforward plan, almost identical to the one Parry had tried some fifty years earlier. The only real difference was in the choice of the battlefield. Nares's squadron was to attack through Baffin Bay.

By all the laws of probability this expedition should have resulted in a disaster on the scale of the Franklin tragedy. But such were the qualities of endurance and stubborn courage in the men involved that it turned out to be the most successful polar expedition to this time.

Luck had a good deal to do with it, of course. It always did in polar voyages. Taking advantage of favourable ice conditions, Nares worked the *Alert* north to winter quarters on the very shore of the Arctic Ocean, near Cape Sheridan on Ellesmere Island. *Discovery* went into winter quarters on the north shore of Lady Franklin Bay in a support role. Then, briskly, the parties of ratings, led by jaunty junior officers, set off with sleds to do some work. They accomplished a surprising amount before scurvy incapacitated and crippled nearly half the expedition's complement of 120 men. One party explored and mapped the whole north coast of Ellesmere Island, west to Alert Point, a distance of nearly 300 miles. Another had a look at the north coast of Greenland, but was turned back by scurvy. It was left to Albert Markham to lead a party of sailors, dragging boats and sleds, out over the ice toward the Pole. They did not get far, but when they turned back at 83° 20′ N. they had set a new world record for high northern latitudes.

The expedition was equipped and supplied for two full years, but by the end of the first winter it was so far gone with scurvy that Nares wisely elected to retreat. He managed to extricate both his vessels and get them out into Baffin Bay, then home. Luck had remained with the Nares expedition to the very end, although not with all its members, since four men died of scurvy or accidents.

But luck turned her face resolutely against the next would-be conquerors of the Pole.

The polar passion had by now heated up to a state of near-frenzy. The British held the record, and the Americans were determined to wrest it from them. James Gordon Bennett, the owner of the New York *Herald*, had become increasingly interested in polar exploration, having noted (as a by-product of the Stanley and Livingstone saga) how such exploring ventures could increase newspaper circulation. He now bought the small yacht *Pandora* in which Sir Alan Young had unsuccessfully attempted the Northwest Passage in 1876, renamed it *Jeanette*, and dispatched it to bring the Pole home to the United States in general; and to the New York *Herald* in particular.

This was an unofficially official expedition since the ship was manned by the U.S. Navy and under the command of young Lieut. DeLong, USN. Bennett's instructions were that the *Jeanette* was to sail via the Bering Strait. Both he and DeLong appear to have believed the wild conceit of a German armchair geographer named Peterman that Greenland stretched northward across the Pole, and thrust an arm southward on the other side of the world, almost to the northeast coast of Siberia. DeLong was to march north along this convenient causeway.

What followed was unmitigated disaster. As soon as she reached the ice in the autumn of 1879, *Jeanette* was beset, and never again escaped. She drifted aimlessly about the polar sea for eighteen months before the ice stopped playing, and sank her. Her people escaped to the floes not far from the New Siberian Islands; then in a most tragic and harrowing ordeal on ice, water and land, they attempted to make their way to the mouth of the Lena River. Twenty-four succeeded, but DeLong and eleven others, including two Chinese messboys, perished. The passage of a bill in the United States Congress in 1882 to appropriate $25,000 to bring the bodies home to America – the few that could be found – did nothing to reduce the magnitude of the disaster. Bennett got his story, though hardly the one he had counted on.

News of the *Jeanette* disaster was not received until 1881 and by that time the United States Army had dispatched its own polar expedition up through Baffin Bay. Theoretically this was a purely scientific endeavour, under instructions to establish a base in Lady Franklin Bay in order to collect data for a species of International Polar Year. It is not generally admitted that, while this provided an excuse to enter the publicity-rich polar arena (where the Navy had so far managed to hold the lion's share of attention), the commander was under instructions to compete with the sister service in the drive to reach the Pole itself.

From the start the Army expedition, commanded by Lieut. Adolphus Greely, was ill-starred. Originally it was to have departed in 1880, but the Navy refused to sanction the use of the ship purchased by the Army and in the inter-service feuding that ensued Lieut. Greely resigned his command. The ship sailed anyway, but got only as far as Disco where the doctor, Octave Pavey, landed to spend a winter studying natural history.

In the spring of 1881 the on-again, off-again Army expedition finally surmounted the difficulties of an obstructionist Navy, and a Secretary of War who was on the Navy's side, and went into action. Greely was re-appointed but did not get his instructions and authority until two months before he was due to sail. Supplies were short and often of the wrong kind. Most of the appropriation of $25,000 (the same amount voted a year later to bring back the bodies of the Naval expedition) went to pay the one-way charter of the Newfoundland sealer *Proteus*, commanded by Capt. Pike and a crew of fellow Newfoundlanders. *Proteus* was only hired to deliver the party to Lady Franklin Bay; but Greely's orders informed him that a supply ship would be sent north in 1882, and a relief expedition would be dispatched in 1883.

Proteus sailed to Greenland where Greely picked up Dr. Pavey, signing him on for a year's service in the Army. He also bought twenty-seven dogs (of whom more than half died early that winter), and hired two Eskimos, Frederick Christiansen and Jens Edward. The party totalled twenty-three men in all.

Proteus duly carried the expedition north to Discovery Harbour (where

Nares's *Discovery* had wintered). Greely's men celebrated their arrival at the site they were to name Fort Conger by slaughtering a herd of eleven musk-ox that were placidly watching them disembark.

Just before *Proteus* was due to leave, Greely's second-in-command, Lieut. Kislingsbury, asked to be relieved and sent home since he did not feel it proper that the officers should be expected to rise at the same hour in the morning as the enlisted men. Greely complied, but settling the protocol took so long that Capt. Pike got tired of waiting, and Kislingbury was forced to remain at Conger, although in "an unofficial capacity."

A house was built at Fort Conger and during the autumn Greely was busy sending out advance depot parties to facilitate his lunge for the Pole. But the loss of most of his dogs put a crimp in his plans. Nevertheless when spring came Lieut. Lockwood (who was a magnificent traveller), Sergeant Brainard, and Frederick Christiansen, the Eskimo, made a dash along the northwest coast of Greenland to reach 83° 24′ – four miles better than Markham's British record. It was the major geographical accomplishment of the expedition.

The summer of 1882 passed and no supply vessel appeared. Winter came and Fort Conger gradually became more and more inactive as the effects of bad food and too few dogs put an end to any real travelling. By the summer of 1883 Greely was becoming seriously worried. He was also having trouble with his people. Dr. Pavey protested against wasting food, energy and effort in futile exploring trips during the early spring of 1883, insisting it would be better to conserve energy for a retreat to the south in case no ship appeared. Bitter rancour developed between Greely and Pavey and when the doctor refused to sign up for another year of service in "Greely's Army," Greely placed him under arrest, which was an act of imbecility even for the military mind. The doctor of the expedition stayed under open arrest from that time forward.

When no ship had appeared by August 9, 1883, Fort Conger was belatedly abandoned (as were the surviving dogs) and the retreat was begun, a steam-power launch being used to tow three whaleboats.

The whole story of the expedition is one of constant indecision, never better illustrated than in this attempt to escape to the south. Having left things dangerously late in the season, the flotilla meandered along, stopping at frequent intervals, until it was inevitably beset by new ice. It was then forced to spend the next month drifting in Kane Basin. Greely seemed unable to decide whether to make for Greenland or Ellesmere Island. In the event a storm broke up the ice and the party lost much equipment (including all but one of its boats) before being driven off the pack at a point on Ellesmere south of Cape Sabine. They landed almost opposite the Eskimo settlement of Etah and only thirty-three miles from it, and less than that from Littleton Island, which was the designated rendezvous point with the relief squadron. Even if no relief had come, the party could have survived the winter in comfort as the guests of the always hospitable Etah Eskimos, had they only made up their minds to strike out for Greenland when they had the chance.

The rest of the story is told by Greely; the excerpts being from his diary, with a few additions from the diaries of Lieut. Lockwood and Sergeant Brainard.

September 30: Sergeant Rice proposed to take a one-man sleeping bag and endeavour, with Jens [the Eskimo], to reach Cape Sabine on foot. I gave the necessary orders for his outfit and journey, and prepared records which were to be left in the cairn [established on the way north] at Brevoort Island.

Rice and Jens started at 8:40 a.m. for Cape Sabine. They carried with them a large single-man sleeping bag into which the two can barely crowd, and four days' rations, expecting to subsist at Cape Sabine and during their return upon the English supplies at that point [left by the Nares expedition].

Long killed a walrus in a water pool near camp and was able to touch him with a pole but, unfortunately, could not get him within reach before he sank. This encouraged us, as we could live through the winter if we could secure a couple of walruses. I decided to remain here for the present, and so I sent the officers and Sgt. Brainard to examine and report on the various projected sites for a winter hut.

If we had a second boat [he had lost all but one on the ice] I should not hesitate as to the course to be pursued. I should cache everything not indispensable for a boat journey and follow the coast of Ellesmere Land south to the Carey Islands where we would be safe.

With one boat this idea is futile, however, and, during Rice's journey to look for succour or provisions, I deem it best to build permanent huts, while our hunters, searching for game, may obtain two or three walruses which would ensure our safety here. With the latter view Bender is now trying to fashion a harpoon head from a piece of my sword, with which to kill and secure them.

I was obliged to reprimand Elison severely in the presence of the party for reflections made by him upon Lieutenant Lockwood in my absence, and which Lieutenant Lockwood brought to my notice. This indiscretion on the part of one of my best men illustrates forcibly the demoralizing influence of the improper criticisms already made by his superiors [criticisms of Greely by Dr. Pavey and Lieut. Kislingsbury].

Lieutenant Lockwood says: "We have now three chances for our lives; first, finding American caches sufficient at Sabine or Cape Isabella; second, of crossing the straits when our present rations are gone; third, of shooting sufficient seal and walrus nearby here to last during the winter. Our situation is certainly alarming in the extreme."

October 7: Mrs. Greely's birthday, a sorry day for her and a hard day for me to reflect on the position of my wife and children should this expedition perish as did Franklin's. However, I hope in faith that we shall succeed in returning. We would at least place our records where our work will live after us. I drank Mrs. Greely's health in a half gill of rum which I had saved from previous issues. Reprimanded Salor for his part in recent complaints, for which he expressed the most sincere regret. Was also obliged to take Connell seriously to task for frequent and similar expressions of discontent.

October 9: An Eventful Day! Sergeant Rice, who Lieutenant Kislingbury had gone over the glacier to meet, was reported returning from the front of the glacier. He brought both good and bad news. The *Proteus* sank July 24 this year. Her crew, and Lieutenant Garlington, had gone south hoping to meet the United States steamer *Yantic* or a Swedish steamer. There are about 1,300 rations at or near Cape Sabine.

I have decided to move to Sabine, abandoning our temporary winter quarters here. It is impossible for us to haul the ten to twelve thousand pounds of articles at Cape Sabine to this place as I could wish. Our chances for game are superior here, but we look for possible assistance at that point. I am so thankful to be assured of the health of my wife and children, from the note [left by Garlington], "Your friends are all well."

These records make our fate seem somewhat brighter, and the party is in very high spirits over them, feeling certain we can get through somehow. I, however, am fully aware of the very dangerous situation we are now in, and foresee a winter of starvation, suffering, and probably death for some. The question is, did the *Yantic* reach Littleton Island; if so, we are safe. Our fuel is so scanty that we are in danger of perishing for want of that alone. I am determined to make our food last until April 1, and shall so divide it; supplementing it from any game that we may kill. Rice discovered three caches – the English one of 240 rations, the Beebe cache of 1882 [a supply ship that failed to reach Greely], and the wreck cache of the *Proteus*.

The record brought back by Rice comprised a notice of the proceedings of the Beebe expedition of 1882, and the following note from Lieutenant Garlington as to the loss of the *Proteus* and his intended movement:

"The steamer *Proteus* was nipped midway between this point and Cape Albert, on the afternoon of the 23rd instant, while attempting to reach Lady Franklin Bay. She stood the enormous pressure nobly for a time, but had to finally succumb to this measureless force. The time from her being beset to her going down was so short that few provisions were saved. A depot was landed from the floe at a point about 3 miles from the point at Cape Sabine as you turn into Buchanan Strait. There were 500 rations of bread, sleeping bags, tea, and a lot of canned goods; no time to classify. This cache is about 30 feet from the water line and 12 feet above it on the west side of a little cove under a steep cliff. Rapidly closing ice prevented it being marked by a flagstaff or otherwise; have not been able to land there since. A cache of 250 rations in same vicinity, left by the expedition of 1881 [left by Greely on his way north]; visited by me and found in good condition, except boat broken by bears. There is a cache of clothing on a point of Cape Sabine, opposite Brevoort Island, in a jam of the rock and covered with rubber blankets. The English depot on a small island near Brevoort Island in damaged condition, not visited by me. Cache on Littleton Island, boat at Cape Isabella. All saved from the *Proteus*. The USS *Yantic* is on her way to Littleton Island with orders not to enter the ice. A Swedish steamer will try to reach Cape York during this month. I will endeavour to communicate with these vessels at once, and everything within the power of man will be done to rescue the brave men at Fort Conger from their perilous position."

This record speaks in varying ways; but to the party and to me it meant that we could rely upon it that "everything within the power of man" would be done to rescue us, and on the strength of that promise I at once decided to proceed to Cape Sabine and await the promised help. My journal shows that I looked forward to privation, partial starvation, and possible death for a few of the weakest, but I expected no such thing as an abandonment to our fate.

We now had four boats [counting those at various caches] and, although the sun was about leaving us for the winter, we could yet travel southward, there being open water visible at Cape Isabella. Had I been plainly told that we must now depend upon ourselves, that trouble and lack of discipline prevailed among the *Proteus* crew, that the *Yantic* was a fair weather ship and that its commander and Lieutenant Garlington were acting independently of each other, I should certainly have turned my back to Cape Sabine and starvation, to face a possible death on the perilous voyage along the shore to the southward.

fm The orders Greely carried stated that if he was not relieved during the summer of 1883, a strong support party, with ample supplies and the best equipment, would be landed at Littleton Island and would proceed north as soon as ice conditions permitted. Greely had every reason to believe that these orders, issued by the Secretary of War, Robert Lincoln, would be carried out.

In 1882 a supply ship was in fact sent north but penetrated only a short distance into Smith Sound. Instead of unloading all its cargo, it left a bare 250 rations (a ration equalled food for one man for one day) and fled south, with the rest still under hatches in the hold. Then in the spring of 1883 the *Proteus* came north. She was nipped and sank. The relief party commander, Lieut. Garlington, promptly fled south carrying all the food his boats would hold, in a frantic sweat to escape the Arctic. He intercepted the USS *Yantic*, bound for Littleton Island, but did nothing to encourage the naval officer in command to land supplies and a rescue party on that island. On the other hand there is evidence to show that the Navy was still livid with indignation at the way the Army had attempted to intrude into the field of polar exploration. The *Yantic's* commander was far too easily persuaded to turn his ship about and head for home. A chartered Swedish steamer (she lurks like a ghost in all the accounts) never did materialize. Thus Greely and his men were left to their fate, convinced that it would only be a matter of time before a relief expedition appeared from the direction of Littleton Island, which lay *a bare thirty miles away* to the southeast. □ FM

October 15: I left the main party with orders to follow me, and started with Sergeant Gardner and Jens to visit the Garlington cache and determine the point at which it would be best to make our winter quarters. I reached the cache in about two hours and examined its contents as far as was practicable. I was very much disappointed in the contents, there being scarcely a hundred rations of meat instead of 500, as I had supposed from Lieutenant Garlington's record. Passing onward I visited the 1882 cache which, covered by a huge drift, had apparently not been disturbed but, having no shovel, we were unable to uncover its contents. I went down within a mile of Cape Sabine and then returned to meet the party. From an examination of the entire coast it was evident that no better place afforded for quarters than a lake, inland from, and near to the wreck [*Proteus*] cache [on the shores of Rice Strait, behind Pim Island].

About an hour after we reached camp, Rice and Christiansen surprised me by their appearance. Rice reported that he had visited Cape Isabella, that no whale boat could be found, and only 144 pounds of English meat were cached there. The spirits of the party were generally depressed at this announcement, as the greater part of the men were confident that some stores must have been landed on Cape Isabella for us.

With great difficulty we partly cleared the site for our house and commenced its construction by laying the corner stone. It is to be 25 feet by 18. We call the place Camp Clay.

October 19: A whale boat was brought from our old camp and put across the walls of the house this morning [as a roof] and a snow wall was commenced around the stone wall already erected. The spaces between these walls are to be filled in with snow, sand and gravel.

The rock walls of the house were about 2 feet thick and 3 feet high, outside of which was an embankment of snow at first 4 feet in height, but eventually the winter gales buried the whole house in snow. The whale boat just caught on the end walls, and under the boat was the only place in which a man could even

get on his knees and hold himself erect. Sitting in our bags, the heads of the tall men touched the roof. Holes were cut in the side of the boat in which oars were inserted, which, reaching to the side walls and fastened by ropes, supported the canvas and overlying blocks of snow which formed the outer roof. Compared with our previous quarters at Fort Conger the house is warm, but we are so huddled and crowded together that the confinement is almost intolerable. The men, though wretched from cold, hard work and hunger, yet retain their spirits wonderfully. I broached today the question as to what should be our winter ration, but leave the point undecided until the English cache, reported damaged by Lieutenant Garlington, is visited by us. God only knows what we shall do if it is spoiled, this hut will be our grave; but until the worst comes we shall never cease to hope for the best.

October 22: Ellis's birthday has been celebrated by a punch, which consisted of half a gill of rum – regularly issued of late – flavoured with a couple of lemons and a can of cloudberries. This indulgence, though a small one, greatly benefits the men, improving their spirits. Rice's party on their return brought, amongst other things, a newspaper article written by Henry Clay, May 13, 1883. A reference to DeLong shows the loss of the *Jeanette* and his party. Of this, Lieutenant Lockwood writes: "We infer the loss of the *Jeanette*, and the alarming view which must be taken at home of our own situation. We all think that our friends regard us as lost."

October 25: Sledge broke again yesterday and was temporarily patched up, but it was found to be in such bad order that it must be carefully repaired before being fit for further use. As no sledging could be done, I directed Brainard to open the dog biscuits and ascertain their condition, which was evidently bad. His journal says: "When this bread, thoroughly rotten and covered with a green mould, was thrown on the ground, the half famished men sprang to it as wild animals would. What, I wonder, will be our condition when we undergo a still greater reduction in our provisions?"

I recall most vividly my efforts to persuade the men to let alone that mass of corruption, pointing out that the injury from eating such food must be far more certain than any possible benefit could be. In accordance with my instructions, the slimy, mouldy substance was thrown away, but I learned later that a few ate all of it.

October 26: Our last day of sunlight for 110 long days, and how to pass this coming arctic night is a question that I cannot answer.

During the evening I announced to the party what my intended programme was, and invited the opinion of the men concerning it and also asked for suggestions. I said that the present ration would be continued until November 1, after which it would be reduced to about 6 ounces of bread, 4 ounces of meat, and 4 ounces of vegetables, aggregating in all about 14 ounces. By this means the party could be provided for until March 1, at which date there would be remaining 10 days' rations, on which to cross Smith Sound by sledge [to Littleton Island or Etah]. There was a warm and animated discussion regarding the reduction.

I quote what Lieutenant Lockwood says on the subject: "The doctor urged that a great objection to the reduction of the ration was that our strength might be reduced, the disease scurvy might be brought on, and only too late would we find it impossible to recover. I remarked that the general view taken by the party, as far as I could get it, was that our ration should be reduced to the very lowest limit, and afterwards increased enough, if necessary, rather than the contrary. So it seems to be fixed upon that we are to try to make out on our food until March 1. Then we shall try to cross the straits on 10 ounces of pemmican, 10 ounces of bread, and tea included."

October 27: Lieutenant Lockwood says: "This is miserable; we have insufficient supplies of everything. Even the blubber will support but one poor light, and that hardly for the winter. We must rely on the whale boat and barrel staves mostly for fuel, the alcohol being almost exhausted. Cold, dampness, darkness, and hunger are our portion every day and all day. Here in the hut one has to grope around in the darkness to find anything laid down."

October 31: A fox around our camp this morning, but too dark to shoot him. Sent a sledge party in a temperature of 2°, for a load which we abandoned 3 miles from the hut a couple of days ago. They were gone about 5 hours. Dr. Pavey today objected strongly to the ration fixed by me, which commences tomorrow. He says that we cannot possibly live on it. It is very trying to have the opinion of my medical officer put so strongly before me at a time when I must depend on my own judgment alone, as the responsibility rests solely upon me.

Our rations were now all collected, and it remained to be seen if we could supplement them by our own exertions sufficiently to eke out an existence until spring and help should come. I had, however, decided on the necessity of a journey to obtain from Cape Isabella, 40 miles to the southward, the 144 pounds of beef cached there by Nares in 1875. It would give nearly an extra ounce of meat to each of us daily, which in the coming winter, might mean life or death.

THE TRIP TO ISABELLA

The account of the journey to Cape Isabella, to obtain the English meat, is drawn largely from the recollections of Frederick, a participant, and of Brainard, the advance guard of the rescuers.

The party, consisting of Rice, Frederick, Elison and Lynn left on November 2, in a temperature of –9° below, with a light sledge, a four-man sleeping bag, a tent-fly, rifle, cooking lamp, and pot. As the arctic night had commenced a week before, the darkness drove them to take to their bags on the ice in Rice Strait the first day out; but on the second day, they had reached, tired and hungry, Eskimo Point where they camped in our old quarters. The third day rough ice impeded their progress and exhausted Lynn and Elison so that they camped before Cape Isabella was reached. On this day Elison and Lynn, in their great thirst, resorted, despite warnings, to eating snow. On November 7, taking only their sledge and leaving their tent behind, they found the ice so bad that they were 7 hours in reaching Isabella. They took up the cache of meat and started immediately on their return, but the rough ice on the north of Isabella was so difficult to travel over that it was 14 hours before the exhausted party reached their sleeping bags. Rice had expected to make the trip in a few hours and the day's work had been done on a cup of tea and no food. On reaching their camp, Frederick said, "Elison had frozen both his hands and feet and our sleeping bag was no more nor less than a sheet of ice. I placed one of Elison's hands between my thighs and Rice took the other, and in this way we drew the frost from his poor frozen limbs. The poor fellow cried all night from pain. This was one of the worst nights I ever spent in the Arctic."

Elison was altogether helpless on the morning of the 9th and so, to save his life, it became necessary not only to abandon the meat for which they had laboured and suffered so hard, but also a rifle which was stood up to mark the

A soldier at 17, Greely was a U.S. Army lieutenant at 37 when he took his expedition of 23 men north in 1881. Only six survived, including Greely who won the Medal of Honor and, later, the rank of major-general.

The first supply ship sent north didn't get close
to Greely's camp at Fort Conger. The second (the
Proteus) was crushed by the ice. Dissension in
the party mounted and Greely's leadership was
threatened. He decided to move to Cape Sabine.

spot. Ten hours struggle with a helpless, frozen man brought them to our abandoned winter quarters at Eskimo Point.

On November 10 they started for Camp Clay, Lynn going ahead with Elison while the others dragged the sledge. The low temperature, about −25°, soon froze Elison's limbs and face, and glued together his eyelids. Frederick says: "We tried to keep Elison in front of us, but to no avail. He would stagger off to one side and it seemed every moment that the frost was striking deeper into the poor man's flesh. We fastened a rope to his arm and the sledge, as it now took 3 men to haul our load, but every few rods the poor fellow would fall and then sometimes he was dragged several feet. No person can imagine how that poor man suffered."

In consequence they were obliged to camp. A northward gale with a temperature of −22° prevailed, so that Rice and Frederick froze their fingers in an unsuccessful attempt to kindle a fire while the sleeping bag was laid in the only possible place, exposed to the full fury of the gale. They decided that Rice should start for Camp Clay to obtain assistance, and he at once left. As he reached Buchanan Straight the moon fortunately shone and a broken, exhausted man, his staggering footsteps awakened me at midnight, and inspired me with new horror before his frozen lips could separate to say, "Elison is dying in Ross Bay."

In gloom and depression we heard the story. I sent Brainard and Christiansen at 4:30 a.m. with brandy and food to relieve the immediate necessity of the party.

Of the night passed by the men, Frederick says: "We tried to keep Elison warm but as we laid helpless and shivering with the cold, and poor Elison groaning with hunger (his frozen lips did not permit him to gnaw the frozen meat) and pain, you can imagine how we felt. Lynn was a strong, able-bodied man, but the mental strain caused by Elison's sufferings made him weak and helpless. In fact I was afraid that his mind would be impaired at one time. We were but a few hours in the bag when it became frozen so hard that we could not turn over, and we had to lay in one position 18 hours until, to our great relief, we heard Brainard's cheering voice at our side. There was nothing more welcome than the presence of that noble man, who had come in advance with brandy for Elison and food for all."

Frederick and Lynn were sent in alone to Camp Clay, which they reached safely, although Frederick broke through the young ice at one point. Lieutenant Lockwood arrived at 2:00 a.m. bringing Elison, alive but in a very critical condition. Not only were Elison's hands and feet frozen solid, but his face was frozen to such an extent that there was but little semblance of humanity in the poor fellow as we dragged him through the narrow door of our wretched hut. He begged piteously for death the first week, but within a month was a bright and cheery member of our party, despite his utter helplessness and great pain.

It is best here to break that silence mantained by me for the many months since my return, through the long and bitter discussions regarding the responsibility for our great disaster. There exists no doubt that in 1881 I should have done more than arrange for a retreat to Cape Sabine if we should not be reached at Conger. Although not under orders to do so, I should have provided against shipwreck and all other mischances.

The neglect of these points would have been uncriticized had the *Proteus* disaster not occurred. The neglect of Lieutenant Garlington to replenish the stores he knew to be damaged, although he was under orders to do so, would have been unnoticed. His action in taking every ounce of food he could carry when turning southward cannot be justified, nor his retaining and feeding a large dog under such circumstances. He acknowledged the dangerous condition in which we were situated, promised us all the assistance in the power of man, tied us down to Cape Sabine, and as events have proved never even asked a National ship to turn its prow northward to our rescue or relief.

The *Proteus* disaster and the subsequent failure of Commander Wildes of the *Yantic* to extend relief did not alone determine the fate of the party. I concur in the views and opinions of the sealers of Newfoundland, that our relief was practicable during the autumn of 1883. Had a stout sealer – and there were many available – left St. John's, under a competent officer within 10 days after the return of the *Yantic*, the entire Lady Franklin Bay expedition, in my opinion, would have safely returned.

LIFE IN THE WINTER QUARTERS

November 9: Lieutenant Lockward discovered an open but full can of milk hidden away. It had evidently been concealed by someone who, surprised, had been unable to eat it after opening. It appears from the marks that the can was opened by a knife broken in a peculiar manner. It was afterwards ascertained that the knife belonged to Pte. Henry, but he claimed to have lent it to Schneider.

November 14: Elison very bad all day; he suffers excruciating pains in his hands and feet. The men are slowly recovering from their exhaustion on the late severe trip.

November 17: I have been casting about for some means to amuse and divert the party during the weary time now upon us. The entire work of the party does not require more than an hour's labour from two or three people, and the remainder, by choice or necessity, remain almost continually in the sleeping bags. As we have fairly entered upon an arctic night of nearly four months' duration, it is absolutely necessary that the spirits of the men should not be allowed to flag. After much thought and some consultation, I have decided to give, daily, a lecture of from 1 to 2 hours in length upon the physical geography and the resources of the United States in general; followed later by similar talks on each state and territory in particular. I commenced today by talking on the physical geography of the United States, particularly with reference to its mountains and river systems.

Brainard today put up a signal pole on the adjoining cliffs which should be seen by any party travelling along the coast. I have not now the faintest expectation of such a party this winter. But some of the rest have, and I am unwilling to depress their spirits by destroying any hopes they may nourish.

November 19: Long shot a blue fox weighing 4¼ pounds; Jens, our Eskimo, shot one weighing 3⅞, which has much encouraged us. The entrails of the foxes go as an addition to, or flavour for, the stew. Talked for an hour or two on the grain and fruit products of the United States. Later I gave an hour to the mineral productions of the United States. It was interesting to note the lack of interest shown by the party regarding the production of gold and silver.

December 4: During last night someone took bread from Corporal Elison's bread can. I was awake and plainly heard it done. In this entry of the most unfortunate experience of the month, the name of Dr. Pavey was omitted. I was shocked that the surgeon of the expedition should so fail in his duty to the men and his commanding officer, and this discovery gave me great anxiety. Realizing that an open charge would result in a denial and bitter discussion, I

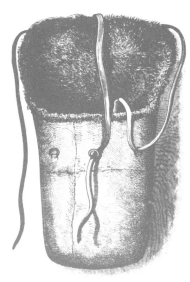

A three-man buffalo sleeping bag.

committed my knowledge of the fact to Lieutenant Lockwood, as my successor in command, and to Sergeant Brainard, who doled out the provisions. The importance of the Doctor's services to us at that time was manifest to the entire party; nearly everyone but myself having been treated medically since reaching Sabine, and the demand for medical treatment was increasing. Whether right or wrong I felt the necessity of pursuing conciliatory methods.

December 9: Two blue foxes were shot today weighing over 5 pounds. The large number of foxes killed lately encourages us to hope that the supply may continue.

December 10: A strong westerly gale with drifting snow. Dr. Pavey informs me that Elison's feet will be saved. Part of one hand must be eventually lost, but no amputation will be made in our present camp. The patient is cheerful, talks much and has his face healed to such an extent that he enjoys smoking. Bierderbick, who does not agree with the doctor, told Lieutenant Lockwood that Elison would lose his feet and part of his hands, as the line of demarcation is quite plain, being just below the angles in the feet, and through the fingers of the hand.

December 13: Trouble in Lieutenant Kislingbury's mess today;† they accuse Frederick, their cook, of unfairness in dividing the rations. Dr. Pavey, Henry, and Whisler stated they had plotted to catch Frederick dealing unfairly. At my request Lieutenant Kislingbury listened to all the members of his mess had to say on the subject. After hearing all the testimony Lieutenant Kislingbury decided that the complaints were unfounded, and he desired that Frederick should remain on duty as their cook.

One bit of flame, affording about as much light as a poor tallow candle, suffices for the entire hut. The steam and smoke which are produced in cooking are so dense that but few of the party are able to even sit up on their bags while cooking is going on, and only on favourable occasions can a man see the face of his neighbour touching him. In the midst of these dense clouds of smoke or steam, without any additional light, the cooks are obliged to divide the stews, tea, and other food. I do not believe that either cook has intentionally shown partiality to any member of the mess, or retained an extra quantity for himself. The ravenous, irritable condition in which the entire party are at present, cannot but have the effect of making most men morbid and suspicious. Sergeant Gardner lately said to me that he objected very decidedly to passing Rice's ration to him, if it could be avoided. He declared that he realized the fairness of the cooks, but that in allowing a cup of tea or a plate of stew to pass through his hands, he could not prevent himself from mentally weighing the food as it passed by, comparing it to the portion which came to himself. Such a comparison, he knew, was small and petty, but his starving condition must explain and excuse it. I readily understood his feelings, as I myself have avoided handing another man's portions for similar reasons.

January 2: Owing to a defective cartridge, Connel missed a fox today. The Doctor severed the fragment of skin which held Elison's right foot to his ankle, unknown to the patient.

January 3: Brainard wounded a fox, but he escaped. Dr. Pavey cut off one of Elison's fingers. Brainard reports that a hole has been cut through the canvas roof of the storehouse and a small piece of bacon fished out. This bold attempt to steal our food gives me great uneasiness for the future.

January 7: Biederbick talked this evening upon home life in Germany, and I discoursed an hour or more this forenoon regarding Minnesota, my remarks being supplemented by Kislingbury.

†*Although they were all living cheek-by-jowl in one tiny hut, Greely insisted on separate messes, a division of the party into two groups.*

Brainard discovered today that someone had made a hole with an axe in one of the barrels of bread and had taken out several pounds. He suspects the thief but has no direct proof. Quite a number of our men offered [to contribute] an ounce of bread a day to keep the thief from temptation if he would only confess and repent. The guilty man kept his counsel. It appears that someone in Lieutenant Kislingbury's mess has taken a piece of bacon from one of their pots, where it was put by their cook. Complaints have been made that in the darkness of night, after the Eskimo lamp is put out, someone has been in the habit of scraping the rancid oil out of the lamp and eating it.

January 10: I ordered everyone to carry out instructions as to their health given any man by Dr. Pavey. In consequence Ralston and Ellis are to stop smoking tea leaves, a solace I am loath to deprive them of but which cannot be safely indulged. Elison is 34 years old today. He is cheerful and doing wonderfully well, although both feet and the greater part of both hands are now gone. I gave him half a gill of rum to celebrate the day.

January 13: Lieutenant Lockwood gave me much anxiety all night through, as at times he seemed to be decidedly out of his head. It appears that he has been saving up small amounts from each day's food, and from his own account he ate today 24 ounces of solid food, an imprudence which has tended to break him down.

January 15: Lieutenant Lockwood is in the sleeping bag with me, and I had conversation with him today. He no longer sees double as he has been doing for the past two days. He admitted being very much depressed, and laments it as one of his characteristics. In consequence of the necessity of melting ice for our water, I was obliged to reduce the quantity of tea today so that hereafter we have but half allowance. It comes very hard upon many of the men. I talked for an hour about the Indian territory. Conversations of this character are not so popular as they have been, and they are exceedingly trying upon me, leaving me perfectly exhausted when I am through.

January 17: Lieutenant Lockwood still in my bag. He slept well last night but is exceeding weak. I have been obliged to assist him every time he finds it necessary to change his position, no matter if it is even to turn from one side to the other. The Doctor told me this morning that Lockwood was in a dangerous condition and in consequence I urged him to write to his family.

It is interesting to note that Elison does not yet know of the loss of his feet, but frequently complains of pain in the sole or toes.

January 18: Cross died today at about 2:00 p.m. My attention was called to him by Jewell who slept next to him. On lighting the lamp, Jewell found Cross to be unconscious and partly out of his bag. The Doctor examined him and, by his advice, I ordered some brandy and soup to be given him which were taken with great difficulty. He never recovered his entire consciousness. The Doctor, after examining the body, reported to me in French that there were very pronounced signs of scurvy, and that his death must be attributed most particularly to that cause.

January 20: The weather remains calm, clear and very cold, the temperature being below the scale of the thermometer. Lieutenant Lockwood made up his mind today to leave me and return to his own bag. He is exceedingly weak; too weak in my opinion to be alone. I had been able in a manner to care for him.

Brainard discovered today that at some time 12 cans of milk had been stolen. There is an intense feeling amongst the party over this news. In order to counteract the depression caused by Cross's death and by the loss of the milk, I decided to increase the seal blubber and hard bread ration slightly.

January 23: A very strong gale has prevailed today, which sent the temperature within the house to below 20°. I have spent some time in giving a very elaborate account of San Francisco and also read a great deal to the party from Spofford's American Almanac. The statistics regarding crops and articles of food are extremely interesting, as well as tantalizing to us.

I was obliged to forbid the practice of eating tea leaves, which the Doctor thinks injurious in our present condition; only a few of the party have indulged in the practice. Jewell is in an apathetic and very depressed condition, and I have exhausted my patience and ingenuity in trying to revive his former courage and energy. I commenced feeding up Rice and Jens for a proposed trip to Littleton Island. They now receive daily 16 ounces of bread and the same amount of meat. Frederick, our cook, and Schneider, are working their best to get the travelling gear into proper condition for this forlorn hope [that they would find a rescue party].

January 28: Drilled Brainard and one or two others this evening in the chronological table. The novel *Coningsby* was finished last night and our attention is now directed to reading Kane, whose record of his starvation diet creates in us an indescribable longing for even half as much food as his men had. The bluntness of our taste at this time is instanced by the fact that on one occasion our cook forgot to put the tea in the pot, and no one detected the omission, not even the cook himself, until he found the tea measured out in the can after he had drunk the dirty water.

Most of the party believe that Lieutenant Garlington is at Littleton Island with ample supplies from the *Yantic;* but I have announced that I count on nothing but a very small cache.

The end of January was an important season to us. We had already passed three months of darkness with a mean temperature of −23°, and looked on our troubles as almost past though the sun was to be absent 16 days longer. Twenty-four men yet remained alive, of whom twenty-two were in comparative health and strength. Though haggard, emaciated, and suffering, we were yet confident and hopeful. We hoped that Smith Sound was frozen over, and that if Garlington failed us at Littleton Island, yet Rice would bring to our help the gentle natives of Etah, who never failed Kane and Hayes in their hours of need and danger. Once among these Eskimo Arctic Highlanders we knew our safety would be assured.

February 1: Bender showed an insubordinate disposition today, and refused to obey my orders when I interfered to stop a violent and bitter discussion between him and Whisler. In consequence I sent him out of doors with directions that he remain there until he was willing to obey my orders. He remained out about an hour before he would submit.

I have given letters, records and his orders to Rice, who leaves in the morning to attempt to cross Smith Sound to Littleton Island.

February 2: An important day for us. I called the cooks at 5:00 a.m. Rice said that his outfit was perfect. I gave him and Jens 4 ounces extra of beef for breakfast this morning. Long killed a blue fox shortly before their departure, which we considered a good omen. They got away at 8:45 a.m. Brainard says of Rice's departure: "A tremulous God bless you, a hearty grasp of the hand, and we turned away in tears from those two brave souls who were daring and enduring so much for us. We waited until their receding forms were lost to view in the bewildering confusion of the ice fields and then slowly retraced our steps to the hut."

February 4: Frederick had the misfortune to spill the rice belonging to his mess this morning, but gathered it up without any considerable loss. It is remarkable that the cooks have been able to prepare their food with so few accidents considering the darkness and other great disadvantages under which they have necessarily laboured.

The Doctor informs me that Brainard's symptoms look towards kidney trouble and are very bad; and his chest, from certain indications, seems to be affected. He says that Brainard is in danger unless he avoids exposure to the cold and violent exercise. Lieutenant Lockwood was much better this morning, being able to get up, but in going out he fell down in the passageway and also after re-entering the hut. He fears our projected journey across the straits saying we could cross, however, if we had enough meat and bread. Connell reported today that from the hill behind camp he could see the opposite side of the straits without any sign of open water. We all wonder where Rice is, and what results will flow from his trip.

February 6: We were very much surprised by the return of Rice and Jens about 2 o'clock today, quite well but much exhausted by their trip. Rice reports that he saw open water extending from ten miles off Wade Point, as far north into Kane Basin as the eye could reach. Happily our party does not appear to be very much affected by this unfortunate report. Rice said that at no time did he see the Greenland shore. There was much moving ice with dense water clouds along the edge of the fast ice. He thinks he reached a point as far south as Littleton Island, and about 10 miles distance from it. The only sign of game seen was some old bear tracks.

Lieutenant Lockwood expressed the condition of affairs and the prevailing spirit when he wrote: "Of course we are all very much disappointed; the party takes a bold front and are not wanting in spirit. So here is the upshot of affairs. If our fate is the worst, I do not think we shall disgrace the name of Americans and of soldiers."

February 7: Increased the rations slightly today to counteract the effect of Rice's return, and announced publicly that hereafter we shall have next week nearly 18 ounces weekly of blubber and lard combined, in addition to our usual ration of several ounces. It is all a pitiful game of brag, and I shall have to reduce everything materially the coming week, but it has had the desired effect.

Mercury froze in the thermometer again. Sergeant Brainard overhauled our remaining provisions and found a considerable less quantity of rum than was expected, as we had calculated on the barrel holding the quantity certified on it. I was very much worried over the matter, as it could not be explained, until Israel suggested that our English measure differed from the American one, which satisfactorily accounted for the deficit. I ought to have thought of the difference in the measures as it leaves us now with such a small quantity of liquor.

Lieutenant Kislingbury and Dr. Pavey had a very bitter discussion which barely stopped short of personal violence. I have found that the most certain manner of retaining my influence over the men is to refrain from interference, except in official quarrels. Bitter talk relieves the mind at times and no blow has ever been struck, a remarkable record for 25 tortured and irritable men who have not known a moment of comfort in these many months.

February 13: Dr. Pavey and Bender had violent words, in consequence of which the Doctor told me he would never again prescribe for Bender unless he publicly apologized, which I told Bender he must do. Later Dr. Pavey had a quarrel with Whisler and wished me to publicly reprimand him, which I declined, as there was no cause, the trouble having been commenced by the

Many arctic explorers raised
rock cairns. This one contained
papers left by the lost Franklin.

Eskimo Jens Edward, "a Christian of
whom no evil word had ever been
spoken," was drowned in his kayak.

In a snowstorm Sergeant Frederick warmed Sergeant Rice is his arms until the starved man quietly died.

The funeral of Cross, the first man to die at Cape Sabine. Dr. Pavey reported that scurvy was the cause of death.

Doctor. These continuous quarrels wear on me for I never know how they will end, or what violence the wretched men will be tempted to commit, for in many ways death is preferable to life. I thought it best today to turn over to Lieutenant Lockwood a favourite pistol of his, which I brought down on my person at his personal request, and of which he spoke yesterday. His mention of it gave me an unpleasant feeling, for it looks as though he were putting his house in order. Lieutenant Lockwood said; "The sun does not make us very enthusiastic. We are too near the end of our rations, with a very poor prospect of increasing them at Littleton Island. I see no chance of the straits being closed with ice by the end of the month. To my mind we must find game here, or else receive help from Littleton Island. It will soon all be decided, thank God."

February 19: Brainard's journal says: "Smith Sound was an open sea today; no ice of any kind was visible on its surface and the waves and whitecaps were rolling in against the edge of the fast ice with a dismal roar, which sounded in our ears as the knell of our impending doom."

The sun has not yet actually been seen by any of the party, but its rays have appeared to the northward, gilding the mountains.

Another violent scene between the Doctor and Lieutenant Kislingbury. Better this than mental apathy. We are trying to delude ourselves with the idea that we will have some opportunity of using the sledges and the foot and hand gear we have prepared for crossing Smith Sound.

March 1: Today is the one which was [long since] fixed upon for crossing the strait. We have lived through to this time on a ration thought to be impossible for sustenance of life, but now the fates appear to be against us. The straits are wide open, and if we had only sufficient strength to remove the boat from the roof of our building we could now attempt a passage partly by sledge and partly by boat.

I informed the party that we could hold out here without any material reduction in the rations until the early days of April, and could stay until March 16 and still have sufficient food to try to cross. My announcement seemed to have a good effect.

Brainard asked if I could promote Frederick to Cross's position. I have promoted him to sergeant, hoping the action will have a stimulating effect by keeping before the man a keener realization that there is yet a world and something worth striving for.

Lieutenant Lockwood is in a very morbid and unsettled condition of mind. Bender is in a fit of passion again. I cannot endure this state of affairs much longer I am afraid.

March 13: Long returned at 7:15 p.m. from Alexander Harbour where he and Christiansen, the Greenlander, had gone in search of game. They saw no game and no tracks, except of a single fox. They travelled nearly 70 miles and, their sleeping bags having frozen up, they were unable to get into them farther than the hips, and were compelled to get what rest they could alternately, one resting while the other walked. We are all terribly disappointed over the result as I had counted with some confidence upon obtaining game.

The fates seemed to be against us — an open channel in Smith Sound, no game, no food, and apparently no hopes of rescue from Littleton Island. We have been lured here to our destruction. If we were now the strong, active men of last summer, we could cross Smith Sound where there is much open water; but we are a party of 24 starving men, of whom two cannot walk, a half dozen cannot haul a pound. We have done all we can to help ourselves and shall ever struggle on, but it drives me almost insane to face the future.

March 16: Lieutenant Lockwood is weaker than yesterday but he seems now to be in good mental condition. Long and Christiansen with the kayak went to the open water. They returned about 2 o'clock having killed 4 dovekies. They weigh 4 pounds, exactly, after being plucked. The entire party are delighted and feel much encouraged at the prospects. Brainard made an improvement on my plan of last autumn to dredge for mussels, and suggests that we try to catch shrimps. Certainly our men are full of devices and we shall yet make a brave fight for our lives.

March 21: A net was made in which to catch shrimps.† Gardner was anxious to do something for the commonweal and so fixed up a rake for dredging, hoping to get some mollusks or seaweed. It is surprising with what calmness we view death, which, strongly as we may hope, seems now inevitable. Only game can save us. We have talked over the matter very quietly, and I have always exhorted the men to die as men and not as dogs.

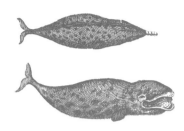

March 22: Rice tried the shrimp net today and brought in about a pint of minute shrimps. He thinks he can get a quart daily, which will be a considerable help to us. Long and Jens went hunting. Ellis carried out the kayak for them. Long reports that the ice extends about 3 miles farther out than on March 17. This is very encouraging since it indicates that the strait may be closing, but I have given up the idea of crossing, as our strength and rations would not permit such hard work now and we must be even weaker when the straits close over, if at all. I have concluded that on April 1st I shall reduce the rations to a basis which will enable us to live till May 1st.

March 24: The entire party nearly perished by asphyxiation from the fumes of the alcohol lamp used in cooking. It has been the custom to close with rags the tin can which formed the chimney through the boat, so that as much heat as possible could be retained in the hut at night. The cooks had forgotten to remove the rags and in consequence the alcohol lamp burned poorly. About this time Sergeant Israel complained of nausea and dizziness. I spoke to Dr. Pavey and he advised Israel to lie down, saying he would be better in a few minutes. Shortly after, Bierderbick, on the other side of the hut, fainted, and the Doctor went to his assistance. Sergeant Israel then became unconscious; while I was devoting my energies towards restoring him another man became faint. Sergeant Gardner called out, "It is the alcohol. Open the door. Open the door!" The door opened, everyone who was able, with one or two exceptions, crawled out of the hut, some fainting by the way. On emerging from the passageway I saw Brainard stretched upon the snow perfectly white and apparently dead. Whisler fell down and I went to his assistance; but, before reaching him lost my strength and fell to the ground. Gardner came to my assistance and with difficulty got me on my feet and tried to put a pair of mittens on my hands, which had already commenced freezing. Whisler also tried to assist me but, Gardner falling to the ground, we turned our attention to him. By this time Brainard had recovered consciousness and was able to rise. Strength and consciousness returning to us, we realized that we were freezing, the temperature being about –25° Dr. Pavey and one or two others were not affected, but Bierderbick and Israel were very near unto death. Several of the men were sharply frostbitten; Sergeant Brainard suffering the most of anyone except myself. My hands were frozen so severely above the second joint that a week passed before I was able to even feed myself, and nearly two weeks before I could use my fingers without great suffering.

After order was restored and the breakfast cooked, it was found that a piece of bacon had been stolen. Curses loud and deep were heaped upon the man

† *These were "krill," tiny shrimp-like creatures about ¾ of an inch in length. They form the basic food of the baleen, or whalebone, whales.*

who would be base enough to steal the food from his comrades who were striving against death in another form than by starvation. A few hours afterwards I gathered in conversation that suspicion rested upon Henry, and later learned that "our little man" (as we called Eskimo Jens) had seen him take the bacon and conceal it within his shirt. In the meantime those who suspected Henry kept watch on him. Just toward dinner he complained of nausea. The meat for dinner was divided and Henry, in my hearing, said on taking his portion, "I'll put this away." In a minute or two afterwards, becoming sicker, he vomited. Frederick found, when it was emptied, that the can of vomit contained a considerable quantity of undigested, scarcely masticated bacon.

There was much suppressed talk of proceeding to violence, but I remarked that it was a military command, and that I would take extreme measures when needful. Since I had spared an officer (Dr. Pavey) these many months on grounds of indispensable service, I was unwilling to deal otherwise with a private.

THE BEGINNING OF THE END

April opened favourably, for Long killed 11 dovekies and 2 ptarmigan and saw a seal and walrus. On the 3rd we had remaining 5 pounds of meat, 3 of bread, and nearly 2 of fat to each man. Rice, too, was bringing in from 20 to 30 pounds of shrimps daily and reported that seaweed, or kelp, was visible and might be reached, he thought, at the spring tide. Our first really depressing day came with April 5th. The night before, Chrstiansen, one of the Greenland Eskimos, had been somewhat delirious; but in early morning he grew worse and at 9 o'clock he died. His body was examined by Dr. Pavey. The Doctor reported that a few ill-defined signs of scurvy were visible but that death resulted from the action of water on the heart induced by insufficient nutrition. We dreaded to use or hear the word starvation, but that was the plain meaning of it. His death could not fail to have a very injurious effect on the weak and despondent.

On Sunday, April 6, Lynn became unconscious and died at 7:00 p.m. He asked for water just before dying. We had none to give. It was very noticeable, in after cases, that almost invariably from 6 to 12 hours before conciousness ceased, thirst began and a request for water was repeatedly made. Lynn's death affected us all deeply.

Near midnight of April 6, Sergeant Rice and Private Frederick started southward towards Baird Inlet. They went to attempt the recovery of the 100 pounds of English beef which had been abandoned in November, 1833. The abandonment, it will be remembered, was necessary to save the life of Sergeant Elison, then dangerously frost-bitten. The journey had been proposed by the two men about the middle of March, but I had persistently objected to it, foreseeing the great chances of a fatal result.

After a final consultation with me about the trip, Rice, in default of another sleeping place (since his bag was on the sledge), crept in with his comrade, Lynn, who had just died. He slept for a time with the dead, unconscious that in a few hours he too would pass away.

The details of the journey, told us in simple touching words by Frederick on his return, was substantially as follows:

On starting out a heavy gale was experienced. The high wind and blinding snow rendered the lighting of the lamp for tea impossible, and so without drink of any kind they stretched their sleeping bag on the ice and, taking a few

Greely made a few attempts to
achieve his aims before supplies
failed. Lt. Lockwood reached 83° 24'.

Steam and smoke from the cooking fire
made conditions intolerable inside
the hut. There was no other light.

The ordeal ends. When the rescue expedition led
by Commander W. S. Schley finally reached the
Greely camp on Bedford Pym Island, off Cape Sabine,
the few survivors had eaten the covers of their
sleeping bags. One man had been shot for cannibalism.

The emaciated survivors had to be carried to the
rescue ship. Indecision was a big factor in
the tragedy: Greely could have struck out
early for Etah, Greenland, only 33 miles from
his last camp instead of waiting for rescue.

Bearded Major A. W. Greely (he had been promoted during
his long absence) later gathered the survivors for
this early photograph. The seventh member, Elison, had died
soon after rescue. Greely later directed government
relief work after the great San Francisco earthquake of 1906.

ounces of frozen pemmican, crawled into it for rest. They were confined to the bag for 22 hours by a violent storm which buried them completely under snow. About 6:00 a.m. on the 8th they got out of their bag, but were too cold to cook until they had travelled an hour. The warm meal with tea refreshed them very much, as they had been nearly 36 hours without drink. About 7:00 p.m. that evening, dark and blustering weather drove them to camp. Their sledge was drawn up between a large iceberg and the face of a glacier. The morning of April 9 broke calm and clear and an hour's travel brought them to our old camp at Eskimo Point. Being within 6 miles of the place where the meat had been cached, they decided to drop their sleeping bag and a portion of their rations, expecting, with their lightened sledge to reach the meat and return in one march.

About 11:00 a.m. a strong north-west gale sprang up with drifting snow. In a short time they were unable to see any considerable distance. Struggling on, by 3:00 p.m. they had reached the place where the meat had been abandoned; but notwithstanding a very careful and extended search they were unable to find any traces of it. Frederick proposed that they return to their sleeping bag and resume the search on the morrow. Rice favoured remaining, hoping that it would soon clear and that the meat would be found. About 4:00 p.m. Frederick noticed indications of weakness in Rice and reminded him of their mutual agreement to give timely warning of approaching exhaustion so as to avert disaster. Rice said that if they travelled a little slower he would soon be rested, but in a short time he showed such signs of exhaustion that Frederick called a halt and gave him a quantity of spirits of ammonia in rum, until some tea could be cooked. After warm food and drink, Frederick in vain urged him to start to avoid freezing. His condition had now become alarming. He was too weak to stand up. Frederick did all possible for him. Although a driving storm of wind and snow, with a temperature of 2° prevailed, he stripped himself of his jumper in which to wrap poor Rice's feet. In his shirt sleeves, sitting on the sledge, he held his dying comrade in his arms until a quarter of eight when Rice passed away. Frederick's condition may be more readily imagined than described. Starved by slow degrees for months, weakened by his severe and exhausting labours, chilled nearly to numbness, he was alone on an extended icefield with his dead comrade. His sleeping bag was miles from him and to reach it he must struggle against a cutting blast filled with drifting snow.

He reached Eskimo Point and his sleeping bag, too weak to open it until he had laid down a while and revived himself by a mixture of ammonia and rum. As soon as he awoke, benumbed and stiff, he immediately got out of his bag, travelled on until he was thoroughly warmed up, then prepared tea and food and marched on as far as possible. In this way he managed to bring back to us everything hauled out, and, astonishing to say, he turned in all of Rice's rations, having done this work on the food allotted to himself alone.

The condition of affairs had changed much during Frederick's absence. Lieutenant Lockwood's condition after Christiansen's death alarmed me very much and on April 6 I commenced issuing him extra food – four ounces of raw dovekie, all, and really more than, we could spare. On the 8th he fainted and his mind wandered much during the evening. He became unconscious at 4:00 a.m. of the ninth and died 12 hours later, calmly and peacefully, without suffering, as passed away most of our party.

Jewell failed after Lockwood's death and, despite extra food, died on the 12th, becoming unconscious in my arms. I fed him for several days before his death, and laboured assiduously to inspire him with new courage and vigour.

A scraping device used on the sea ice by Eskimos to attract seal.

On Easter Sunday we heard on our roof a snow bird chirping loudly – the first harbinger of spring. All noise stopped as by magic, and no word was said until the little bird passed. His coming on that Sabbath morn was thought a good omen, and did much to cheer us through the day.

On Rice's departure, Salor had attempted the work of catching shrimps, but, breaking down, had been relieved by Brainard who was very successful, bringing in from 20 to 30 pounds daily, thus enabling us to keep body and soul together.

On the 11th Brainard fell breathless in the passageway, calling out: "A bear, A bear!" He had seen one coming up the icefoot and, being unarmed, returned as rapidly as his feebleness would permit to the hut. Lieutenant Kislingbury, Long, and Jens, immediately started in pursuit. Long and Jens proceeded cautiously, but the bear, catching sight of them, turned and made for the open water. The hunters divided, one travelling a little south, the other a little north of the route taken by the bear. The rough ice favoured them and as the animal stopped occasionally, they got within rifle shot before it reached the water. Both fired within a few seconds of each other, from a distance of 250 yards. The bear proved to be a young one, weighing about 400 pounds dressed. This game seemed to insure our future. Jens received an allowance of rum and tobacco, while as a reward for Long's coolness and skill he was conditionally promoted to sergeant.

On April 13 I increased the ration of the party to a pound of meat daily, which with the shrimps improved us generally.

On April 14th my journal says: "Lieutenant Kislingbury shows very decided mental derangement, and the Doctor informs me that my heart is in a very dangerous condition. I had been previously urged by a number of the party to issue myself extra allowances, such as had been granted to various other members of the party. But I had not been willing to do so. The death of Lieutenant Lockwood and the mental incapacity of Lieutenant Kislingbury materially changed the condition of my affairs. My death seemed imminent. If I should die Sergeant Brainard would be my legal successor, as Dr. Pavey had refused to renew his contract the preceding July, and had become a civilian. I therefore wrote a letter transferring the command in such case to Sergeant Brainard. My journal April 15 says: "Bierderbick made oath today about the truthfulness of his statements charging Dr. Pavey with taking Elison's bread, last autumn, and appropriating to his own use 4 cans of extract of beef."

April 19: Sgt. Long detected Dr. Pavey this morning drinking part of Schneider's allowance of rum. The Doctor complained very bitterly of Elison's ingratitude to him for the kindness and attention he has shown him. I cannot blame Elison for giving vent to his feeling, as he has long realized the part the Doctor has played towards him. Bierderbick and Ellis were much worse today, being unable to eat the shrimps. It worried me a great deal, for if one cannot eat them he must certainly die soon.

April 22: This evening Schneider broke down morally, if I may use the word, and refused to obey my orders to prepare supper. The Doctor reported him well, yet Schneider said that he could not do it.

April 23: Schneider cooking again. I told him yesterday that if he did not cook the breakfast he could have none; that if he could not work here, he could not eat here. I pity the man's condition but deem it necessary that he should cook. I plead with him as a man, as a soldier, and as a German, but for a long time in vain. We used the last of the fat for cooking this evening and begin on the boat in the morning. We have yet 7 gallons of alcohol, but I think it better to use it as food to eke out our remaining rations, of which we have about 330 pounds. Our chances are still fair of getting through.

April 24: I have a terrible attack of illness this morning, losing much blood and experiencing great pain, with resulting physical weakness. A bad day for hunting; Long saw but one seal. Party generally are in poor spirits. Brainard was too much run down by previous work to enable him to go for shrimp this afternoon and his trip was taken by Frederick who got about 7 pounds. I am taking a grain of mild chloride of mercury a day. Suffering much pain and in consequence am depressed in spirits and physically very weak. My bowels seem to have completely lost their power. Private Henry took advantage of my illness and of others being down in their bags this morning to make some moonshine and drank extra alcohol to such an extent as to become helplessly drunk. His condition was discovered by Lieutenant Kislingbury who was next to him. The disgust of everyone at such baseness is excessive. Yesterday Long saw a dozen white whales, which were travelling from the north; unfortunately they did not come within shooting distance.

April 29: A fatal day for us. Jens and Long got away at 6:45 a.m. to go hunting. Jens appeared to be in particularly good humour, and for the first time in many weeks came and shook hands with me before he left, laughing pleasantly the while. At 2:30 p.m. Long returned and reported that Jens was drowned, losing the kayak and our only reliable rifle. Everyone grieves over the "little man's" death, not alone on account of the critical condition in which we are left as regards food, but on account of the strong affection we all had for his great heart, unvarying truthfulness and integrity. Jens Edward, though an Eskimo, was a man and a Christian of whom no evil word had ever been spoken, and on whom no shadow of fault rested in his three years' service with us.

THE FINAL DAYS

May opened dismally with a snow-storm. Brainard continued indefatigably his work of catching shrimps, of which he brought in 450 pounds from April 8th to 30th. On May 3rd, however, our last bread was gone, and but 9 days' meat remained, even at the small ration then issued.

The early days of May I was very ill and expected hourly to pass away. When I was in the worst condition, Whisler was detected by Bender and Henry with bacon from the storehouse. The three men were outside, and Whisler claimed that the door was forced by the others, and, he, passing by, saw the food and was too ravenous to resist. Bender and Henry said that Whisler forced the door open and they detected him. I was too sick to do much in the matter.

May 6: A violent storm commenced at 3 o'clock this morning and gradually abated, dying away at noon. Dr. Pavey made trouble today by false statements on three different points as regards his reports made daily to me in French, and an acid discussion followed. I ordered him four times to drop the matter, and finally told him were he not the doctor I would kill him. Private Bender attempted to defend the Doctor and, despite repeated orders, would not be quiet. A mutiny seemed imminent and I would have killed him could I have got Long's gun. Things have come to such a point that my orders, by these two men, are considered as binding or not at their pleasure. I fear for the future.

May 11: The temperature at 2:00 a.m. when Frederick returned from hunting was minus 4°, an extremely low one for this time of year. Frederick succeeded in killing a seal in a water pool, but, unfortunately, he sank instead of floating into the fast ice.

A couple of days earlier an ounce of Long's lunch was stolen. Extremity is demoralizing some of the party, but I have urged on them that we should die like men and not as brutes.

May 18: Very stormy last night. I heard a raven croaking this morning and called Long who succeeded in killing him. Gave Long the liver, and concluded to use the bird for shrimp bait, thinking we could obtain more from him that way than in eating him. A violent storm kept everybody in the hut today except Brainard who went for shrimp. Ellis very weak. Bender treated him brutally, so that even Henry rebuked him. I reprimanded Bender sharply for his lack of feeling, although he is probably somewhat insane and not entirely responsible.

May 19: Frederick going out to get ice to cook breakfast this morning returned immediately reporting that he saw a bear within a few yards of the house. Long and Frederick dressed for the hunt and started after him but returned about 10:30 having been unable even to get a shot at it. Their weakened condition was such that the bear easily outstripped them. Our agony of hope and fear while the hunters were absent cannot be adequately expressed by language. The last alcohol was issued today, except a few ounces for medicinal purposes which the Doctor will prescribe. Israel and Whisler have quite broken down, the whole party is in lower spirits than ever before. Private Ellis died at 10:15 a.m.

A saxifrage plant seen in blossom. We are now mixing saxifrage in our stews; fully 19/20 of it is the dead plant with but the faintest tinge of green at the ends. My appetite and health continue good. It is evident that I shall die as have the others of lack of food, which induces dropsy of the heart. Kislingbury and Ralston are very weak.

May 22: It is now 8 days since the last regular food was issued. It is astonishing to me how the party holds out. I have been obliged to feed Ralston for a couple of days past. About 2:00 p.m. he succeeded in eating a part of his dinner, but the rest he could not force down. When tea came I asked him if he wanted it, and he said yes. I raised him up but he became unconscious in my arms and was unable to drink it. The strength of the party has been devoted today to pitching the wall-tent some 300 yards southeast of the present hut on a level, gravelly spot in the sun's rays. The Doctor says that the party will all die in a few days unless we succeed in moving from this wretched hut. Melting snow rained down such a quantity of water upon us that we are saturated to the skin and are in a wretched condition.

Ralston died about 1:00 a.m. Israel left the bag before his death, but I remained beside him until driven out about 5:00 a.m., chilled through by contact with the dead. The weakest of the party moved to the tent upon the hill this afternoon.

May 24: The temperature reached 39° inside the tent this morning. Whisler was unconscious and died about noon.

The storm was so bad on the 26th that Brainard could not go shrimping. Owing to his failure to obtain shrimps, we had a stew last night and this morning of the sealskin thongs which had been used in lashing together the sledge. Israel is now in an exceedingly weak condition and unable to even sit up in his bag. He talks much of his home and younger days, and seems thoroughly reconciled to go. I gave him a spoonful of rum this morning, he begged for it so exceedingly hard. It was a great comfort and relief to him and I did by him as I should like to have been done by in such a time.

May 27: Long killed a dovekie which he could not get. Israel died very easily about 3 o'clock this morning. I gave him, yesterday evening, the last food he ate.

Very unpleasant scene occurred today. Dr. Pavey in the afternoon took all the remaining iron from the medicine chest. I ordered him to return it there, he having been accused to me by Steward Bierderbick, Sergeant Elison, and others of tripe de rochet and lichens and found them very nutritious; they certainly iron to the party as promised. There was a violent scene and Lieutenant Kislingbury, as usual, thought Dr. Pavey right.

Summer opened wretchedly with a howling gale and driving snow and a temperature near the freezing point. For a day and a-half an unbroken fast depleted our little strength. We were still 14 in number but it was evident that all must soon pass away unless our hunters were more fortunate, or relief came speedily. Everybody was wretched, not only from the lack of food but from the cold to which we are very sensitive. Lieutenant Kislingbury, who was exceedingly weak in the morning at breakfast, became unconscious at 9:00 a.m. and died at 3:00 p.m. The last thing he did was to sing the doxology and ask for water.

June 6: Fine, warm, clear day. Frederick detected Henry stealing shrimps out of the general mess pot when his back was turned. Later Henry made two trips to our old winter quarters, and when returning from the second trip, while passing me, I stopped him and questioned him as to what he had been doing, and what he had with him. After a while he admitted he had taken from there, contrary to positive orders, sealskin thongs and, further, that he had in a bundle concealed somewhere, sealskin. He was bold in his admissions and showed neither fear nor contrition. I ordered him shot, giving the order in writing.

Near Cape Sabine, June 6, 1884.

To: Sergeants Brainard, Long and Frederick;
Notwithstanding promises given by Private C. B. Henry yesterday, he has since, as acknowledged to me, tampered with seal thongs, if not other food at the old camp. This pertinacity and audacity is the destruction of this party, if not at once ended. Private Henry will be shot today, all care being taken to prevent his injuring anyone, as his physical strength is greater than that of any two men. Decide the manner of death by two balls and one blank cartridge. This order is imperative, and absolutely necessary for any chance of life.†

(Signed) A. W. Greely
1st Lieutenant, 5th Cavalry,
U.S.A. and Commanding L.F.B.
Expedition

About 2 o'clock shots were heard, and later the order was read to the general party. Everyone acknowledged without exception that Henry's fate was merited. On searching his bundles, very considerable quantities of sealskin were found, as well as a pair of my sealskin boots which I had loaned to Long a short time since, and which had been stolen from him two nights before. There was found in his pocket a valuable silver chronograph left by me with other scientific instruments at Fort Conger, and stolen by him on our departure. Fully twelve pounds of sealskin were found cached amongst his effects.

I learned this afternoon from Steward Bierderbick that Dr. Pavey, while at the medicine chest yesterday, took away the extract of ergot and has since drunk all in the bottle, about 3 ounces. Bierderbick says that after Dr. Pavey left the medicine chest he examined it to see what had been taken, but did not notice the absence of the ergot bottle as it was a medicine for which he had no use. Dr. Pavey is now, at 5:00 p.m., at the point of death, which has doubtless been

†*Private Henry's real crime was cannibalism, the horror of which nearly unhinged Greely, who could not bear to admit that such a thing could have taken place in the Army, and in a unit under his command. Neither then – in his orders to the sergeants – nor later, could he bring himself to admit that this most terrible of all degradations had come upon his expedition. He preferred, instead, to run the risk of public censure himself for having had a man shot on the flimsiest of excuses.*

hastened a day or two by this action on his part. Bender is also dying.

Later – Bender died at 5:45 p.m. very easily. I think his death was hastened by Henry's execution. Dr. Pavey died at 6:00 p.m. His death had evidently been hastened by the narcotics. There are now but 9 left. Long killed a dovekie which I ordered to be divided between the hunters and Frederick. Long saw many ducks today. Brainard was out nearly 7 hours and got less than 3 pounds of shrimp. We must begin to eat our sealskin clothing. Today I got a large quantity of tripe de roche† and lichens and found them very nutritious; they certainly are very palatable.

June 9: Calm, fair day. The party succeeded in getting the bodies of Dr. Pavey and Bender into the ice crack. We are all very weak. Connell shows signs of scurvy and bleeding gums, and Schneider in his swollen, stiff knees, while Gardner and Bierderbick are weaker. I was out on the rocks 50 yards distant for 6 hours, and got a quart of tripe de roche; and Bierderbick the same. Had nothing but tripe de roche, tea, and sealskin gloves for dinner. Without fresh bait we can do little in shrimping, and so live on lichens and moss alone.

June 10: Gardner is suffering very much. Long killed last night a Brant goose which he lost, and a dovekie. The dovekie went to the hunters today although there were some unpleasant remarks made about it. Very few shrimps were obtained. In the evening we had only a stew of tripe de roche which was gathered by Bierderbick. I was out nearly 5 hours until driven from the rocks thoroughly chilled. The stewed tripe de roche today was delicious. It leaves a sweetish taste in the mouth.

June 12: Long came in with no game and Brainard brought back the news that the floes at his shrimping grounds had broken up and been driven out by the late gale so that he had lost not only the shrimps but the net and the ropes. In consequence we had for breakfast only tea and such roasted sealskin as each one had left from the part issued a few days ago. The misfortunes of the day are very discouraging and affected the spirits and tempers of some of the party. Gardner died today of inflammation of the bowels and starvation. He was apparently dead at 11:00 a.m. and was removed from the tent, but, showing signs of life, was deposited on an old buffalo robe where he died about 5:00 p.m.

June 13: Formally discharged Bierderbick today, his term of service having expired. Having no proper blanks, I gave him a written certificate of discharge to be replaced by a regular one. Re-enlisted Bierderbick as a hospital steward of the 1st class, subject to approval.

June 16: It was too cold and cloudy in the forenoon to pick lichens. The party now eating oil-tanned skins, which is very repugnant to us. All are weaker and much discouraged. I do not know how we live except on our hopes and expectations of a ship. Schneider last evening begged for opium pills with which he could end his life, but found no one to help him to them. He was in better spirits this morning but had to be handled like a child this afternoon, being as helpless physically as Elison.

June 18: Schneider was very weak and out of his head in the morning and later became unconscious. He wandered a good deal but not unpleasantly, and died at 6:00 p.m. Brainard got no shrimp. I am afraid we'll have to give it up until we get birds or other bait. He is now collecting tripe de roche with all the rest of us.

June 20: Six years ago today I was married, and three years ago I left my wife for this expedition; what contrast! When will this life and death end? During this day the gale continued with unabated violence. Our tent gradually gave way inch by inch before the gale and all our efforts to straighten it or to improve

†*A lichen that grows upon rocks.*

it proved futile owing to our enfeebled condition. By evening the front portion of the tent rested on the ground pinning Brainard, Long and myself in our sleeping bags so we could hardly stir. At 8:30 a.m. it commenced snowing. Connell's legs paralyzed from knee down. Bierderbick suffering terribly from rheumatism. Buchanan Strait open this noon a long way up the coast.

With these words my Journal ends.

By the morning of the 22nd we were all exhausted, and it was only through the energy and devotion of Frederick or Brainard, I do not remember which, that we obtained about noon some water. That and a few square inches of soaked sealskin was all the nutriment which passed our lips for 42 hours prior to our rescue. Connell was very feeble and the end of all was approaching. I tried with indifferent success to read from my prayer book but the high wind and lack of food made it too exhausting.

Near midnight of the 22nd I heard the sound of a whistle. I could not distrust my ears, and yet I could hardly believe that ships would venture along that coast in such a gale. I feebly asked Brainard and Long if they had strength to get out, to which they answered, as always, that they would do their best. I directed one to return with the news if any vessel could be seen. Brainard came back in about 10 minutes from the brow of the hill, some 50 yards distant, reporting in a most discouraging tone that nothing was to be seen, and said that Long had gone over to set up the distress signal a short distance away, which had blown down. Brainard returned to his bag while a fruitless discussion sprang up as to the cause of the noise, wherein Bierderbick suggested that the vessel was in Payer Harbour, which I could not believe, as I thought the whistle must be from a ship running along the coast. We had resigned ourselves to despair, when suddenly strange voices were heard calling me; and in a frenzy of feeling as vehement as our enfeebled condition would permit, we realized that our country had not failed us, that the long agony was over, and the remnant of the Lady Franklin Bay expedition saved.

fm When the rescuers reached the tent they slit it open and met the cold gaze of a dead man. "Directly opposite, on his hands and knees was a dark man with a long, matted beard, in a dirty dressing gown with a little red skull cap on his head, and brilliant staring eyes. . . . He raised himself a little and put on a pair of eye-glasses.

" 'Who are you?' The man made no answer, staring vacantly. 'Who are you?' again.

"One of the men spoke up. 'That's the Major – Major Greely.'[†] Lieut. Colwell crawled in and took him by the hand, saying to him, 'Greely, is this you?'

" 'Yes,' said Greely in a faint, broken voice, hesitating and shuffling with his words, 'Yes – seven of us left – here we are – dying – like men. Did what I came to do – beat the best record.' Then he fell back exhausted."

Greely had beaten Markham by four miles, and he had paid a fearful price. There was payment yet to make. The savagely crippled Sergeant Elison died as the ships reached Godhavn on the way south; and Brainard and most of the others never fully recovered from their ordeal.

The rescue was accomplished by two Newfoundland sealers, *Thetis* and *Bear*, bought by the United States Government. They went north with the Scots whaling fleet in early spring, 1883. Commander Schley, in charge of the two ships, gives scant notice to the assistance of the whalers, but Greely is more generous.

"No relief vessels ever ventured, at so early a date, the dangers of Melville

†He had been promoted during his absence.

Bay . . . and the perils of that ice which is never entered except by the hardiest and most fearless navigators of the present day – the Scotch whalers. I may be pardoned for differing from my friend and rescuer, Captain Schley, in believing that the remnant of the expedition owes much to the influence of those bold navigators. Not only did the Scotch whalers set forth on their voyage many days earlier than usual, but with their usual skill and energy improved every opportunity and, by their numbers, searched out the only available passage. . . . Had the whalers delayed their voyage, or had they looked unkindly on the work, the relief squadron must have missed some of their opportunities and . . . reached Sabine days later, which meant the extermination of the party." □ FM

CHAPTER 6 THE INLAND ICE

The macabre fate of DeLong's and Greely's expeditions cooled the polar passion so thoroughly that for more than a decade nobody else took up the challenge. Nevertheless the Arctic itself still retained its old allure and, if the North Pole seemed temporarily out of reach, there remained other goals. There was, in particular, the mysterious world of the Greenland Icecap.

By far the largest glacier in the world, this remnant of the Ice Age broods over Greenland like a titanic white beast. It is so massive that its weight has depressed central Greenland until parts of it are actually below sea-level. Thus the great island has become a mountain-rimmed bowl, its centre mounded high with ice, which in places is two miles thick.

Prior to the late nineteenth century nothing whatever was known about the real nature of the Inland Ice, or about the interior regions of Greenland. It was then, and still remains, singularly difficult to approach, for its edges are guarded first by ramparts of rugged mountains and then by steep glacial slopes so criss-crossed with almost bottomless crevasses as to turn them into death traps for those who venture on them. This much was known for a long time before the mystery of what lay beyond those coastal slopes was solved.

The problem was first seriously attacked by a Dane named Henry Rink who was a government official in south Greenland between 1853 and 1869. Rink studied the edges of the Inland Ice but could not gain the interior. In 1878 Lieut. Jensen of the Danish Army broke through the outer defences and, after suffering agonies from snow-blindness and exposure, reached some nunataks (isolated mountain peaks thrusting up through the ice) about forty-five miles in from the west coast. Then, in 1883, the great Swedish explorer, Nordenskiöld, grew interested. He believed that the ice formed a rim *within* the mountain rim, and that the centre of Greenland was a vast and ice-free valley. After eighteen days of struggling to gain the gale-swept, snow-whipped, frigid heights, Norden-skiöld's party had advanced seventy-three miles and was at the end of its tether. However, there were two Lapps in the expedition, both expert skiers, and they were sent on to make a fast reconnaissance to the "central valley." The Lapps may have gone as much as a hundred miles farther before returning to announce that they had found nothing but ice, which still sloped slowly but steadily upward.

Nordenskiöld's return to Sweden coincided with a wave of general revulsion against polar expeditions, growing out of the horrors of the DeLong-Greely debacles. The Greenland Icecap had emerged into public view at just the right time to give would-be arctic venturers a substitute objective. As a consequence, the story of the exploration of the Inland Ice bears an integral relationship to the polar story. Three of the men who went to the Icecap in the 1880s later competed with each other for that final prize – the Pole itself. They were Fridtjof Nansen, Frederick Cook and Robert Peary. All three served their arctic apprenticeship in the attempt to solve the mysteries of the Inland Ice.

Fired by Nordenskiöld's account, Peary made an attempt on the Inland Ice from Disco in 1884. This was his first northern venture, and was a failure. It seems to have temporarily dampened his interest in the Arctic before it had really begun to develop, and Peary retreated south.

Meantime a young Norwegian, Fridtjof Nansen, had also read about the Nordenskiöld expedition, and had been mulling the matter over in his mind.

Fridtjof Nansen was only 27 when he crossed Greenland on skis. Later in the Fram, he drifted across the Pole.

In the summer of 1882 I was on board the *Viking*, a Norwegian sealer, caught in the ice off the east coast of Greenland in an area still unexplored. For more than three weeks we were absolutely fixed and every day, to the terror of the crew, we drifted nearer to a rocky coast. Many times a day from the main top my glasses were turned westward, and it is not to be wondered at that a young man's fancy was drawn irresistibly to the charms and mysteries of this unknown world of eastern Greenland. I pondered plans for reaching this coast which so many had sought in vain, and I came to the conclusion that it must be possible to reach it, if not by forcing a ship through the ice, which was the method tried hitherto, then by crossing the floes on foot and dragging one's boat with one.†

One autumn evening in 1883 I was sitting listening indifferently as the day's paper was being read aloud. Suddenly my attention was roused by a telegram telling me that Nordenskiöld had come back safe from his expedition to the interior of Greenland (from the west) on which his Lapps were said to have covered an extraordinarily long distance on ski in an astonishingly short time. The idea flashed upon me at once of an expedition crossing Greenland on ski from coast to coast.

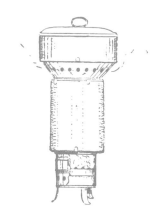

The cooker used by Nansen's party.

My notion was that if a party of good skiers were equipped in a practical and sensible way they must get across Greenland if they began from the east side, this latter point being of extreme importance. If they were to start, as all other expeditions have done, from the west side, they were practically certain never to get across. They would have all the fleshpots of Egypt behind them and in front the unexplored desert of ice, and the east coast, which is little better. Furthermore if they did get across, they would have the same journey back again in order to reach home. So it struck me that the only sure road to success was to force a passage through the floe-belt ice, land on the desolate and ice-bound east coast, and thence cross over to the inhabited west coast. In this way one would burn all one's ships behind one, there would be no need to urge one's men on as the east coast would attract no one back, while in front would lie the west coast with all the allurements and amenities of civilization. There was no choice of routes, "forward" being the only word. The order would be: "death or the west coast of Greenland."

I applied to the government for assistance but they answered they could not see their way to give the scheme any support, and one of the newspapers even went so far as to maintain that there could be no conceivable reason why the Norwegian people should pay five thousand kronen in order to give a private individual a holiday trip to Greenland. Most people who heard of the scheme considered it simple madness, asking what was to be got in the interior of Greenland, and were convinced that I was either not quite right in the head or was simply tired of life.

In spite of warning voices and in spite of the general opinion that the whole scheme was simple madness there were, nevertheless, plenty of men who wished to join me. Finally I chose three Norwegians: Otto Sverdrup; Oluf Dietrichson, and Kristian Trana. I also took two mountain-Lapps, Samuel Balto and Ole Ravna.

I proposed to reach the east coast of Greenland by getting a Norwegian sealer to pick us up in Iceland and take us on farther. My agreement with the captain of the *Jason*, Mauritz Jacobsen, a cool-headed and experienced arctic skipper, was that on his way to Denmark Strait, after the season was over in the Jan Mayen waters, he should call for us in Iceland about the beginning of June.

†*Up to this date the east coast of Greenland north of Angmagssalik was almost unknown because explorers had been unable to penetrate through the east Greenland pack ice. This ice flowing south on the east Greenland current formed an almost impenetrable barrier cutting off the land from the sea.*

On June 3rd we met Captain Jacobsen in Iceland and lost no time in getting ready. There was no lack of willing hands to bring our goods on board. Amid general interest a little pony of ours was led onto the landing stage. He did all he could to resist, poor little fellow, and almost had to be carried. Had he but known the sad fate in store for him I scarcely think we should have got him on board at all.

When all was done and we had said farewell we steamed out of the fiord and to sea northward. The very next day, June 5th, 1888, we reached the ice, which this year had come a long way south. Borne on the polar current, the ice is carried southward along the east coast of Greenland. Here it meets the swells of the sea and the larger solid masses are broken into smaller and smaller floes as they come farther south. By the pressure of waves and packing the floes are sometimes piled one upon another and then form hummocks or crags of ice which may often rise twenty or thirty feet above the water. It is this broken and scattered polar ice which the sealer meets in Denmark Strait, and it is amongst these floes, which can indeed be dangerous obstacles, that he forces his way.

On Thursday June 7th we got into a tongue of open ice and saw here and there seals upon the floes. There is life on board the *Jason* at once. Visions of a real handsome catch, as in old Greenland days, arise in the lively imagination of many a sealer. The men are all deeply interested in the success of the vessel as their earnings are dependent thereon.

We saw more seals and the boats of one watch were sent out. We soon heard reports on various sides of us but only a shot now and again – no lively firing. In the afternoon when this detachment returned we found they had got 187 seals altogether that day, which is no great bag.

That day too we saw several sealers in the ice to the west of us and the next day had a talk with some of them. They all wanted to talk with the *Jason*, which had the Greenland expedition on board. The postal system of the arctic sea is managed in a somewhat remarkable way. If any of the vessels touch at Iceland they carry off the post for the rest of the fleet. The reader will perhaps think it is doubtful that one vessel would find the others in these parts but it is not really so. The sealing grounds are not so extensive. The sealers like to keep close together and none will separate any distance from the rest for fear the others may come in for a haul while he is away.

Late in the afternoon we passed the *Geysir* of Tonsberg. The captain came on board and had supper with us. He was in such high spirits that none of us had the heart to tell him that he had lost three of his children of diphtheria since he sailed from home. Captain Jacobsen had been told it in a letter which he got in Iceland but the father had heard nothing of it, nor did he learn it from us. One's joys and sorrows are bound up in the seal and sealing, and the whole of Europe might well collapse without the knowledge or regard of this section of its population.

On June 11th we got a sight of land, the first alluring sight of the east coast of Greenland. We see high jagged mountain tops. We are not so far away as we expected, perhaps rather more than sixty miles.

We find a narrow inlet cutting deep into the ice. We have the wind in our favour and make our way in quickly. We soon find the way blocked, but a sealer does not lose heart at such trifles. We force a passage, and the floes have to give way before the stout bows of the *Jason*. Then we get into a large open pool with no ice in sight between us and land. This looks promising. But after steaming inward for another couple of hours at good speed we again sight ice right in front of us. We are now forty miles from land and, as the ice ahead is heavily packed and rough, it scarcely seems advisable to try to land now.

The next few days we beat up to the northeast along the edge of the ice, but make little way, as the wind is strong against us and the current carries us back.

The seal season begins in June, at which time the sealers arrive in Denmark Strait. While the vessel is being driven with all the speed she can bear onwards amongst the floes, the crew begin to suspect that seal have been sighted and there is life on board. The men gather in the bows and along the ship's sides. All hands are set to work to get the boats ready. Every detail is seen to, the skinning knives have their last edge put on, then up the men go on deck to have another look forward. Meanwhile the captain sits in the crow's-nest feasting his eyes on the crowds of seal ahead and laying his plan of campaign while directing the vessel's course. It is an exciting time.

By this time after several hours steaming through the ice the ship is well amongst the seal, which are lying on all sides about her. But still she pushes on until she is in the very middle of them, and the final order for the hunt is given. At once all hands drop into the boats which are hanging clear in their davits over both sides of the ship. Then the shooters – there is only one in each boat crew, and he takes command – receive their orders from the captain and the boats are lowered away.

When the seals are reached the fusillade begins. If the day be fine and sunny and there are plenty. of seal around there is a fascination about the scene which will never cease to charm the mind of one who has been present at it. If there are many seals on the same floe a large number may be shot then and there. But the chief point is to hit the first ones so as to kill them on the instant. If this is done one can proceed at one's leisure. When I was out in 1882 I remember shooting my whole boat's load on the same spot, and could have multiplied the number again and again if I had been able to go on shooting. For when one is well in amongst the seal, and has the dead bodies of those one has shot lying around on all sides, the others lie quietly gazing at their dead comrades who they still think to be alive.

As soon as the seal are shot they are skinned. Only the skin and the thick layer of blubber which lies between it and the flesh are taken, the rest of the animal being left on the ice as food for the sea birds.

The capture of the bladder-nose seal in Denmark Strait is not an industry of long standing. It was inaugurated by the Norwegians in 1876 and their example was followed by a few English and American vessels. For the first eight years the venture was an unprecedented success. During this period something like five hundred thousand were captured and it is possible that quite as many were killed and lost. After these years of plenty came a change and ever since, the pursuit has been practically a failure, all the vessels alike being equally unsuccessful. Here on the very same grounds where in 1882 I saw seal on all sides as soon as we had pushed a little way into the ice, and where I helped to shoot them down by thousands, there was now scarcely a sign of life to be seen.

So tame and confiding had the seals been during the first few years that it was not necessary to shoot them. They were simply knocked upon the head where they lay, and some captains did not even allow their men to take rifles in the boats with them. The bladder-nose had not yet learned the danger threatened by vessels with their crow's-nest on the main top and swarms of boats. The most remarkable thing was that it was not only the old seals that grew shy, but the youngest animals were now astonishingly wary. The parents must have imparted their experience to their offspring.

On July 11th the ice was moving violently, as we had come into one of the

Since earliest times, artists have been
fascinated by the spectacle of the "Midnight
Sun." At the North Pole, the sun never sets
between March 21 and September 23, appearing to
travel in a circular path above the horizon.

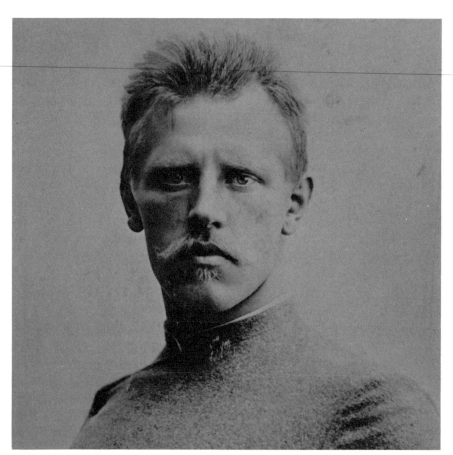

The hero as a young man: When
Nansen set out he was asked why should
Norway pay for his "holiday trip."

The hero as a statesman: In later
life Nansen was an ambassador and
especially concerned with refugees.

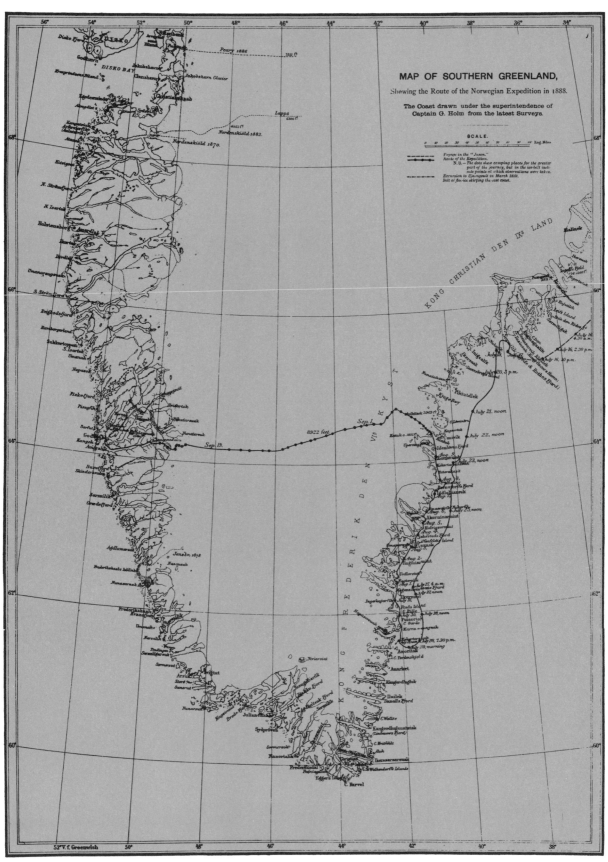

MAP OF SOUTHERN GREENLAND,

Shewing the Route of the Norwegian Expedition in 1888.

The Coast drawn under the superintendence of
Captain G. Holm from the latest Surveys.

SCALE.

Dotted line indicates Nansen's path across the icy middle of Greenland.
The actual journey took 41 days. The party crossed or skirted many
crevasses of "depths unfathomable."

stronger currents. As two or three of us were sitting in the mess room the *Jason* was struck so heavily by a floe on the bows that she was literally driven back. We rushed out and saw another big floe advancing with great speed upon her quarter. The shock comes, the whole vessel quivers and heels over, we hear a crash and the rudder is gone, but luckily the damage is no worse. Had the floe struck us full in the side there is no telling what might have happened as it would have then found the sealer's weakest point.

The next day we spent fixing a spare rudder which these vessels always carry, and we were soon as seaworthy as before. But the summer was now so far advanced that there was little prospect of getting more seals. So on July 13th it was resolved, to the satisfaction of us all, to leave the ice and make way westward for Greenland.

Our baggage is brought up upon deck, all preparations are made for our departure. Towards dinner time I hear the magic word "land" from the deck. I rush up and a glorious sight meets my eyes. Right before me through a veil of mist lies the sunlit shores of Greenland, a glorious array of peaks which lie to the north of Cape Dan.

We were probably about thirty-five miles from land and it looked as if we could get right into shore. But as we get nearer we find there is more ice than we expect. On our way south we passed several enormous icebergs. We could make no attempt to land that day nor on the next. There was too much ice.

When I came on deck on the morning of the 17th I saw that the landing must be attempted that day. The mountains lay enticingly before us. Further west we could see the "Inland Ice," the goal of our aspiration, stretching inward in a white undulating plain.

We had brought one boat with us. But as this would have been too heavily laden with the voluminous equipment of the expedition I accepted the Captain's kind offer of one of the *Jason's* smaller sealing boats. We had the two lowered and brought alongside. Sermilikfjord lies straight west of us about nine miles. I go up to the masthead to see where the ice looks easiest to what will be our best course. The hour of departure is at hand.

As the boats rush through the dark water before the first vigorous strokes the air rings with three lusty cheers. At first we advanced quickly. The ice was mostly open but there were a few places where we had to drag our boats over the ice. The ice now grew more difficult and we had often to mount a hummock to look out the best way. From the top of one of these I waved a last farewell to the *Jason* with our flag, which she answered by dipping hers.

Shortly afterwards we drift suddenly into a tearing millrace which is driving the floes pell mell, jamming them together and piling them one upon another. Both our boats are in danger of destruction. By our united efforts we reach a large open pool in the lee of an iceberg and are for the time secure.

We now find a many good lanes of open water; the ice jams only once or twice. Our prospects are good and our hearts are light. Long stretches of water lie in front and I fancy I can see the open water beyond the ice. It does not seem possible that anything can stop us landing and we are self-confident. Just at this moment a sharp edge of ice cuts through a plank on one boat's side. She would no longer float and there was nothing to be done but unload her and put her on the floe for repairs. While we were at work the ice packed, the clouds gathered, and rain began to pour in torrents. The only thing to be done was to get up our tent and wait.

Before we turned in we caught sight of the *Jason* far away. She was getting up full steam and a while later disappeared in the distance no doubt comfortably believing that we were safe on shore. When Ravna, the Lapp, saw the ship for the last time he said: "what fools we were to leave her to die in this place."

We were now in a fatal current. With irresistible force it first carried us westward into the broader belt of ice and then took a more southerly direction and bore us straight away from shore at a pace that rendered all resistance futile. That a current existed was well known, but I had no suspicion of its real strength. Now it was our fate to see how well we might manage.

For the first time we can now hear clearly the sound of breakers on the edge of the ice towards the sea, but pay no particular attention to that fact. We seem to be drifting straight away from land and the tops of the mountains gradually diminish. Next morning, July 20th, I was roused by violent shocks to the floe on which we were camped and thought the motion of the sea must have increased. When we got outside we discovered the floe had split in two not far from the tent. The Lapps now shout that they can see the open ocean.

We load our sledges and try to drag them inward toward land, but soon see that the pace we are drifting at is too much for us. We begin to look around for a safer floe to pitch our camp on, as our present one seems somewhat shaky. Meanwhile the breakers seem to be drawing nearer, their roar grows louder, the swell comes rolling in washes over the ice all around us and the situation promises before long to be critical.

Poor Lapps! They are not in the best of spirits. They go through their dinner in perfect silence, but the rest of us talk and joke as usual, the violent rolls of our floe giving rise to witticisms. As far as the Lapps were concerned, however, these jests fell on anything but good ground. They plainly thought that this was not the proper time and place for such frivolity.

We have scarcely half a mile left now and none of us have any doubt that before another couple of hours we shall find ourselves rocking on the open sea, making our way along the ice southwards, or sinking to the bottom.

If we are going to sea we shall need all our strength in case we have to row for days in order to keep clear of the ice, so all hands are ordered to bed in the tent which is the only thing we have not yet packed into the boats. Sverdrup, as the most experienced and cool-headed amongst us, is to take the first watch and turn us out at the critical moment.

After sleeping for a while I am wakened by the sound of water rushing close by my head outside the wall of the tent. I feel the floe rocking up and down like a ship in a heavy sea. I could distinctly hear Sverdrup's familiar steady tread up and down the floe between the tent and the boats. I remember no more as I dozed off to sleep again. I did not wake again until it was full morning. Then I started up in astonishment for I could hear nothing of the breakers but a distant thunder. When I got outside the tent I saw that we were a long way from the open sea. Our floe, however, was a sight to remember. Fragments of ice, big and little, had been thrown upon it by the waves till they formed a rampart all around us. The ridge on which our tent and one of the boats stood was the only part that the sea had not washed.

Sverdrup now told us that several times he stood by the tent door prepared to turn us out. We were then right out on the extreme edge of the ice. The surf was washing us on all sides, but the rampart that had been thrown up did us good service. Then matters got still worse. Sverdrup undid some of the hooks on the tent. Just as things looked worse and our floe's turn came to ride out into the middle of the breakers, she suddenly turned her course, and with astonishing speed we were once more sailing in towards the land.

Items of an Eskimo wardrobe.

July 22nd: In the night a fog comes on and hides everything from us. We cannot tell which way we are drifting but the breakers sound no less distinct than they have been. In the afternoon it clears and we seem to be possibly a little nearer to land. We see a number of big seals lying on the floes around us. We could easily shoot them but as we do not want them now we leave them in peace. We have enough fresh meat as yet, a big haunch of our little horse which we brought off the *Jason.* Through the afternoon the ice remains packed.

July 25th: No change, except that we are nearer the edge of the ice and the open sea. We are drifting southward along the coast apparently at great speed. We have to encourage the two Lapps, who seem to lose their spirits more and more, because they think we shall end by being driven out into the Atlantic. We agree that in any case we shall be able to manage a landing at Cape Farewell.

We are now just off the mountains of Tingmiarmiut. Along the whole of this magnificent coast of East Greenland one group of wild alpine peaks exceeds the other, each more beautiful than the last. Really it is not so bad after all to lie drifting here on the ice. We see more of the coast and more of the beauties of nature than we should have otherwise.

July 28th: Yesterday we did nothing and the same is the case today. Our fear of being driven out into the breakers was by no means groundless. Yesterday we were less than half a mile, and yet we almost wished to go, as by putting out to sea we should bring this life in the ice to an end. However we were not to go to sea after all. We began to move inward in a field of floes extending away to the south. The icebelt here is very narrow and we found that we were not more than eighteen miles from land.

In the morning I happened to be lying awake watching Ravna's bearded little face as it peeped through the opening into the tent. It struck me that there was a peculiar, uneasy expression in his face which was not familiar. So I said at last: "Well, Ravna, can you see land?" And he answered eagerly in his queer, naïve way: "Yes, yes, land too near."

I jumped out of the bag and saw land much nearer than we had ever had it before. Ravna was indeed right. I turned the others out and it was not long before we dressed and breakfasted. The boats were launched and loaded and we were soon ready. It is strange how quickly one's fate changes. It was quite plain that we should now soon be on shore, and, had this been told us yesterday, not one of us would have allowed the possibility of such a thing.

We started off and pushed quickly landward. The water was open enough for us to row pretty well the whole way, there being only two or three places where we had to force a passage. We felt as if we had escaped from a long and weary imprisonment and now all at once saw a bright and hopeful future lying before us.

At last our boats glided under a steep cliff, the dark wall of which was mirrored in the bright water. Beyond the cliff we found a harbour. We scrambled out, each striving to get first to land and feel real rocks and stones under his feet. The two Lapps went straight up the mountainside, and for a long while we saw nothing more of them.

After a grand dinner we embarked again and started to try to make our way back towards the north along the coast. The whole night we worked north through loose ice. We passed Cape Rantzau and reached Cape Adelaer where things were bad even to despair. The floes lay jammed together against the shore huge and unwieldy and refusing to move. Floe by floe we inch our way on to the next floe where the same performance is repeated. Sverdrup's boat, which followed mine, was nipped between the floes till her sides writhed and bulged under the pressure; but her material was elastic and she was brought through without real mishap.

My diary of the next day records the occurrences thus:

"Yesterday, July 30th about noon, we put into Cape Garde. While we were having dinner I heard amidst the screams of the gulls a cry of a different kind. Just as we were finishing our meal there came a shout so distinct and close that we sprang to our feet. Balto soon had the glass upon two black objects moving amongst the floes. At last they came straight toward us and I could see the paddles going like windmills – it is evidently two small men in kayaks. When they came close our first impression was distinctly favourable. We saw two somewhat wild but friendly faces smiling at us. One of the men was dressed in a jacket as well as breeches of sealskin. The other had, to our surprise, some garments of European origin. We gave them each a bit of biscuit, at which they simply beamed with pleasure. Then with expressive gestures telling us it was too cold to stand about there on the rocks, they prepared to go down to their canoes again. By signs they asked whether we were coming northward, and as we answered yes, they warned us against the perils of Puisortok Glacier. We had never expected to fall in with people here, where according to previous travellers' experience the coast was uninhabited.

Snow goggles used by Nansen.

We were soon afloat and steering northward for the dreaded glacier. I was in constant fear that things would be worse farther on and lost no time. But the ice up here consisted chiefly of glacier floes which are much better to deal with than sea floes since boats are not cut by their sharp edges. Without meeting serious obstacles we passed the glacier, sometimes rowing right under the perpendicular cliffs of ice. Earlier writers record the excessive dread which Eskimos have for this dangerous glacier, which is always ready to fall upon and crush the passer-by and far away from which, out at sea, huge masses of ice may suddenly dart up from the depths and annihilate both boat and crew. The name Puisortok means "the place where something shoots up." The Eskimos dread any passage by glaciers of this kind which are continually calving, or dropping masses of ice from their upper parts, and the danger to passing craft is by no means imaginary.

As we drew near Cape Bille we discovered a number of skin tents perched amongst the rocks and at the same time became aware of a noteworthy smell of oil which followed the offshore breeze. At the moment we turned our boat towards shore groups of human beings began to shriek and yell pointing and rushing down to the shore. Their faces, one and all, simply beamed with smiles. All about the ledges of rock stood long rows of strangely wild and shaggy looking creatures – men, women, and children, all in scanty dress.

As we stopped in front of the largest tent we were invited in by signs. The sight and smell was, to put it mildly, unusual. My attention was first arrested by the number of naked forms in standing, sitting, and reclining positions. All the occupants were attired in their so-called "natit" or indoor dress, the dimensions of which are so extremely small as to make them practically invisible to the stranger's inexperienced eye. The dress consists of a narrow band about the loins, which in the case of the women is reduced to the smallest possible dimensions.

Of false modesty, of course, there was no sign, but the unaffected ingenuousness with which all intercourse was carried on made a very strange impression upon us Europeans. Blushes rose to the checks of some amongst us when we saw a party of young men and women who followed us into the tent at once proceed to attire themselves in their indoor dress. The Lapps especially were much embarrassed at the unwonted sight. This particular tent housed four or five different families. Each of them had its own partition marked off upon the common couch, and in each of the stalls so formed man, wife and children would be closely packed, a four-foot space thus having sometimes to accommodate husband, two wives, and six or more children.

They began to explain to us the mutual relations of the occupants of the tent. A man embraced a fat woman, and thereupon the pair with extreme complacency pointed to some younger individuals, giving us to understand that the party together formed a family of husband, wife, and children. The man then proceeded to stroke his wife down the back and pinch her here and there to show us how charming and delightful she was and how fond he was of her, the process giving her, at the same time, evident satisfaction.

They were all friendliness and hospitality. The hospitality, indeed, of this desolate coast is quite unbounded. The man will receive his worst enemy, treat him well and entertain him for months if circumstances throw him in the way. The nature of their surroundings and the wandering life they lead force them to offer and accept universal hospitality.

When the time of our departure drew near a man came up and asked whether we were going northward. When we said yes his face brightened and it proved that he was bound in the same direction with his party. The camp was now a scene of lively confusion while we and the Eskimo vied with one another in our haste. The great skin tents were soon down and packed away in oomiacks [skin boats]. The oomiacks preceded us as did a company of kayakers. But one kayaker remained behind, no doubt wishing to show us the civility of escorting us.

fm From this point until August 10 Nansen and his party travelled north up the Greenland coast rowing or sailing as opportunity offered. Having met several other groups of Eskimos and having finally got clear of the shore ice, they pitched their camp on August 10 at what was to prove their last camping place on the east coast of Greenland. □ FM

On August 11th, from our tent, we could see blue sea stretching away to the horizon. To the east of us or in front of us was a huge conical mass of Kiatak mountain stretching from the blue sea at its foot to the pale August sky above. Beyond this and to the north lay the white snowfields of the Inland Ice which grew bluer and bluer and more and more scarred as it fell into the sea, ending in lofty cliffs of seamed and fissured ice.

Most of the party are at work scraping the rust off the sledge runners and off the steel-shod skis. In their present state, after the ravages of salt water and damp, they are all absolutely useless. Sverdrup and I are about to set out on our first journey on the Greenland ice. We must discover if an ascent is possible here, and which will be the best course to take. We are consumed with impatience for the first sight of this undiscovered country in which the human foot has as yet never trodden.

With our glacier rope and ice axes we start up the mountainside on which our tent stands. We are soon at the head of it and could now see that the country beyond was not so level as it had looked from the sea. The whole surface was seamed with numerous crevasses on every side. These were especially plentiful in the two streams of ice that lay on either side of us. At first it was hard and rough, with a rugged surface which crunched beneath our feet. Then we reached softer and wetter snow in which we sank. It was not long before we came to crevasses. They grew broader and opened a view to depths unfathomable. They were not to be jumped and we must needs skirt them either to the right or to

This portrait of Nansen was drawn
by Eric Werenskiold as the explorer
neared the peak of his fame. In 1895
Nansen (with F. H. Johansen) reached
86° 14′, the farthest north at that
time, and wrote a book about it.

Nansen's camp on the east coast of
Greenland. They left their boats
when they set out across the ice.

The Greenland coast was still
swarming with seal in the 1880s. The
drawings on this page are by Nansen.

A walrus is flayed on the ice.
Introduction of firearms into the
Arctic was disastrous for this animal.

When a bear attacked his colleague
Johansen, Nansen just managed
to reach his shotgun in time.

the left. Often, too, we crossed them on snow bridges or narrow strips of ice. As long as the covering layer of snow was thin, there was no danger, as we could see when we had firm ground beneath us. As we went farther the snow got deeper. Neither of us had any bad falls although it was nasty now and again when one or other sank to the armpits and felt his legs dangling in space. This was a performance of which we soon got tired. We doubled our efforts and determined not to be beaten. At last, after we had thought again and again that we were at the top and found the ground still rising in front of us, we reached the top of the long-sought ice ridge. A great white snowfield lies before us in all its majesty. The whole surface seems smooth and crevasseless right to the horizon. This we had expected, but we had not expected the number of "nunataks," or peaks, small and large, which protuded from the great field of snow for a long distance inland. We reckoned the distance to the farthest of them to be twenty-five or thirty miles. The gradient was even and slight as far as we could see but the going was anything but good as we had already learnt. It was five o'clock in the morning before we got back to our camp, well satisfied with our first excursion on the much discussed and much dreaded Inland Ice.

We spent the next day or two overhauling and rearranging our equipment. On the morning of the 15th the boats were hauled up to their last resting place. It is quite possible that the Eskimos have already found them. If this be so it is not easy to imagine what kind of supernatural beings they must take us for, who have thus abandoned our valuable possessions and so mysteriously disappeared. On a small piece of paper I wrote a short account of the expedition so far.

At first our progress was slow. The snow came nearly down to the sea so we could begin hauling at once but the gradient was steep and we had to put three men to each sledge. Our loads were heavy, each sledge weighing something more than 200 pounds.

After our first stage of some two or three miles we pitched our tent at a height of about 500 feet. The evening of the next day we continued on, travelling in darkness in order to get the benefit of colder snow. We crossed ice of the same rough kind. Towards morning it began to rain and things grew worse and worse and existence to us less joyous. Crevasses were plentiful so we had to go warily. We could not rope together, as that made the hauling work too difficult. If one went through the snow bridges which crossed the fissures one was left hanging securely [by the hauling line] as long as the sledge did not follow.

For three whole days, from noon August 17th to the morning of August 20th, we were confined to the tent by a violent storm and uninterrupted rain. The whole time we only left our sleeping bags for the purpose of getting food or for other small errands. Rations were reduced to a minimum, the idea being that as there was no work to do there was not much need for food.

On the morning of August 20th the weather had so far improved that we could resume our journey. The ice was still much fissured and as we were about to ascend a ridge which lay in front of us we found the crevasses so numerous and formidable that there was no possibility of passing them. Here they ran not only parallel but also across each other, a combination before which one is completely powerless. We had to turn back and try to move to the north, and sitting on the sledges we slid down the slope again between the crevasses.

Next morning, August 21st, we turned out at 4:00 a.m. The crust on the snow was now sufficiently hard to bear us. The gradient was still steep and the crevasses large and numerous, but we pushed on fast and without mishap in the most glorious weather, until well in the morning when the blazing sun began to make the snow softer and softer. This work under such conditions is terribly exhausting, and we suffered from an unquenchable thirst. We had already passed the limit of thawed water and were destined to find no more till we reached the west side. All we get is what we can melt by the warmth of our own bodies in tin flasks which we carry inside our clothes next to the skin.

About eleven we reached the top of a ridge which we had set as our goal for the day's march, a distance of some three or four miles. Beyond, the ice sloped gently inward and was free from crevasses. So we thought we must have already overcome the first difficulty of our ascent.

At two o'clock in the morning of August 22nd we went on again. There had been nine degrees of frost in the night and the snow was as hard as iron, but by nine o'clock the sun had such power that we were obliged to halt after having again accomplished a stage of three or four miles. We presently reached a steep incline and our work was worse than ever. We had to put several men to each sledge, but even then the labour was cruelly exhausting. Consequently our astonishment and joy knew no bounds when we had climbed some hundreds feet higher and suddenly found the surface stretching flat in front of us as far as we could see in the moonlight, and the snow as hard and level as the ice on a frozen lake. About eleven o'clock we stopped and pitched our tent having done a stage of nine or ten miles. At half-past six the next morning we were on the move again. As we advanced things altered for the worse and the icy surface was covered with a coat of freshly-fallen snow.

We had already begun to see that we should have more frost at night than we cared about, for on the dusty new snow and in the fifteen degrees of frost we now had, the steel runners of the sledge did not go better than upon sand. Seeing the folly of now doing our work in the night instead of daytime we halted until ten o'clock.

We were speculating on whether it was advisable to lighten our load by abandoning things. The first things to sacrifice were the oilcloth covers of our sleeping bags as now that we had advanced so far there was no moisture to be afraid of. It would have been too stupid to leave them behind. Oilcloth was combustible. Using the oilcloth we now managed to get so much snow melted that over and above a good supply of hot soup, we were able for once to get thoroughly the better of our thirst. This was the last really satisfying drink we had before we found water on the other side. Our small supply of fuel would not allow us any indulgence in this way.

We had reached the height of some six thousand feet above the sea when we were halted [by a storm] on the evening of August 26th. We had soon learned to take measures against storms and the penetrating, dust-like snow. We dug a hole which gave us a bank on the weather side and we furthermore turned one of the sledges over and covered it with tarpaulins. We thus had fairly good shelter and were in excellent spirits as we sat around the singing tea kettle and lamp.

There was no abatement in the wind when we woke next morning. I was by this time tired of plodding along against the wind in this deep loose snow and resolved this morning to rig the sledges and try a sail.

We soon found there was no question of tacking up against the wind. But I had not really been very hopeful on this score and had, as a matter of fact, other ends in view. I now saw plainly that with this heavy going and the persistent foul wind there was no chance of reaching our original destination of Kristianshaab by the middle of September when the last ship for Copenhagen would sail and with it vanish our last chance of getting home this year. I argued

Nansen's ski party on the march.
His main colleague was Otto Sverdrup
· later to win renown of his own.

Deep snow made progress arduous.
The party climbed to 7,930 feet before
descending towards Davis Strait.

that we would have a better chance of catching the last boat if we made for one of the southern ports, for preference Godthaab. The rest of the party hailed my change of plan with acclamation. They seemed to have already had more than enough of the island ice, were longing for kindlier scenes. So the sails were hoisted and about three in the afternoon we got under way, keeping as well up to the wind as we could.

For the next two days the weather remained unchanged; there was the same storm and driving snow. At night I often feared the tent would be torn to pieces. In the morning when we proposed to start, the sledges had to be dug out of the drifts and unloaded. When we at last managed to get under way it was a case of tramping the whole day in the deep snow – a heavy and exhausting business.

On the afternoon of August 29th the wind so far dropped out that it no longer paid to sail, and we therefore unrigged our vessels and set to work in the old way, taking a course straight for Godthaab. This day the snow was so loose and deep that Sverdrup and I took to the Canadian snowshoes. They caused us a good deal of trouble at first as we had no practice with them previously. When we grew accustomed to them we found them of great practical use. They bore us up well in the snow and gave us good and firm foothold and we regretted that we had not taken to them before.

All this time, or for more than three weeks on the whole, our life was inordinately monotonous with not a trace of any important occurrence. About ten in the morning of August 31st we saw land for the last time. We were upon the crest of one of the great waves or gentle undulations in the ice surface and had our final glimpse of a little point of rock which protruded from the snow.

At the end of August we were still ascending. We were always hoping to reach the uppermost plateau, and that the ascent we were just then making would prove our last; but when we came to the top we always found a level stretch and then another rise behind. However, on the evening of September 1st we reached the top of a long slope and saw before us a huge flat plain. Everything seemed to point to the conclusion that we had reached the high plateau of the interior. The announcement of this to the party produced general rejoicing. According to our aneroid barometers the height we had now reached was 7,930 feet.

We now hoped to begin to enjoy the long descent, but the expected change of level would not come. For days – I might almost say weeks – we toiled across an interminable flat desert of snow. One day began and ended like another and all were characterized by nothing but a wearisome, wearing uniformity. Flatness and whiteness were the two features of this ocean of snow. We looked like a diminutive black line feebly traced upon an infinite expanse of white. There was no break or change in our horizon, no object to rest the eyes upon, and no point by which to direct the course. Our days were short, varying between five and ten miles. The reason for this was the persistently heavy going. On the whole, the going was so unconscionably heavy that it was only by the exertion of all our strength that we were able to make any progress at all, and work at this high altitude is of course very wearying.

On September 8th my diary says: "The snow was incredibly heavy going today, heavier than it has ever been before. The wind-packed snow is no better than sand. We had the wind to pull against too." The next day I wrote: "It began to snow in the middle of the day and our work was heavier than ever. It was worse than yesterday and to say that it was like hauling in blue clay will scarcely give an idea of it."

It is remarkable the extraordinarily rapid fall of the temperature during the night on the inland ice. Professor Moon has calculated that our lowest records must have reached something like $-50°$. On these days the temperature of the air at noon rose to between $-4°$ and $+5°$. This was in the middle of September and these temperatures are without any comparison the lowest that have ever been recorded at this time of year anywhere on the face of the globe. Constant exposure to the cold was by no means pleasant. The ice often formed so heavily on our faces that our beards and hair froze fast to the coverings of our heads and it was difficult to open the lips to speak. This inconvenience had to be endured because we had no way of shaving.

During the night of the 6/7th of September we had a tremendous storm. On the morning of the 7th as I awoke and lay half conscious I heard something go outside. It was a guy rope on the east side. I expected the tent wall to give way at any moment but by the help of some bags we made the weak side somewhat stiffer. Samuel Balto crawled out the tent door but it was not many seconds before he came plunging in again, absolutely breathless. The wind had completely taken his breath away and the first words he said when he had recovered himself were, "There is no going on this day!" So we had to stay where we were. When Kristian went out to put some storm guys on the weather side of the tent, the wind fell upon him with such force that he had to go down on all fours.

Suddenly, a little after mid-day, the wind dropped all at once as abruptly as if the current had been cut off with a knife. There was absolute calm and an uncomfortable silence for we knew that the wind would presently come again from the opposite quarter. Presently there came a gentle gust from the northwest, the door side of our tent, and this was soon followed by blast upon blast, each more furious than its predecessor. The storm overwhelmed us with greater fury than before and the inside of the tent was a mist of flying snow. Next morning the wind had dropped so much that we found we could move on again. But it was no easy matter to get out of our prison; the tent was buried so deep that only the ridge of the roof remained above the snow and we had to dig our way through the drifts that blocked the door. Of the sledges there was nothing to be seen and we had a good deal of work to do before we got them out. When we did get off we found the going, as usual, heavier than ever.

As the middle of September approached we hoped every day to arrive at the beginning of the western slope. On September 12th we were about 8,250 feet above sea level and our reckoning made us out to be about seventy-five miles from the nearest bare land with the ground at last falling well and continuously. The very pronounced fall of the slope on September 17th was a comfort to all of us and when the thermometer that evening just failed to reach zero we found the temperature quite mild and felt we had entered the abode of summer again.

In the middle of the afternoon of September 19th, as we were sailing our sleds along at their best and fastest, we heard a cry of joy from the party behind us, Balto's voice being prominent as he shouted "Land ahead!" And so there was. Through the mist of snow we could see away to the west a long dark mountain ridge and to the south of it a smaller peak. The land was soon hidden in the snow but we went on with the wind straight behind us for the rest of the afternoon. The wind grew stronger and stronger, we flew down slope after slope, and everything went famously. It was already growing dusk when I saw in the general obscurity something dark lying in front of our path. I took it for some ordinary irregularity in the snow and unconcernedly steered straight ahead. The next moment, when I was within no more than a few yards, I found it to be something very different, and in an instant swung around sharp and brought the vessel up into the wind. It was high time for we were on the very edge of a chasm broad enough to swallow comfortably sledges, steersmen and passengers. Another second and we should have disappeared for good and all.

My diary says: "This was the first crevasse but was not likely to be the only one and we must now go warily. It was suggested that it was hardly safe to sail any further that evening but I thought it too early to stop yet, as we must take advantage of the wind. So I left the sledges and went on in front to reconnoitre. The wind was strong enough to blow me along on my skis. When the snow looked treacherous I had to go cautiously and use my staff to see whether I had solid ground underfoot. In spite of all precautions Sverdrup and Kristian all but came to grief once as the snow fell in behind them just as they had passed over an unsuspected crevasse. It was getting dark, but the full moon was now rising. It was a curious sight for me to see the four sleds come rushing along behind me, with their square Viking-like sails showing dark against the white snowfield. Presently I cross a broad crevasse and can see in front of me a huge black abyss. I creep cautiously to its edge on the slippery ice, here covered by scarcely any snow, and look down into the deeps. Beyond it I can see another crevasse running parallel. I tell the others to stop as this is no ground to traverse in the dark and we must halt for the night. I now discover for the first time that I had got the fingers of both hands frozen during the afternoon sail. It was too late now to rub them with snow as they had begun to thaw on their own account, and that night the pain they gave me was almost unendurable.

When we looked out of the tent in the morning we could see the whole country to the south of Godthaabsfjord lying spread out before us, a rough mountainous tract with many deep valleys and lofty peaks. It was a fine country, wild and grand as the western coast of Norway. Fresh snow lay sprinkled about the mountain tops between which were deep black gorges. At the bottom of these were the fiords, which we could fancy, but could not see. A journey to Godthaab in this kind of country looked anything but a simple matter.

Presently we reached the top of a long, steep slope which had to be descended. Sverdrup and I started down on our skis and had a fine run. But our sledge was difficult to steer, and we had huge crevasses on each side, so at last we were constrained to take our skis off for safety's sake. We then went on, standing each of us on a runner of the sledge, and scraping and braking with our feet in order to keep clear of the crevasses. The Lapps during this run were especially reckless and let their sledge rush ahead as much as it pleased.

We had a nasty experience when our sledge came lengthwise upon a crevasse, the snow cornice of which gave way under one of the runners and we only managed to drag it onto firm ground just as the whole mass of snow was falling in beneath it.

Next day, September 21st, snow was falling and we could see nothing of the land or the ice around us. Our position was a little more northerly than I should have liked. We now had to pay a penalty. We soon found ourselves in the middle of some terrible crevasses. They were worse than any we had hitherto had to deal with and we were very glad to get clear of them and bear away more to the south. Here there was an abrupt fall and the ice was uncomfortably rough. The place looked all but impracticable and it was clearly no use trying to push on any further while the weather was so thick.

Sverdrup, Kristian, and I decided to go ahead and see whether this broken ice would allow of a passage. We had not gone far when I saw a little dark spot

Once, Nansen slipped into a crevasse
when alone. "*I was left hanging by
my arms,*" he wrote in his journal.

At journey's end, Nansen sketched
this Eskimo. The last boat had left,
so the party wintered in Greenland.

down below us. It looked amazingly like water. But it was quite possibly only ice so I said nothing to the others. However, when I reached it and, putting my staff in, met with no resistance our surprise and delight was unbounded. We threw ourselves down, put our lips to the surface, and sucked up the water like horses. After a month of incessant thirst the pleasure of an abundance of drink was indescribable.

We now found ourselves amongst the roughest ice I have ever seen. Absolutely impassable it was not, but ridge upon ridge, each sharper and more impracticable than its neighbour, lay in all directions while between them were deep clefts often half full of water, which was covered with a thin skin of ice not strong enough to bear us. A cheering smell of good pea soup met us as we arrived back at the little tent where we found the others squatting around our stove.

After breakfast on the 22nd Sverdrup and I went out again to explore the ice to the west. The others were meanwhile to follow us with four sledges as far as they could in the same direction. Sverdrup and I started off with the wind behind us and ran fast on our slippery oak skis. Then the crevasses began, but at first ran parallel, and we pushed a good way farther on. Presently things became utterly hopeless. Even the fancy could form no idea of the depth of these chasms, and the sight of the riven and chaotic mass was unearthly in the extreme. Not a step farther could we go. There was nothing for it but to return to the others.

On the way back I had the ill luck to fall into a crevasse. I was left hanging by my arms, and the position was neither easy nor pleasant. The fissure was narrow but it was very difficult to get a footing with my ski on the slippery edges. I was alone as Sverdrup had taken a different route and saw nothing of my disaster. However, after struggling for a while I at last managed to scramble out by myself.

On the 23rd Sverdrup went out upon a prospecting expedition and came back with reassuring intelligence. He thought it would be possible to get on if we put three men to each sledge. We set out then upon the heaviest ice travelling which we had yet had. In many places we had to carry each sledge bodily up the steep slopes of the ridges we had to cross while, as we descended the other side, the unfortunate man that went behind had to hold it back with all his might. Sometimes we were lucky enough to hit upon the course of a frozen river which gave us an easy, though somewhat winding, passage amongst the hummocks and ridges of ice which often formed cliffs with nearly perpendicular walls.

Next day, September 24, we turned out early and pushed on fast as the gradient was tolerably steep. I went on in front and soon found myself upon the brow of an ice slope which overlooked a beautiful mountain lake, the surface of which was covered with a sheet of ice. Beyond was a gorge through which a river from the lake ran downward. Here was an easy descent for us and no obstacles to separate us from our goal. The sledges went gaily and soon we were safe upon the frozen lake with the Inland Ice forever left behind.

It was high time to think of dinner. Neither the highest spiritual enjoyment nor the overwhelming sense of an end obtained is sufficient to make one oblivious of bodily wants. There was now a trace of gladness to be discovered even in Ravna's face. He had over and over again abandoned all hope of getting solid earth beneath his feet again, poor fellow. The first thing he and Balto did when they brought their sledge safe on to the lake was to run straight away up the mountainside.

Nansen and his men were equipped with "the Canadian snowshoe."

fm The first crossing of the Inland Ice was now completed. Making their way laboriously down through the mountain valleys the little party reached the head of Godhan fiord. Here they built a tiny boat out of sled runners and tarpaulins in which Sverdrup and Nansen paddled down the fiord to obtain help. Near Godhan they encountered a group of Eskimos among whom was a Dane. When they landed the stranger asked them their names. "My name is Nansen, and we have just come from the interior." "Oh then, allow me to congratulate you on taking your doctor's degree." It was an odd plaudit to receive at the end of such a remarkable journey. Nansen and his party did not catch any of the homebound boats and were forced to spend that winter in Greenland. But the experiences gained during the winter contributed very largely to Nansen's later design for the famous voyage of the *Fram* in the ice of the polar sea. □ FM

CHAPTER 7 THE PASSION QUICKENS

Nansen's successful crossing of the Inland Ice won him world-wide adulation and gave him towering stature as an arctic explorer. This, in turn, fuelled his ambitions to increase that stature, and at the same time ensured that he would have no trouble raising support for a new arctic venture.

It also goaded the American Robert Peary into renewed interest in the Icecap. He concluded that anything the Norwegian could do he could do better. So he sailed north again in 1891, intending to redeem his failure of five years earlier by crossing the Inland Ice where it was widest, from Whale Sound (on Smith Sound), to the unknown northeast coast. Peary was accompanied by his wife; by a Norwegian named Eivind Astrup; by a Negro (most often described as "Peary's coloured man") named Matthew Henson; and by Dr. Frederick Cook. Making use of the other men as a support party, Astrup and Peary managed to cross the remainder of the Icecap diagonally, reaching land at the base of what is now called Independence Fiord, but which Peary called Independence Bay. This was a notable achievement – but Peary gilded the lily by pronouncing that the northern portion of Greenland was a vast independent island (which he modestly called Peary Land) separated from the main island by a great channel (which he modestly called Peary Channel.) He also reported the existence of an East Greenland Sea which extended into northeast Greenland to the base of Independence Bay.

None of these "discoveries" were real. Peary Channel did not exist, and therefore the great island named Peary Land could not exist. Where Peary had mapped the East Greenland Sea, several thousand square miles of dry land rose into mountains and glaciers. But before these errors could be put right they provided Peary with the reputation he needed to help drum up support for his polar ventures. They also resulted in Mylius-Erichsen, leader of the "Denmark expedition" of 1906-08, and two of his men losing their lives. The three Danes went to their deaths as a direct result of having been misled by Peary's imaginative additions to the map.

Peary returned to the United States in the late summer of 1892 to announce his discoveries to the world and, on the strength of them, to obtain backing for a new project. This was to be the establishment of a supply route running across the Icecap to the northernmost tip of Greenland – a point which, theoretically, ought to have provided an excellent jumping-off point for a run to the Pole. At this juncture nobody was yet talking openly about renewed polar expeditions – the memory of the Greely and DeLong shambles was still too clearly etched in the public mind. Nevertheless the passion was burning bright again in Nansen, Peary, Cook – and other less well-known men.

Two of these "unknowns" made an attempt to reach the Pole in 1892. Alfred Björling, a twenty-one-year-old Swede, was the nominal leader of a two-man expedition of which the other half was a fellow-countryman named

E. G. Kallstenius. The expedition was vaguely described as a "botanizing expedition to northern Greenland." In fact it seems to have been a wildly romantic endeavour to snatch the Pole from under the very noses of the professional explorers. Originally the young men hoped to get north on a whaler (à la Charles Hall) but their plans misfired. Nothing daunted they bought a small, ancient, and unseaworthy schooner called the Ripple in St. John's, Newfoundland. Hiring three Newfoundlanders as crew, they set out for their distant goal.

A pall of mystery hangs over the subsequent history of the expedition, but it seems to have been their plan to sail to Etah and there enlist the help of a group of Eskimos to carry them Poleward. It was a good plan, and was to bear fruit – for other men at another time.

They were desperately short of supplies even at the start and so they put in to the Carey Islands, which stand well out into Baffin Bay, to stock up from an old cache left there by the Nares expedition. While they were doing this the little Ripple was driven ashore and wrecked.

The five men then attempted to sail a small open boat north to Etah, but something went wrong. Björling's letters only record that: "we were compelled from several causes, to give up this voyage." They returned to the Carey Islands where, about October 12, one of the men died under circumstances that remain unspecified. Shortly thereafter the survivors set out in their boat to the westward, intending to cross eighty miles of open water to Cape Clarence on Ellesmere Island. Why they should have chosen such a suicidal course, instead of sailing to the Greenland coast twenty-five miles distant, and then making their way north to Etah or south to Upernavik, is unexplained. Perhaps they hoped to coast south from Cape Clarence to Pond Inlet where they might have encountered Eskimos.

Björling left a packet of four letters in a cairn on the Carey Islands with a request that the finder should visit Cape Clarence "where I shall leave a cairn relative to our fate during the winter." No cairn was ever found and no trace of the missing men ever turned up. The polar passion had claimed five more victims; but hardly a mention of the Björling disaster was made in the world's press, and it had no effect upon many plans then maturing.

It certainly had no effect upon Peary. In 1893 the Newfoundland sealer Falcon, commanded by Newfoundlander Harry Bartlett, carried Peary and a large, well-equipped expedition back to Whale Sound. The party included such unusual elements as a pregnant Mrs. Peary and her ageing nurse, as well as Peary's servant, Matthew Henson. The rest of the men were volunteers, drawing no pay, and some of them even paying their own way. In the spring of 1894 Peary set out for Independence "Bay" supported by five Eskimos and eighty dogs, and accompanied by seven of his own men. In his impatience he began the journey too early in the season. Atrocious weather conditions resulted in the death of all but twenty-five of the Eskimo dogs before the party turned back, having gone only 128 miles.

In August of 1894 Bartlett and the Falcon returned and picked up all of the party except Peary, Henson and Hugh Lee. Harry Bartlett carried the rest safely back to Philadelphia, but while returning to St. John's the ship and all her crew were lost without a trace.

In April of 1895 Peary, Henson, Lee and six Eskimos, with sixty dogs, had another go at the northeast route. This time Peary tried to force both the pace and the issue, refusing to be turned back by the loss of a number of vital caches which had disappeared under the winter snows. The upshot was that he and his party came within a whisker's breadth of losing their lives. Peary managed

For 23 years Robert E. Peary was
obsessed by the desire to be the
first man to reach the North Pole.
The author says: "He was an incredibly
ruthless and self-dedicated man."

Peary's Falcon leaves New York in
1898 for his first attempt on the Pole.
On this two-year expedition, he failed
to advance beyond 84° 17′N., short
of the record of Nansen in 1895.

The Falcon at Cape York. Eskimos
played their part in the Peary "machine."
At least eight died in his service.

When the U.S. Congress recognized
Peary's polar claims he was promoted
rear-admiral. He died in 1920.

to reach the bottom of Independence "Bay" again, but did not correct a single one of his geographical errors of 1892. He and his companions almost literally crawled back across the Inland Ice, reaching their base camp more dead than alive (only one dog survived), having accomplished nothing for three years of effort. However, Peary was now convinced that the northeast route over the ice was not a feasible path toward the Pole.

By this time Peary had demonstrated, to those with eyes to see, the three salient aspects of his character. He was an incredibly ruthless, hard-driving, tough and self-dedicated man. He displayed pathological jealousy of anyone who trespassed on any field he chose to make his own. And he was icily unscrupulous about the methods he adopted to gain his ends. During the 1895 journey clear symptoms of the messianic compulsion which allowed him to exploit other people with precious little regard for their rights and well-being, had made themselves apparent. From this time forward Peary considered that all the resources of the region, including the musk-ox, sea mammals, Eskimos and dogs, existed to further his ambitions. He assumed a proprietory air toward them and toward the entire district, which he now referred to as "The American Route to the Pole." He used the people and the resources ruthlessly. More than 400 Eskimo dogs, two white men and at least eight Eskimos died in Peary's personal service. The lives of the Etah people were completely disrupted. These Eskimos were not only used on the expeditions, but provided a supply of white fox and narwhal ivory, which helped finance Peary's expeditions. Peary's records tell of more than a thousand musk-ox and innumerable caribou, seals, walrus and polar bears which were sacrificed to fuel his polar machine.

The year 1893 had also seen the beginning of a second polar venture which became one of the most remarkable exploring endeavours in history. Having carefully reviewed all that had been done by his many predecessors, Fridtjof Nansen concluded that the best way to reach the Pole was to *deliberately* drive a ship into the arctic pack at a carefully chosen point on the perimeter of the frozen sea, and then let the drift carry her across the Pole. The main difficulty with this plan was that nobody had ever built a ship that could withstand such a voyage. Most people, including almost all the "old arctic hands," did not believe such a vessel *could* be built. Nansen put the problem in the hands of the venerable Scottish designer Colin Archer who in due course produced a strange little vessel which was christened *Fram*. She was designed and built in such a way that, when the ice began to nip, it would be unable to grip her rounded hull but would squeeze her up and out of danger rather as someone might squeeze a water-melon seed between his fingers.

With a crew of thirteen, including Otto Sverdrup who had been with him on the Icecap, Nansen sailed the *Fram* north and east during the summer of 1893 until she reached a position near the New Siberian Islands not so far from where the *Jeanette* had sunk. Here he put her in the ice. Throughout the next year she drifted slowly north and west, confounding the prophets of doom who had assured the world that, though she just might survive the summer pack, the heavy winter pack would crush her to a pulp. Apparently she was never in any real danger, though she was several times squeezed out of her ice bed and lifted so high that daylight could be seen beneath her keel.

While the balance of the party worked steadily at oceanographic studies, Nansen fretted. The drift was not following his predicted course but was carrying the ship past the Pole and to the south of it. By November of 1894 Nansen had gloomily concluded that *Fram* was not going to get much closer to the Pole than 83°. So he began preparing to make a dash northward with sleds and dogs as soon as the spring of 1895 should bring sufficient light to see by.

After several false starts Nansen and one companion, Johansen, departed from the ship on March 14. The polar dash was not very successful. Starting from about 83° 30', the two men reached 86° 13' on April 8, at which point Nansen decided they must turn back. He made no attempt to rejoin the ship. It would appear that his patience had been severely strained by two years' drifting, and so he headed for Franz Josef Land. Killing a dog every day or so in order to feed the survivors, he pushed south until open water was reached, whereupon the two men launched kayaks and, after killing the last two dogs, began working south through the channels between the Franz Josef Islands. By the end of August they had made so little progress against storms and drift ice that they decided they had better winter where they were.

They built a combination stone cave and hut on one of the small islands and here they hibernated, amply supplied with walrus and bear meat, but with not much else.

In the spring of 1896 they began working their way south again, but progress was desperately slow. They would have had either to endure another winter in Franz Josef Land or to take the very real risk of perishing while trying to make the long open-water passage to Spitsbergen or Novaya Zemlya in kayaks, had they not had the good luck to fall in with the Jackson-Harmsworth Expedition. This was a British group engaged in mapping and exploring Franz Josef Land, hoping to find land extending beyond it to the Pole, and with the steam whaler *Windward* as a supply ship.

The story of Nansen's lunge for the Pole, and the aftermath, is replete with fascinating incidents and exciting adventures. It may have been the most daring, if not the rashest sled journey ever undertaken across the polar ice. But it took its genesis from a desire to satisfy national and personal ambition, rather than from any deep desire to provide the world with new knowledge. The voyage of the *Fram*, under command of the phlegmatic Otto Sverdrup, was another story. Day after interminable day, as *Fram* drifted slowly to the westward, Sverdrup kept his people occupied in their routine studies of the arctic sea, its bottom, the ice, the currents, the weather and so on. *Fram* remained locked in the ice *for almost three full years* during which time she drifted right across the polar basin. The information amassed during the voyage has not been surpassed in quality or quantity and remains the foundation of our knowledge of the great frozen ocean.

Nansen deserves much credit for having fathered this expedition, even if it is true that he organized it primarily as a springboard from which he hoped to become the first man to reach the North Pole. Otto Sverdrup deserves even more credit. Having left the glory-bid to Nansen, he devoted himself to the true work of discovery. *Fram*'s voyage dissolved much of the mysterious aura that still hung over the polar basin. It demonstrated that there was no new land in the entire eastern portion of the Arctic Ocean and that, far from being the shallow sea of the theorists, it was immensely deep — sometimes exceeding 11,000 feet; and, once and for all it gave the lie to the myth of an open polar sea.

The year following upon *Fram*'s return from the ice saw the playing out of an even more extraordinary attempt to reach the Pole. When the *Windward*, with Nansen aboard, touched in at Spitsbergen on her way home, passengers and crew were amazed by the sight of an immense wooden barn housing a huge balloon. By means of the balloon *Eagle*, three Swedes, Salomon Andrée,

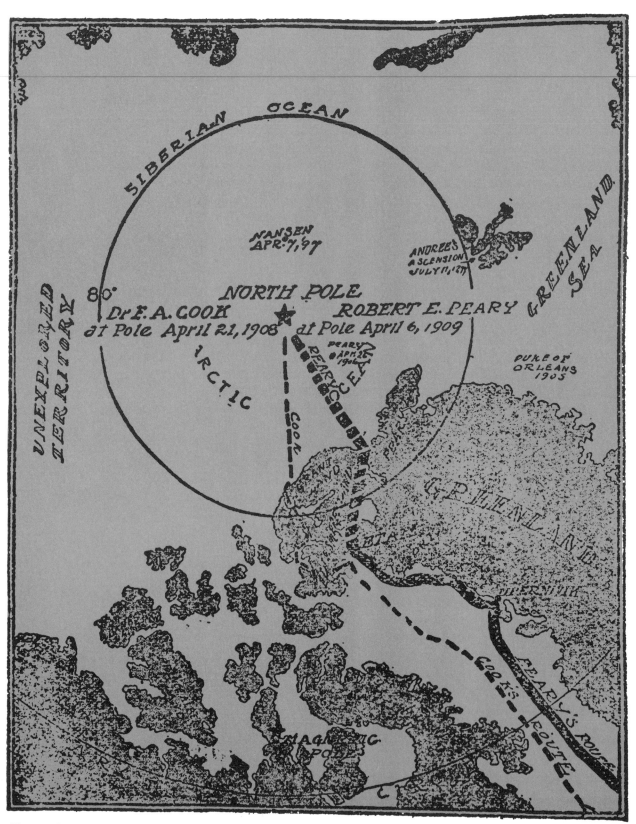

The most bitter controversy developed over the rival claims of Robert Peary and Frederick Cook. The latter (who had been a member of an earlier Peary expedition) announced his success only five days before Peary returned to Labrador with his news. Map shows both Cook and Peary routes.

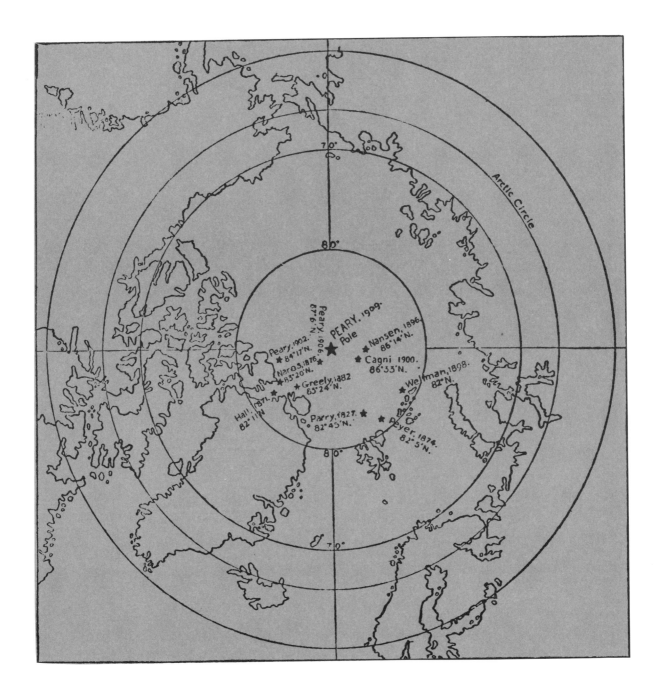

Polar expeditions recorded on this chart,
drawn after Peary's final 1909 voyage,
do not include Dr. Cook's. The little-known
exploit of the Italian party,
under the leadership of the Duke
of Abruzzi and Capt. Umberto Cagni,
in 1900, resulted in the closest
approach to the Pole at that time.

Fram, *the most famous of all polar*
ships, is in a museum near Oslo.
In her, Nansen and Sverdrup drifted
right across the polar basin. Later,
she took Amundsen to the Antarctic.

This English polar expedition never
got off the ground but, in 1897,
three Swedes did take off in a gasbag
called Eagle. Their bodies were found
by chance on White Is. in 1930.

Nils Strindberg and Knut Fraenkel, hoped to conquer the North Pole from the sky.

They were unable to make the attempt in 1896 due to unfavourable winds, so they returned south for the winter, not realizing that they had been granted a year's stay of execution.

In mid-July of 1897 the *Eagle* was at last cut free from the bonds of earth, with the three men swinging in a wicker basket below the great gas bag. The voyage lasted sixty-five hours, and during most of that time the *Eagle* dragged the gondola along the surface of the floes. When she finally came to rest it was at latitude 82° 56′. Abandoning the *Eagle*, her crew set out hauling sleds toward Franz Josef Land, but after three weeks' hard work they were stopped by a great open lead. They turned back for Spitsbergen but found they were being drifted away from it almost as fast as they could march toward it.

On September 17 they glimpsed isolated and lonely White Island (the most easterly of the Spitsbergen group) and on October 1 finally gained its steep shores. Here they set up their tent and began to get ready to endure the long winter. . . .

In 1930 the sealer *Bradtvaag* brought a small Norwegian exploring party to White Island. One August day two young men were crossing a snowbank when they stumbled on the bow of a canvas boat protruding from the ice below. Not far off, a human corpse leaned against a rocky cliff. Within a few hours the macabre discovery had been identified – this was the last camp of the three men who had ballooned clear of Spitsbergen in 1897 and then vanished from human ken.

Through a remarkable freak the doomed men had chosen to camp in a place that was temporarily clear of snow but into which the snow drifted through the succeeding years and packed to form hard ice. Within this ice most of the human remains, diaries, and even the photographic films of the Andrée expedition had been preserved. Entries in the diaries stop short twelve days after the landing on White Island, although the men were then in reasonably good health. In all likelihood they died of carbon monoxide poisoning from burning one of their pressure stoves for too long a time in a tent too well sealed.

Fate may have been merciful to them. Had they not died so swiftly, they probably would have died a slow and agonizing death from starvation during the long months ahead.

By 1898 new plans to assault the Pole were being publicly announced. In that year two major expeditions were launched. One, with Otto Sverdrup in command of a large party of scientists, saw the sturdy *Fram* voyaging into Smith Sound. The other, led by Robert Peary, consisted of a few volunteers his man-servant Henson, and a large number of Etah Eskimos.

Sverdrup was destined to spend the years from 1898 to 1902 exploring, discovering and accurately mapping nearly 100,000 square miles of new lands, while his scientific corps gathered a massive body of information on meteorology, biology, botany, palaentology, geology and many kindred sciences. Peary was to spend those same years in the same quarter of the North, and to accomplish nothing more useful than a hurried sled journey along the north Greenland coast to its most northerly point, which he named Cape Morris Jesup; and to descry – far to the eastward – a large island which he named Wyckoff Island. Wyckoff Island was later demonstrated (by other explorers) to be no more of an island than was Peary Land but, while it lasted, it served as an example of the kind of geographical immortality which Peary bestowed on those rich men at home who made generous donations to his expeditions.

Peary's 1898-1902 expedition had two other results. Following almost exactly in Markham's path, Peary pushed due north to 84° 17′ – fifty-seven miles farther than Markham had gone but a long way short of Nansen's record. The third result was the claim – made some time *after* the return of the expedition – that Peary was the first to see Axel Heiberg Island and therefore claimed primacy for the name he had given it – Jesup Land. Many years later it was shown, from Peary's own books, that he could not have been in a position to have even glimpsed this distant land when he claimed to have done so. Sverdrup's prior claim was never in serious dispute, and the wealthy Morris Jesup had to be content to rest his hopes of geographical immortality on a mere headland in north Greenland.

Sverdrup made an attempt to force *Fram* up through Robeson Channel in 1898. But it was a bad year for ice, and neither *Fram* nor Peary's *Windward* (on loan from Harmsworth) was able to get beyond Kane Basin. Sverdrup thereupon concluded that his time and that of his men would be best spent exploring the great unknown area lying to the west. This included south and central Ellesmere Island, northwest Devon Island, Jones Sound, and the Sverdrup Group – Axel Heiberg, Ellef Ringnes and Amund Ringnes Islands. (Sverdrup was not innocent of the deplorable practice of naming new features after sponsors. The jaw-breaking names of these three islands are derived from the names of a Norwegian consul and two brothers who owned a brewery in Norway; these three men having contributed most of the money which made the expedition possible.)

Sverdrup was delighted to find a fellow explorer in the area and was happy to cheer Peary on. Peary, on the other hand, was fearfully disturbed by the presence of the Norwegians and looked upon them as interlopers and dangerous competitors. It would hardly be possible to devise a more revealing contrast than that between Sverdrup, the true explorer, quietly engaged in enlarging the store of human knowledge; and Peary, the monomaniac, furiously determined to burn his name indelibly into the folk memory of mankind.

In 1900, while Peary was still striving unsuccessfully to get north from Greely's old Fort Conger, which Peary had adopted as his polar base, the Italians stole a march on everyone and launched an expedition north from Franz Josef Land. Their ship, the *Polar Star* (the ex-whaler *Jason*) under Captain Evensen, carried the Duke of Abruzzi, Captain Cagni and ten other members of the Italian Navy north to about 82°. In mid-February of the following year Abruzzi and Cagni with their supply parties started north. On April 24 Cagni and two companions managed to reach 86° 34′, thereby bettering Nansen's record. The price of this new record was the lives of three of Cagni's men who disappeared while returning from a support journey.

The success of the Italian expedition was gall and wormwood to Peary. Grimly he went to work raising the very large sums of money which he now decided he must have if he was to reach the Pole. A Peary Arctic Club was formed by a number of wealthy and influential Americans (the question of national pride was now looming very large in connection with the polar passion) and enough money was raised to build a special ice-ship, the *Roosevelt*, and to provide Peary with the best of everything. In 1905 the *Roosevelt* sailed north under command of Capt. Robert Bartlett, and reached Cape Sheridan on the shores of the Arctic Ocean not far from where Nares's *Alert* had wintered in 1875-76. She carried 200 Eskimo dogs and fifty Etah Eskimos who were to drive the sleds, break the trail, hunt meat, sew clothing, build igloos, and in general do most of the labour of the expedition. In the spring of 1906, using twenty-nine men and 120 dogs to advance supplies and break trail for him, Peary made his second direct bid for the Pole. He was stopped at 87° 6′ by a broad lead of open water.

The great expedition had not been a complete failure. Aside from bettering the record of the Italians by thirty-two miles, Peary made a side trip to the north tip of Axel Heiberg Island, from which point of vantage he discovered a large, new land lying off to the northwest. He named it Crocker Land in honour of one of his most important supporters. Crocker Land did not, and does not exist – a fact which did not become known until 1914.

The *Roosevelt* had suffered considerable damage during this voyage, and the repairs required to make her seaworthy were so extensive that it was found she could not be ready to sail north again in 1907 as Peary had hoped. Consequently his next try for the Pole had to be delayed a year. This left the quest for the Pole in a temporary vacuum.

Into this vacuum stepped Dr. Frederick Cook.

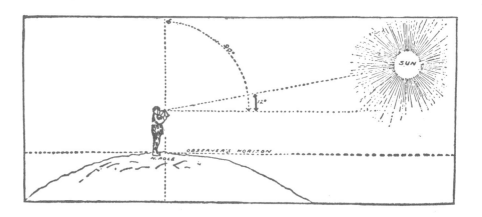

CHAPTER 8 THE TOP OF THE WORLD

Robert Peary was a career naval employee who, since he belonged to it, recognized the value of having the Establishment on his side. He understood the fundamentals of success so well that, very early in his adult life, he set about interweaving his own reputation and personal fortunes with those of such rich and influential men as Morris Jesup, Thomas Hubbard and the Colgates, and with such powerful commercial organizations as the National Geographic Society (a privately-owned publishing house of great wealth and influence). Peary always saw to it that his supporters had a vested interest in forwarding his work and in enhancing and protecting his reputation, if only to enhance and protect their own. Had it not been for the monomania that channelled all his truly remarkable energy into the quest for the Pole he could have had a brilliant career in either finance or politics.

Cook, on the other hand, was a lone wolf and an outsider first and last. His hard and rather grubby childhood did give him a powerful egocentric urge to accomplish something of great moment; but he had neither Peary's rapier-like ability to strike straight for what he wanted, nor his iron-bound conviction that the end justified the means. Where Peary was naturally amoral, and therefore icily effective, Cook laboured all his life under the restraints imposed by his quaint conviction that a man should live by an ethical code and that human relationships were essentially warm, just and meaningful. Cook was naive in the extreme; consequently it was as easy for his enemies to make his claims appear fraudulent as it was for the massed might of Peary's supporters to make Peary's frauds appear as facts.

Cook lived his life outside the Establishment and we can understand the contempt of its members for a man who was essentially a romantic. He would have fitted into the Establishment about as readily as a Zen Buddhist would fit into the Mafia. He was essentially a pariah in his own times as was Charles Francis Hall in his. Indeed these two men had a great deal in common.

Not only did Cook lack Peary's no-nonsense practicality, he seemed to choose deliberately to flaunt his addiction to the idealistic way of life. He was forever volunteering to assist in other men's expeditions – usually without pay and sometimes at his own expense. He was incapable of realizing how important it was to use his fellows as pawns in Peary's "great game of life." He persisted in playing fair with those he should have used – even when they happened to be Eskimos. He liked all sorts of things which could not possibly advance his expeditions: small birds that were no use for the pot; lemmings not big enough to merit attention from the hunter; old stories; moss on an arctic rock; clouds in a distant mirage. One of the most frequent and telling cricitisms of him is that his book, *My Attainment of the Pole*, is full of extraneous details about man, his thoughts, and the world he lives in. Such trivia found no place in the business-like communiqués issued by Robert Peary.

Perhaps Cook was most vulnerable in his apparent lack of "method." Peary tackled the Pole in the best modern manner, massing machines (as far as he was concerned Eskimos and their dogs were mere machines) and equipment until he felt he could force a victory over nature by brute strength. But Cook clung to the concepts of C. F. Hall, believing that the best way to succeed against natural forces was not to struggle, but to flow with them. Instead of spending over a million dollars of other peoples' money organizing an exploring venture designed to make use of the very latest in American technology, like that which sent Peary's army marching toward the Pole, Cook went north as companion to a wealthy sportsman, prepared to take advantage of the opportunity – if it should present itself – of finding his own way to the Pole. When he set out it was with about three thousand dollars' worth of equipment, paid for out of his own pocket, and accompanied by two Eskimo companions. For Cook to tackle the Pole in such a casual manner when Peary had demonstrated to the world that only the most determined mobilization of American resources could do the job was to mortally insult not only Peary and his supporters, but the whole of the United States. Yet this is what Cook, in his incurable innocence, chose to do.

There were many reasons why Cook should not have reached the Pole – *should* not, it will be noted. He represented no great body of savants and no consortium of wealthy interests; his methods were insultingly simple; he represented the wrong set of values. Asking no man's permission and no man's blessing he sailed off to Etah (which Peary claimed as his own personal preserve) and then, while Peary was busy in New York lecturing on the tremendous hazards of the polar attempt, and of how he would "bring the Pole home to the United States" despite them, Cook was quietly *bringing* the Pole home to the United States.

It is impossible not to feel some sympathy for Peary. To have been forestalled and made to look like a fool by such an insignificant fellow was enough to have unhinged a much less egocentric man than Peary. It did temporarily derange him and he suffered a nervous breakdown which resulted largely from his inability to properly express his rage. And it is small wonder that the very name of Cook was sufficient to transform the elegant admirals, dignified men of science, suave men of politics, shrewd men of publishing, and the "practical" men of high finance who, together, formed the Peary Arctic Club, into savage character assassins.

It is little wonder that for thirty years after the "discovery" of the Pole an unceasing and unbelievably vicious and unprincipled campaign of slander was unleashed against Cook by Peary's supporters. What is not so easy to understand is that otherwise intelligent men and women of our day can still be misled by the discredited and discreditable attempts to destroy Cook, his work and his character. Presumably these blind adherents to the verdict of the Establishment remain unaware that modern scientific investigations have established beyond reasonable doubt that if Frederick Cook did not reach the top of the world he at least came as close to that elusive goal as any other man, including Peary, and he properly deserves (for whatever it may be worth) the title of discoverer of that peculiarly non-objective yet passionately desired Holy Grail of so many men – the North Pole.

On July 3, 1907, the schooner *John R. Bradley* withdrew from the pier at Gloucester, Massachusetts, and, turning her prow oceanward, quietly started on her journey to the arctic seas. No whistles tooted after her departure. No visiting crowds of curiosity seekers ashore waved her good-bye.

An arctic expedition had been born without the usual clamour. Prepared in one month, and financed by a sportsman whose only mission was to hunt game animals in the North, no press campaign heralded our project, no government aid had been asked, nor had large contributions been sought from private individuals. Although I secretly cherished the ambition, there was as yet no definite plan to essay the North Pole.

At the Holland House in New York a compact was made between John R. Bradley and myself to launch an arctic expedition. Because of my experience Mr. Bradley delegated to me the outfitting of the expedition and turned over to me money enough to pay the cost. A Gloucester fishing schooner had been purchased by me and was refitted and strengthened for ice navigation. So far as the needs of my own personal expedition are concerned, I had with me on the yacht plenty of hard hickory wood for the making of sledges; instruments, clothing and other apparatus gathered during my former years of exploration, and about 1,000 pounds of pemmican. These supplies, necessary in any case to offset the danger of shipwreck and detention by ice, were also all that would be required for a polar trip. When, later, I finally decided on a polar campaign, extra supplies contributed from the ship's stores were provided.

My background was not particularly well fitted for polar adventure. Abject poverty and hard work marked my school days. After the death of my father I came to New York where I sold fruit at one of the markets. I saved my money, enjoying no luxuries. Later I worked at a dairy business in Brooklyn and on the meagre profits undertook to study medicine. At that time the ambition which beset me was undirected; it was only later that I found, almost by accident, what became its focusing point. I graduated in 1890. I felt (as what young man does not?) that I possessed unusual qualifications and exceptional abilities. I fitted up an office and my anxiety over the disappearing pennies was eased by the conviction that I had but to hang out my shingle and the place would be thronged with patients. Six months passed. There had been three patients.

I recall sitting alone one gloomy winter day. Opening a paper I read that Peary was preparing his 1891 expedition to the Arctic. I cannot explain my sensations. It was as if a door to a prison cell had opened. I felt the first commanding call of the northland. The impetus of that ambition born in childhood, which had been stifled and starved, surged up within me.

I volunteered and accompanied Peary on this, the expedition of 1891-92, as surgeon. Whatever merit my work possessed has been already cited by others. I might note that on this as on all subsequent expeditions I served without pay.

On my return from that trip I managed to make ends meet by meagre earnings from medicine. I was nearly always desperately hard pressed for money. I tried to organize several co-operative expeditions to the Arctic but these failed. I then tried to arouse interest in antarctic exploration but without success. Finally came an opportunity to join the Belgian Antarctic Expedition, again without pay.†

A summer in the Arctic followed my antarctic trip and I returned to invade Alaska. I succeeded in scaling Mount McKinley. After my Alaskan expedition the routine of my Brooklyn office work seemed like the confinement of prison.

†Cook was knighted by the King of Belgium for his work during this expedition.

I fretted and chafed at the thought. I convinced myself that in some way the attainment of one of the Poles would become possible. My work in exploration had netted me nothing and all my professional income was soon spent. I waited, and fortune favoured me in that I met Mr. John R. Bradley. His interest in the trip was that of a sportsman eager to seek big game in the Arctic. My immediate purpose was to return again to the North. He and I had talked, of course, of the Pole; but it was not an important incentive to the journey.

Skippered by Captain Moses Bartlett of Newfoundland, we headed north. After an uneventful journey, with hunting en route, we entered Foulke Fiord and steered for the settlement of Etah. A tiny settlement it was, for it was comprised of precisely four tents. Inside the point was sheltered water for the Eskimos' kayaks and also a good harbour for the schooner. In favourable seasons it is possible to push north of this through Smith's Sound and Kane Basin into Kennedy Channel, but the experiment is always at the risk of the vessel. As there was no special reason for us to hazard life in making this attempt we decided to prepare the schooner here for the return voyage.

Some days later we decided to make a launch trip to Anoatok, twenty-five miles to the northward, and the northernmost settlement of the globe, a place beyond which even the hardy Eskimos attempt nothing but brief hunting excursions. Passing inside Littleton Island, we searched for relics along Lifeboat Cove. There the *Polaris* was stranded in a sinking condition in 1872, with fourteen men on board.

Ordinarily Anoatok is a town of only a single family, or perhaps two, but we found it unusually large and populous, for the best hunters had gathered here for the winter bear hunt. Their summer game catch had been lucky. Immense quantities of meat were strewn along the shore under mounds of stone. More than a hundred dogs, the standard by which Eskimo prosperity is measured, yelped a greeting, and twelve long-haired, wild men came out to meet us as friends.

For the past several days, having realized the abundance of game and the auspicious weather, I had thought more definitely of making a dash for the Pole. With all conditions in my favour, might I not, by one powerful effort, achieve the thing that had haunted me for years? I confess the task seemed audacious, but with these advantages so fortunately placed in my hand it took on a new fascination. I informed Mr. Bradley of my determination. He was not over-optimistic about success but shook my hand and wished me luck. From his yacht he volunteered fuel, food, and other supplies for local camp use and trading for which I have been thankful.

Besides the good location and the abundance of food, there was gathered at Anoatok the best Eskimos in all Greenland, from whom by reason of the rewards from civilization which I could give them, such as knives, guns, ammunition, old iron, needles and matches, I could select a party more efficient, because of their persistence, tough fibre, courage and familiarity with arctic travelling, than any party of white men could be.

My party, so far as civilized men were concerned, was to be an unusually small one. That was not from lack of volunteers, for when I had announced my determination many of the crew had volunteered to accompany me. Captain Bartlett himself wished to go along, but generously said that if it was necessary for him to go back with the schooner he would need only a cook and an engineer, leaving the other men for me. However, I wanted only one white companion since I knew that no group of white men could possibly match the Eskimos in their own element. I had the willing help of all the natives, and

Frederick Albert Cook accompanied both Peary and Amundsen
on polar expeditions before mounting his own in 1907.
Peary wrote of him: "I owe much to his professional skill
and unruffled patience and coolness in an emergency."
Later, he attacked the doctor savagely.

more than that was not required. I made an agreement with them for their assistance through the winter in getting ready, and then for as many as I wanted to start with me towards the uttermost north. For my white companion I selected Rudolph Francke, one of the arctic enthusiasts on the yacht.

Early in the morning of September 3, I bade farewell to Mr. Bradley and not long afterwards the yacht moved slowly southward and faded gradually on the southern horizon. I was left alone with my destiny, seven hundred miles from the Pole.

Why did I desire so ardently to reach the Pole? The attainment of the Pole meant at the time simply the accomplishing of a splendid, unprecedented feat – a feat of brain and muscle in which I should, if successful, signally surpass other men. This imaginary spot held for me the revealing of no great scientific secrets. I never regarded the feat as of any scientific value. The real victory would lie, not in reaching the goal itself, but in overcoming the obstacles which exist in the way of it.

At Anoatok we erected a house of packing boxes. The building of the house, which was to be both storehouse and workshop, was a simple matter. The walls were made of the packing boxes, specially selected of uniform size for this purpose. Enclosing a space 13 by 16 feet, the cases were quickly piled up. The walls were held together by strips of wood, the joints sealed with pasted paper, with the addition of a few long boards. A good roof was made by using the covers of the boxes as shingles. A blanket of turf over this confined the heat and permitted at the same time circulation of air. Our new house had the great advantage of containing within it all our possessions within easy reach. When anything was needed in the way of supplies all we had to do was open a box in the wall.

I now had time to plan my journey. I aimed to reach the top of the globe through a new and lonesome region which had not been tried, abandoning what has come to be called the "American route." I should strike westward across Smith Sound to Ellesmere Island and then northward, working new trails. With Anoatok as a base of operation I planned to carry sufficient supplies to Ellesmere Island to get me to game country in the west where I would find sufficient supplies en route to the shores of the polar sea. This journey to land's-end would also afford a test of every article of equipment. It would also enable us to choose finally from a selected number of Eskimos those most able to endure the rigours of the journey which lay before us.

To start from my base with men and dogs in superb condition, with their bodies nourished with wholesome fresh meat instead of the nauseating laboratory stuff too often given to men in the North, was of vital importance. If the men and dogs could afterward be supported in great measure by the game of the region through which we were to pass, it would be of importance more vital still. If my information was well founded and my general conjectures correct, I should have advantages which had not been possessed by any other leader of a polar expedition.

According to my plan, a large party of picked natives would accompany me to land's-end and somewhat beyond on the polar sea, when I started my dash in the coming spring. As spring is the best hunting season it was therefore imperative to secure sufficient advance provisions for the families of these men, in addition to preparing requisites for my expedition. So the days of the winter would have to be busily occupied by the men in a ceaseless hunt for game. Later, even when the darkness had fully fallen, the moonlight days and nights would thus have to be used also.

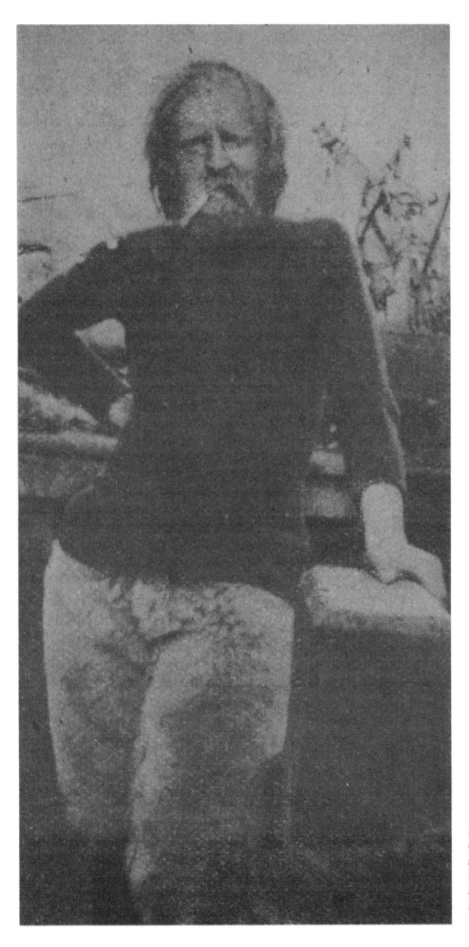

Rudolphe Francke, a tough young German, was selected by Cook as his sole European companion. For the final dash, Cook was accompanied only by two Eskimos, Etukishook and Ahwelah.

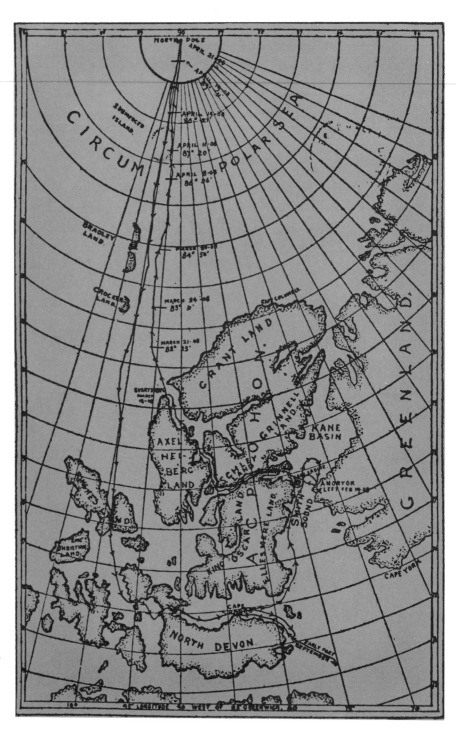

Dr. Cook's own sketch of his route to
and from the Pole, as published in
his journal in 1913. Note that map
includes Crocker Land – a "discovery"
by Admiral Peary that does not,
in fact, exist at all.

During the months of September and October the Eskimos were engaged in a feverish quest for reserve supplies. Shortly after my arrival, word had been carried from village to village that I was at Anoatok and intending to make a dash for the "Big Nail," and desired the help of the entire tribe. Intense and spontaneous activity followed. Knowing the demands of the North and of such work as I planned, the natives, without specific instructions from me and with only a brief outline of the planned polar campaign, immediately got busy gathering the necessary things. They knew better than I where to go for certain game, and where certain desirable things were obtainable. This relieved me of a great responsibility. Thus, in one way or another, every man and woman and most of the children of this tribe of 250 people were kept busy in the service of the expedition. The work was well done, and with much better knowledge of the fitness of things than could have been possessed by any possible gathering of alien white men.

Great quantities of meat, including narwhal, white whale, walrus, caribou, seal and lesser game was gathered. A full force of men were put to the work of devising equipment; the women were making clothes and dressing skins.

In planning for the polar dash I fully appreciated the vital importance of sleds. These, I felt, must possess to an ultimate degree the strength of steel with the lightness and elasticity of the strongest wood. They must neither be flimsy or bulky, nor heavy or rigid. After a careful study I came to the conclusion that the sled should be made of the best hickory wood and fitted with iron shoes. All joints were made elastic by the use of seal thong lashings. The sledges were 12 feet long and 30 inches wide; the runners 1⅛ inch wide. For dog harness the Greenland Eskimo pattern was adopted. But canine habits are such that when rations are reduced to minimum limits the leather straps disappear as food. To obviate this, the shoulder straps were made of folds of strong canvas, while the traces were cut from cotton log line.

A boat is an important adjunct to every sledge expedition which hopes to venture far from its base. It is a matter of necessity, even when following a coast line. Sectional boats, aluminum boats, skin floats and many other devices have been tried, but all these have the same objection on a polar trip, of impossible transportation. It seems odd that the ordinary folding canvas boat has not been previously pressed into service.† We had such a canoe-boat made to fit the situation exactly. The slats, spreaders and floor pieces were used as parts of our sledges. The canvas cover served as a floor cloth for our sleeping bags. Thus the boat did useful service for a hundred days and never seemed a needless encumbrance. When the craft was finally put into use as a boat, in it we carried the remains of the sledge, in it we sought game for food, and in it or under it we camped. Without it we could never have returned.

Even more vital than the choice of sledges on such a trip as I proposed is the care of the stomach. In this respect, as in others, I was helped very much by the natives. The Eskimo is ever hungry but his taste is normal. Things of doubtful value in nutrition form no part of his diet. Animal food, consisting of meat and fat, is entirely satisfactory as a steady diet without any other adjuncts. This food requires neither salt nor sugar, nor is cooking a matter of necessity.

By the time Christmas approached I had reason indeed for rejoicing. Our equipment was now almost complete. In the box house were tiers of new sledges, rows of boxes and piles of bags filled with clothing, canned supplies, dried meats, and sets of strong dog harnesses. The food, fuel and camp equipment for the polar dash were ready. Everything had been thoroughly tested

†*Peary never carried any sort of boat, which was the reason he had to turn back on his 1906 try for the Pole, after being stopped by an open lead.*

and put aside after final examination. Filled with gratitude to the natives I declared a week of holidays, with rejoicing and feasting. Feasting was a good thing, especially desirable, for we had now to fatten up for the anticipated race.

THE JOURNEY TO THE POLE BEGINS

By the end of January preparations were complete for a journey across Smith Sound. Francke asked to join the party, and prepared for his first camp outing. Four sledges were loaded with two hundred pounds each of expedition advance supplies. Four good drivers volunteered to move the sledges to the American [Canadian] side. This party reached Cape Sabine after a long run of twenty hours, being forced to make a considerable detour to the north by open water. The ice offered good travelling but the cold was bitter, the temperature being −52°F.

Another party, of eight sledges, led by Esseyou, Kudla, and Netek, started on February 5. The object was to carry advance supplies to the head of Flagler Bay and to hunt musk-oxen to feed the sledge teams as they moved overland. We were to meet this party in Flagler Bay. The light was still too uncertain to risk the fortunes of our major force. With a hundred dogs, a delay of a day would be an expensive loss, for if fed upon the carefully guarded food of the advance stores a rapid reduction in supplies would follow which could not be replaced, even if abundant game were secured later. It was therefore desirable for us to wait the rising sun. So we made our last arrangements and waited impatiently for the sunrise at this northern outpost of human life, just 700 miles from the Pole, but almost 1,000 miles as our route was planned. One thousand miles and return, or 2,000 miles in all, allowing for detours across icy and unknown wastes.

On the morning of February 19th, 1908, I started on my trip to the North Pole. Eleven sleds carried 4,000 pounds of supplies for use on the polar sea, and 2,000 pounds of walrus skin and fat for use before we procured the fresh game we anticipated. The eleven sledges were to be driven by Francke, nine Eskimos and myself. They were drawn by 103 dogs, all in fine condition. The dogs had been abundantly fed with walrus skin and meat for several weeks and would now be fed only every second day on fresh supplies.

When we started, a few stars were seen between the clouds but the light was good. A soft wind came up from the south; the temperature was −36°F. The Greenland icecap was outlined; a belt of orange in the south heralded the rising sun. The ice was covered with about three inches of soft snow over a hard crust which made speed difficult. Before noon the sky grew grey but the light remained good enough for travelling until four p.m. Our course was northwest because a water-sky to the west and south denoted open water in the centre of the strait.

The next day brought still air with a temperature of −42° and brilliant light at eight o'clock. We had made twenty miles air-line distance from Anoatok, and Cape Sabine was but thirty miles away, but we had been forced so far north that we still had thirty miles before us to reach the Cape. We made only about three miles an hour. At noon we stopped and coffee was served from our ever-hot coffee box. A can had been placed in a box and so protected by reindeer skins that the heat was retained for twelve hours during the worst weather. While we sat regaling ourselves a ball of fire appeared on the icy horizon. Our hearts were glad. The weather was bitterly cold, the temperature was −51°F., but the sun had risen, the long night was at an end.

Although Cape Sabine was in sight we still headed for the Bache Peninsula. Impassable ice and open water pushed us farther and farther north. It was three o'clock before the Cape was seen over the dogs' tails. Soon after four the light failed, the land coloured to purple and gold toward the rim of the horizon and we were left to guess the direction of our course. But Eskimos are somewhat better than Yankees at guessing, for we got into no troubles until nine o'clock when we tried to scale the rafted ice against Cape Sabine. With only the camp equipment and dog food, the dogs crept up and down in the black hills of ice while we followed like mountain sheep. Here had been the camp of the ill-fated Greely expedition. It occurred to me that it was a curious whim of fate that this ill-starved camp of famine and death in earlier days should mark the very outset of our modern effort to reach the Pole.

The morning of February 22nd the thermometer registered −58°. We were evidently passing from the storms and open water of Smith Sound to a still, dry climate with very low temperature. At noon the sun showed half of his face over the cliff as we crossed the bay and sought better ice along Bache Peninsula. Here we saw hares staring at us and four were secured for our evening meal. In the very low temperature of −64° the hunters suffered from injuries like burns, due to the blistering caused by the cold metal of their guns. Dog food had also to be prepared. In efforts to divide the walrus skins, two hatchets were broken. The Eskimo dog is a tough creature but he cannot be expected to eat food which breaks an axe. Petroleum and alcohol were used liberally and, during the night, the skin was sufficiently softened by the heat to be cut with the hatchet. This skin seems to be good for the dogs. It is about one inch thick and contains little water, the skin fibre being a kind of condensed nutriment, small quantities of which satisfy the dogs. It digests slowly and therefore has lasting qualities.

The lamps burning at full force made the night camp igloos comfortable although the temperature fell to −68°.

On the morning of the 23rd we met the advance party, who came to our igloos at breakfast. One musk-ox and eleven hares had been secured. The valley had been thoroughly hunted but no other game was sighted. This was sad news for us for we had counted on game with which to feed the dog train en route to the polar sea. If animals were not secured here our project would fail at the very start, and this route would be impossible. To push overland rapidly to the west coast of Ellesmere Island was now our only chance, but the report of insufficient snow on the passes seemed to forbid this. Something, however, must be tried. We could not give up without a fight. The strong probability of our failing to find musk-oxen and therefore forcing the extension of the expedition for another year, over another route, made me decide to send Francke back to headquarters to guard our supplies. There was no objection to the return of most of the other party as well, but we took their best dogs and sledges, with some exchange of drivers.

With this change in the arrangements, and the advance supplies from Cape Sabine and Cape Viele, each sled now carried eight hundred pounds. Beyond Flagler Bay the ice became smooth and almost free of snow. Our increased number of dogs, with good travelling, enabled us to make satisfactory progress despite a steadily falling temperature. The head of the bay was reached late at night after an exhausting march of twenty-five miles, against a hard wind, with a temperature of −60° that almost paralyzed the dogs. The men only kept alive by running with the dogs. Comfortable [snow] houses were soon built and preparations made for a day of rest.

On the morrow we intended to begin crossing the central glacier of Elles-

From a Greenland Eskimo woodcut.

mere Island. We had intended to cross to Cannon Bay but on February 25th, when the dogs were harnessed to their sleds and we pushed into the valley of mystery ahead, I discovered that nowhere did it offer a safe slope for an ascent. I realized that our only hope was to push overland to Bay Fiord. The easy slopes on this route were enlivened with hares. Some sat motionless with long ears erect, others danced about in frisky play. The temperature was –62° but there was no wind. Following the winding of a stream we advanced about twenty miles. The valley looked like a pass. At various places we noticed old musk-ox paths. I knew that where game trails are well marked on mountains one is certain to find a good crossing. At any rate there was no alternative.

On the morning of the 27th slow progress was made up the rising bed of the stream. The side slopes were grassy and mostly swept bare of snow by strong winter winds. Here, I knew, were excellent feeding grounds for musk-ox and caribou but a careful scrutiny gave no results for a long time. To us the musk-ox was now of vital importance. If the product of the chase gave us no reward, then our polar venture was doomed at the outset.

One day, with a temperature of 100 degrees below the freezing point and a light but sharp wind driving needles of frost to the very bone, we searched the rising slopes of ice-capped lands around us in the hopes of spotting life. For three days the dogs had not been fed. Only meat and fat in large quantities could satisfy the wants of over a hundred empty stomachs. After a hard pull we entered a narrow gorge-like valley. Strong winter gales had bared the ground and we sat down to rest. The dog noses suddenly pointed to a series of steep slopes to the north. They were scenting something, but were too tired to display the animation of the chase. Soon we detected three dark, moving objects on a snowy sun-flushed hill, under a huge cliff about a thousand feet above us. "Ah-Ming-Nah!" shouted Etukishook. The dogs jumped to their feet; the men grasped their glasses; in a second the sledge train was in disorder. Fifty dogs were hitched to three sleds. Rushing up three different gulches, the sleds, with tumbling human forms as freight, advanced to battle. The musk-oxen, with heads pointed to the attacking forces, quietly waited the onrush. Within an hour three huge, fat carcasses were down in the river bed. A temporary camp was made and before the meat froze most of it had passed down hungry throats.

Continuing our course we cross the divide in a storm.† Beyond, in a canyon, the wind was more uncomfortable than it had been in the open. Something had to be done. We could not go on breathing that maddening air, weighted by frost and thickened by snows. The snow banks gave no shelter whatever and a rush of snow came over which quickly buried the investigators.   But it was our only hope.

"Dig a hole," said Koolootingwah.

Now to try to dig a hole without a shovel, and with snow coming more rapidly than the power of man could remove, seemed a waste of needed vital force. But I had faith in the intelligence of my savage companions, and ordered all hands to work. They gathered in one corner of the snow bank while I allowed myself to be buried in a pocket of the cliff to keep my tender skin from turning to ice. Every few minutes someone came along to see if I was safe. A kind of buried igloo was progressing. Two men were now inside. In the course of another hour they reported four men inside; in another hour seven men, and the others were piling up the blocks, cut with knives from the interior. Inside the men were sweating. Soon after, the igloo was completed and I lost no time in seeking its shelter. The lamps sang cheerily of steaming musk-ox steaks. The dogs were brought into the canyon and a more comfortable night was impos-

†*At an altitude of about 3,600 feet.*

sible to imagine. We were fifty feet under the snow. The noise of the driving storm was lost. The blinding drift about the entrance was effectually shut out by a block of snow used as a door.

When we emerged in the morning the sky was clear. A light wind came from the west with a temperature of −78° F.† Two dogs had frozen during the storm. All the rest were buried in the edge of a drift that was piled fifteen feet high. An exploration of the canyon ahead showed other falls and boulders, impossible for sledge travel. A trail was therefore picked over the hills to the side. It was a severe day. How we escaped broken legs and smashed sleds was miraculous. But somehow, in our plunges down avalanches, we always landed in a soft bed of snow. We advanced about ten miles and made a descent of five hundred feet, camping on a glacier lake. The temperature was now −79°. We were glad indeed when the candle was at last placed inside the dome of an igloo to reveal the last cracks that needed to be stuffed.

The following dawn we saw that our advance was blocked by a large glacier. A way would have to be cut into this barrier of icebergs for about a mile. This required the full energy of all the men for the day. The weather seemed beautiful. For the first time I felt the heat of the sun. It came through the thick fur on my shoulders with the tenderness of a warm human hand. The mere thought of the genial sun brought a glow of warmth but at the same time the thermometer was very low, −78½°. One's sense of cold under normal conditions is a good instrument in its bearing upon animal functions, but as an instrument of physics it makes an unreliable thermometer. If I had been asked to guess the temperature of the day I should have placed it at about −25°. Nevertheless the igloo failed to become warm that night so we fed our internal fires liberally with warming courses. We partook of super-heated coffee, thickened with sugar, and later took butter chopped in squares which was eaten as cheese with musk-ox meat chopped by our axe into splinters. Hare loins and hams cooked in pea soup served as dessert. The amount of fat and sugar which we now consumed was quite remarkable. In this low temperature I found considerable difficulty in jotting down the brief notes of our day's doings. The paper was so cold that the pencil scarcely left a mark. To economize fuel the fires were later extinguished. In the morning we were buried in the frost falling from our own breath.

It was difficult to work with fur-covered hands, but the Eskimo can do much with his glove-fitting mittens. Some damaged sledges were soon repaired. After tumbling over irregular ice along the face of the glacier, the frozen river offered a splendid highway over which the dogs galloped with speed. We rode until cold compelled exercise. The stream descended amongst picturesque hills but the most careful scrutiny found no sign of life except the ever-present musk-ox trails of seasons gone by. As we neared the sea-line near the mouth of the river we began to see a few fresh tracks. Passing out on the south into Bay Fiord we noted bear and wolf tracks. We had already gone twenty-five miles and were looking forward to our next camping place when all my companions, seemingly at once, espied a herd of musk-oxen on the skyline of a whale-backed mountain to the north.

The cumbersome loads were quickly pitched from three sledges. Rifles and knives were fastened and in a few moments the long lashes snapped and away we rushed with two men on each of the sledges and with double teams of twenty dogs. It took but a brief time to cover the three miles between us. The musk-ox did not take alarm until we were ready to attack them from three separate points.

All but five dogs from each sledge were now freed from harness. They darted

†The alcohol thermometers available to Cook were not intended for use at such phenomenally low temperatures and, as he reported, the readings they gave could only be considered approximate.

towards the oxen with speed. The oxen tried to escape through a ravine but it was too late. The dogs were on every side of them and all the oxen could do was grunt fiercely and jump into a bunch with tails together and heads directed at the enemy. There were seven musk-oxen in all, and they tried to keep the dogs scattered at a safe distance. After a few bold efforts the bulls, with lowered horns, merely held to the position, while the dogs, not actually daring to attack, sat in a circle and howled. Meanwhile the Eskimos and myself were hurrying up. The battle was soon over. One old bull broke through the dogs and, followed by a group of them, was driven over a cliff in a plunge of five hundred feet.

It was very cold and no time could be lost in dressing the game. While this was being done I noticed on neighbouring hills three other herds of musk-oxen. I did not tell the hunters for they would not have rested until all were secured. Living in a land of cold and hunger, the Eskimo is insatiable for game. We had as much meat as we could possibly use for the next few days and it was much easier to fill up, and secure more when we needed it, than to carry almost impossible loads.

I looked at the enormous quantity of meat and wondered how it could be transported to camp, but no such problem troubled the Eskimos. Piece after piece went down the canine throats with a gulp. The dogs had not yet reached their limit when the snow was cleared of its weight of dressed meat and a canine wrangle began for possession of the cleaned bones. It was midnight before camp was pitched. Two comfortable snow houses were built and in them our feasts rivalled those of the dogs.

March 2nd was bright and clear and still. The ice was smooth, with just snow enough to prevent the dogs cutting their feet. The temperature was −79°. Yet we found it comfortable to walk along behind the upstanders of the sledges. Some fresh bear tracks were crossed. These denoted that bears had advanced along the coast on an exploring tour, much as we aimed to do. Scenting their tracks, the dogs forgot their distended stomachs and braced into the harness with full pulling force. We were still able to keep pace by running. But hard exercise brought no perspiration.

During our daily marches north from Bay Fiord [through Eureka Sound] and up Nansen Sound the shadow became a thing of considerable interest and importance. The Eskimo's soul is something apart from his body. He believes it follows in the shadow. For this reason, stormy sunless days are gloomy times to the natives, for the presence of the soul is then not in evidence. The night has the same effect, though the moon often throws a clear-cut shadow. The native believes the soul wanders from the body at times. When it does this, the many rival spirits, which in their system of beliefs tenant the body, get into all sorts of trouble.

The shadow does not quickly return with the returning sun. Continuous storms so screen the sunbeams that only a vague, diffused light reaches the long night-blackened snows. When the joy of seeing the first shadows exploded amongst my companions I did not know what intoxication infected the camp. With stomachs full of newly acquired musk-ox meat we had slept. Suddenly the sun burst through a maze of clouds. The temperature was very low but, only half-dressed, the men rushed outside dancing with joy. Their shadows were long, sharp-cut, and of a deep purple hue. They danced with them. This brought them back to the normal life of Eskimo hilarity.

For a while we advanced north over an easy trail. But, beyond, the snow increased rapidly in depth with every mile. In two difficult marches we reached

Eureka Sound. Bear tracks were numerous. We were, however, too tired to give chase. Etukishook noted two bears wandering over the land not far away. Watching for a few moments with the glasses, we noted that they were stalking a sleeping musk-ox. Now we did not care particularly for the bears, but the musk-ox was regarded as our own game and we were not willing to divide it. Our packs were pitched into the snow and the dogs rushed off through deep snow, over hummocks and rocks, towards the creeping bears.

As the bears turned, the rear attack seemed to offer sport and they rose to meet us. But as one team after another bounced over the nearest hills towards them, their heads turned and they rushed up the steep slopes. We now saw twenty musk-oxen asleep in scattered groups. These interested us much more than the bears. The dogs were seemingly of the same mind, for they required no urging to change their noses from the bears to the musk-oxen. All the musk-oxen rose at once, shook off the snow, rubbed their horns on their knees, and then formed a huge star. In a short time the entire herd was ours. The meat was dressed, wrapped in skins, the dogs were lightly fed and the carcasses hauled to camp. Then we completed building our igloos. Bears and wolves wandered about camp all night, but with a hundred dogs, whose eyes were on the swollen larder, there was no danger from wild beasts. A holiday was declared. It would take time to stuff the dogs with twenty musk-oxen. Furthermore our clothing needed attention. Boots, mittens, and stockings had to be dried and mended. Some of our garments were torn. Much of the dogs' harness required fixing. The Eskimo sledges had been slightly broken. Later, the same day, another herd of twenty musk-oxen were seen. Now even the Eskimo's thirst for blood was satisfied. The pot was kept boiling, and the igloos rang with primitive joys.

On March 7 we began a straight run up Nansen Sound to the polar sea, a distance of 170 miles. The weather was superb and the ice again free from heavy snow. In six marches we reached Schei Island, which we found to be a peninsula.† We halted here and a feast day was declared. Twenty-seven musk-oxen and twenty-four hares were secured in one hunt. This meat guaranteed a food supply to the shores of the polar sea. A weight was lifted from my load of cares for I had doubted the existence of game far enough north to count on fresh meat as far as the sea. The temperature was still low (−50° F.) but the nights were brightening and the days offered twelve hours of good light. Our outlook was hopeful indeed.

The land whose coast we were following to the shores of the polar sea [Elles-mere Island] is part of the American hemisphere and one of the larger islands of the world, spreading 30° in longitude and rising 7° of latitude. What is its name? The question must remain unanswered, for it not only has no general name, but numerous sections are written with names and outlines that differ with the caprice of the explorers who have been there. Thus the south is called Lincoln Land; above it, Ellesmere Land. Then comes Schley Land, Grinnell Land, Arthur Land, and Grant Land, with other lands of later christenings. No human beings inhabit the island. No nation assumes the responsibility of claiming or protecting it.‡

We had now advanced beyond the range of all primitive [human] life. No human voice broke the frigid silence. Yet there was no good reason why men should not have followed the musk-oxen here. I found an inspiration in being thus alone at the world's end. The barren rocks, the waste of snow fields, the mountains stripped of earlier ice sheets, and every phase of the landscape, assured a new interest. There was a note of absolute abandon on the part of nature. If our own resources failed, or if a calamity overtook us, there would

†*Incorrectly mapped as an island by Sverdrup.*

‡*Canada had not yet made an effort to exert sovereignty over it, but did so the following year.*

be no trace to mark icy graves forever hidden.

When we passed Snags Fiord the formation changed and for several marches game was scarce. The temperature rose as we neared the polar sea. Camping in the lowlands just south of Svartevoeg Cliffs we secured seven musk-oxen and eighty-five hares. Here were immense fields of grass and moss bared by persistent winter gales. It was a great surprise that here on the shores of the polar sea we found a garden spot of plant luxuriance. This assured, in addition to the caches left en route, a sure food supply for the return from our mission to the north.

Svartevoeg is a great cliff, the northernmost of Axel Heiberg Island, which leaps precipitously into the polar sea. Its negroid face of black scarred rocks frowns like the carven stone countenance of some hideously mutilated and enraged Titan. It is 520 miles from the North Pole.

From this point I planned to make my dash in as straight a route as possible. The supplies we had brought with us from Anoatok were practically untouched. Eating to repletion on unlimited game, our bodies were in excellent trim for the exigencies of the difficult travel. As a man's mental force is the result of yesteryear's upbuilding, so his strength of today is the result of last week's eating. With the surge of ambition which had been formulating for twenty years, and my body in the best physical shape for the supreme test, the Pole now seemed almost near.

Having reached the end of Nansen Sound, with Svartevoeg on my left, and the tall, scowling cliffs of Lands-Lokk on my right, I viewed for the first time the rough and heavy ice of the untracked polar sea over which, knowing the conditions of the sea-ice, I anticipated the most difficult part of our journey lay. Imagine before you fields of crushed ice which have been slowly forced downward by great currents from the north, and pounded and piled into jagged mountainous heaps for miles about the land. Beyond this difficult ice, as I knew, lay more even fields, over which travelling would be comparatively easy.

I now decided to reduce my party into the smallest possible number consistent to the problem in hand. An extra sled was left at a cache at this point to ensure a good vehicle for our return in case the two sleds which we were to take should be badly broken en route. I decided to take only two men on the last dash, plus a support party of two other men who would turn back soon after we had left the land. I had carefully watched and studied every one of my party, and had already selected Etukishook and Ahwelah, two young Eskimos, each about twenty years old, as best fitted to be my companions in the long run of destiny.

Twenty-six of the best dogs were picked to haul two sleds and upon these when we left the advance support party, were to be loaded all our needs for a trip estimated to last eighty days. The camp equipment selected included the following articles: one blow fire lamp, three aluminum pails, three aluminum cups, three aluminum teaspoons, one tablespoon, three tin plates, six pocket knives, two butcher knives, one saw knife, one long knife, one Sharps rifle, one Winchester .22 rifle, 110 cartridges, one hatchet, one Alpine axe, extra line and lashings, and three personal bags.

The sled equipment consisted of two sleds weighing fifty-two pounds each; one twelve-foot folding canvas boat, the wood of which formed part of the sled; one silk tent, two canvas sled covers, two caribou skin sleeping bags, floor furs, extra wood for sled repairs, screws, nails and rivets.†

The personal bags contained four extra pairs of kamiks (skin boots) with fur stockings, a woollen shirt, three pairs of sealskin mittens, two pairs of fur

†Cook also carried a complete set of scientific instruments including everything necessary to obtain accurate position fixes.

mittens, a piece of blanket, a sealskin coat, and repair kit for mending clothing as well as other necessary materials. On the march, we wore snow goggles, blue fox coats and birdskin shirts, bearskin pants, sealskin boots, bearskin stockings, and a band of fox tail around the knee and about the waist.

The food supply was mostly pemmican: 850 lbs. of beef pemmican, 130 lbs. of walrus pemmican, 50 lbs. of musk-ox meat, 25 lbs. of musk-ox tallow, 2 lbs. of tea, 1 of coffee, 25 of sugar, 40 of condensed milk, 60 of milk biscuit, 10 of pea-soup powdered and compressed, 50 lbs. of surprises, 40 lbs. petroleum, 2 lbs. wood alcohol, 3 lbs. candles and 1 lb. matches.

We planned our future food supply with pemmican as practically the sole food; the other things were to be mere palate satisfiers. Of the twenty-six dogs, we had at first figured on taking sixteen over the entire trip to the Pole and back to land, but in this last calculation only six were to be taken. Twenty, the least useful, were to be used one after the other as food on the march, as soon as reduced loads and better ice permitted. This, we counted, would give 1,000 pounds of fresh meat over and above our pemmican supply.

THE DASH FOR THE POLE

After making several trips about Svartevoeg arranging caches for the return, studying the ice and land, I decided to make the final start on the polar sea on March 18th, 1908.

The time had come to part with many of our faithful Eskimo companions. Taking their hands, in my manner of parting, I thanked them as well as I could for their faithful service to me. "Tigishi Ah Yaung-Uluk!" (The Big Nail!), they replied, wishing me luck.

Then in a half gale blowing from the northwest and charged with snow, they turned their backs upon me and started upon the return track. They carried little but ammunition because we had learned that plenty of game was to be found along the return course. Even after they were out of sight in the drifting snow-storm their voices came clearly back to me. They had followed me until I told them I could use them no longer; and it was not only for their simple pay of knives and guns, but because of a real desire to be helpful.

With a snow-charged blast in our faces it was impossible for us to start immediately. We climbed into our bags and slept a few hours longer. At noon the horizon cleared and the wind veered to southwest. Doubly rationed the night before, the dogs were not to be fed again for two days. The time had come to start.

Our journey was begun. Swept of snow by the force of the storm, the rough ice crackled under the swift speed of our sleds. Even on this uneven surface the dogs made such speed that I kept ahead of them only with difficulty. The hard irregularity of the ice at times endangered our sleds. We climbed over ridges like walls. We jumped dangerous crevasses, keeping slightly west by north. The land soon sank in the rear of us. Drifting clouds and wind-driven snow soon screened the tops of the black mountains. On every side ice hummocks heaved their backs. Behind me followed snugly loaded sleds, drawn by forty-four selected dogs under the lash of four expert Eskimo drivers.

We pitched camp on a floe berg of unusual height. About us were many big hummocks, and to the lee of these, banks of hardened snow. Away from land it is always difficult to find snow suitable for cutting building blocks. There, however, was an abundance. We busily built, in the course of an hour, a comfortable snow igloo. Into it we crept, grateful for shelter from the piercing wind.

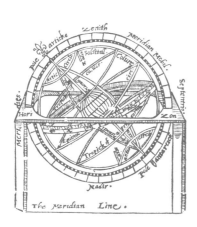

The Meridian Line.

†On Franz Josef Land in 1901-02. Cook anticipated an easterly drift, whereas he actually encountered a westerly one.

‡This is the first description of the thick land-shelf ice north of Ellesmere and Axel Heiberg Islands and is conclusive proof that Cook was where he said he was.

Already I had begun to think of our return to land. It was difficult to approximate any probable course. Much would depend upon conditions to be encountered in the northward route. Although we had left caches of supplies with the object of returning along Nansen Sound and over Arthur Land, I entertained grave doubts of our ability to return this way. I knew that if the ice should shift strongly to the east we might not be given the chance. In such an event we would be carried helplessly to Greenland. The drift, in my opinion, would not necessarily mean dangerous hardships, for the musk-oxen would keep us alive to the west, and to the east it seemed possible to reach Shannon Island where the Baldwin-Zeigler expedition had abandoned a large cache of supplies.† I fell asleep while pondering these things. By morning the air was clear. It was intensely cold, not only because of a temperature of −56°, but a humid chill which pierced to the very bones.

Hitching our dogs we started off. For several hours we seemed to soar over the white spaces then the ice changed in character, the expansive, thick fields of glacier-like ice‡ giving way to floes of moderate size and thickness. These were separated by zones of crushed ice thrown into high pressure ridges, which offered serious barriers. Chopping the pathway with an ice-axe we managed to make fair progress. We covered twenty-one miles of our second run on the polar sea.

I expected, at the beginning of this final effort, to send back the two extra men, Koolootingwah and Inugito, who had remained to help us over the rough pack ice. But progress had not been as good as expected so, although we could hardly spare any food to feed their dogs, the two volunteered to push along for another day without dog feed. Taking advantage of big, strong teams and the fire of early enthusiasm, we aimed to force long distances through the extremely difficult ice jammed against the distant land. The great weight of the supplies intended for the final two sleds were now distributed over four sleds. With increasing difficulties we camped after making only sixteen miles. Although weary, we built a small snow house and I prepared a steaming pot of musk-ox meat and broth. After this our two helpers prepared to return. To have taken them further would have put a serious drain on our supplies and an increased danger for their lives in a longer return to land.

The way before Koolootingwah and Inugito, who had so cheerfully remained to the last possible moment that they could be of help, was not an entirely pleasant one. Their friends were by now well on their journey back to Anoatok, and they had to start after them with sleds empty of provisions and dogs hungry for food. There were no formalities in our parting. Yet as the three of us who were left alone gazed after our departing companions we felt a pang. About us was a cheerless waste of crushed, wind- and water-driven ice. A sharp wind stung our face. The sun was obscured by clouds. My Eskimos already showed anxiety – an anxiety which the aboriginal involuntarily feels when land disappears on the horizon. But before leaving us, one of the two departing Eskimos had pointed out a low-lying cloud to the north of us. "Noona" (land), he said, nodding to the others. The thought occurred to me that, on our trip, I could take advantage of the mirages and low clouds on the horizon to encourage a belief in a constant nearness of land, thus maintaining the courage and cheer of my companions.

We had now advanced by persistent high-pressure efforts over the worst possible ice conditions, somewhat more than sixty miles. Of the nine degrees between land's end and the Pole we had covered one.

Although, being only three, the isolation was more oppressive, there was the advantage of the greater comfort, safety, speed and convenience that came from only a small band. The large number of men in a big expedition increases responsibilities and difficulties. In the early part of a polar venture this disadvantage is eliminated by the ability to augment supplies by the game en route, and by the ultimate advantage of the law of survival of the fittest. But after the last supporting sleds return, the men are bound to each other for protection and can no longer separate. A disabled or unfitted dog can be fed to his companions, but an injured or weak man cannot be eaten or left alone to die. An exploring venture is only as strong as its weakest venture, and increased numbers, like increased links in a chain, reduce efficiency. Moreover personal idiosyncrasies always shorten a day's march and, above all, a numerous party quickly divides into cliques, which oppose each other. With but two savage companions, to whom this arduous task was but a part of an accustomed life of frost, I did not face many of the natural personal troubles which contributed to the failure of former arctic explorations. In my judgment when you double a polar party its chances of success are reduced by one-half; when you divide it, strength and security are multiplied.

We had been travelling about two and a half miles per hour. By making due allowance for detours and halts at pressure ridges, the number of hours travelled gave us a fair estimate of the day's distance. Against this my pedometer offered a check, and the compass gave a course. Thus, over blank charts, our course was marked. By this kind of dead reckoning our position on March 20th was latitude 82° 23'; longitude 95° 14'. We had evidently passed beyond the zone of ice crushed by land pressure. Behind were the great hummocks and small ice; ahead was a cheerful expanse of larger, clearer fields, offering a promising highway.

Our destination was now about 460 miles beyond. Our life now assumed another aspect. Previously we permitted ourselves some luxuries. A pound of coal oil and a good deal of musk-ox tallow were burned each day to heat the igloo and cook food. Extra meals were served when occasion called for them and for each man there had been all the food and drink he desired. If his stockings and mittens were wet there was fire enough to dry them out. All of this had now to be changed.

Hereafter there was to be a short daily allowance of food and fuel – one pound of pemmican a day for the dogs, about the same for the men, with just a taste of other things. Fortunately we were well provided with fresh meat for the early part of the race. At first no great hardship followed our routine. We filled up sufficiently on two cold meals daily, and also depended on superfluous bodily tissue.

Such a journey as now confronted us is a long, continued, hard, difficult, sordid, bodily-exhausting thing.

Until now the strange white world had been one of grim reality. As though some unseen magician had waved his wand it was now transformed into a land of magic. Leaping into existence from beyond the horizon, mirages wove a web of delusional pictures. Peaks of snow were transformed into volcanoes belching smoke; out of the mist rose marvellous cities with strange castles; in the clouds waved golden pennants from pinnacles and domes of many-coloured splendour. Huge creatures, misshapen and grotesque, writhed along the horizon and performed amusing antics. Beginning now, and rarely absent, these spectral denizens of the North accompanied us during the entire journey. Later, when fagged of brain and sapped of bodily strength, I felt my mind swimming in a sea of half-consciousness, they filled me almost with horror, impressing me as do the monsters one sees in a nightmare. All of these things happened whenever the atmosphere was in the right condition to elevate the terrestrial contours by refracting the sun's rays.

The snow was hard and the ice, in fairly large fields separated by pressure lines, offered little resistance. On March 21st at the end of fourteen hours the register indicated a progress of twenty-nine miles. Too weary to build an igloo we threw ourselves thoughtlessly upon the sleds for a short rest and fell asleep. I was awakened by a feeling of compression as if stifling arms gripped me. This was the wind. I breathed with difficulty. I struggled to my feet and about me hissed and wailed a dismal sound. It was a sharp warning that to sleep without the shelter of an igloo would probably mean death.

The wind blew fiercely throughout the night. By the morning of March 22nd the storm had eased to a steady breeze. The temperature was −59°. We emerged from our igloo at noon. Although the cheerless grey veil had been swept from the frigid dome of the sky, to the north there appeared a low black line which gave us much uneasiness. This was a belt of "water-sky," which indicated open water or very thin ice at no great distance.

In the course of a brief time our noses became tipped with a white skin and required nursing. My entire face was now surrounded with ice but there was no help for it. If we were to succeed, the face must be bared to the cut of the elements. We continued, urging the dogs and struggling with the wind just as a drowning man fights for life in a storm at sea. About six o'clock as the sun crossed the west, we reached a line of high pressure ridges. Beyond these the water-sky widened. We laboriously picked a way amongst hummocks which seemed impossible from a distance. Our dogs panted with the strain. In a few hours we arrived at the summit of an unusual uplift of ice. Looking ahead my hopes sank within me. Twisting snakelike between the white fields, and separating the packs, was a tremendous channel several miles wide which seemed to bar all further progress. This was the Big Lead, that great river separating the land-adhering ice from the vast fields of the central polar pack beyond. Of course we had our folding canvas boat on the sleds; but in this temperature of −48° I knew no craft could be lowered into water without fatal results. All of the ice about was firmly cemented together, and over it we made our way toward the edge of the water line.

Camp was pitched on a secure old ice field. Cutting through huge cliffs, the dark channel seemed like a long river winding between palisades of blue crystal. A thin sheet of ice had already spread over the mysterious deep. On its ebony surface a profusion of fantastic frost-crystals arranged themselves in bunches resembling white and yellow coloured flowers.

In exploring the shoreline, a partially bridged place was found about a mile from camp, but the young ice was too elastic for a safe crossing. The temperature, however, fell rapidly with the setting sun, and the wind was just strong enough to sweep off the heated vapours. I knew that better atmospheric conditions could not be afforded to quickly thicken the young ice.

On the morning of March 23rd the Big Lead was mottled and tawny-coloured like the skin of a great boa constrictor. We stood and looked over its broad expanse to the solid floes two miles off. Would the ice bear us? If not, our fate would almost certainly be death. But whatever the luck, we must try to cross. Delay would be fatal, for at any time a light wind or change in the drift might break the new ice and delay us long enough to set the doom of failure upon the entire venture.

Every precaution was taken to safeguard our lives. The important problem was to distribute the weight so that all of it would not be brought to bear on a small area. We separated our dog-teams from the sleds, holding to long lines which we fastened about our bodies and also to the sleds. Running from sled to sled, from dog to dog, and man to man, the line would afford a pulling chance for life should anyone break through the ice. Gingerly testing the ice before me with the end of my axe, with spread legs on snowshoes and with long sliding steps I slowly advanced.

A dangerous cracking sound peeled in every direction under my feet. The Eskimos followed. With every tread the thin sheet of ice perceptibly sank under me and waved in small billows, like a sheet of rubber. Stealthily, as though we were trying to steal some victory, we crept forward. We rocked on the heaving ice as a boat on waves of water. Now and then we stepped upon sheets of thicker ice and hastily went forward with secure footing. None of us spoke during the dangerous crossing. I distinctly heard the panting of the dogs and the patter of their feet. We covered the two miles safely, yet our snail-like progress seemed to cover many anxious years.

Starting forward in the afternoon of March 24th we crossed many small floes separated by narrow belts of new ice. Our speed increased. The temperature rose to −41°. Along the horizon remained misty appearances resembling land. This low-lying fog continued during our entire second hundred miles over the polar basin. Under it we dearly hoped to see new land.

Signs of a gale from the west appeared before we were quite ready to camp. Suitable camping ice was sought and in the course of an hour we built an igloo. We made the structure stronger than usual on account of the threatening aspect of the storm. We constructed double tiers of snowblocks to the windward. A little water was thrown over the top to cement the blocks. We fastened the dogs to the lee of the hummocks. The sleds were securely lashed and fastened to the ice.

We expected a hurricane and had not to wait very long to taste its fury. Before we were at rest in our bags the wind lashed the snow with a force inconceivable. Dogs and sleds in a few minutes were buried under banks of snow, and great drifts encircled the igloo. The cemented blocks of our dome withstood the sweep of the blast yet, now and then, small holes were burrowed through the walls by the sharp wind. Drift snow entered and covered us. I lay awake for hours. I felt the terrible oppression of that raging, life-sucking vampire force sweeping over a desolate world.

Early in the morning of the 25th, the storm ceased as suddenly as it had come. A stillness followed which was appalling. It seemed as if the storm had heard my thoughts and paused to contemplate some more dreadful onslaught. The dogs began to howl desperately, as if being attacked by a bear. We rushed out, grabbing our guns. There was no approaching creature; it was a signal of distress that we had heard. The dogs were in acute misery. The storm snows had buried and bound them in unyielding ice. They had partly uncovered themselves but united by trace and harness they were imprisoned in frozen masses. Few of them could even rise or stretch; they were in severe torment.

As it was still too early to start we released the dogs, then slipped into the bags and sought some quiet slumber. Out of the blankness of sleep I suddenly awakened again. Half dazed, I heard beneath me a series of thundering noises one feels on a tossing ship at sea. In the flash of a second I saw Ahwelah leap to his feet. In the same dizzy instant I saw the dome of the snow house open I felt the ice floor on which I lay quivering; I experienced a sudden giddiness above me and caught a vision of streaked sky. I tried to rise, when suddenly everything seemed lifted from under me; I experienced a suffocating sense of falling and next, with a spasm of indescribable horror, felt about my body a terrific tightening pressure like that of a chilled and closing shell of steel.

In an instant it was clear what had happened. A crevasse had suddenly opened through our igloo directly under the spot where I slept. I, a helpless creature in a sleeping bag, with tumbling snow blocks and ice and snow crashing about and crushing me, with the temperature 48° below zero, was floundering in the sea!

I think I was about to faint when I felt hands beneath my armpits and heard laughter. Adroitly my two companions were dragging me from the water and while I lay panting on the ice, recovering from my fright, they rescued our possessions.

All this happened so quickly so that I really had been in the water only a few seconds. My two companions saw the humour of the episode and laughed heartily. A sheet of ice surrounded my sleeping bag but fortunately the reindeer skin was found to be quite dry when the ice was beaten off. The experience, while momentarily terrifying, was instructive, for it taught us the danger of spreading ice, especially in calms following storms.

Henceforth, one day was to be much like another. Beyond the 83rd parallel life is devoid of pleasure. The intense objective impressions of cold and hunger assailing the body rob even the mind of inspiration. Even the best day of sun and gentle wind offers no balm.

One awakes realizing the wind has abated and sees the cheerless sun. One then kicks the victim upon whom, that morning, duty has fixed the misfortune to be up first – for we tried to be equals in sharing the burdens of life. Upon him to whose lot this hardship falls there is a loss of two hours' repose. He chops ice, fills the kettle, lights the fire, and probably freezes his fingers doing so. Then he wiggles back into his bag, warms his icy hands on the bare skin of his stomach or, if he is in a two-man bag, and the other fellow is awake, arctic courtesy permits the icy hands on the stomach of his bed fellow.

In due time the blood runs to the hands and he sets about tidying up the camp. First the hood of his own bag which is loaded with icicles and frost, the result of the freezing of his breath while asleep. The ice has settled in the kettle in the meantime; more ice must be chopped and put in. The chances are that he now breaks a commandment and steals what to us is a great luxury – a long drink of water to ease his parched throat. Because of the need of fuel economy, a limit is placed on drinks.

Then the fire needs attention; the flame is imperfect and the gas hole needs cleaning. He thoughtlessly grips the little bit of metal at the end of which the cleaning needle is attached. The metal is so cold that it burns and he leaves a piece of his skin on it. Then the breakfast ration of pemmican must be divided. It is not frozen, for it contains no water, but it is hard like granite. Heat would melt it – but there is no fuel to spare. The two slumberers are given a thump and their eyes open to the stone-like pemmican. Between yawns the teeth are set to grind at it. The water boils, the tea is tossed in, and the kettle is removed. We rise on elbows, still in the bags, to enjoy the one heavenly treat of our lives – a cup of tea which warms the hands and the stomach all at once.

Then we dress. It is remarkable how cold compels speed in dressing. The door of the snow house is now kicked out – all tumble about to warm up and stop chattering teeth. Breaking camp is a matter of but a minute, for things fall almost automatically into convenient packs. The sledges are loaded and lashed in a few minutes. Then the teams are gathered to the pulling lines and off we go with a run. The pace for dog and man is two and a half miles an hour, over good ice or bad, hard snow or soft. There is no stop for lunch, no riding or rest, or anything else. It is drive – drive.

On March 27th a half gale was blowing and as the sun settled into the west the wind increased in fury and forced us to camp. Before the igloo was finished a steady rasping wind brushed the hummocks and piled the snow in large dunes about us. The snow house was not cemented as usual with water. The tone of the wind did not seem to indicate danger and furthermore, there was no open sea water near.

Not particularly anxious, we sought the comfort of the bags. Awakened in the course of a few hours by drifts of snow about our feet, I found that the wind had burrowed holes in weak spots through the snow wall. We were bound, however, not to be cheated of a few hours' sleep and with one eye open, we turned over. I was awakened by falling snow blocks soon after.

Forcing my head out of my fur hood I saw the sky, cloud-swept and grey. The dome of the igloo had been swept away. We were being quickly buried under a dangerous weight of snow. Tearing and burrowing at the fallen snow blocks I made violent efforts to free my companions, buried in their bags under the fallen snow blocks. I was surprised a few moments later, as I was working to keep their breathing place open, to feel them burrowing through the snow. They had entered their bag without undressing. Half clothed in shirt and pants but with bare feet, they wiggled out of the bag and up through the breathing hole. After a little digging their boots were uncovered and then, with protected feet, their bag was freed and placed at the side of the broken igloo. Into it the boys crept fully dressed, with the exception of coats. I rolled out beside them in my bag. Thus we lay in the open sweep of furious winds, impotent to move, for twenty-nine hours.

As we pushed on into the sterile wastes, our eager eyes constantly searched the plains of frost but there was no speck of life to grace them. The sense of covering distance gave me only a dull satisfaction. Only some catastrophe, some sudden and overwhelming obstacle, would have aroused me to an intense mental emotion, to a passionate despair, or to the anguish of possible defeat. I was now becoming the unconscious instrument of my ambition; almost without volition my body was being carried forward by a subconscious force which had fastened on a distant goal. Sometimes the wagging of a dog's tail held my attention for a long time; it afforded a curious play for my morbidly obsessed imagination. In an hour I would forget what I had been thinking.

We forced marches day after day. We travelled until dogs languished or legs failed. Ice hills rose and fell before us. Mirages grimaced at us daily. The incidents and our positions were recorded, but our adventures were promptly forgotten in the mental bleach of the next day's effort.

We had now followed the sun's northward advance from its first peak, at mid-day, above the southern ice of the polar gateway, to its sweep over the whole northern ice at midnight. From the end of the polar night, late in February, to the first of the double days and the midnight suns, we had forced a trail through darkness and over the irregularities of an unknown world of ice to a spot almost exactly 200 miles from the Pole.

Now that we had the sun unmistakably at midnight, its new glory was an incentive to onward efforts. Observations on April 8th placed camp at latitude 86° 36′, longitude 94° 2′. Although we had made long marches and really great speed, we had advanced only 96 miles in the nine days. Much of our hard work had been lost in circuitous twists around troublesome pressure ridges and high, irregular fields of old ice.

We had lived for weeks on a steady diet of withered beef and tallow. There was no change, we had no hot meat, and never more to eat than was absolutely necessary. We became indifferent to the aching pain of the stomach. The depletion of energy, the lassitude of overstrained limbs, manifested themselves. The Eskimos grew lax in the swinging of the whip and indifferent in urging on the dogs. The dogs displayed the same spirit by lowering tails, limp ears, and drooping noses, as their shoulders dragged the sled farther and ever farther from the land of life.

As we passed the 86th parallel, the ice increased in thickness. Great hummocks and pressure ridges became less frequent. A steady progress was gained with the most economical human drain possible. The temperature ranged between 36° and 40° below zero, with higher and lower mid-day and midnight extremes. Only spirit thermometers (alcohol) were useful, for the mercury was at this degree of frost either frozen or sluggish.

In camp a grip of the knife left painful burns from cold metal. To the frozen fingers ice-cold water was warm. With wine spirits the fire was lighted, while oil delighted the stomach. In our dreams heaven was hot, the other place was cold. All nature was false; we seemed to be nearing the chilled flame of a new Hades.

Our observations on April 11th gave latitude 87°, 20′, longitude 95°, 19′. The pack disturbance was less and less noted as we progressed in the northward movement. Fewer troublesome old floes and less crushed new ice was encountered. We had now passed the highest reaches of all our predecessors. The inspiration of being "Farthest North" for a brief time thrilled me. The time was at hand, however, to consider seriously the possibility of an early return. Nearly half of the food allowance had been used. Now our dog-teams were also much reduced in number. Because of the cruel law of the survival of the fit, the less useful dogs had gone into the stomachs of their stronger companions. Owing to food limitations and the advancing season, we could not prudently continue the onward march more than a fortnight longer.

We had dragged ourselves 300 miles over the polar sea in twenty-four days. Including delays and detours this gave a daily average of nearly thirteen miles. There remained 160 miles to the pole itself. There was fuel and food enough to risk the adventure. But a prolonged storm, a deep snowfall, or an active ice pack would mean failure. I watched daily for possible signs of falling in the strength of any of us, because a serious disability would now mean a fatal termination. A disabled man could neither continue nor return.

Our tremendous exertions provoked intense thirst. Following the habit of the camel we managed to take enough water before starting to keep sufficient liquid in the stomach and veins for the ensuing day's march yet it was painful to await the melting of ice at camping time. In two sittings, evening and morning, each of us took an average of three quarts of water daily.

Day after day we pushed along at a steady pace over plains of frost and through a mental desert. As the eye opened at the end of a period of shivering slumber, the fire was lighted little by little, the stomach was filled with liquids and solids, mostly cold – enough to last the day, for there could be no halt or waste of fuel for mid-day feeding. We got into harness, and under the lash of duty, paced off the day's pull, working until standing became impossible. As a man in a dream I marched, set camp, ate and tried to rest. The arduous task of building a snow house meant only physical hardship. There was no pleasurable mental recreation to relieve us; there was nothing to arouse the soul from its icy enclosure. To me there was still the inspiration of ultimate success; but for my young savage companions, it was a torment almost beyond endurance.

On the morning of April 13th, the strains reached the breaking point. For days there had been a steady cutting wind from the west which drove despair to its lowest reaches. The west again blackened. The frost burn of sky colour changed to a depressing grey, streaked with black. The path was absolutely cheerless. All this was a dire premonition of a storm and greater torture.

No torment could be worse than a never-ceasing rush of wind. It gripped us and sapped the life from us. Ahwelah bent over his sled and refused to move. I walked over and stood by his side. His dogs turned and looked inquiringly at us. Etukishook came near and stood motionless, like a man in a trance, staring blankly at the southern skies. Large tears fell from Ahwelah's eyes and froze in the blue of his own shadow. I knew that the dreaded time of utter despair had come. With a tear-streaked and withered face, Ahwelah slowly said with a strange wail, "It is well to die – beyond is impossible – beyond is impossible!"

I shall never forget the mournful group before me, in itself an awful picture of despair, of man's ambition failing just as victory is within his grasp. Ahwelah, a thin, half-starved figure in worn furs, lay over his sled, limp, dispirited, broken. It was a critical moment.

"Yesterday I, too, felt that way," I said. "Beyond tomorrow it will be better. Cheer up!" I urged, trying to essay a smile.

"Return will I; the sky and weather I do not understand. It is very cold," said Ahwelah.

"A little farther come," I pleaded. "Only a little farther."

I knew my companions were brave and I was certain of their fidelity. Could their mental despair be alleviated, I felt convinced they could brave themselves for another effort. I told them what we had accomplished, that they were good and brave, that their parents and their sweethearts would be proud of them, and that as a matter of honour, we must not now fail.

"The Pole is near," I said. "At the end of five sleeps it is finished, beyond all is well, we return thereafter quickly."

"On ice always, is not good. The bones ache," they replied. But I noticed that Ahwelah had wiped his eyes.

"Come walk a little further," I went on. "Beyond tomorrow within two moons we return to Eskimo lands."

"At last, then it is to laugh! There we will meet father and mother and little wives!" said Ahwelah.

"Yes, in two moons there will be water and meat and all in plenty," I returned.

Etukishook gazed at me intently. His eyes brightened. And as I spoke, my own spirits rose to the final effort. My lassitude gave way to a new enthusiasm. I felt the fire, kindling for many years, aglow within me. The goal was near; there remained but one step. I spoke hurriedly. The two sat up and listened. Slowly they became inspired by my intoxication. Never did I speak so vehemently.

Ahwelah, determined but grim, braced his body and shouted to the dogs – "Huk, Huk, Huk"; and then to us he said, "Aga – Ka!" (Go – Come).

With snapping whip, we were away on that last 100 miles.

In the forced effort which followed, we frequently became overheated. The temperature was steady at 44° below zero. Perspiration came with ease and with a certain amount of pleasure. Later followed a train of suffering for many days. The delight of the birdskin shirt gave place to the chill of a wet blanket. Our coats and trousers hardened to icy suits of armour. It became quite impossible

On the ceaselessly moving polar sea, explorers
attempting the Pole found ice thrown up in strange
shapes, a nightmare world of crags and chasms. Cook travelled
for 20 days at one period without knowing his position.
"Beyond is impossible," one of his Eskimos insisted.

to dress after a sleep without softening the stiffened furs with the heat of our bare skin. Mittens, boots and fur stockings became quite useless until dried out.

Signs of land, which I encouraged my companions to believe were real, were seen every day, but I knew, of course, they were deceptive. It now seemed to me that something unusual must happen, that some line must cross our horizon to mark the important area into which we were passing. Daily, by careful measurements I found that our night shadows shortened and became more uniform during the passing hours of the day.

Nearing the Pole my imagination quickened. A restless, almost hysterical excitement, came over all of us. My boys fancied they saw bears and seals. I had new lands under observation frequently, but with a change in the direction of the light the horizon would clear. We became more and more eager to push further into the mystery.

At eight o'clock in the morning of April 19th we camped on an old field of ice with convenient hummocks, to the top of which we could climb for the frequent outlook we now maintained. We pitched our tent, silenced the dogs by blocks of pemmican. New enthusiasm was aroused by a liberal pot of pea soup and a few chips of frozen meat. Ahwelah and Etukishook were soon lost in profound sleep, the only comfort of their hard lives. I remained awake to get nautical observations. Our longitude calculations lined us up at 94°, 3′. At noon the sun's altitude was carefully set on the sextant, and the latitude, reduced, gave 89°, 31′. The drift had carried us too far east. I put down the instrument, wrote the reckonings in my book. Then I gazed with a sort of fascination at them. My heart began to thump wildly. I rose jubilant. We were only twenty-nine miles from the pole!

I suppose I created quite a commotion. Etukishook awoke and rubbed his eyes. I told him that in two marches we should reach the "Tigi-Shu" – the Big Nail. He kicked Ahwelah, none too gently, and told him the glad news. They went out to the hummock to see if they could locate the mark. If but one sleep ahead it must be visible. So they told me, and I laughed. The sensation of laughing was novel. I had not laughed for many days.

We were excited to fever heat. Even the dogs caught the infection. They rushed along at a pace which made it difficult for me to keep a sufficient advance to set a good course. The horizon was still eagerly searched for something to mark the approaching centre of the North but nothing unusual was seen. The same expanse of moving seas of ice on which we had gazed for 500 miles swam about us as we drove onward.

Late at night, after another long rest, we hitched the dogs and loaded the sleds. When action began, the feeling came that no time must be lost. Cracking our whips we bounded on. The boys sang and the dogs howled. Midnight of April 21st had just passed. Etukishook and Ahwelah, though thin and ragged, had the dignity of the heroes of a battle which had been fought through to success.

We were all lifted to the paradise of winners as we stepped over the snows of a destiny for which we had risked life and suffered the tortures of hell. Constantly I watched my instruments in recording this final reach. Nearer and nearer they recorded our approach. At last we touched the mark! We were at the top of the world! The flag is flung to the frigid breezes of the North Pole!

My mental intoxication did not interfere with the routine work which was now necessary. Having reached the goal it was imperative that all scientific observations be made as carefully as possible. To the taking of these I set myself while my companions began the routine work of unloading the sledges and building an igloo. Our course when arriving at the Pole, as near as was possible to determine, was on the 97th meridian of longitude. The day was April 21, 1908. It was local noon. The tent pole, marked as a measuring stick, was pushed into the snow, leaving six feet above the surface. This gave a shadow twenty-eight feet long.

Several sextant observations gave a latitude a few seconds below 90°. (Other observations the next day gave similar results, although we had shifted camp four miles towards magnetic south.)

The ice about was nearly the same as it had been continuously since leaving the 88th parallel. It was slightly more active and showed, by new cracks and over-sliding young ice, signs of recent disturbance. The field upon which we camped was about three miles long and two miles wide. Measured at a crevasse the ice was sixteen feet thick.

In a geographic sense we had now arrived at a point where all meridians meet. The longitude was therefore zero. Time was a negative issue. The hour lines of Greenwich, New York, Peking, and of all the world here run together. Figuratively it is possible here to have all meridians under one foot and therefore it is possible to step from mid-day to midnight, from the time of San Francisco to that of Paris, from one side of the globe to the other.

Here there is but one day and one night each year, but the night of six months is relieved by about one hundred days of continuous twilight. There was here but one direction. It was south on every line of the dial of longitude – north, east and west had vanished. It was south before us, south behind us and south on every side.

The puzzled standpoint of my Eskimos was amusing. They tried hard to appreciate the advantages of finding this suppositious "Tigi Shu" (Big Nail), but actually here, they could not, even from a sense of deference to me and my judgment, entirely hide their feelings of disappointment.

We spent two days about the North Pole. After the first thrill of victory the glamour wore away. We rested and worked. I could get no sensation of novelty as we pitched our last belongings on the sleds. The intoxication of success had gone. During those last hours I asked myself why this place had so aroused an enthusiam through the years. Why, for so many centuries, had men sought this elusive spot? What a futile thing, I thought, to die for! How tragically useless all those heroic efforts – efforts in themselves a travesty, an ironic satire on much vain-glorious human aspiration and endeavour!

With my two companions I could not converse fully; in my thoughts and emotions they could not share. I was alone. I was victorious. But how desolate, how dreadful was the victory. About us was no life, nothing to relieve the monotony of frost and a dead world of ice. A wild eagerness to get back to land seized me.

Before leaving I enclosed a note, written the previous day, in a metallic tube. This I buried in the surface of the polar snows. With few glances backward we now started homeward in haste, on a course along the 100th meridian.

RETURN FROM THE POLE

With correct reasoning, all former expeditions had planned to return to land and secure line of retreat by May 1st. We could not hope to do this until early in June. It seemed probable that, therefore, the ice along the outskirts of the polar sea would be much disrupted and that open water and rapid drifts would seriously interfere with our return.

Considering the difficulties and possibilities, I came to the conclusion that to endeavour to get back by our outward trail would not afford great advantage. Much time would be lost seeking the trail. The almost continuous low drift of snow during some part of nearly every day would obliterate our tracks and render the trail useless as a beaten track in making travel easier. I also had an eager desire to ascertain what might be discovered on a new trail farther west. It was this eagerness which led us to be carried adrift.

The first days, however, passed rapidly. The ice fields became smoother. On April 24 we crossed five crevasses. With fair weather and favourable ice, long marches were made. On the 24th we made sixteen miles, on the 25th fifteen miles, on the 26th, 27th and 28th, fourteen miles a day. The fire of the homing sentiment began to dispel our overbearing fatigue. The dogs sniffed the air, the Eskimos sang songs of the chase.

My lonely march ahead of these sledges continued day by day, compass in hand. Progress was satisfactory. We had passed the 89th and 88th parallels. The 87th and 86th would soon be under foot.

The long strain of the march had established a brotherly sympathy amongst the trio of human strugglers. The dogs had taken us into their community. We now moved among them without hearing a grunt of discord, and their sympathetic eyes followed until we were made comfortable on the cheerless snows. If they happened to be placed near enough, they edged up and encircled us, giving the benefit of their animal heat. To remind us of their presence, frost-covered noses were frequently pushed under the sleeping bags, and occasionally a cold snout touched our warm skin for a rude awakening. The bond of animal friendship betwen us had drawn tighter and tighter in a long run of successive adventures. Now there was a stronger reason than ever to appreciate the power, for together we were seeking an escape from a world which was never intended for creatures with beating hearts.

Much very heavy ice was crossed near the 88th parallel and the weather changed considerably. The inducement to seek shelter in cemented walls of snow was very great but such delay would mean certain starvation. We could not do otherwise than force ourselves against the wind with all possible speed, paying no heed to unavoidable suffering. The hard work of igloo-building was now a thing of the past – only one had been built since leaving the Pole, and in this a precious day was lost hiding out from the fury of a storm. The little silk tent protected us sufficiently from the icy airs.

On May 6th we were stopped at six in the morning by the approach of a gale. The wind had been heavy and strong all night but we did not heed it. When the strongest blast came we threw ourselves over the sled behind hummocks and gathered new breath to force a few miles more.

Finally, when no longer able to force the dogs through the blinding drifts, we sought the lee of an unlifted block of ice. Here suitable snow was found for a snow house. Blocks were cut but the wind swept them away as if they were chips. The tent was tried but could not be made to stand in the rush of the tumult. In sheer despair we crept into it without erecting the pole. Creeping into our bags we allowed the flapping silk to be buried by the drifting snow. Soon the noise and discomfort of the storm were lost and we enjoyed the comfort of an icy grave. A breathing hole was kept open and the wind was strong enough to sweep off the weight of a dangerous drift. Several days of icy despair now followed one another in rapid succession. The wind did not rise to the full force of a storm but was too strong and too cold to travel in. The food supply was noticeably decreasing. With such weather, starvation seemed inevitable. Camp was moved nearly every day, but ambition sank to the lowest ebb. To the atmospheric unrest was added the instability of broken ice and the depressing mystery of an unknown position. For many days no observations had been possible. Our location could only be guessed at.

Through driving storms, with the wind wailing in our ears and deafening us even to the dismal howling of the hungry dogs, we pushed forward in a maddening daily struggle. The route before us was unknown. We were in the clutch of a drifting sea of ice. I could not guess whither we were bound. At times I even lost hope of reaching land. We were now almost insensible to the mad hunger of our stomachs. We were living on a half-ration of food, and daily becoming weaker.

On May 24th the sky cleared long enough to permit me to take observations. I found we were on the 84th parallel, near the 97th meridian. [About 160 nautical miles north and slightly west of Axel Heiberg Island.] The ice was much crevassed and many open spaces of water were denoted in the west by patches of water-sky. The pack was sufficiently active to give us anxiety, although open water did not at the time seriously impede our progress.

Scarcely enough food remained on the sledges to reach our caches unless we should average fifteen miles a day. On the return to this point we had been able to make only twelve miles daily. Now our strength did not seem equal to more than ten. The outlook was threatening, and even dangerous. Still counting on a steady easterly drift of the pack a course was set somewhat west of Svarte-voeg. The ice changed rapidly to smaller fields as we advanced. The temperature rose to zero and the air really began to be warm. Our chronic shivering disappeared. With light sledges and endurable weather we made fair progress over the increasing pack irregularities.

As we crossed the 83rd parallel we found ourselves to the west of a large lead extending slightly west and south. Immense quantities of broken and pulverized ice lined the shores to a width of several miles. The irregularities of the surface and the uncemented break offered difficulties over which no force of man or beast could move a sledge or boat. Compelled to follow the line of least resistance, a south-westerly course was set along the ice division. The wind had now changed and came from the east but there was no relief from the heavy bank of fog that surrounded us.

The following days were days of desperation. The food for man and dog was reduced, and the difficulties of ice travel increased dishearteningly. We travelled twenty days, not knowing our position. A grey mystery enshrouded us. The grey world of mist was silent. My companions gazed at me with faces shrivelled, thinned and hardened as those of mummies. My own vocal power seemed to have left me.

After the long mental torment of threatened starvation and after heartbreaking marches and bitter hunger, and unquenched thirst, the baffling mist that had shut us from all knowledge at last cleared away on the morning of June 14th. I felt such a relief as a man buried alive must feel when, after struggling in the stifling darkness, his grave is suddenly opened. Land loomed to the east and south of us.

Yet we found we had been hardly dealt with by fate. Since leaving the 84th parallel, without noticeable movement, we had been carried astray by the ocean drift. We had moved with the entire mass covering the polar waters. I took observations. They gave latitude 79° 32′ and longitude 101° 22′. I had discovered our whereabouts and found that we were far west from where we ought to be. We were in Crown Prince Gustav Sea. To the east were the mountains and valleys of Axel Heiberg Land, along the farther side of which was our pre-arranged line of retreat, with liberal caches of good things and big game everywhere; but we were effectually barred from all this. Between us and Axel Heiberg lay fifty miles of small crushed ice and impassable lanes of open water. In hard-fought efforts to cross these we were repulsed many times. I knew that if by chance we should succeed in crossing, there would still remain an unknown course of eighty miles to the nearest cache on the eastern coast of Axel Heiberg.

The land to the south was nearer. Due south there was a wide gap which we took to be Hassel Sound. On each side were the islands which Sverdrup had named Ellef Ringnes Land and Amund Ringnes Land. The ice southward was tolerably good and the drift was south-south-east.

The march on June 14th was easy. In a known position, on good ice and with land rising before us, we were for a brief period happy and strong even with empty stomachs. We were far enough south to expect bears and seals, and expecting the usual luck of the hungry savage, we sought diligently.

At about six o'clock we heard a strange sound. Our surprised eyes turned from side to side. Not a word was uttered. Another sound came – a series of soft, silvery notes. It was a snow bunting trilling its ethereal song – the first sound of life heard for many months. We were hungry but no thought of killing this little feathered creature came to us.

We were now on immovable ice attached to the land [they were approaching an island off the Isachsen Peninsula of Ellef Ringnes Island]. We directed our course uninterruptedly landward, for there was no thought of further rest or sleep after the visit of the bird. Our chances of getting meat would have been better by following the open water, but the ice there was such that no progress could be made. Furthermore the temptation to set foot on land was too great to resist. At the end of a hard march – the last few hours of which were through deep snow – we mounted the ice edge and finally reached a little island – a bare spot of real land. We sat down, and the joy of the child in digging the sand of the seashore was ours.

We resolved to keep henceforth from the waste of the terrible polar sea. In the future the position of land must govern our movements. For, along a line of rocks, although we might suffer from hunger, we should no longer be helpless ships on the ocean drift, and if no other life should be seen, at least occasional shrimps would gladden the heart.

The land was low, barren and shapeless. Part of its interior was blanketed with ice. Its shoreline had neither the relief of a cliff nor a picturesque headland. There was only dull uninteresting slopes of sand and snow separating the frozen sea from the land ice. A most careful scrutiny gave no indication of a living creature. Yet it aroused in us a deep sense of enthusiasm. A strip of tropical splendour could not have done more. The spring of man's passion is sprung by contrast, not by degree of glory.

A disabled dog which had been unsuccessfully nursed for several days was now sacrificed on the altar of hard luck, and the other dogs were given a liberal feed, in which we shared. To our palates the flesh of the dog was not distasteful, yet he had been our companion for several months. We had killed and were eating a living creature which had been faithful to us.

We were hard-looking men at this time. Our fur garments were worn through at the elbows and at the knees. Ragged edges dangled in the wind. Our stockings were in tatters. The birdskin shirts had been fed to the dogs and strips of our sleeping bags had, day by day, been added to the canine mess. It took all our spare time now to mend clothing. Dressed in rags, with ugly brown faces seamed with many deep wind fissures, we had reached the extreme limit of degradation in appearance. At the Pole I had been thin, but now my skin was contracted over bones offering only angular eminences. The Eskimos were as thin as myself and my face was as black as theirs.

As we passed out of Hassel Sound the ice continued to drift southward. Here we saw the track of a lemming – the first sign of a four-footed creature – and we stopped to examine the tiny marks with great interest. Next, some old bear tracks were detected. These signs showed that the possibilities of food were at hand and the thought sharpened our senses into savage fierceness. We continued southward following, wolf-like, in the bear's footprints. We were not more than ten miles beyond land when Ahwelah located a spot to leeward. After a peek through the glasses he shouted. The dogs understood, they raised their ears and jumped to the full length of their traces. We hurried eastward to deprive the bear of our scent, but soon saw that he was as hungry as we were, for he made a bee-line for our changed position. We were hunting the bear – the bear also was hunting us. When he was within a hundred yards the dogs were freed. In a few moments the gaunt creatures encircled the bear. Almost without a sound they leapt at the great animal and sank their fangs into his hind leg. Ahwelah fired. The bear fell.

Camp technique and the advantages of fire were not considered – the meat was swallowed raw. No cut of carefully roasted bullock ever tasted better.

The immediate threat of famine was removed and the day was given over to filling up with food. After that a liberal supply of fresh meat rested on the sledge for successive days of feasting. In the days which followed, other bears, intent on examining our larder, came near enough to enable us to keep up a liberal supply of fresh meat. With the assurance of a food supply, a course was set to enter Wellington Channel and push along to Lancaster Sound where I hoped a Scottish whaling ship could be reached in July or August. We were then to the west of North Cornwall Island but a persistent local fog gave only an occasional view of its upper slopes. The west was clear, and King Christian Land appeared as a low line of blue. The sea was bright, the air was delightfully warm with the thermometer at 10° above zero.

The drift carried us into Penny Strait between Bathurst Land and Grinnell Peninsula. At Dundas Island the drift stopped and we sought the shores of Grinnell Peninsula. Bears no longer sought our camp but seals were conveniently scattered along our track. A kindly world had spread our waist-bands to fairly normal dimensions. Three caribou were also secured. Usually we took only the choice parts of the game but every eatable portion of caribou that we could carry was packed on the sledges.

As we neared Pioneer Bay working along the coast of North Devon, it became evident that further advance by sledge was impossible. A persistent wind had jammed the channel with small ice over which sledging was a hopeless task. On the 4th of July we began climbing the highlands of North Devon in order to cross the land to Jones Sound. In bright cold weather we made a descent to Jones Sound on July 7th. Here a diligent search for food failed. Open water ran the range of vision. Sledges were no longer possible, game was scarce, ammunition nearly exhausted. Our future fate had to be worked out in the canvas boat. What were we to do with the faithful dog survivors? We could not stay with them and live. Two had already left to join their wolf progenitors. We gave the others the same liberty. One sledge was cut up and put into the canvas boat which we had carried to the Pole and back.

Advancing eastward in the boat we camped on ice islands in the pack but the pack ice soon became too insecure. Sometimes we made camp in the boat. We pulled with great anxiety to reach the land at Cape Sparbo before a storm entrapped us.

After midnight one day we scented a storm coming. We pulled desperately while the swells shortened and rose. There was no alternative but to seek the shelter of the disrupted pack and press landward as best we could. We had hardly landed on the ice when the wind struck us with such force we could hardly stand against it. The ice immediately started in a westward direction moving slowly seaward. It was no longer possible to press toward the land for the leads were too wide and were lined with whitecaps while the tossing seas hurled mountains of ice and foaming water over the pack edge.

From some distance to windward we noted a low iceberg slowly gaining on our floe. It was a welcome sight for it alone could raise us high enough above the rush of icy water.

Bearing down upon us it touched a neighbouring piece and pushed away. As the berg passed us, however, it left a line of water behind it. We threw boats and sledge into this, paddled after the berg, reached it and leaped to its security.

It was an old remnant of a much larger berg. There were three pinnacles, but too slippery and too steep to climb. Along these the sea had worn grooves leading to a central concavity filled with water. The only space which we could occupy was the crater-like rim around this lake. To prevent us being thrown about we cut holes in the pinnacles and spread lines about them to which we clung. The boat was securely fastened in a similar way. Although the temperature was only at the freezing point it was bitterly cold and we were in a bad way to weather a storm.

When all was snug and secure on the berg we began to take a greater interest in our wind- and sea-propelled craft. Its exposed surface was swept along by the winds while its submarine surface was pushed by tides and currents giving it a complex movement at variance with the pack ice. It plowed up miles of sea-ice, crushing and throwing it aside.

After several hours of this kind of navigation the berg suddenly took a course at right angles to the wind and pushed out of the pack into the seething seas. This rapid shift to the wild agitation of the black waters made us gasp. The seas, with boulders of ice, rolled up over our crest and into the concavity of the berg, leaving us no safe part. We cut many other anchor holes, doubly secured our life-lines and shifted our boat to the edge of the berg. The hours of suspense and torment thus spent seemed as long as the winter of the Eskimo. We were now rushing through a seething blackness, made more impressive by the blue of the berg and the white, ice-lined crests of the seas.

Twenty-four hours elapsed before there was any change. We maintained a terrific struggle to keep from being washed into the sea. We were not far from the twin channels, Cardigan Strait and Hellgate, where the waters of Pacific and Atlantic meet. We were driving for Cardigan Strait past the fiord into which we had descended from the western seas two weeks before. We had lost an advantage of two weeks in one day, and had probably lost our race with time to reach the life-saving haunts of the Eskimos.

At midnight the wind eased and the ice started seaward. This was our moment for escape. We quickly prepared the boat and with trepidation pushed it into the black and frigid waters. Suddenly and to our horror, an invisible piece of ice jagged a hole in the port quarter. In a few minutes the frail craft would have filled; we should sink to an icy death. Fortunately there was a floe near and while the canoe rapidly filled we pushed for the floe, reaching it not a moment too soon. A boot was sacrificed to mend the canoe. Patching the cut, we put again to sea and proceeded.

As we neared the land, ice birds became numerous. Still nearer we noted that the body of land ice was drifting away. We pointed for Cape Vera and to our joy made land on a ledge of lower rocks. I cannot describe the relief I felt in reaching the land after the spells of anguish through which we had passed.

We lost no time trying to regain the distance lost by the drifting berg. We sought our way along the shore. Here, over ice with pools of water and slush, we dragged our sledge with the canvas boat ever ready to launch. Early in August we reached the end of the land pack, about twenty-five miles east of Cape Sparbo. At the end of the last day of sledge travel a camp was made on a small island. Here we saw the first signs of Eskimo habitation. Old tent circles and stone foxtraps in abundance indicated an ancient village. On the mainland we discovered signs of musk-ox, partridge and hare, but no living thing was detected.

As we were packing our things onto the edge of the ice we spied a oogzuk seal. Upon it one of our last cartridges was expended. All of its skin was zealously taken, for this would make harpoon lines which would enable the shaping of Eskimo implements to take the place of the rifles, which, with ammunition exhausted, would soon be useless. Our boots could also be patched with bits of skin. Of the immense amount of oogzuk meat and blubber we were able to take only a small part.

fm During the balance of August every attempt was made to push eastward towards the mouth of Jones Sound, but all efforts were frustrated by the condition of the ice and by the weather. It became obvious that the only possible chance to escape death was to go back to Cape Sparbo or some other suitable area and establish a winter camp in the country. □ FM

We were near the land where Franklin and his men starved. They had ammunition. We had none. We had seen nothing to promise sustenance for the winter. In our desperate straits we even planned to attack bears, should we find any, without a gun. Life is never so sweet as when its days seem numbered. The development of a new art of hunting, with suitable weapons, was reserved for the dire needs of later. The problem was begun by this time. We fortunately had the material of which harpoons and lances could be made and the boys possessed the savage genius to shape a new set of weapons. The slingshot and the loop-line had served a useful purpose already in securing birds and continued to be of prime importance. In the sledge was excellent hickory which could be utilized in various ways. Along shore we had found musk-ox horns and fragments of whale bones. Out of these the points of both harpoon and lance were made. A part of the sledge shoe was sacrificed to make metal points for the weapons. The nails of the cooking box served as rivets. The sealskin which we had secured months earlier was carefully divided and cut into suitable harpoon lines. Our folding canvas boat was strengthened by the leather from our old boots. Ready to engage in battle with the smallest or the largest creatures that might come within reach, we started for Cape Sparbo. Death on our journey never seemed so near.

Pursuing our search for food along the southern side of Jones Sound early in September, we were in starving condition, yet land and sea had been barren of any living thing. Our situation was desperate. One day when we were passing a glacier with waves dashing against its side, something white and glittery pierced the bottom of the boat! It was the tusk of a walrus, gleaming and dangerous. Before we could grasp the situation he had disappeared and water gushed into our craft. An impulse, mad under the circumstances, rose to give him chase. But each second the water rose higher. Instinctively Ahwelah pressed to the floor of the boat and jammed his knee into the hole. He looked mutely to me for orders. The glacier offered no stopping place. Looking seaward I saw a small pan of drift ice. Before the boat was pulled to its slippery landing on this, several inches of water had flooded the bottom. Once again with a piece of boot the hole was patched.

We launched the boat and pulled for land. A school of walrus followed us for at least half the distance. Now followed a long run of famine luck. We searched land and sea for bird or fish. A different stage of starvation was at hand when we were awakened one morning by the sound of distant walrus calls. Through the glasses the group was located far off shore on the pack. Our bodies were fired with a light that had been foreign to us for many moons. Quickly we dropped into the water with our implements and pushed from the famine shores. The pack was about five miles northward. In our eagerness to reach it, the distance seemed spread to leagues. The animals were on a low pan. We aimed for a little cut of ice to the leeward where we hoped to land and creep up behind hummocks. The splash of our paddles was lost in the noise of the grinding ice and the bellowing of walrus calls. The boat finally shot up on the ice and we scattered amongst the ice blocks. Everything was in our favour. We did not for the moment entertain the thought of failure, though our project was tantamount to attacking an elephant with pocket knives. Ten huge animals were lazily stretched out before us. With a firm grip on a harpoon and line, we started. Suddenly Etukishook shouted "nanook!" (bear). We halted. Our implements were no match for a bear but we were too hungry to retreat. The bear paid no attention to us. Slowly he crept up to the snoring herd while we watched with a mad, envious anger swelling up within us. All the creatures woke, but too late to give battle as his glistening fangs closed and a young walrus struggled in the air. The other walruses sank into the water and the bear moved off to a safe distance where he sat down to a comfortable meal. We were not of sufficient importance to interest either the bear or the disturbed herd of giants.

On land that night we were cheerless and cold. We were in no mood for sleep. In a lagoon we discovered small moving things that proved to be fish. A diligent search under stones brought out a few handfuls of tiny creatures. Seizing them we ate the wriggling things raw.

Next morning we saw a number of groups of walrus sound asleep on the ice. We ventured out with a savage desire sharpened by a taste of raw fish. Several groups were in the water and gave us much trouble. They did not seem ill-tempered but were dangerously inquisitive. We experienced several love-taps, however, with but one narrow escape from drowning, and we had no further desire for walrus courtship. Fortunately we could maintain a speed almost equal to theirs.

From an iceberg we studied the various groups of walrus for the one best situated for our primitive methods of attack. All together we counted more than a hundred snorting creatures arranged in black lines along a line of low ice. Here was food in massive heaps. We had had no breakfast and no full meal for many weeks. We took our position in the canvas boat behind a floating cape of ice and awaited the drift of the sleeping monsters on pans bearing down on us.

We now had time to arrange our battle tactics. The most vital part of our equipment was the line. It was a new, strong sealskin rawhide which had been reserved for just such an emergency. Attached to the harpoon, with float adjusted, it is seldom lost, for the float moves and permits no sudden strain. To safeguard the line a pan of ice was selected only a few yards in diameter. This was to do the duty of float and drag. With the knife two holes were cut, and into these the line was fastened near its centre.

The harpoon was set to the shaft and the bow of our little twelve-foot boat cleared for action. Peeping over a wall of ice we saw the black-littered pans slowly bearing down on us. Our excitement rose to a shouting point. It was evident the pan would go by at a distance of about fifty feet. The first group of walrus were allowed to pass. They proved to be a herd of twenty-one mammoth creatures and, aside from the danger of the pack, their unanimous plunge would have raised a sea that would have swamped us.

On the next pan were but three spots. At a distance we persuaded ourselves they were small, for we had no ambition for formidable attacks. As they neared the point, the oars of the boat were gripped and out we shot. They all rose to meet us, displaying the glitter of ivory tusks from little heads against huge wrinkled necks. They grunted viciously but the speed of the boat did not slacken. Etukishook rose. With a savage thrust he sank the harpoon into a yielding neck. The walrus tumbled over themselves and sank into the water on the opposite side of the pan. We pushed upon the vacated floor without leaving the boat, taking the risk of an ice puncture rather than walrus bumps. The line caught up with a snap. The ice-pan began to plow the sea. It moved landward. What luck! I wondered if the walrus would pull us and his own carcass ashore. Other animals had awakened to his battle call and now the sea began to seethe and boil with the enraged monsters. The float took a zigzag course and we watched the movement with anxiety. Our next meal and our last grip on life were at stake. But for the time being nothing could be done.

The struggle was prolonged. In six hours, during which the sun had swept a quarter of the circle, our two floes were jerked through the water with the rush of a gunboat. The lance was thrust in and withdrawn time and time again; the line was shortened; a cannonade of ice blocks was kept up; but the animal gave no signs of weakening. Seeing that we could not inflict dangerous wounds, our tactics were changed to a kind of siege and we aimed not to permit the animal any breathing spells.

The line did not begin to slacken until midnight. The battle had then been on almost twelve hours. Bits of ice quenched our thirst and the chill of night kept us from sweating. With each rise of the beast for breath now, the line slackened and gently it was hauled in and secured. Then a rain of ice blocks drove the spouting animal down. Finally after a series of spasmodic encounters lasting fifteen hours the enraged snout turned blue, the fiery eyes darkened and victory was ours.

As the battle ended we were not far from a point three miles south of our camp. A primitive pulley was arranged by passing the line through slits in the walrus's nose and holes in the ice and the great carcass, weighing perhaps three thousand pounds, was drawn onto the ice and divided into portable pieces.

With ample blubber a fire was now made between two rocks. Soon pot after pot of savoury meat was being consumed. We ate with a vulgar insatiable hunger, speaking little. When eating was no longer possible, sleeping dens were arranged in the little boat and like other gluttonous animals after an engorgement we closed our eyes.

At the end of about fifteen hours a stir about our camp awoke us. We saw a huge bear nosing about our fireplace. We had left there a walrus joint weighing about one hundred pounds. We all of us jumped up shouting and making a pretended rush and the bear took up the meat in his forepaws and walked off, manlike, on two legs, with a threatening grunt. We did not accept the challenge. With lances, bows, arrows, and stones we next crossed a low hill beyond which was located our precious cache of meat. Here, to our chagrin, we saw two other bears with heads down and paws busily digging about the cache. We were not fitted for hand-to-hand encounter but our lives were equally at stake whether we attacked or failed to attack. With a shout and a fiendish rush we attracted the brutes' attention. They raised their heads, turned, and to our relief grudgingly walked off to seaward, each with a piece of our meat. Advancing to the cache we found it absolutely depleted. Many other bears had been there. The snow and sand were trampled down. Our splendid catch of the day previous was entirely lost. We could have wept with rage and disappointment. We realized that life was now to be a struggle with the bears for supremacy. With but little ammunition we were not at all able to engage in bear fights so, baffled, we packed our few belongings and moved westward to Cape Sparbo.

We reached Cape Sparbo on the shores of Jones Sound, early in September. Our dogs were gone. Our ammunition except four cartridges which I had secreted for use in a last emergency was gone. Our equipment consisted of a half sledge, a canvas boat, a torn silk tent, a few camp kettles, tin plates, knives and matches. Our clothing was slitting to shreds.

THE LONG NIGHT

When we landed we found to our surprise that it was the site of an ancient Eskimo village. We sought a place protected from wind and cold where we might build a winter shelter. Our search disclosed a cave-like hole, part of which was dug from the earth, and over which, with stones and bones, had been constructed a roof which now was fallen in.

The long winter was approaching. We were over 300 miles from Anoatok, and the coming of the long night made it necessary for us to halt. We must have food and clothing. We now came upon musk-oxen and tried to fell them with boulders, and bows and arrows made of the hickory of our sledge. Day after day the pursuit was vainly followed. Had it not been for occasional ducks caught with loop-lines and slingshots we should have been absolutely without any food.

By the middle of September snow and frost came with such frequency that we gave up hunting to dig out the ruins in the cave, and cut sod before permanent frost made such work impossible. Bone implements were made from skeletons found on the shore, for the digging. Drifts of sand and gravel were slowly removed from the pit. We found under this, to our great joy, the underground arrangement which we most desired: a raised platform, about six feet long and eight feet wide with suitable wings for the lamp, and foot space, lay ready for us. The pit had evidently been designed for a small family. The walls, which were about two feet high, required little alteration. Another foot was added which levelled the structure with the ground. A good deal of sod was cut and allowed to dry in the sun for use as a roof. On the shore we secured additional whale ribs and made the framework for the roof. This was constructed of moss and blocks of sod. We built a rock wall about the shelter to protect ourselves from storms and bears. Then our winter home was ready. Food was now an immediate necessity. On land were bear and musk-ox; in the sea walrus and whales. But what could we do without either dogs or rifles?

The first weapons we had devised were the bow and arrow. We had in our sledge hickory wood of the-best quality; we had sinews and seal lashings for strings but there was no metal for tips. We tried bone, horn and ivory but all proved ineffective.

Harpoons and lances were next made and with them we hastened to retrieve our honour. After all, the musk-ox alone could supply our wants. Winter storms were coming fast. We were not only without food and fuel but without clothing. One day when Etukishook had secured a hare with the bow and arrow, we ascended a rocky eminence and sat down to appease our stomachs without a camp fire. From here we detected a family of four musk-oxen asleep. This was a call to battle. We were not long in planning our tactics for the wind was in our favour permitting an attack from the side opposite the rocks, to which we aimed to force a retreat. We also found small stones in abundance, these being now a necessary part of our armament. The musk-oxen were simply chewing their cud when we approached and rose to form a ring of defence. We stoned them with stones and they took to the shelter of the rocks. We continued to advance slowly upon them throwing stones occasionally. Besides the bow and arrow and the stones we now had lances and these we threw as they rushed to attack us. Two lances were crushed to fragments before they could be withdrawn by the light line attached. They inflicted wounds but not severe ones. Ahwelah now threw the harpoon. It hit a rib, glanced off a rock and was also broken. Fortunately we had a duplicate point which was quickly fastened. Then we moved about to encourage an onslaught by the musk-oxen. Two came at once, an old bull and a young one. Etukishook threw the harpoon at the young one and it entered. The line had previously been fastened to a rock. The animal ran back to its associates, apparentlly not severely hurt, leaving the line slack. Our problem now was to get rid of the other three while we dealt with the one at the end of the line. Our only resort was a fusillade of stones. The three scattered and ascended the boulder-strewn foreland of a cliff, where the oldest bull remained to watch our movements. The young bull now made violent efforts to escape, but the sealskin line was strong and elastic. A lucky throw of a lance at close range ended the strife. Then we advanced on the old bull, who was in a good position for us.

A 19th century Eskimo Apollo and Venus, carved in wood in Greenland.

We gathered stones and threw them at him. This did not enrage him but prevented his making an attack. As we gained ground he gradually backed up to the edge of the cliff, snorting but making no effort to escape along a lateral bench, or to attack. Suddenly we made a combined rush into the open, hurling stones. Our storming of stones had the desired effect. The bull, annoyed and losing his presence of mind, stepped impatiently one step too far backward and fell over the cliff, landing on a rocky ledge below. Looking over we saw he had broken a foreleg. The cliff was not more than fifteen feet high. From it the lance was used to put the poor creature out of his suffering. We were rich now and could afford to spread out our stomachs, contracted by long spells of famine. The bull dressed out about 300 pounds of meat and 100 pounds of tallow.

We left most of the meat carefully covered with heavy stones to protect it from bears, wolves and foxes. The following day we returned with the canvas boat, landing about four miles from the battlefield. As we neared the cache we found to our dismay numerous bear and fox tracks. Bears had opened the cache and removed our hard-earned game while the foxes and ravens had cleared up the very fragments and destroyed even the skins. Here was cause for ven-

geance on the bear and fox. The fox paid with his skin later, but the bear out-generalled us in nearly every manoeuvre.

Having tried bows and arrows, stones, the lance and harpoon, we now tried another weapon. This was the lasso. We tried, but not successfully, to throw it over the head. Then we tried to entangle their feet with slip-knots just as we trapped gulls. This also failed. We next extended the loop idea to their horns. The bull's habit of rushing at things hurled at him caused us to think of this plan.

A large slip-loop was now made in the centre of the line and the two natives took up position on opposite sides of the animal. They threw the rope, with its loop, on the ground in front of him, while I encouraged an attack from the front. As the head was slightly elevated the loop was raised and the bull put his horns into it, one after the other. The rope was now fastened to stones and the bull tightened the loop by his efforts to advance or retreat. With every opportunity the slack was taken up until no play was allowed the animal. During this struggle all the other oxen retreated except one female. When we had the bull where we could reach him with the lance at arm's length and plunge it into his vitals he soon fell over, the first victim to our new art of musk-ox catching.

Our art of musk-ox fighting was now completely developed. In the course of a few weeks we secured enough to assure comfort and ease during the long night. By our own efforts we were lifted suddenly from famine to luxury. The musk-ox now supplied many wants in our "Robinson Crusoe" life. From the bone we made harpoon points, arrow pieces, knife handles, fox traps and sledge repairs. The skin, with its remarkable fur, made our bed and roofed our igloo. Of it we made all kinds of garments, but its greatest use was for coats with hoods, stockings and mittens. From the skin with the fur removed we made boots, patched punctures in our boat, and cut lashes. The hair and wool which were removed from the skins made pads for the palms in our mittens, and cushions for the soles of our feet in lieu of the grass formerly used.

The meat became our staple food for seven months without change. It had a flavour slightly sweet, like that of horse flesh, but still distinctly pleasing. It possessed an odour unlike musk but equally unlike anything that I know of. The live creatures exhale the scent of domestic cattle. Just why this odd creature is called a "musk-ox" is a mystery, for it is neither an ox nor does it smell of musk. The bones were used as fuel for outside fire, and the fat as both fuel and food.

At first our wealth of food came as a surprise and delight to us for, in the absence of sweet or starchy food, man craves fat. Sugar and starch are most readily converted into fat by the animal laboratory, and fat is one of the prime factors in the development and maintenance of the human system. It is the confectionery of aboriginal man, and we had taken up the lot of the most primitive aborigines, living and thriving solely on the product of the chase without a morsel of civilized or vegetable food. Under these circumstances we especially delighted in the musk-ox tallow and more especially in the marrow, which we sucked from the bones with the eagerness with which a child manages a stick of candy.

In two months, from the first of September till the end of October, we passed from a period of hunger, thirst and abject misery, into the realm of abundant game. But although our larder was now well stocked with meat for food and blubber for fuel, we were still in need of furs and skins to prepare new equipment with which to return to Greenland. The animals whose pelts we

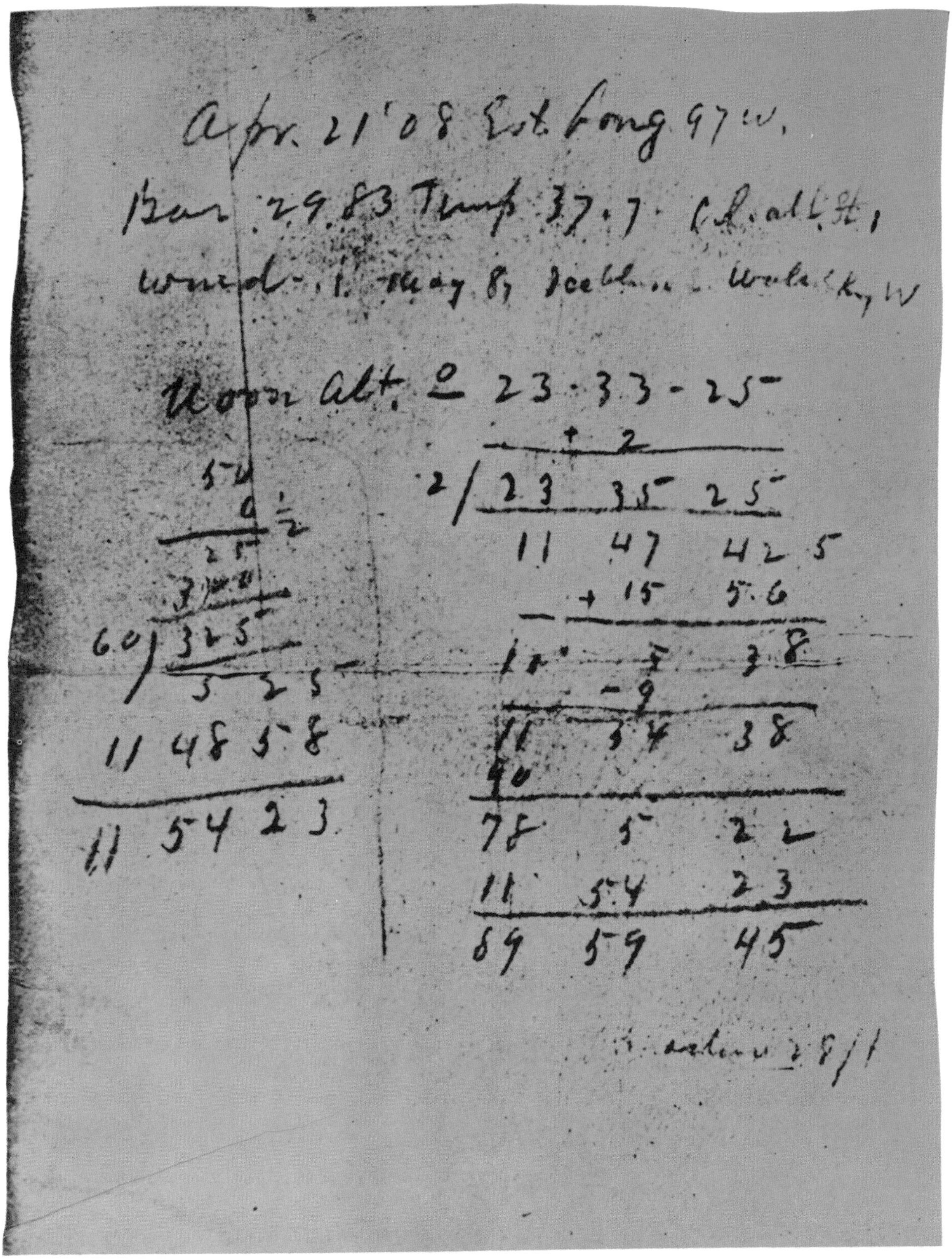

Apr. 21'08 Est. Long. 97 W.

Bar. 29.83 Temp 37.7 Cd. alt. St.

wind... May 8, Icebln.. Wk. sky W

Noon Alt. ⊙ 23·33·25

$$\begin{array}{r} + 2 \\ \hline 2\,/\,23\ \ 35\ \ 25 \end{array}$$

11   47   42 5

+ 15   5·6

11   5   3 8

− 9

11   54   38

40

78   5   2 2

11   54   2 3

69   59   45

5
9 ½
25
3 0
6·0) 3 2 5
5   2 5
11   48   5 8
11   54   2 3

Facsimile of page in Cook's notebook, recording his exact arrival at
the North Pole. He wrote: "Here there is but one day and one night
each year . . . Figuratively, it is possible here to have all meridians
under one foot . . . to step from one side of the globe to the other."
Peary's comment was: "He has simply handed the people a gold brick."

required were abundant everywhere. But they were too active to be caught by the art and the weapons evolved in the chase of the walrus and the musk-ox.

A series of efforts, therefore, was directed to the fox, the hare, the ptarmigan and the seal. The hare was perhaps the most important, not only because of its delicate meat, but also because its skin is not equalled by any other for stockings. The hare was a good mark for Etukishook with his slingshot, and many fell victim to his primitive genius. Ahwelah, never an expert at stone-slinging, became an adept with the bow and arrow. Usually he returned with at least one hare from every day's chase. But our main success resulted from a still more primitive device. Counting on its inquisitiveness we devised a chain of loop-lines arranged across the hare's regular line of travel. In playing and jumping through these loops, the animals tightened the lines and became our victims.

The ptarmigan chase was possible only for Ahwelah. The bird was not shy but it was too small a mark for the slingshot and only Ahwelah could give the arrow the direction for these feathered creatures. Altogether fifteen were secured and all served as dessert for my special benefit. According to Eskimo custom, a young unmarried man or woman cannot eat the ptarmigan. That pleasure is reserved for the older people, and I did not for a moment risk the sacrilege of trying to change the custom.

We caught the fox more diligently. We had a more tangible way of securing it. Furthermore we were in great need of its skin. We had no steel traps and with its usual craft the fox usually managed to evade our crude weapons by keeping out of sight. Little stone domes were a raised imitation of caches, with trap stone doors. In these we managed to secure fourteen white and two blue animals. After that they proved too wise for our craft.

Up to the present we had failed in the quest for seal. As the winter and the night advanced we were too busy with the land animals to search for blow-holes in the new ice. Now that the winter had sheeted the black ice with a white cover, the seal holes, though open, could not be found. We were not in need of fat or meat, but the seal skins were to provide the boots and sled lashings from their thin, tough hide. How could we get it?

From our underground den we daily watched the wanderings of the bears. They trailed along certain lines which we knew to be favourable feeding grounds for seal, but they did not seem to be successful. Could we not profit by their superb scenting instinct and find the blow-holes? The bear had been our worst enemy, but it also proved to be our best friend. We started out to trail the bears' footprints. By these we were led to the blow-holes, where we found the snow had been circled with a regular trail. Most of these had been abandoned, for the seal has a scent as keen as the bear, but a few "live" holes were located. Sticks were placed to mark these and after a few days' careful study and hard work we harpooned six seals. Taking only the skins and blubber we left the carcasses for Bruin's share of the chase. We did not hunt together with the bear — at least not knowingly.

Late in September the nights became too dark to sleep in the open, with inquisitive bears on every side. Storms, too, increased thereafter and deprived us of the cheer of coloured skies. Thus we were now forced to seek a retreat in our underground den. We took about as kindly to this as a wild animal does to a cage. For over seven months we had wandered over vast plains of ice with a new camp site almost every day. We had grown accustomed to a wandering life but had not developed a hibernating instinct.

Early in November the storms ceased long enough to give us a last fiery vision. With a magnificent cardinal flame the sun rose, gibbered in the sky and sank behind the southern cliff on November 3rd. It was not to rise again until February 11th of the next year. We were doomed to hibernate in our underground den for at least a hundred double nights before the dawn of a new day.

We stood watches of six hours each to keep the fires going, to keep off the bears and to force an interest in a blank life. We knew that we were believed to be dead. Our friends in Greenland would not ascribe to us the luck which came after our run of abject misfortune. This thought inflicted perhaps the greatest pain of the queer prolongation of life which was permitted us. It was loneliness, frigid loneliness. I wonder whether men ever felt so desolately alone.

We could not have been more thoroughly isolated if we had been transported to the surface of the moon. I find myself unable to outline the emptiness of our existence. In other surroundings we never grasp the full meaning of the world "alone." When it is possible to put a foot out of doors into sunlight without the risk of a bear-paw on your neck, it is also possible to run off a spell of blues. But what were we to do with every dull rock rising as a bear, and with the torment of a satanic blackness to blind us?

There were no discussions, no differences of opinion. We had been too long together under bitter circumstances to arouse each other's interest. A single individual could not live long in our position. A selfish instinct tightened a fixed bond to preserve and protect one another. As a battle force we made a formidable unit, but there were no matches to start the fires of inspiration.

The half darkness of mid-day, and the moonlight, still permitted us to creep from under the ground and seek a few hours in the open. Visiting the stone and bone foxtraps and some trap caves for bears which we built during the last glimmer of day offered an occupation. But we were soon deprived of this.

Bears headed us off at every turn. We were not permitted to proceed beyond an enclosed hundred feet from the hole of our den. Not an inch of ground nor a morsel of food was permitted us without a contest. It was a fight of nature against nature. We either actually saw the little sooty nostrils with jets of breath rising, and the huge outline of the beast ready to spring on us, or imagined we saw it. With no adequate means of defence we were driven to imprisonment within the walls of our own den.

From within, our position was even more tantalizing. The bear thieves had dug under the snow over our heads and snatched blocks of blubber fuel from under our very eyes, without a consciousness of wrong-doing. Occasionally we ventured out to deliver a lance, but each time the bear would make a leap for the door and would have entered had the opening been large enough. In other cases we shot arrows through the peep-hole. A bear's head again would burst through the silk covered window near the roof, where knives at close range and in good light could be driven home with sweet vengeance.

As a last resort we made a hole through the top of the den. When a bear was heard near, a long torch was pushed through. The snow for acres about was then suddenly flashed with a ghostly whiteness which almost frightened us. But the bear calmly took advantage of the light to pick a larger piece of the blubber upon which our lives depended, and then with an air of superiority he would move into the brightest light, usually within a few feet of our peep-hole, where we could almost touch his hateful skin.

We were lonely enough to have felt a certain delight in shaking hands even with Bruin if the theft of our blubber had not threatened our very existence. In the night we could not augment our supplies and without fat, fire and water were impossible. But one night after Bruin's steps had passed out of hearing we heard noises from inside our hut. There was a scraping and scratching. We had a neighbour and companion. We were kept in suspense for some time. When all was quiet after midnight a small blue lemming came out and began to tear the bark from our willow lamp-trimmer.

I was on watch, awake, and punched Etukishook without moving my head. His eyes opened with surprise at the busy rodent, and Ahwelah was kicked. He turned over and the thing jumped into a rock crevice.

In the course of two days it came back with a companion. They were beautiful creatures hardly larger than mice. They had fluffy fur of a pearl-blue colour, with blue eyes. They had no tails. A few days were spent in testing our intentions, then they arranged a berth just above my head and became steady boarders. They were good, clean, orderly camp-followers, always kept in their place and never ventured to borrow our bed furs nor did they disturb our eatables. They passed our plates of carnivorous food without venturing a taste and went to their herbivorous piles of sod delicacies. About ten days before midnight they went to sleep and did not wake for more than a month. Again we were alone. Now even the bears deserted us.

Meanwhile our preparations for return were being accomplished. This work kept us busy during the wakeful spells of the night. Although real pleasure followed efforts of physical labour, the balking muscles required considerable urging. Musk-ox meat was cut into portable blocks, candles were made, fur skins were dressed and chewed, boots, stockings, pants, shirts, sleeping bags were made, the sledge was relashed, things were packed in bags. All was ready about three weeks before sunrise. But although the fingers and jaws were thus kept busy, the mind and the heart were left free to wander.

In the face of all our efforts to ward aside the ill effects of the night we gradually became its victims. Our skin paled, our strength failed, the nerves weakened, and the mind ultimately became a blank. The most notable physical effect however, was the alarming irregularity of the heart.

About two weeks before sunrise the lemmings woke and began to shake their beautiful blue fur but they were not really alive and awake in a lemming sense for several days. The foxes now began to bark from a safe distance and advanced to get their share of the camp spoils. Wolves were heard away in the musk-ox fields but did not venture to pay us a visit.

On the 11th of February the snow-covered slopes of North Devon glowed with the sunrise of 1909. The sun had burst nature's dungeon. Cape Sparbo glowed with golden light. The frozen sea glittered and we escaped to a joyous freedom. With a reconstructed sled, new equipment and newly acquired energy we were ready to pursue the return journey to Greenland.

On February 18, 1909, the sledge was loaded for the home run. We had given up the idea of journeying to Lancaster Sound to await the whalers. There were no Eskimos on the North American side nearer than Pond Inlet. It was somewhat farther to our headquarters on the Greenland shore, but all interests would be best served by a return to Anoatok.

During the night we had fixed all our attention upon the return journey and had prepared new equipment with the limited means at our command; but, travelling in the coldest season of the year, it was necessary to carry a cumbersome outfit of furs, and furthermore, since we were to take the places of the dogs in the traces, we could not expect to transport supplies for more than thirty days. In this time, however, we hoped to reach Cape Sabine, where the father of Etukishook had been told to place a cache for us.

We were dressed in heavy furs. The temperature was −49°. A light air brushed the frozen mist out of Jones Sound and cut our sooty faces. The sled was overloaded and the exertion required for each movement over the snow was tremendous. A false, almost hysterical, enthusiasm lighted our faces, but the muscles were not yet equal to the task ahead of them.

Our camp life now was not like that of the polar campaign. Dried musk-ox meat and strips of musk-ox fat made a steady diet. Moulded tallow served as fuel in a crescent-shaped disc of tin in which carefully prepared moss was crushed and arranged as a wick. Over this primitive fire we managed to melt enough ice to quench thirst and also to make an occasional pot of broth as a luxury. While the drink was liquefying, the chill of the snow igloo was also moderated and we crept into the bags of musk-ox skin, where agreeable repose and home dreams made us forget the cry of the stomach and the torment of the cold.

At the end of eight days of forced marches, we reached Cape Tennyson. The disadvantage of manpower, when compared to dog motor force, was clearly shown. With the best of luck we had averaged only about seven miles daily. With dogs, the entire run would have been made easily in two days.

From Cape Tennyson to Cape Clarence the ice near the open water proved fairly smooth. A persistent northerly wind brought the humid discomfort of our breath back to our faces with painful results. During several days of successive storms, we were imprisoned in the igloos. By enforced idleness we were compelled to use a precious store of food and fuel without any advance. Serious difficulties were encountered in moving to Cape Faraday. Here the ice was tumbled into mountains of trouble. Tremendous snow drifts and persistent gales from the west made travelling next to impossible and, with no gain and no food supplies in prospect, I also knew that to remain idle would be suicidal. The sledge load was lightened and every scrap of fur which was not absolutely necessary was thrown away. Wet boots, stockings and seal skin coats could not be dried out, for fuel was more precious than clothing. All of this was discarded and with light sledge and reduced rations we forced our way on. In all of our polar march we had seen no ice which offered so much hardship as did this so near home shores. With overwork and insufficient food our furs hung on bony eminences over shrivelled skins.

At the end of thirty-five days of ceaseless toil we reached Cape Faraday. Our food was gone. We were far from the haunts of game and had seen no living thing for a month. In desperation we ate bits of skin and chewed tough walrus lines. While trying to masticate this I broke some of my teeth.

Travelling in a circuitous route there was still a distance of 100 miles between us and Cape Sabine, and the distance to Greenland might, by open water, be spread to 200 miles. Where, I asked in desperation, were we to obtain subsistence for that last thirty days?

Staggering along one day we saw a bear track. These mute marks in the half dark of the snow filled us with a wild resurgence of hope. On the evening of March 20th we prepared cautiously for the coming of the bear. A snow house was built somewhat stronger than usual. In front of it a shelf was arranged with blocks of snow and on this were bits of skin to imitate the dark outline of a recumbent seal. Over this was placed a looped line, through which the head and neck must go in order to get the bait. Our lances and knives were carefully sharpened. When all was ready, one of us remained on watch while the others sought sleep. We had not long to wait. Soon a crackling sound gave the battle call and with a little black nose extended from a long neck the creature advanced.

He looked gigantic. Apparently as hungry as we were he came in straight rushes for the bait. The run port was open and Ahwelah and Etukishook emerged, one with a lance, the other with a spiked harpoon shaft.

During the previous summer, when I foresaw a time of famine, I had taken my four last cartridges and hid them in my clothing. Of the existence of these the two boys knew nothing. They were to be used at the last stage of hunger to kill something – or ourselves. That desperate time had not arrived till now. I jerked the line. The loop tightened about the bear's neck. At the same moment the lance and spike were driven into the creature. A fierce struggle ensued. I withdrew one of the precious cartridges from my pocket, placed it in my gun and gave the gun to Ahwelah who took aim and fired. When the smoke cleared, the bear lay on the ground.

Here was food and fuel in abundance. We were saved! But we did not sit down. Greenland was in sight and, to an Eskimo, Greenland was heaven. When more eating was impossible we began to move for home shores, dragging a sled overloaded with the life-saving prize.

A life of trouble still lay before us. Successive storms, mountains of jammed ice, and deep snow interrupted our progress and lengthened the course. When, after a prodigious effort, Cape Sabine was reached, our food supply was again exhausted. Here an old seal was found. It had been caught a year before and cached by Panicpa, the father of Etukishook. With it was found a rude drawing that told the story of a loving father's fruitless search for his son and friends. The seal meat had the aroma of limburger cheese, and age had changed its flavour but, with no other food possible, our palates were satisfied.

Smith Sound was free of ice and open water extended sixty miles northward. A long detour was therefore necessary to reach the opposite shore. With light hearts and cheering premonitions of hope we pushed along Bache Peninsula to a point near Cape Louis Napoleon. The horizon was now cleared of trouble. The ascending sun had dispelled the winter gloom of the land. As it lay in prospect, Greenland had the charm of Eden. It was a stepping-stone to my home, still very far off. It was a land where a man had a fighting chance for his life.

In reality we were now in the most desperate throes of the grip of famine which we had encountered during all our hard experience. Greenland was but thirty miles away. But we were separated from it by impossible open water. To this moment I do not know why we did not sit down and allow the blood to cool with famine and cold. We had no good reason to hope that we could cross.

Nevertheless, we started. We were as thin as it is possible for men to be. The scraps of meat, viscera, and skin of the seal, buried for a year, was now our sole diet. We travelled two days northward over savage uplifts of hummocks and deep snow. Then we reached good, smooth ice, but open water forced us still northward ever northward from the cliffs under which our Greenland homes and abundant supplies were located. The days were prolonged, the decayed seal food ran low, water was almost impossible to obtain. Life no longer seemed worth living.

So weak that we had to climb on hands and knees, we reached the top of an iceberg on the eastern side, and from there saw Anoatok. Natives who had thought us long dead rushed out to greet us. There I met Mr. Harry Whitney. As I held his hand the cheer of a long-forgotten world came over me. With him I went to my house, only to find that during my absence it had been confiscated. From Mr. Whitney I learned that Mr. Peary had reached Anoatok about the middle of August, 1908, and had placed a boatswain named Murphy, assisted by William Pritchard, a cabin boy, in charge of my stores which Mr.

Harry Whitney, an American sportsman
who was in the Arctic after bear,
met Cook on his return from the Pole.

Captain J. E. Bernier, who had
formally claimed the arctic islands
for Canada, left supplies for Dr. Cook.

Peary had seized. According to Mr. Whitney, the stores were said to be abandoned. The men, under Peary's orders, went to Koolootingwaht and forced from him the key with which to open the guarded stores. Murphy was given a letter of instruction to make a trading station of my home and to use my supplies. Now if Mr. Peary had required my supplies for legitimate exploration, I should have been glad to give them to him. But to use my things for commercial gain was bitter medicine.

Fortunately at Etah was a big cache which had been left a year before by Captain Bernier, the commander of a northern expedition sent out by the Canadian Government, and which had been placed in charge of Mr. Whitney. In this cache was food, new equipment, and clean underclothes which Mrs. Cook had sent out on the Canadian expedition. With this new store of suitable supplies I completed my equipment for the return to civilization.

fm Whatever else it may have been, and whatever it may have achieved, there is no gainsaying the fact that this was one of the most remarkable journeys in the history of arctic exploration. Cook's ability to make a near-total adaptation to the harsh environment in which he found himself has perhaps never been surpassed, even by that famed exponent of the art, Vilhjalmur Stefansson. It is too bad that the story could not have ended as Cook returned to Anoatok. Even as he enters that little settlement we feel the overtones of the bitterness, jealousy and hatred that were to make the rest of Cook's life a nightmare for him. It is a dark passage, but one we need not delve into deeply.

After leaving Etah, Cook made his way south along the coast in a small boat until he arrived near Upernavik, where he found the Danish ship *Hans Egede*. He was offered a passage in her to Denmark. The alternatives were to hope for a ride home with Peary (a chilling and unlikely prospect) or to try to charter a small schooner to carry him across to Labrador. It seemed probable that he would reach New York more rapidly by way of Denmark, so Cook sailed to the south and east.

When John Bradley returned home in the late summer of 1907 he carried with him a letter from Cook to the Explorers Club‡ in New York. The letter stated that Cook had decided to try for the Pole, and hoped to report back to the Club in the following year.

Peary was informed of Cook's intentions, but seems to have been incapable of believing it at the time. He sailed north in the spring of 1908, with the personal blessing of President Teddy Roosevelt, with two good ships, and with the most expensive privately equipped polar expedition ever launched. He stopped briefly at Anoatok, where certain obscure events took place. Cook was gone, of course, but Rudolph Francke remained. Peary took over the entire settlement and made it clear to Francke that he would be well advised to return south immediately on one of Peary's ships. He was not permitted to take with him any of the furs or other materials he and Cook had trapped, nor was he allowed to take any of Cook's supplies or equipment. Everything belonging to Cook was confiscated by Peary, who put two of his men in Cook's house with orders to use Cook's supplies as trade goods with which to obtain fox furs for Peary. Meanwhile Peary and the *Roosevelt*, with 260 dogs and fifty Eskimos, continued north to Cape Sheridan. Advance depots were then pushed out to Cape Columbia, ninety miles to the northwest, at the extreme northern tip of Ellesmere Island.

On February 15, 1909, the first teams set out from Cape Columbia toward the Pole, with Peary following a week later. Several white men, nineteen

†The Eskimo whom Francke left in charge, when Francke returned south on Peary's ship.

‡Of which both Cook and Peary were members.

Eskimos, twenty-eight sledges and 140 dogs powered this polar thrust. Peary followed behind sucessive leaders, who broke trail until they were exhausted and then turned back for the land. At latitude 87° 47′ Peary sent back his last remaining support party, commanded by Captain Bartlett. Peary continued on, with Henson to drive his sled and three Eskimos with their teams and sleds to break trail for him. Six days later, having averaged 42 miles a day he claimed to have reached the Pole.

Late on April 7th he started back, reaching the *Roosevelt* on April 25, having averaged 45½ miles a day and, *during two marches 75½ miles a day!* According to Henson, Peary rode the entire distance home from the Pole in Henson's sled – which makes the speeds even more notable. But the most remarkable fact of all is that young Capt. Bartlett, one of the best dog-drivers in the North, returning over a beaten trail, only managed to beat Peary back to the *Roosevelt* by three days, although the distance he had to travel was 300 miles shorter than that travelled by Peary.†

The *Roosevelt* started south as soon as the ice opened, and at Anoatok Peary heard the details of Cook's exploit from the wealthy sportsman Harry Whitney. At Whitney's suggestion Cook had left all his instruments and some of his rough journals in the sportsman's care, rather than risk everything on the small boat trip south to Upernavik. Peary now forbade Whitney to bring anything of Cook's aboard the ship, and Whitney buried the instruments and records – or, at any event, this is how he later accounted for their disappearance. Peary had Cook's two Eskimo companions brought before him and interrogated them for a long time; "asking us many strange things, and showing us papers we did not understand."

Peary was now in a tearing hurry to get under way. Course was laid for the nearest telegraph station, at Smokey Tickle on Labrador, and from this point Peary sent his telegram of triumph on September 6: "I have the Pole, April 6, 1909."

But five days earlier Cook had sent a wire from Denmark: "Reached the North Pole April 21st, 1908."

When the *Roosevelt* reached Battle Harbour, Labrador, there was a message from Reuters telling of Cook's message, and asking for Peary's comments. He was glad to give them.

"Do not trouble about Cook's story . . . the affair will settle itself. He has not been at the Pole on April 21st, 1908, or any other time. He has simply handed the people a gold brick . . . when he makes a full statement over his signature to some geographical society or other reputable body, if that statement contains the claim that he has reached the Pole, I shall be in a position to furnish material that may make distinctly interesting reading for the public."

Peary's material turned out to be interesting, but unconvincing. It consisted of statements allegedly made to Peary by Cook's two Eskimo companions, to the effect that Cook had never been more than two days out of sight of land. Knud Rasmussen and other Danish authorities later said that the two Eskimos were either badly misquoted or badly misunderstood by Peary, and that their stories corroborated Cook's claim. The Royal Danish Geographical Society presented Cook with its Gold Medal in recognition of his discovery of the Pole; and this Society has never since seen cause to withdraw the award.

During the frightful furor that ensued, almost any club was good enough to clout Cook over the head with. Typical of the kind of accusation used to discredit him is the statement that a photograph of Cook's two Eskimo companions at the Pole shows them dressed in musk-ox trousers, whereas no such

†Nansen, on his polar dash and the return to Franz Josef Land, considered that nine miles a day dog-sledding over the polar pack was better than average.

materials were available before the party left Anoatok and *by Cook's own admission in his book*, no musk-oxen were encountered until after Cook returned from the Pole! Two of the most authoritative current books dealing with arctic exploration, *To The North* by Jeanette Mirsky, and *The White Road* by L. P. Kirwan, Director of the Royal Geographical Society (which supported Peary from the first) repeat this statement. It is painfully apparent that the authors of what are, in most respects, very careful and admirable texts, were so prejudiced against Cook that they did not even read his book. Another major criticism is that, had Cook followed the route he claimed to have followed, and if his given positions were accurate, he must have seen Meighen Island, which was first reported, plotted and mapped by Stefansson in 1916. But the latest air-photographic maps of this region, Canada's National Topographic Series, 1:500,000, Sheets 650 S½, 69 N½ and 59 N½, demonstrate irrefutably that if Cook was where he said he was, he could not, under any circumstances, have seen Meighen Island which was, in fact, incorrectly plotted by Stefansson.

Attempts have been made from time to time to show that Cook failed to reach the top of Mt. McKinley and that, consequently, his claim that he reached the Pole must also be false. However, there is no valid reason to believe that he failed to scale the peak of McKinley. The accusations against him are very much a matter of opinion. On the other hand, four major geographical claims made by Peary are demonstrably incorrect and have been stricken from all modern maps. Peary's strange failure to take Capt. Bartlett all the way with him to the Pole (Bartlett was the one man who could have confirmed the observations for latitude at the Pole) together with Peary's incredible speeds on his final run and on his return to the *Roosevelt*, have led most unbiased observers to conclude that Peary's own claim rests on exceedingly shaky foundations.

Oddly enough, Frederick Cook never questioned Peary's claim. He seems to have been content to accept Peary's word for it although it would surely have been to his advantage to have helped prove Peary a liar. To the end of his life, Cook never understood the rules of the game in which he found himself a player. Many years after the trip to the Pole, Cook was arrested for having allegedly made false representation about the value of oil lands which he had acquired in the southwest United States. He was convicted, against all the evidence, and given a positively savage sentence.† While he was in jail, agencies of the Government (which had seized his lands) proved them to be even more valuable than Cook had ever claimed by selling them at auction for several millions of dollars. Eventually this miscarriage – or deliberate perversion – of justice was brought to the notice of President Franklin D. Roosevelt, who granted Cook a full pardon.

The pardon came a little late. It was received on May 16, 1940. On August 5, 1940, Frederick Cook died at the age of seventy-five years. □ FM

†*Fourteen years in Leavenworth —
the longest sentence on record
for misrepresentation.*

EPILOGUE

The polar passion burned low after the incandescent violence of the conflict between Cook and Peary. But this singular passion, which had led to the display of many of mankind's most admirable attributes before it devolved into a savage, pointless and often tragic competition between man and nature, and then between man and man, had not yet run its allotted course.

For fifteen years the bitter aftermath of the Cook-Peary struggle masked the North Pole's indefinable powers of attraction. Then, in the mid-twenties, the old fires flickered briefly back to life, revived by the advent of the age of the airplane. Although much of the Arctic had already been explored on foot, by ship, or by dog-team, leaving little for the new means of transport to accomplish in that field, the glamour of polar flights loomed irresistibly, and so men set out to conquer the North Pole all over again.

In 1925 the insatiable Roald Amundsen (who already had the Northwest Passage and the discovery of the South Pole to his credit) set out with an American, Lincoln Ellsworth, in two big Dornier flying boats from King's Bay in Spitsbergen to add the North Pole to his string of victories.

On May 21 the lumbering aircraft, grossly overloaded with fuel and emergency supplies, staggered into the air and rumbled northward on a tedious eight-hour flight. When the explorers calculated that they were over the Pole the pilots circled, found a convenient open lead, and landed. Filled with jubilation at this easy conquest, these men of the new age climbed out on the ice to confirm their position by solar sights. The results were somewhat disillusioning. The planes had landed at about 87° N. latitude, and the Pole lay 120 nautical miles to the north.

Before the six men in their two aircraft could take off again the lead closed, and they were trapped. Ellsworth's aircraft was completely wrecked, but there seemed to be some hope of escaping in Amundsen's plane if a long enough strip could be cleared across the ice. The alternative was a 400-mile walk to Greenland, and all the men were fully aware that there was almost no chance of surviving such a journey.

So they laboured through twenty-four miserable and fear-filled days to build an ice runway, using wooden shovels and whatever other tools they could improvise. On the twenty-fifth day the surviving aircraft with all six men aboard skidded down the icy surface and rose uncertainly into the air. Her crew did *not* complete the remaining 120 miles to the Pole. They headed back for Spitsbergen with all seemly haste. This expedition, largely sponsored by the National Geographic Society in the United States, had cost $150,000 and had added nothing to man's knowledge of the Arctic, nor had it been intended that it should. Like the DeLong venture of so many years before, it had been sponsored as a publicity venture with the hope that it would produce good magazine copy.

However, the flight had one major side effect. It stirred up all sorts of personal and national jealousies. Half a dozen nations now announced plans to be the first to send one of their citizens to the North Pole by air. A spirit of juvenile competition ran high. An American Navy pilot, Richard Byrd, determined that he would beat the field. He managed to get a plane to King's Bay by May 9, 1926, and he then flew to the Pole, turned around and flew back. It seems a singularly pointless performance until one realizes that he was successful in beating Amundsen and Ellsworth *by two days* which, surely, was achievement enough.

Amundsen and Ellsworth were already at King's Bay when Byrd arrived, preparing to make a new attempt to conquer the North Pole, in the Italian-designed airship *Norge*. On May 11 the *Norge* got under way carrying a crew of seventeen and piloted by her designer, Umberto Nobile. Although Byrd had beaten them to the Pole, they had a trick of their own to play. After reaching the Pole the *Norge* sailed sedately on and in due course raised the north coast of Alaska. Here the big airship got lost and fumbled blindly about for a considerable length of time before finally making a landing about ninety miles north of Nome. She had been airborne for seventy-two hours, and her crew had seen a great deal of ice and snow – from a distance. They had also seen the beginning of a bitter professional dispute between Amundsen and Nobile. The rancour that developed from this rift was to lead directly to one final flare of tragedy.

In April of 1928 a sister ship to the *Norge*, named *Italia*, set out for the North. She was commanded by General Umberto Nobile, who was bent on demonstrating his arctic exploring abilities as opposed to those of Amundsen. The expedition was nominally sponsored by the Royal Geographic Society of Italy, but it was in fact intended by Mussolini to be a demonstration of the capabilities of the New Italy.

The *Italia* carried fifteen Italians, one Swedish and one Czech meteorologist – and a small black and white mongrel dog named Titina. This dog has been undeservedly ignored by most polar historians; but she was the first dog to fly over the Pole, having previously been on the *Norge* expedition.

On May 23 the *Italia* flew to the Pole where she cruised about for an hour or so to let her passengers have a good look. It had originally been intended to land a party of six men at the Pole for an extended visit; but this plan had been abandoned after the six hurriedly booked passage home from Spitsbergen on a tourist ship rather than accept this opportunity to garner fame and glory.

A head wind plagued the *Italia*'s return to Spitsbergen. Then she got lost in a fog, and her pilots were still feeling their way when, on May 25, she began to ice heavily and to sink by the stern. Shortly after 10:00 a.m. she suddenly plunged fifteen hundred feet to crash into the pack below. After the first impact the wreckage went bounding away over the ice, but the navigation gondola had split open, spilling out its complement of nine men, Titina, and a considerable amount of supplies and equipment. Several of the men were injured, notably Nobile who had a leg broken. One man was crushed in the motor gondola and the remaining five were carried off to the southward inside the disintegrating airship. The only clue to their fate was a plume of black smoke seen by the survivors on the far horizon. Since she was filled with hydrogen it is probable that she caught fire and exploded.

The fate of the dirigible and her crew remained a mystery to the outside world until June 2, when a Russian amateur radio enthusiast near Archangel caught a faint s.o.s. transmitted from a hand-powered radio which had been spilled out on the ice with the survivors.

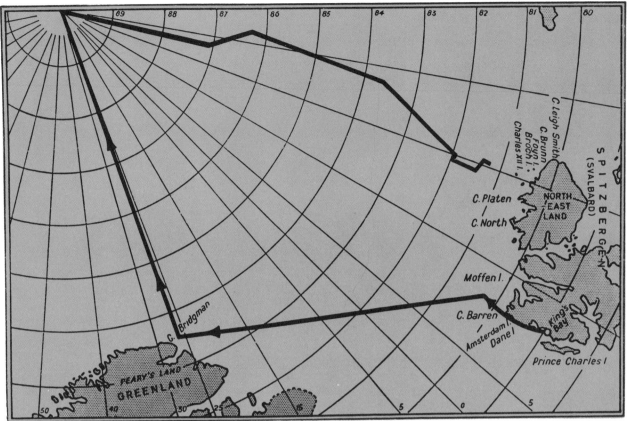

In April 1928 the hydrogen-filled airship
Italia flew from Spitsbergen to the Pole. On the
return journey (see chart) she crashed, setting
off an epic rescue that cost the life of Norway's hero,
Roald Amundsen. He vanished in a French aircraft.

General Umberto Nobile had designed the airship
Norge which carried Amundsen safely across the Pole in 1926.
After his own exploit, he autographed this
photograph for his rescuer, Captain Einar Lundborg.

The Italia flew over Stockholm on
May 3, 1928, on her way north. General
Nobile dropped a letter of greetings.

Roald Amundsen was the first man
to reach the South Pole in 1911. He
was 56 when lost in the Arctic.

*Nobile (in sleeping bag) feeds a
morsel to his dog Titina, after his
rescue by Captain Lundborg.*

*General Nobile (left) being assisted to
the rescue plane. His leg was broken
in the Italia crash. Twelve men died.*

A rescuer needed rescuing when Capt.
Lundborg's plane flipped. The rubber
boat was dropped from another plane.

With the whole world caught up in
the drama, the Russian Krassin picked
up the survivors of the Italia.

A massive rescue campaign now got under way, which eventually included two Norwegian ships, three French ships, two Swedish ships, two Russian ships and more than twenty aircraft.

By June 16, when Norwegian aircraft began searching the ice north of Spitsbergen, the Swedish meteorologist Finn Malmgren, and two Italian naval officers had already left the disaster camp in a bid to reach land on their own.

An Italian aircraft discovered the main party on June 20 and dropped supplies, being unable to land. The discovery came two days too late to avert another tragedy.

On June 18 Roald Amundsen personally joined the search for his rival, Nobile, by taking off from Tromso, Norway, in a large French amphibious aircraft. Amundsen and the four-man French crew were never heard of again. The only trace of them that has ever been discovered consists of part of a wingtip pontoon which drifted to the coast of Norway in September of 1928.

All the Norwegian aircraft were now diverted to search for Amundsen, while the Swedes took over the attempt to rescue the *Italia* survivors. On June 24 Captain Einar Lundborg made a risky landing on the small floe where the survivors clustered, and brought Nobile and the dog Titina back to the Italian base ship at Spitsbergen. While making a second flight the next day, Lundborg's plane was wrecked and he was forced to join the *Italia* castaways until he could be rescued by another Swede on July 6.

It was now obvious that aircraft were not the answer to the problem of rescuing the *Italia* survivors. In those days airplanes were still far too fragile and unreliable to cope with the difficulties of landings and take-offs from the arctic pack.

However, on receipt of the first s.o.s. two Soviet ice-breakers, *Krassin* and *Malygin*, began steaming toward the scene. Without fanfare these ships fought their way steadily into the pack. On July 7 the *Krassin* launched a scout aircraft whose pilot, Tyuchnosky, located men moving on the ice and radioed their position back, enabling the *Krassin* to pick up the two Italians who had tried to walk to shore with Malmgren. Malmgren was not with them. The truth of what happened will probably never be known, but it was widely reported that Malmgren either died, or was killed, and was eaten by one of the two Italians. One Italian was certainly in good condition when rescued; the other was very nearly dead and, in fact, died a few months later.

The *Krassin's* pilot also located two members of an over-ice rescue party who, with dog sleds, had got to Foyn Island where they had been marooned by the spring thaw. Finally the pilot located the main body of castaways but, while attempting to return to his ship, he was forced down by a fog and had to crash-land his aircraft. All this kept the *Krassin* busy, and it was not until July 20 that she had picked up everyone who was marooned or adrift and brought them all into King's Bay.

The *Italia* expedition gave rise to almost as much bitterness and vituperation as the Cook-Peary controversy. The Norwegians were enraged against the Italians in general, and against Nobile in particular, since they held the *Italia* Expedition responsible for the loss of their national hero, Roald Amundsen. Mussolini was much chagrined by the disaster, and made Nobile the scapegoat, demoting him for having been the first to be rescued. This in turn annoyed the Swedes since it was on Capt. Lundborg's orders that Nobile (against his own firmly expressed wishes) had been flown from the ice floe. Mussolini was enraged by the reports that one of his naval officers had indulged in cannibalism, and the Swedes were enraged at what had reputedly been done to Finn Malmgren. The Soviets suggested that the *Italia* disaster was all that could be expected from a fascist state, and Mussolini was horribly embarrassed by the fact that his nationals had had to be rescued by Communists. The only individual who seems to have emerged unruffled from the entire affair was Titina. Twelve men did not emerge at all – having died upon the frozen sea.

The over-all effect was to strip from the North Pole a little more of its ancient allure. Through the next decade the Pole was left severely alone. The polar passion had finally burned down to a mere glow.

When the next visitors arrived, they had no interest in the Pole itself. During May and June of 1937 a squadron of four-engined aircraft operating on skis landed a party of Russian scientists and a mountain of equipment at the Pole. The men established a hydrographic and meteorological observatory on the ice and floated with the pack for 274 days, gradually drifting southward until they were taken off by Soviet ice-breakers near the mouth of Scoresby Sound, on the east coast of Greenland, in late February of 1938. They had by then drifted about 1,300 miles and had made a thorough hydrographic survey of the polar basin.

Twenty years later the Americans wrote a postscript to the polar story when the nuclear-powered submarine *Nautilus* crossed the polar basin far beneath the pack and, as her historian puts it, "pierced the pole." This was doubtless a remarkable technical achievement, but it had nothing in common with the achievements of those many men who, up to the time of Cook and Peary, had striven with the ice on its own chosen battlefield. The following passage written by *Nautilus*'s commander makes this quite clear:

"Uncertain of the thickness of the ice, we descended to several hundred feet, set a course due north and, several minutes later, *Nautilus* passed far beneath the edge of the pack ice. In the crew's mess the last watch was routinely eating dinner. In the background I could hear the strains of Pat Boone's 'Love Letters In The Sand,' one of a hundred records on our juke box.

"This, I thought, is the way to explore the Arctic!"

Today the famous goal no longer attracts much attention from explorers or adventurers, although a few years ago one optimistic glory-hunter set out to try and reach it on a motor-cycle; and during the spring of 1967 a more sober attempt was made from Ellesmere Island to "recapture" the Pole by means of motorized sleds supported by air drops.

The true polar passion burns no longer. Scheduled passenger aircraft fly Great Circle routes across the polar ocean every day but the champagne-sipping passengers are seldom stirred to stare into the white wastes where men of another time, and almost of another breed, once dared and died. Several years ago the pilots of a European airliner were instructed by their company's publicity department to make a diversion and fly over the North Pole. At the appropriate moment the passengers were told they were approaching the historic point and some of them looked out the windows. They were apparently unimpressed. When the aircraft landed, two Chicago businessmen made a complaint about the diversion, which had resulted in the flight's being prolonged by something over half an hour. The airline company concluded that, even as a tourist attraction, the North Pole held no interest for the new generations of mankind.

SOURCES AND ACKNOWLEDGEMENTS

The sources from which material in this book has been taken are shown below. Special thanks are due to Helene Cook Vetter for her permission to use the excerpts from her father's book, *My Attainment of the Pole*.

ROBERT BYLOT AND WILLIAM BAFFIN
Clements R. Markham (editor), *The Voyages of William Baffin, 1612-1622*;
London, 1881, Hakluyt Society.

ELISHA KENT KANE
Arctic Explorations in Search of Sir John Franklin; London, 1902,
Thomas Nelson.

CHARLES FRANCIS HALL
Arctic Researches and Life Among the Esquimaux;
New York, 1865, Harper.

GEORGE TYSON
E. Vale Blake (editor), *Arctic Experiences, Containing Capt. Geo. E. Tyson's
Wonderful Drift on the Ice-Floe etc.*;
New York, 1874, Harper.

ADOLPHUS GREELY
Three Years of Arctic Service;
London, 1886, Richard Bentley and Son.

FRIDTJOF NANSEN
The First Crossing of Greenland (translated by Hubert Gepp);
London, 1893, Longmans.

FREDERICK COOK
My Attainment of the Pole;
New York and London, 1913, Mitchell Kennerley.

The Author wishes to express his gratitude to Alan Cooke, of Centre d'Études Nordiques, Université Laval, Québec, and of Scott Polar Research Institute, Cambridge University, England, for expert assistance in the checking of the manuscript.

INDEX

PICTURE CREDITS

This volume was designed by Hugh Michaelson.
The type for the text, composed by London Typesetting Limited,
is 10 pt. Electra. It was designed for the Linotype
by W. A. Dwiggins in 1935 as an effort
to produce a *fast moving* type face, hence the name Electra.
This book was printed in Canada on Lucerne paper by Ashton-Potter Limited.
It was bound by The Ryerson Press.